THE INTERNATIONAL BOOK OF
The FOREST

The golden cat, *Profelis temmincki*, which has an extensive range in South East Asia, has a uniformly tawny coat and two distinctive stripes on its yellowish cheeks. Like their relatives elsewhere, the smaller cats of the Asian forests are expert hunters and seldom go short of food. Most of them are agile tree climbers and they prey successfully on creatures ranging in size from monkeys to birds.

THE INTERNATIONAL BOOK OF
The FOREST

SIMON AND SCHUSTER

The North American wood thrush, *Hylocichla mustelina*, is reluctant to leave the cool shade of the deciduous forest where, as its plumpness shows, it can find a varied and protein-rich diet of insects and berries. The wood thrush is an accomplished songbird and at dawn and dusk it serenades its bountiful environment with flute-like melodies.

Consultants and Contributors

P. W. Allen, DPhil, FRSC, Malaysian Rubber Producers' Research Association
Bernard L. Archer, PhD, DIC, Head of RRIM Biochemistry Unit, Malaysian Rubber Producers' Research Association
Peter J. Banyard, MA
W. R. Beath, MScTECH, Courtaulds Ltd
David Black
Su Braden
Robert Burton, MA, MIBiol
Keith Crabtree, PhD, Lecturer in Geography, University of Bristol
Dougal Dixon, MSc
Dr Carl M. Gallegos, Senior Research Forester Central and South American Species, International Paper Co.

Joseph Gennaro, Editor *Viewpoints* Magazine, International Paper Co.
P. Hilton, BSc
R. E. Holttum, SCD, Honorary Research Associate, Royal Botanic Gardens, Kew
Richard H. Kirby, OBE, BCom, PhD, formerly of the Tropical Products Institute, London
Michael Janson, BSc
Alison Klein
Scott Leathart, MBE, MA(For) Oxon; FLS, Editor Quarterly Journal of Forestry. Formerly Secretary, Royal Forestry Society
William T. Michaels, Manager News Services, International Paper Co.
Morley Penistan, MA, FIFor, FIUSF, Conservator of Forests, Forestry Commission (ret.)

© 1981 Mitchell Beazley Publishers
The International Book of the Forest
Edited and designed by Mitchell Beazley International Ltd.
87/89 Shaftesbury Avenue, London, W1V 7AD

Published in the United States
by Simon and Schuster
A Gulf + Western Company
Simon & Schuster Building
Rockefeller Center
1230 Avenue of the Americas
New York, New York 10020

Library of Congress Cataloging in Publication Data Main entry under title:

The International book of the forest.

1. Forest ecology. 2. Forests and forestry.
QH541.5.F6157 1981 574.5'2642 80–6105
ISBN 0–671–41004–0

Photosetting in Great Britain by
Jolly & Barber Ltd, Rugby
Colour separations in the Netherlands by
Koninklijke Smeets Offset b.v.
Printed and bound in the Netherlands by
Koninklijke Smeets Offset b.v.

W. G. Potter, Press Officer, Timber Research and
Development Association
E. F. Roberts, Editor-in-Chief, Timber Trades
Journal
John A. Roberts
David E. Rose
Bryan Sage, Environment and Wildlife
Consultant
L. A. Spong
Dr Andrew Sugden
M. F. Walsh
Constance Webster, AIWSc
Ralph Whitlock, FZS
Dr James G. Yoho, Manager International
Development, Wood Products & Resources
Group, International Paper Co.

Researched, designed and edited by
Michael A. Janulewicz
Leonard Roberts

Margaret Mulvihill

Lesley Ellis
Sean Keogh
Zuza Vrbova

Nicholas Law
David Rowley

Margaret Little

Photographic Research
Marilynn Zipes

Photographic Research Manager
Brigitte Arora

Production   Peter Phillips

Contents

In the heart of the Mato Grosso rain forest in Brazil
Xingu women and youths plant sweet potatoes. Such
clearings are created by cutting and burning the forest,
an ancient practice that is common among the
contemporary peoples of the tropical forests and which
was once intrinsic to all forest-originating human cultures.

Foreword

"Dark behind it rose the forest
Rose the black and gloomy pine-trees"
Dark behind *us* rises the forest. The force of
Longfellow's image is universal. The forest is
the world in which our primate-ancestors
evolved. Beneath its branches the sense of
awe is inescapable. We feel at home under its
great familiar canopy, yet at the same time as
aware as animals, our senses alert to its
innumerable whispers and flickers of
mysterious life. It produces emotions and
reactions with deep roots in the early history
of humankind—roots that nourish a world-
wide tradition of art, of folk-tales, literature
and music with the forest as its inspiration
and its theme.

The realm of trees seems as elemental as
the ocean. True, in the forest you do not
drown, but you get lost; sunlight is reduced
to slanting shafts and distant glimmers high
in the shadowy branches; the forest floor is
barren and infertile; beasts roam at large.

For nearly all of our history we have
regarded the forest as an enemy. An enemy to
be despoiled by plundering its timber, or
simply to be destroyed to make way for
sunshine and crops. There was so much
forest that the idea of it coming to an end was
simply laughable. The Earth's small human
population could not consume timber at the
rate it was growing, in every tree, every year.
Its use for houses, ships, charcoal, firewood
made no impression. Natural wastage by fire,
disease, insects and storms accounted for far
more trees than mere humankind.

Then all at once the local demand for
particular trees of particular ages began to
outstrip supply. Ship builders found it hard
to procure the huge crooked boughs of two-
hundred-year-old oaks they needed for
brackets and angle-pieces. In the seventeenth
century it became obvious that the navy
would have to plan ahead for its future
warships by planting trees.

There are earlier examples of forest-
management. Regular lopping for fuel led to
the discovery that regrowth is more vigorous
than first-growth, and often straighter, giving
valuable poles for building.

But just as pressure on the forests of the
Old World began to make replanting and
management—the modern term is
conservation—essential for supplies,
colonization of the New World offered an
easier alternative: apparently limitless new
forests to cut, with trees of sizes, and timber
of qualities, never seen before.

Logging performed the double role of
providing timber and clearing land for
farming. Overenthusiastic logging soon
cleared not only the trees but the soil,
too, as erosion by wind and water ravaged
the unprotected earth.

It is only in the twentieth century that we
have come to realize that man and the forest
are mutually dependent. The combination of
advancing technology and booming
population means that the old philosophy of
cut-and-move-on has no future. There is
nowhere to move to. We must crop the forest
we have, and crop it in such a way that new
timber is always ready for our needs.

The developed world now sees the forest as
the world's greatest renewable resource: a
perpetual spring pouring out materials and
energy; fragile only if it is abused. It is vital to
the interests of all of us that the developing
world rapidly learns the same lesson.

For the modern forester need no longer be
passive, a mere spectator with an axe, waiting
for the trees to grow. He can develop faster,
straighter and stronger trees. We have been
selecting and improving our cereals and
roots, our food and our flowers, for
thousands of years. Now the breeding of
trees has begun—opening up astonishing
possibilities for productivity.

The progress of the forester, from plunder
to partnership, is the great sub-plot of this
book. It is the first book, so far as I know,
ever to take tally of the whole world's woods
and tell their story. All the more important,
then, that it is aware of the pressures on
them—and positive about their future.

HUGH JOHNSON

13

THE FOREST PAST AND PRESENT

. . . Our forests are undoubtedly the greatest magazines of the wealth and glory of this nation; and our oaks, the truest oracles of its perpetuity and happiness, as being the only support of that navigation which makes us fear'd abroad, and flourished at home. It has been strangely wonder'd at by some good patriots, how it comes to pass that many gentlemen have frequently repaired or gained a sudden fortune, with plowing part of their parks and letting out their fat grounds to gardeners etc and very wild wood-land parcels (as may be instanced in several places) to dressers of hop-yards etc while the royal portion lies folded up in a napkin, uncultivated and neglected; especially those great and ample forests; where, tho plowing and sowing have been forbidden, a Royal command and design may well dispense with it, and the breaking up of these intervals, advance the growth of the trees to an incredible improvement.

JOHN EVELYN *Silva* 1664

15

The tree

A tree is a woody perennial plant, usually with a single stem or trunk from which limbs or branches sprout some distance from the ground to carry a spreading crown of leaves. Like most plants, a tree starts life as a seed that, under the influence of warmth and moisture, germinates and pushes forth a root that grows downwards into the soil and a stem that grows upwards towards the sunlight. The stem of a seedling tree does not die down as winter approaches but becomes woody and encased in protective bark, standing ready with the next year's leaves securely wrapped up in well-protected buds, to start growth as the welcome spring returns.

Year by year the young tree pushes upwards, adding to its stature, and always with an initial advantage over its herbaceous rivals, which although they grow more quickly, are forever pushed back to the beginning as they die down each autumn. Even woody shrubs with their multiple stems are overtaken by the young sapling that devotes all its energies to its single trunk until, spreading out over all its rivals, it becomes a mature tree.

The tall and massive structures that trees eventually become—some can reach nearly 400 feet in height and can contain as much as 1,000 tons of timber in their trunks—are built up by a wonderful process, powered by the sun's rays, called photosynthesis. The process of tissue-building by photosynthesis is common to all green plants, but trees, because of the dimensions they attain, are unique among plants in the strength of their stems and in the specialized tissues thus required.

Each year a tree adds a new ring of woody sap-conducting vessels. The summer ones are thicker-walled and darker in colour than those formed in spring and are visibly different, thus creating the annual rings so clearly seen in the cross-section of a tree trunk. As the years advance, the vessels from the centre outwards die and become embalmed in tannins and resins to form a strong and lasting core that continues to hold the heavy leafy crown aloft for many years, and provides the timber of commerce.

Timbers, and the trees that form them, fall into two categories—softwood and hardwood. Softwood embraces the timber of coniferous cone-bearing tree species, such as pines, firs and spruces, and hardwood includes the timber of all broadleaved flowering tree species, such as oaks, beeches, elms and ashes. There are softwoods such as yew, however, that are physically harder than many hardwoods, and some hardwoods, including balsa, poplar and willow, that are softer than most softwoods.

The softwood tree species are characteristic of the cold to cool temperate zones of the world. They are adapted both by shape and leaf form to climates that by virtue of latitude or altitude have long cold or dry spells. The stiff narrow, needle-like or flattened scale-like form of their leaves prevents excessive transpiration in times of drought and undue resistance to winter winds. Furthermore, the hardy conifers retain their leaves throughout the year, although there are some exceptions such as the larches and swamp cypresses which have soft needle-like deciduous leaves. All conifers (with the exception of podocarps) bear cones; some huge and conspicuous, others small and secreted among the needles or leaves. Reproduction by wind-borne pollen, without the assistance of birds or insects, enables conifers to start the reproductive process very early in the still bitterly cold spring that comes after a harsh winter.

The broadleaved, or hardwood, trees are more numerous and more diverse. For the most part they are deciduous, shedding their leaves in autumn, the better to withstand wind and cold or, in monsoon climates, at the start of the dry season to prevent desiccation. Yet some species do not lose their leaves at all. Those in tropical rain forests, where seasons do not change, have no need to do so and grow continuously. Others develop thick, leathery, evergreen leaves to withstand the hot dry summers of Mediterranean climates, but must also be capable of functioning as soon as the damper, cooler winter weather arrives. But generally the broadleaved trees, typical of the warmer temperate, subtropical and tropical parts of the world, have soft, wide leaves that expand over a wide expanse of crown to trap the maximum of sunlight.

On the crowns before, or most often after, the leaves have opened, flowers appear, some as hanging catkins, their pollen distributed by the wind, as with willows, poplars, oaks and birches. Others appear as perfect flowers, masterpieces of nature in which both male and female organs are surrounded by an apparatus decked in brilliant colours and exuding nectar. These ingenious natural structures are designed to attract insects and birds that pass on pollen from one flower to another as with cherries, magnolias, some maples and many others.

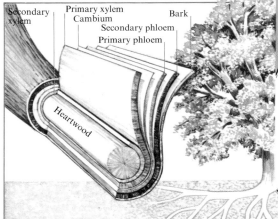

Secondary xylem
Primary xylem
Cambium
Bark
Secondary phloem
Primary phloem
Heartwood

Above *Roots secure trees firmly in the ground and absorb water and minerals from the soil. These are carried up the trunk to the leaves, where food is manufactured and distributed. An active cambial layer of cells, below the bark, produces the xylem vessels on its inner side, which transport the upward flow of the sap to the buds. The phloem on the outer side returns the sap flow to the roots.*

Below *Expanded section of a leaf with the top layers peeled back to expose its components. The epidermis, or skin, protects the cells and numerous veins provide them with water and mineral nutrients. The xylem vessels carry water up from the roots and the phloem vessels carry food manufactured in the leaves to all the other parts of the tree. Air enters the leaf through the stomatal pores, which are usually found on its undersurface.*

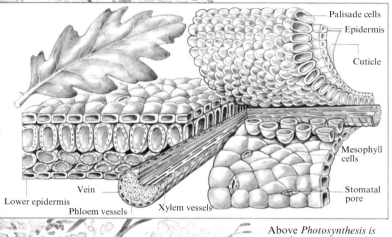

Above *Photosynthesis is mostly carried out in the leaf cells. The green pigment, chlorophyll, is activated by sunlight and it provides the vital chemical energy for carbon dioxide and water to react and combine to form carbohydrates.*

Below *Expanded cross-section of a root. The tiny root hairs, finger-like projections from the epidermal cells, grow out between soil particles, absorbing water and minerals from the soil.*

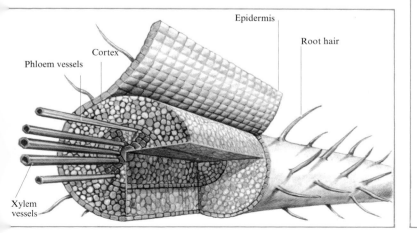

HARDWOODS AND SOFTWOODS

Wood is a complex structure made up of many different kinds of cells. The broadleaved trees, known (by botanists) as angiosperms and popularly as hardwoods, have some different kinds of cells from the conifers or softwoods, known botanically as gymnosperms. The terms "hardwood" and "softwood" often cause confusion because not all hardwoods produce a physically harder timber, nor do all softwoods produce a physically softer timber. Hemlock and yellow pine, for example, yield a hard timber, whereas poplar, basswood and balsa—the favourite wood of modern model makers—yield very soft timber.

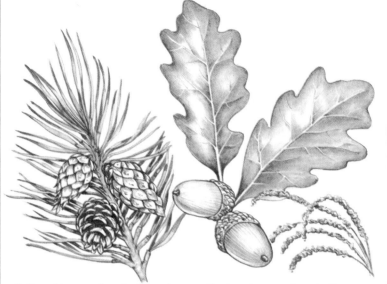

Softwood trees, such as the Scots pine, Pinus sylvestris, include all the coniferous trees. They are mostly evergreen with needle-like leaves and bear "naked" seeds inside cones. The male and female flowers are separate.

Hardwood trees such as the European oak, Quercus robur, have certain defining characteristics. The seeds are enclosed within a fruit, such as this acorn, and flowers sometimes carry both male and female sexual organs.

Above *Pollen being dispersed by wind from the male cones of a Monterey pine, Pinus radiata. Gymnosperms depend on only the wind for their pollination.*

Above *An insect pollinating a cherry tree, Prunus spp. This angiosperm flower has evolved as a specific reproductive organ, having developed from leaves.*

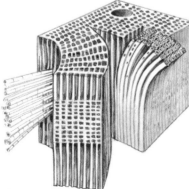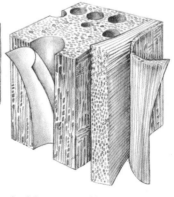

Above *Softwood timbers are simpler in structure than hardwoods, being composed almost entirely of one type of conducting cells known as tracheids, and only a small proportion of food storage cells (parenchyma) and radial conduction cells (medullary rays). Conversely, hardwoods are more highly evolved, because in addition to their greater proportion of parenchyma cells and medullary rays to tracheids, they also possess wide-bore cells or vessels for greater ease of water conduction, as well as thick-walled fibres for strength and support. These separate the two functions combined in conifer tracheids.*

How the forest works

Forests are the world's air-conditioners and Earth's blanket; without them the world would be a bleak and inhospitable place. The great companies of trees that form the forests are complex ecological systems which rid the air of excess carbon dioxide and replenish the oxygen. They also shelter the ground beneath them, and all the animals and smaller plants dwelling there, from the wind and rain and the heat and cold.

Without trees and other green plants there would be no advanced life on Earth. They have the unique ability to photosynthesize: to capture the light energy from the sun, in the presence of their green pigment chlorophyll, and use it to convert water, carbon dioxide and minerals into oxygen and energy-rich organic compounds. Were it not that plants absorb the carbon dioxide that animals exhale (and man creates by burning fossil fuels), and use it to grow and expel oxygen back into the air, the atmosphere would become devoid of oxygen and all life would cease. Forests, with their huge green plants—the trees—raised high up to trap maximum solar energy, play an important role in this recycling process.

This is a role shared by all green plants, but the other roles performed by the forest are unique to it and just as vital. In its protective role the forest is a blanket beneath which life proceeds. No creatures or plants can live without warmth and water, but too much or too little of either or both destroys the mainstream of life. So, where life is protected from these excesses it prospers best.

Beneath the forest canopy dwell immensely complex and interrelated populations of plants and animals. The trees intercept the sun's energy and use it to draw up water and minerals from the soil. With the aid of chlorophyll these substances combine with gases in the air to manufacture the organic compounds that are needed by the tree for both immediate growth and for future use.

The all-important soil in which the forest is anchored contains myriad bacteria and fungi. In return for the shelter from the elements provided by the forest canopy and by means of the raw materials provided by the trees in the shape of discarded leaves and twigs, they keep the soil supplied with important nutrients by "fixing" nitrogen from the air and soil. This they convert into nitrates from which the trees can manufacture protein.

Thus the cycle of life proceeds. Insects and some higher animals eat plants and tree leaves; birds and other animals eat insects. Yet other birds and animals eat their own kind or each other, in life consigning their waste products, and in death their bodies, to the soil to start the process once again.

The greater the area of forest and the warmer and damper the climate the greater is the extent and speed of this inexorable cycle. In the tropical rain forests the temperature never changes from the ideal for growth. There the sun's rays beat down vertically upon an uninterrupted, evergreen forest canopy, dripping and steaming in the frequent rains. It

Above *A forest is like an energy bank. The trees trap energy from sunlight and store it as wood and foliage. They produce food for animals in the form of leaves, fruit and seeds. Ultimately the trees die and fall to the ground, where they eventually decompose and release their stored energy to the earth.*

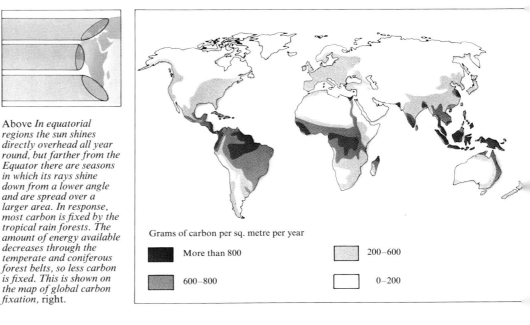

Above *In equatorial regions the sun shines directly overhead all year round, but farther from the Equator there are seasons in which its rays shine down from a lower angle and are spread over a larger area. In response, most carbon is fixed by the tropical rain forests. The amount of energy available decreases through the temperate and coniferous forest belts, so less carbon is fixed. This is shown on the map of global carbon fixation, right.*

Grams of carbon per sq. metre per year

More than 800	200–600
600–800	0–200

THE ELEMENTAL CYCLES

All the components of a forest—the trees, the animals and the soil—interact with each other and with the atmosphere, sustaining a balance of gases, water and nutrients.

THE WATER CYCLE
When it rains some water is taken up from the soil by tree roots and is transpired back into the atmosphere. The rest of the rain water accumulates in the soil and returns to the sea, where some evaporates into clouds.

THE CARBON CYCLE
Trees use carbon dioxide from the atmosphere and, in combination with water taken up from the soil, it is used to make the carbohydrates required for growth. Both trees and animals release carbon dioxide during respiration and return fixed carbon to the earth when they die. Some of this carbon becomes part of the Earth's crust as coal or gas.

THE OXYGEN CYCLE
Oxygen in the air is continually being used by plants and animals for energy during respiration. This is replenished by forest trees because they give out oxygen as a product of photosynthesis.

THE NITROGEN CYCLE
Before nitrogen can be absorbed by trees, it has to be "fixed" by nitrogen-fixing bacteria and fungi in the soil. They use nitrogen to form nitrates, which can then be absorbed by tree roots and used to manufacture proteins.

Solar energy is trapped by the trees, the producers, and it flows through the forest from one component to another: the herbivores feed on trees and they in turn are consumed by predators. Animals play a major role in pollinating and distributing seeds.

Above *Decomposers, such as this beech tuft fungus, Oudemansiella mucida, live on the dead organic matter from the bark of a living tree. They break it down into simpler compounds that can be re-absorbed from the soil by the tree roots.*

Above *Soil-dwelling bacteria, Anabaena, magnified 900 times. They oxidize ammonium compounds, formed from the decomposition of plants, to nitrites. Other bacteria oxidize nitrites to nitrates, which can then be taken up by plant roots.*

is the periods of high or low rainfall that create the seasons. The spongy forest floor receives a permanent and regular supply of discarded forest material that is quickly absorbed to give sustenance to a host of plants and trees, as well as enormous numbers of permanently active creatures great and small.

Farther from the Equator, where a seasonal diminution in temperature below that necessary for tree growth occurs, the temperate forest is very different. A less dense forest results because, in order to ride out the cold season without loss of water or damage from wind, trees shed their leaves and remain mere skeletons until the sun's energy increases once again. The same necessary sheltering of the forest floor occurs when the sun is most intense. But because the canopy is more open and the clearings caused by fire and wind are less quickly filled, the understory of the temperate forest is often thick with shrubs and lesser trees. The temperate forest's floor is carpeted with herbs, all providing a much

more varied habitat than that found in the lower reaches of the tropical forest.

Activity in the life-cycle is greater during spring and summer, for every living thing within the forest must complete its reproductive processes before winter returns, and the forest resounds to the song of birds and the hum of insects. But when the leaves drop the trees can no longer provide the protection required for the life-cycle to proceed at full pitch; life is stilled and the forest takes on a forlorn aspect.

Still farther north, where the summer days are long but few and the winter days short but many, with snow lying thick for months on end, the great conifer forests circle the globe. The trees are evergreen to be ready for the sudden spring and short growing season, they are conical in shape to ward off the snow, and thick upon the ground for mutual protection. Beneath them, often in deep shade, the accumulated needles are slow to decompose in the low temperatures. They can support

few flowering plants, but mosses and lichens abound upon tree stumps or hang from the lower branches of the trees. As the daylight extends to twenty hours and more, insects such as midges and mosquitoes, which breed in water and damp places, proliferate to unimaginable proportions, the insect-eating birds flock in to breed and the evergreen trees quickly add to their stature. The whole process of reproduction is speeded up by the endless food supply and the midnight sun.

Then, quite suddenly, winter comes. All water freezes solid, all sap-flow ceases. Snow slips from the trees to carpet the forest floor, the tempo of life slows and all is silent. The life-cycle has nearly stopped, but not quite. Some birds still find a living in the trees, feeding on seeds in the cones, and some animals, camouflaged in white, still emerge from their lairs to hunt. Beneath the snow under the trees that plethora of tiny creatures in the soil gains enough protection from the forest to survive the worst that winter can do.

The first forests

The first plants were little more than single cells and the first evolutionary steps took place in the sea. The single cells then organized themselves into multi-cellular organisms and eventually evolved to become simple seaweeds—the first plants of any significance. When these ventured out of water to colonize dry land, they faced a forbidding environment. The land was bleak and barren, covered with raw mineral soils which did not contain humus or vegetable material. The atmosphere was hostile too. There was no oxygen and no protection from the lethal ultraviolet rays of the sun.

Then, as now, plants used the carbon dioxide and water that were plentiful in the early atmosphere to manufacture their own food. As a result of this process of photosynthesis, oxygen was given out and the oxygen level on the early Earth gradually increased, until, by the beginning of the Cambrian period about 500 million years ago, there was enough oxygen to support a diversity of primitive life. There was also some free oxygen, or ozone, which formed a layer round the Earth, shielding it from ultraviolet radiation. Animal life, no longer relying on water for protection, eventually followed the plants onto dry land.

For a plant to live on land it must have a vascular system—a network of tubes to bring water up from the ground and food down from the leaves. This is found in an assemblage of psilophytes, primitive fern-like plants that clothed the banks of a lake in Scotland in Middle Devonian times. Although fossils of earlier land-living plants are known, indicating that plants were rapidly evolving during Silurian times, this is the oldest known fossil forest. Its members, however, did not exceed three feet in height. By the end of the Devonian period, the lands of the Earth were dominated by gaunt-branched forests which were an indication of what was to follow.

The following Carboniferous period was a time of giganticism when the ferns, horsetails and club-mosses became more tree-like and assumed heights of a hundred feet or more. They formed huge swamp forests of luxuriant vegetation. All these classes of plant reproduced by means of spores and thus required water for their reproduction.

The giant horsetails, *Cordaites*, flourished in the drier areas of the swamps and possessed fertile branches that bore pollen sacs and ovules at their tips. They are the ancestors of our present-day gymnosperms—the female

cone of a modern pine tree is merely a modification of a fertile cordaite branch. During the course of evolution the branch was shortened and compacted to form a cone, which now bears no resemblance to its cordaite ancestor. The male cones, however, have hardly progressed in evolutionary terms at all.

Fossils of these early forests are found in our present-day coal beds. By looking at the regular pattern of their annual growth rings, one can see that they grew in a warm or hot seasonless environment. One wonders how plants which only thrive in tropical conditions could have existed at the poles of the Earth in the past. The answer lies in the fact that the landmasses on Earth were not always situated where they are now. They are mobile plates floating on the surface of the Earth, continually being broken up and re-formed into different configurations—like pieces of a jigsaw puzzle.

When Alfred Wegener, in the 1920s, first proposed the concept that the continents do actually drift across the surface of the Earth, his idea was regarded as outrageous and preposterous. But, from time to time through the history of science, some outrageous hypotheses are proved to be true: during the past

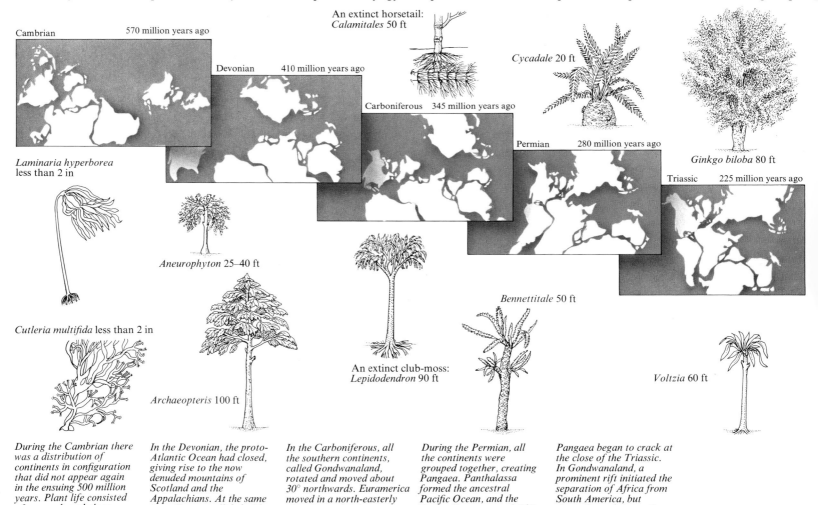

An extinct horsetail: *Calamitales* 50 ft

Cycadale 20 ft

Cambrian 570 million years ago

Devonian 410 million years ago

Carboniferous 345 million years ago

Permian 280 million years ago

Triassic 225 million years ago

Ginkgo biloba 80 ft

Laminaria hyperborea less than 2 in

Aneurophyton 25–40 ft

Cutleria multifida less than 2 in

Archaeopteris 100 ft

An extinct club-moss: *Lepidodendron* 90 ft

Bennettitale 50 ft

Voltzia 60 ft

During the Cambrian there was a distribution of continents in configuration that did not appear again in the ensuing 500 million years. Plant life consisted of seaweeds and algae confined to the sea.

In the Devonian, the proto-Atlantic Ocean had closed, giving rise to the now denuded mountains of Scotland and the Appalachians. At the same time, Europe collided with Asia, producing the Urals.

In the Carboniferous, all the southern continents, called Gondwanaland, rotated and moved about 30° northwards. Euramerica moved in a north-easterly direction and Asia remained in the same spot.

During the Permian, all the continents were grouped together, creating Pangaea. Panthalassa formed the ancestral Pacific Ocean, and the Tethys Sea separated Africa from Eurasia.

Pangaea began to crack at the close of the Triassic. In Gondwanaland, a prominent rift initiated the separation of Africa from South America, but Australia and Antarctica were still joined.

ten years evidence from diverse scientific fields has confirmed the idea that continents do move. The relative positions of the continents have recently been plotted for the past 500 million years of Earth's history, and their varying configurations are shown below.

The ferns and their allies, the horsetails and the club-mosses, that formed the coal swamp floras were not equipped to adapt to new drier, warmer conditions of the Permian period. Unable to maintain their once massive and luxuriant trunks, they reduced in size to the tree ferns of the Tropics and subtropics or they are found hidden away along the banks of streams and in damp ditches, victims of their requirements for abundant moisture.

New groups of gymnosperms flourished and began to dominate the land. These were the *Bennettitales*, *Ginkgoales* and *Cycadales*. They all had palm-like leaves and short stubby trunks, and their method of reproduction, using seeds rather than spores, was better suited to the drier conditions. They rapidly became cosmopolitan at this time because the landmasses were grouped into one huge super-continent known today as Pangaea, and so there were no ocean barriers to prevent their dispersal. Gradually this super-continent began to crack and in the Jurassic period Eurasia, the northern group of continents, and Gondwanaland, the southern ones, began to separate.

The Jurassic was characterized by vast forests of cycads, ginkgos, ferns and primitive conifers that resemble present-day *Araucaria* spp., the monkey-puzzle trees. These were the forests that supported the great dinosaurs. By the end of the Jurassic, the birth of the South Atlantic Ocean had been initiated by the widening of a rift in Gondwanaland. The rotation of the Eurasian landmass had the effect of closing the eastern end of the Tethys Sea, which was the ancestral Mediterranean. At this time, during the Cretaceous period, the flowering plants, angiosperms, came to the fore with their more sophisticated reproductive system. The flower was their major innovation. They were well adapted to the changing climatic conditions and established a flora that has lasted virtually unchanged to this day. Many present-day genera such as oak, sycamore, walnut and fig flourished. They occupied all the important ecological niches, relegating most of the gymnosperms to cold climates and high altitudes, while ferns became water-loving herbaceous plants.

Below *The geological time chart shows the major evolutionary steps made by plants during the past 600 million years. The figures after the geological time period represent millions of years from the present day.*

Pleistocene	2	Arctic plants due to widespread glaciations
Pliocene	7	Temperate trees in the north
Miocene	26	Grasslands increased at the expense of forests
Oligocene	38	Tropical trees in high latitudes
Eocene	64	Temperate and tropical forests widespread
Cretaceous	136	Development and spread of the angiosperms throughout the world
Jurassic	190	Cycads, ferns and conifers were more developed than in the Triassic period
Triassic	225	Ginkgos, cycads and other conifers with palm-like leaves began to develop
Permian	280	Marked development of new coniferous trees and extinction of old Carboniferous ones
Carboniferous	345	Rich coal measure flora of the giant club-mosses and fern-like plants
Devonian	410	True seed plants, *Archaeosperma*, had evolved by the end of the period
Silurian	440	Early vascular plants such as *Cooksonia* appeared
Ordovician	530	Many calcareous and reef-building types of algae, particularly stromatolites that formed dome-like structures in the inter-tidal zones
Cambrian	570	Algae
Pre-Cambrian		Primitive anaerobic unicellular organisms

PRESENT-DAY EQUIVALENTS OF CARBONIFEROUS TREES

Today horsetails, club-mosses and ferns represent relics of a group of plants that were much more important in previous geological epochs. In the Carboniferous they grew to the size of large forest trees, but their present-day relatives exist as the small herbaceous plants, or slightly larger tree ferns.

A horsetail *Equisetum telmateia*

A club-moss *Lycopodium clavatum*

Tree ferns *Cyathea*

Norfolk Island Pine
Araucaria heterophylla 150 ft

Plane tree *Platanus* 110 ft

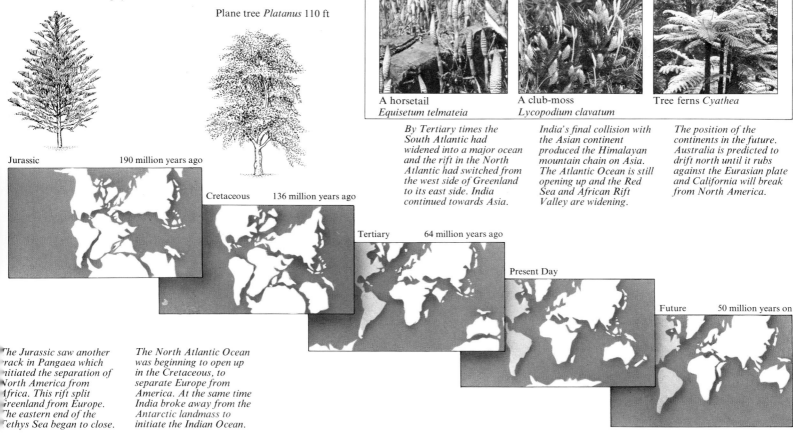

Jurassic   190 million years ago

Cretaceous   136 million years ago

Tertiary   64 million years ago

Present Day

Future   50 million years on

The Jurassic saw another crack in Pangaea which initiated the separation of North America from Africa. This rift split Greenland from Europe. The eastern end of the Tethys Sea began to close.

The North Atlantic Ocean was beginning to open up in the Cretaceous, to separate Europe from America. At the same time India broke away from the Antarctic landmass to initiate the Indian Ocean.

By Tertiary times the South Atlantic had widened into a major ocean and the rift in the North Atlantic had switched from the west side of Greenland to its east side. India continued towards Asia.

India's final collision with the Asian continent produced the Himalayan mountain chain on Asia. The Atlantic Ocean is still opening up and the Red Sea and African Rift Valley are widening.

The position of the continents in the future. Australia is predicted to drift north until it rubs against the Eurasian plate and California will break from North America.

Coal and fossil forests

Forests of the past, their fossilized and compacted remains, provide us with coal today. Their stored energy, in the form of carbon, which is the major component of coal, was manufactured by the leaves of ancient trees. Although these trees have been dead for millions of years, they still provide us with a substantial economic resource.

Coal usually forms in thickly forested swamps where the vegetation is lush and water plentiful. As the trees die, they fall into the loose boggy soil and their remains accumulate in the stagnant waters. Here, decay by bacterial action is inhibited by lack of oxygen and vegetable matter is not broken down completely. For coal to form, these swamplands must be cyclically flooded by seawater. This often occurs if the sea-level rises due to the expansion of polar ice caps and the same effect may occur if the land slowly subsides in response to adjacent mountain building.

The slimy black mass of partially decomposed trees is the first stage in the formation of coal. It is called peat and its constituents are similar in proportion to that of wood except there is more nitrogen. This is due to the activity of the micro-organisms that helped to decompose the original plant tissues. More carbon is present, however, because more of the oxygen and water have been squeezed out by the weight of overlying soil.

Gradually more sediments accumulate that bury the peat. As this happens it undergoes a number of changes. The most obvious effect is that it is compressed to the next grade of fuel. This is called lignite, or brown coal, and contains an even higher proportion of carbon. It is quite soft, weathers rapidly when exposed to air, and contains plant fragments that are still recognizable. Lignite is used extensively in power stations to generate electricity.

Further compaction from the weight of more sediments will render the lignite into bituminous coal, which is black, dense and brittle—in fact the substance that immediately comes to mind when coal is mentioned. The plant structures in this are usually only visible microscopically. The carbon content is now up to about eighty per cent. This coal is characterized by some "bright" and some "dull" constituents, which reflect differences in the plant debris from which they have been derived. There are bright shiny black bands, called clarain, which represent the bark and woody tissue of the former trees. It has a laminated appearance, reflecting the fluctuating conditions that prevailed during the accumulation of the plant debris.

Whenever accumulating peat deposits were partly inundated by shallow water, conditions became more suitable for the formation of durain. This is a dull coal with no lustre and no pronounced lamination, formed from finer plant debris such as spores, leaf cuticles and inorganic mud intimately mixed with the fragmentary plant remains. As this coal is covered by more deposits of later-formed rocks, it is subjected to higher pressures and temperatures by their weight, which causes the hydrogen and water to be expelled and the carbon content to be increased.

Should bituminous coal be involved in mountain-building or other violent Earth movements, it may become metamorphosed, along with the rocks round about, to form anthracite. This is the highest grade of coal and has a carbon content of more than ninety per cent. It is black, hard and brittle and has a glassy lustre. As a rule the higher the quality of coal, the better it is as a fuel. However, the higher grades are almost invariably found at greater depths in the Earth's crust and are consequently more difficult and expensive to reach and extract.

Since coal is formed by swamps being periodically inundated by seawater, it is always found within a specific sequence of rocks—shale, sandstone, seat earth (a thin dark layer of clay containing tree roots) and then coal. Above the coal the shale of the next cycle will be found. It is the thickness of each individual bed of coal that determines whether or not the bed is suitable for extraction by mining.

Most of the world's coal reserves are of bituminous coal and are formed from material laid down during the Upper Carboniferous period between 300 and 280 million years ago. At this time large areas of land that now lie in the northern hemisphere were covered in dense forest. In the waters of the lagoons and streams were dense reed beds of giant horsetails, *Calamites*, growing to heights of about thirty feet. In the shallower water there grew the great club-mosses, *Sigillaria* and *Lepidodendron*, reaching up to one hundred feet. On the dry land the first gymnosperms, *Cordaites*, grew and the undergrowth of small ferns, seed ferns and creeping horsetails was everywhere.

The animal life consisted of anthropods. There were the huge cockroaches, *Aphthoroblattina* and dragonflies, *Meganeura*, which had a wing span of twenty-eight inches. In the waters and among the fallen vegetable matter dwelt a fantastic assortment of amphibians, mostly fairly small and newt-like, but some, such as *Eogyrinus*, were as large as present-day alligators.

The lignite deposits of the world come from younger strata. In some places, for example in the north of Scotland, they are formed from forests of the Jurassic period, 195 to 135 million years ago. Most lignite, however, is younger than this and the extensive rich fields of central Europe and northern Italy were formed less than fifty million years ago during the Tertiary period.

The vegetation at this time was essentially similar to that of today and the brown coal forests consisted of water-loving coniferous trees such as the false cypress, *Chamaecyparis thyoides*, swamp cypress, *Taxodium distichium*, and angiosperms such as *Nyssa*. They grew in an environment almost identical to that of the present-day cypress swamps of the south-eastern United States, complete with water-lilies and palms.

THE FORMATION OF FOSSILS

Our knowledge of ancient extinct forests is derived mainly from fossil evidence. Fossils ca be formed in several ways. The original plant tissues may be replaced molecule by molecule any mineral in abundant supply, such as silica calcite or pyrite, which forms a replica of the original plant.

The trees of the coal swamp floras have bee preserved in a completely different way. The s tissues of the trees have disappeared, leaving nothing but an impression or mould in the ro material that once surrounded it. Sometimes t mould is later filled in with a mineral deposit t produces a nearly perfect cast of the original t specimen.

Amber is a fossil resin produced by conifer trees that flourished on the Baltic coast about twelve million years ago. As the resin oozed o of their barks, it often trapped tiny insects. La the resin hardened, preserving the details of m extinct species. Jet, derived from polished lign coals, is another valued gemstone.

Below *Tropical coastal swamplands, such as the Everglades in Florida, exist in conditions similar to those of the forests that formed the Carboniferous coal deposits. These areas could well form the coal beds of the future.*

Right *Coal-forming swamps grow when the sea-level is relatively low. If there is a rise in sea-level, the incoming layers of marine sediments destroy the trees. When the sea-level drops again, the delta may be deforested.*

Below *Coal is formed by forests that are cyclically inundated by the sea. A characteristic pattern of coal and sedimentary rock is produced. The layer of sedimentary rock* immediately overlying a coal seam contains marine fossils representing an incursion of the sea. Above this freshwater deposits of sandstone occur. Plants first decompose into peat and with increasing pressures, due to the weight of overlying sediments, into the higher grades of coal—lignite, bituminous coal and anthracite.

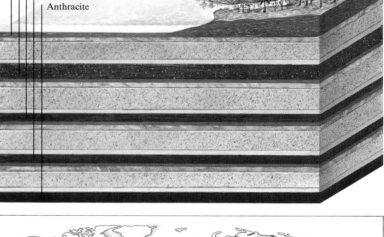

Clay with *Sigillaria* roots
Peat layer
Lignite
Bituminous coal
Anthracite

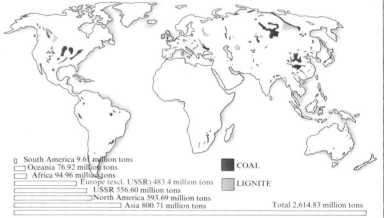

South America 9.61 million tons
Oceania 76.92 million tons
Africa 94.96 million tons
Europe (excl. USSR) 483.4 million tons
USSR 556.60 million tons
North America 593.69 million tons
Asia 800.71 million tons

Total 2,614.83 million tons

COAL
LIGNITE

Below *Recent coal deposits can be cheaply extracted by open-pit mining. However, the deeply seated bituminous and anthracitic coals make mining operations expensive and hazardous,* below right.

Above *The map summarizes the present geographical distribution of the world's commercial coal deposits. It has been formed frequently during the past 300 million years where conditions have been* temporarily favourable. The oldest known coals are preserved in rocks of Devonian age on Bear Island, near Spitzbergen, and in northern Russia. Two-thirds of the world's present coal resources were formed in Carboniferous times. Of the major world regions, Asia was the largest coal producer in 1978, followed by North America, the USSR, Europe, Africa, Oceania and South America.

Above *Far from the site where they once grew, these petrified logs lie scattered in eastern Arizona. They were buried beneath a thick blanket of volcanic debris; silica-* bearing water then replaced the wood with stone. The volcanic surround eventually eroded to reveal perfect replicas of the trees that grew some 40 to 60 million years ago.

Co-existence with the forest

Man is a creature of the forest. He only ventured from the warmth and shelter of the trees twelve million years ago—a relatively late stage in his evolution—to stumble clumsily on feet that had been developed for grasping branches. The forest species from which humankind evolved seem to have been agoraphobic. Although certain dangers might lurk in the forest, its dark interior also offered the safety and security that derives from secrecy and concealment.

The end of the age of reptiles came quite suddenly about seventy million years ago. In a relatively short time, measured geologically, the dinosaurs, brontosaurs, pterodactyls and other huge creatures that lived in the forests and dominated the Earth throughout the Jurassic and early Cretaceous eras (see pages 20–21) vanished, for reasons that are not at present clear. Their disappearance left a vacuum in which mammals, a lowly and comparatively insignificant group of creatures that had been in existence for the previous 130 million years without apparently making much progress, at last had a chance to evolve more rapidly.

Late in the Cretaceous age, some forty to seventy million years ago, the first primates appeared, living in North and South America, Eurasia and probably Africa. The earliest kinds were the prosimians, of which the present-day representatives are the lemurs, tarsiers and allied species (see pages 110–111). They were small, agile mammals that were entirely arboreal.

They and the forest evolved together. The forests of the Jurassic age must have been gloomy places. The trees of that time were gymnosperms that reproduced using wind-borne seeds and so there were no flowers, fruits or berries to relieve the monotonous greenery, and no cheerful sounds of chattering monkeys or singing birds. A welcome change occurred in the Cretaceous era, when angiosperms, or flowering plants, became dominant. The edible fruits and berries they produced provided an attractive diet for arboreal creatures able to reach them, and these in turn performed for the plants the useful service of helping to disperse their seeds.

To this process of adaptation our species owes a number of its most important features. The toes and fingers of the prosimians became elongated until they were ideally suited to grasping branches. Monkeys, with their tails, first appeared about fifty million years ago. The tail served as an excellent balancing organ, and in some species—the New World monkeys such as the spider and howler monkeys (see pages 110–111)—its grasping ability served as a fifth limb. Apes and monkeys developed a new form of locomotion, namely brachiation, which means the power to progress through a tree canopy by use of arms alone. Evolving powerful arm and pectoral muscles, and a shoulder joint so that the arm could rotate a full 180 degrees, these arboreal creatures swung from branch to branch, hardly ever descending to ground level.

Humans have retained this same strength and flexibility in their shoulders and arms. Because leaping through space requires precise judgement, the early primates also developed binocular vision. The necessary co-ordination of limbs, eyes and other organs called for the evolution of a larger brain.

Monkeys and apes retained the characteristics developed by the prosimians over the millennia, but they also evolved new ones of their own, notably thumbs opposing their fingers, which helped them to clutch branches more securely. Some monkeys, though, began to descend from the tree-tops; perhaps they first came down to pick up ripe fruit shed on the ground; perhaps a diminishing rainfall caused the forest to thin out. Whatever the reason, the apes from which man evolved ceased to be entirely arboreal. The ones that remained within the forest, such as the gorillas, have become almost extinct probably due to the more human-like forms that were evolving at the same time. These ventured out of the forest into the drier savannah lands and are our direct ancestors.

Their earliest remains so far discovered are those of a creature named *Ramapithecus* that lived in the Siwalik Hills of India. It was a small, ape-like species, less than half the size of a modern man but apparently able to stand upright. And with that ability came a new advance. The long opposing thumb and fingers could be turned to a new and important use—they could pick up sticks and stones. *Ramapithecus*, who lived some fourteen million years ago, may even have used these as tools for simple tasks. Between two and five million years ago several hominid species developed in eastern and southern Africa. One was a creature known as *Australopithecus*, who seems to have represented a side channel, doomed to oblivion, from the main stream of human development. Another was *Homo habilis*, a creature with a small brain yet able to fashion tools as well as to use the sticks and stones he picked up by chance.

Homo erectus, or upright man, is the name given to our undoubted direct ancestors who lived half a million years ago. Though no more than four or five feet tall he had mastered the art of making tools by flaking chips off stones to make axe-heads, and, of extreme importance, he had discovered how to use fire. Remains in China and Europe of *Homo erectus*, in association with those of animals, reveal that he killed and ate elephants, horses, rhinoceroses, camels, deer and wild boar, as well as the smaller animal species that roamed the more open-canopied forests. The ability to capture and kill such large animals would be beyond the capacity of a single individual and called for the organized efforts of a group. *Homo erectus* had therefore learned the rudiments of speech and co-operation.

So the way was prepared for the emergence of *Homo sapiens*, of which the oldest examples so far discovered are probably about 250,000 years old. The earliest specimen could still be termed dwarfish, but its brain capacity was

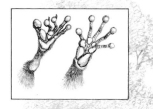

Below *In prosimians, the fingers and toes became lengthened, so the slender, outermost branches could be grasped easily.*

Below *Tree-dwelling apes developed a distinct method of locomotion—brachiation—making them the most acrobatic of all primates. An arm-swing movement propels the body.*

Orang-utan

Gibbon

Below *Ground-dwelling apes such as the chimpanzee and the gorilla can walk by putting weight on their front knuckles. They also have opposable thumbs and big toes to pick up objects.*

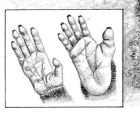

Gorilla

very similar to our own. Man had arrived

To avoid competition from other animals the first hominids ventured out, on two legs, into the drier savannah lands where fruits, nuts and other plant foods were less abundant. To compensate, they learned to use weapons for killing wild animals to supplement their diet. Today most of *Homo sapiens* have abandoned the hunter-gatherer's way of life, but luckily enough communities have survived for explorers and anthropologists to record their culture, which gives us some clues towards understanding our origins.

Deep within the human consciousness, our forest origins have never been forgotten. Man has always been powerfully affected by the mystery of the forest. Many religions enshrine traces of tree cults and some of the earliest religious ceremonies were held in forest groves. Ancient superstitions still half believed today, such as "touching wood" to avert catastrophes, testify to the continuing magic of trees.

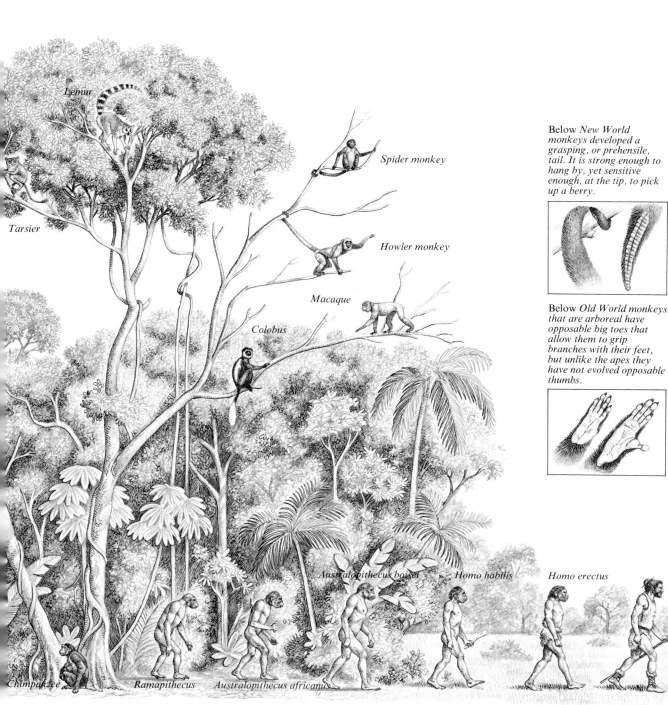

Spider monkey

Howler monkey

Macaque

Colobus

Lemur

Tarsier

Chimpanzee

Chimpanzee Ramapithecus Australopithecus africanus Australopithecus boisei Homo habilis Homo erectus Homo sapiens

Below *New World monkeys developed a grasping, or prehensile, tail. It is strong enough to hang by, yet sensitive enough, at the tip, to pick up a berry.*

Below *Old World monkeys that are arboreal have opposable big toes that allow them to grip branches with their feet, but unlike the apes they have not evolved opposable thumbs.*

During the past 70 million years primates evolved characteristics that were specifically adapted to life in the forest. Each of these left its mark on modern man, who incorporated any new innovations, such as colour vision and improved eye-hand co-ordination, that were essential for an arboreal existence. These, in turn, led to the development of a more complex brain.

The primates made progressive changes in their mode of locomotion. The four-footed gait of the prosimians gave way to tailed monkeys, vestiges of which still appear in the human embryo, to the upright arm-swinging brachiation of apes. No one knows why ape supremacy suddenly ended, about 10 million years ago, but possibly it was due to competition from the more human-like forms that were evolving simultaneously. The new apes adopted bipedalism, typical of man, leaving the hands free to make tools. The ability to walk meant that the hominids, to avoid competition from other animals, could exploit a new niche, the transitional zone between forest and grassland, and become hunter-gatherers.

HUNTER-GATHERERS

Today in several continents hunter-gatherers still inhabit the primeval forest. As recently as 1971 a tribe, consisting of twenty-five people and calling themselves the Tasaday, *right*, was discovered living in the rain forests of the island of Mindanao, in the Philippines. These gentle people live in caves, manufacture simple tools and make cloth by pounding the inner bark of fig trees. Their diet consists of small trapped animals, frogs, crabs and fish and fruits and roots. They live in total harmony with the forest.

In the rain forests of central Africa the Mbuti pygmies live in a similar habitat and enjoy a similar way of life. Their diet includes birds, monkeys, grubs, at least six kinds of antelope, roots, berries, fruit and fungi. Food is always plentiful in the hot, wet woodlands. The Punans are another nomadic tribe who wander through primeval forests, this time in Borneo. They use poison darts propelled from blow-pipes, as do a number of South American forest tribes.

The Ice Ages

No one really knows why the ice came. Changes in the angle of the Earth's axis, excessive volcanism, periodic fluctuations in the amount of heat reaching us from the sun, have all been suggested as causes, but even if one of them could be proved we would still be left wondering why that had happened.

We know that it was a very gradual process, probably beginning in the Pliocene age, between one and fifteen million years ago. The first great glaciation was at its peak early in the Pleistocene era, about a million years ago. The last retreat of the glaciers from what are now temperate lands ended between 10,000–8,000 BC, if indeed it can be said to have ended at all. The Ice Ages must therefore be referred to in the plural. The great ice caps advanced and retreated at least four times, and according to some theories, six.

Although slow, the advance of the ice was inexorable. Winter by winter the glaciers crept a little farther down the mountains. Each spring the snow lingered longer on the upland plateaux, until one spring it failed to thaw at all; each autumn the edge of the frozen sea inched a little farther south. Lengthy, cold winds built up over the frozen lands and resisted the penetration of warmer oceanic air.

Although there were certain exceptions, notably Japan and much of eastern Asia, the Ice Ages were world-wide phenomena. Northern and southern hemispheres were affected simultaneously. A natural consequence was that with so much water locked up in the form of ice, the oceans retreated from the land. According to one theory their level fell by about 400 feet, according to others by twice as much. Vast areas now covered by relatively

shallow seas were then dry land. One of them has been termed Beringia—the land bridge, linking Siberia with Alaska, over which the first people reached North America.

Before the ice came much of the northern hemisphere was enjoying a warmer climate than that of present times. The forests of northern Europe and North America were almost tropical in their profusion of tree species. Where the willow, oak, maple, alder, horse chestnut, redwood and cypress are still found there grew walnut, hickory, sycamore, several species of palm, cedar and maidenhair trees. As the ice advanced, so the trees retreated southwards, and here the geographical formation of the continents played a crucial role.

In North America the mountain ranges, notably the Rockies and the Appalachians, run north and south, so no barrier was interposed in the path of the retreating trees. Nucleus populations, ready to recolonize the north when favourable conditions returned, could survive in southern valleys. But in Europe the mountain ranges tend to lie on an east–west axis. In particular, the Alps and the Pyrenees proved insuperable obstacles. As the ice crept slowly southwards, creating a broad zone of tundra between it and the tree line, the more delicate tree species were trapped against the northern wall of the mountains. So, as the tide of ice ebbed and flowed throughout the long Pleistocene era, there was no hope of these species re-establishing themselves in the mild interglacial periods. North of the mountains they had become extinct. Only on the eastern side of Eurasia were the geographical conditions similar to those of North America, which is why species such as the maidenhair tree (*Ginkgo*), long extinct in Europe, have survived in China.

China and the eastern United States are also the only remaining habitats of the tulip tree (*Liriodendron*), once widely dispersed in the intervening territory. Before the ice came magnificent *Sequoia* trees also formed forests

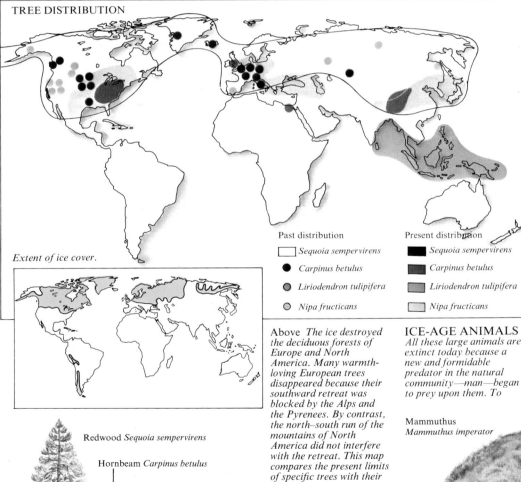

TREE DISTRIBUTION

Extent of ice cover.

Past distribution		Present distribution	
□	*Sequoia sempervirens*	■	*Sequoia sempervirens*
●	*Carpinus betulus*		*Carpinus betulus*
◉	*Liriodendron tulipifera*		*Liriodendron tulipifera*
○	*Nipa fructicans*		*Nipa fructicans*

Redwood *Sequoia sempervirens*

Hornbeam *Carpinus betulus*

Tulip tree *Liriodendron tulipifera*

Palm *Nipa fructicans*

Above *The ice destroyed the deciduous forests of Europe and North America. Many warmth-loving European trees disappeared because their southward retreat was blocked by the Alps and the Pyrenees. By contrast, the north–south run of the mountains of North America did not interfere with the retreat. This map compares the present limits of specific trees with their past range.*

Left *At one time Sequoia sempervirens formed extensive forests across the northern hemisphere, but today it is confined to the Pacific coast of the USA. The hornbeam, too, is more limited in extent than it was. The Nipa palm retreated to Asia and the tulip tree only managed to survive in north-east America and China.*

ICE-AGE ANIMALS

All these large animals are extinct today because a new and formidable predator in the natural community—man—began to prey upon them. To

survive the harsh cold of late glacial times, humans became more expert in luring these massive creatures to their death by using ingenious traps, harpoons and spears.

We can easily imagine the physical appearance of the prehistoric animals of the forest from the graphic representations of stone-age painters and sculptors, and fossils. In addition,

Mammuthus
Mammuthus imperator

Woolly rhinoceros
Coelodonta antiquitatis

right across the northern hemisphere. Fossil remains of a species very similar to *Araucaria* (the monkey-puzzle tree, which is now only native to the southern hemisphere) have been found in Great Britain.

Throughout the Pleistocene age mammals, more mobile than trees, followed the ice tides. Many of the herbivorous species lived on the edge of the forests or on the adjacent grassland, and predators accompanied them. Following the pattern of the extinct dinosaurs, some of them achieved gigantic proportions, much greater than those of their modern counterparts (see below).

Among the richest sources of information about the fauna of 10,000 years ago, when the glaciers of the last Ice Age were receding, are the La Brea tar pits, of Los Angeles, California. Here, asphalt or tar, oozing from the underlying rocks, formed open pools, deceptively covered with a film of water. Animals coming to drink were trapped by the viscous material and their bones were left in the pits. Besides the giant sloths and mammoths the remains of camels and horses (both of which subsequently became extinct in America), tapirs, deer and bison are abundant. Mingled with them are the remains of the fearsome predators that assembled to prey on the struggling animals. Eurasia has no site quite as dramatic as La Brea, but numerous fossils testify to the presence in this period of large mammals such as the aurochs, the giant Irish elk, the woodland musk-ox, the European bison and the mammoth.

Accompanying the herbivorous herds on their treks, in a similar predatory role, were men. Evidently they were not deterred by cold and storms, for many of the earliest discovered sites were quite near the glaciers. Living much of the time in rigorous climates, these early people were becoming increasingly ingenious and adaptable. Their social organization allowed enough free time for development of art and culture.

FOOD GATHERING

Early in spring our forest-dwelling ancestors made oatcakes from the rhizomes of bracken, syrup from tree sap, and bark bread. Later in the year they gathered wild salad plants as well as berries, nuts and forest fungi (some shown below) to supplement their diet.

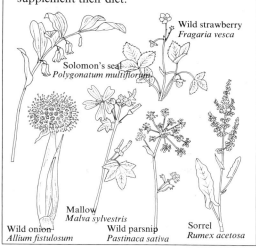

Wild strawberry
Fragaria vesca

Solomon's seal
Polygonatum multiflorum

Mallow
Malva sylvestris

Wild onion
Allium fistulosum

Wild parsnip
Pastinaca sativa

Sorrel
Rumex acetosa

Below As the ice retreated the hunter-gatherers of Europe enjoyed a comfortable and lively existence in the new warm conditions, preying successfully on the multiplying herds of bison. This vigorous bison on the ceiling of the Altamira cave in north-east Spain—the "Sistine Chapel" of Palaeolithic art—was painted by a Cro-Magnon artist about 10,000 years ago. Other animals depicted at Altamira include horses and boars.

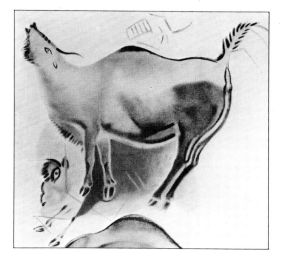

MAMMAL DISTRIBUTION

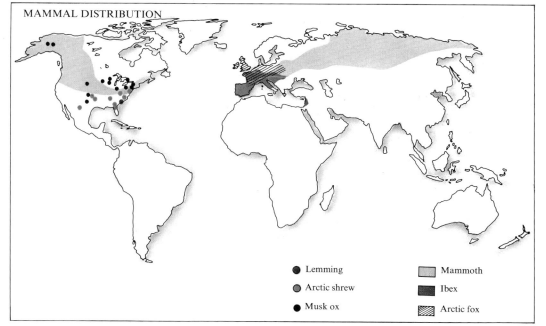

● Lemming
● Arctic shrew
● Musk ox

▨ Mammoth
▨ Ibex
▨ Arctic fox

...perfectly intact but frozen carcasses of mammoths, including a baby mammoth, have been retrieved from the Siberian permafrost. We know, therefore, that the mammoths and rhinoceroses had long shaggy fur and sloping hind quarters, which enabled them to browse comfortably through the boughs of forest trees. Lacking sweat glands, they were better able to retain maximum body heat in the bitter cold of the Ice Ages. The mammoths inhabited the northern coniferous forests of spruce, pine and fir, whereas the elephants and rhinoceroses preferred the more southerly mixed deciduous forests. Farther south again, in forests of yucca trees, lived the massive ground sloths. Slow-moving vegetarians, they were an easy prey for the vicious sabre-toothed cat that pursued them.

Above The map compares the past distribution of certain mammals to that of their present range. Many arctic mammals that are now restricted to circumpolar regions were abundant in central Europe and even as far south as Spain and Moravia, indicating the prevalence of much colder conditions during the Ice Ages.

Woolly mammoth
Mammuthus primigenius

Forest elephant
Palaeoloxodon antiquus

Forest rhinoceros
Dicerorhinus kirchbergensis

Sabre-tooth cat
Smilodon

Ground sloth
Paramylodon

The forest thaws out

The people of the Old Stone Age, with their crude tools and their hunting, gathering and fishing lifestyle, made little impact on the post-glacial forests. As the ice retreated and the climate became warmer birch trees dominated the new landscape, their white spindly trunks stretching endlessly across the rapidly thawing northern hemisphere.

The birch trees became a basic commodity and played an intimate role in everyday life. Birch bark was peeled off in thin strips and sewn like fine leather. It was moulded to make the vessels that were essential before the advent of pottery, and it was made into canoes for transport. In early spring the fresh cambial tissues were ground up to make a nutritious bread, ensuring a reliable source of protein, and the sap was fermented to produce mead. Birch pitch provided the vital glue used by early hunters to fix their flint blades into wooden handles or to secure their arrow and spear heads. This birch-based culture began at the dawn of history and continued well into the early farming communities, but even today some North American Indians use bark for canoes, while some Russian peasants wear birch bark shoes.

The post Ice Age hunters did little harm to the forest trees, but their lifestyle severely depleted the population of certain forest animals. The Irish elk was hunted to extinction. It was probably a docile animal that was easy to kill for meat, and its antlers and hide were used extensively, like the birch, as another essential household commodity. Many other of the larger forest mammals—the mammoths, rhinoceroses and sabre-toothed cats—typical of the cold glacial times and not adapted to the warmer conditions, had become extinct. They were replaced by fast-running animals that were difficult to trap or hunt successfully with primitive spears, slings, bows and arrows.

As supplies of meat began to dwindle, our prehistoric ancestors made a dramatic discovery. Being skilled plant gatherers they ob-

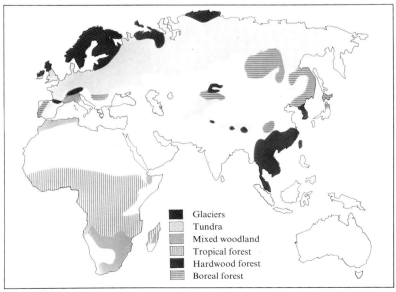

Above *As the continental ice sheets began to melt a new primeval forest, composed mainly of birch trees, flourished in the northern hemisphere. For a while, between 10,000 and 5,000 years ago, birch trees dominated the landscape to such an extent that the time has often been referred to as the "Birch Period".*

Left *The map shows the position of the primeval forest types that began to recolonize different parts of the Earth as the climate gradually became warmer at the end of the last ice age. Although glaciers were still present in northern Europe and on the higher mountains, the lowlands of northern Asia were mostly ice free, because of less rainfall.*

Glaciers
Tundra
Mixed woodland
Tropical forest
Hardwood forest
Boreal forest

THE SLASH AND BURN TECHNIQUE

The knowledge of farming gradually spread to the hunters and gatherers who lived in the forests of northern Eurasia. By 5000 BC the character of the original forest had gradually changed; now being mainly composed of oak and some elm, linden, pine and ash trees. Our understanding of the lifestyle of these people has recently been increased by re-enacting their farming methods.

Above *Prior to its extinction, about 10,000 years ago, the Irish elk, a relatively docile animal, was extensively hunted for its antlers, hide and meat by the people living in the northern birch forests.*

Below *This Egyptian tomb painting depicts practical aspects of ancient farming on the flood plain of the Nile. Workers are shown felling trees, hoeing crops, and their cattle are drawing simple ploughs.*

served that the seeds from such wild plants as wheat and barley could be deliberately planted and cultivated. They began to farm. And this discovery, in terms of human evolution, was as important as coming down from the trees and learning to walk. At first primitive agriculture was a precarious business and, although many people kept domestic animals and grew crops, they still lived in much the same way as their ancestors, supplementing their diet with some fishing and hunting. The gradual transition from a hunting to a farming economy has been termed the Neolithic Revolution, or New Stone Age, in which polished stone axes were used extensively to cut down trees, as opposed to the Palaeolithic or Old Stone Age, when people simply used rough surface-chipped implements.

The forest had a definite influence on human cultural development. The most dominant cultures—the Egyptians of the Nile Valley, the Incas and their predecessors of the High Andes, the Pueblos of North America and the Bantus of Africa—all developed in open savannah country where tree removal posed no great problem, and where wheat, barley or other cereal crops grew abundantly in their wild form before the discovery of cultivation.

The earliest farming communities of which we have knowledge seem to have developed around 10,000 BC on the flood plains of the large river systems of the world: the Tigris, Euphrates, Indus, Nile and Yellow rivers. Tamarisk, acacia, fig and willow trees were scattered sparsely across this fertile crescent and the sandy silty river-plain soils could easily be worked with crude digging sticks. People began to build dwellings around which they could farm, and they mined flint or obsidian with which to manufacture axes for clearing forest trees.

In Eurasia the new knowledge of agriculture spread with the expansion of the population—from its nucleus in Asia and the Middle East, to the Mediterranean Basin and then up the Danube valley, finally reaching the Scandinavian shores about 4000 BC. As the new settlers reached Europe and northern Asia they began to penetrate the thick primeval oak, hazel and beech forests that had begun to replace and grow alongside the birch trees of the northern lands. These great enveloping forests were now seen as potential fields and with the new stone axes they were hacked down to create farmland.

A group of Danish scientists has attempted to re-enact the early Eurasian farming techniques. They used an axe made of a genuine blade, well preserved in the Danish peat bogs, fitted into a copy of an original ash-wood shaft. In the experiment, three men managed to clear six hundred square yards of silver birch forest in four hours, using a blade that had not been sharpened for more than four thousand years.

Tree pollen associated with the Neolithic axes, which has been discovered by archaeologists, suggests that small clearings were hewed in the primeval forest and that the brushwood was ignited using a birch bark torch. Then, small fields of grain were planted in the cleared patch of warm ash-strewn soil. As the forest began to grow back the farmers would move on to hack out a new living in another part of the forest. This "slash and burn" technique is still used in many parts of the world by semi-nomadic tribes. Unfortunately, this method of farming inhibits the regeneration of the original forest as any shoots or seedlings that manage to survive the fire and grow are usually eaten by domestic livestock.

The domestication of plants and animals was an important development because it enabled people to become independent of their environment, rather than being totally at its mercy. Towards the end of the Neolithic era another important discovery was made, the smelting of metals; first copper and tin, then iron were smelted, all of which required large quantities of wood to stoke the furnaces (see pages 30–31).

First, men cleared tracts of the forest. They felled some trees by using axes made of flint and secured in a wooden shaft. These clearings were covered with brushwood and ignited in successive strips so that large areas were burned.

Small fields of cereals were planted in the warm ashy soil and some of the clearing was used for pasturing animals. These events are confirmed by archaeological studies of plant pollen that show the sudden appearance of pollen from herbaceous plants, cereals and new weeds, notably plantain, the plant that North American Indians called "the footsteps of the white man".

As the forest began to grow back, the farmers would move on to a new area. According to the pollen record, after a clearing had been made, different trees—willows, birches and aspens—would spring up. So, the character of the original forest was never to be re-established in quite the same way. Even today, the proportion of elm and linden trees is reduced.

The first civilizations

Below Only remnants of Lebanon's forests of cedar remain today. Their ancestors, which witnessed the rise and fall of empires, played an important economic role in the ancient history of the Middle East.

Farming 2000 BC

Civilizations 3500–2000 BC

Centres of copper smelting 4000 BC

Trade routes

Spread of iron smelting by 2000 BC

The early civilizations tended to grow up in the world's large river valleys where the annual floods and the long, hot, dry summers were ideally suited for farming but were unfortunately adverse to tree growth. The sedentary way of life associated with early farming communities demanded an ever increasing supply of wood to build more permanent settlements and the few hardy, drought-resistant trees were inadequate for the growing needs of the people. Wood became a vital resource and quickly assumed a status similar to that of oil today, encouraging the early powers to strive to gain control of areas that were forested.

The ancient Egyptians of the Nile valley looked towards the mountains of Lebanon, whose now barren slopes were once clad with tiers of fragrant cedar trees. Cedar wood is remarkably durable and was used to build houses, palaces, temples and fleets. Wooden rollers were needed to manoeuvre the vast stones to build the pyramids of their pharaohs. Cedar sawdust was occasionally used in mummification and cedar resin, which imparts the decay resistance to the wood, was perfect for embalmment and as a coating for coffins and papyrus. Thus, the Phoenicians, who lived in the Lebanon, became prosperous. They were skilled woodworkers and renowned boat builders, exporting most of their products to Egypt in exchange for precious gold, metal artefacts and papyrus, which they could not manufacture themselves.

Cedar wood was used lavishly in the construction of King Solomon's temple built between 965 and 926 BC in Jerusalem. Solomon conscripted a huge army of men to harvest and transport the cedar trees from the Lebanon. In return for the wood and the aid of skilled Phoenician craftsmen Solomon promised an annual supply of pure oil and wheat to King Hiram of Phoenicia while the temple was being built. But, unforeseeably, the temple took twenty years to build and Solomon fell behind in his annual payments. To compensate for his debts, Solomon had to concede Eliothia, eastern Africa and western Asia plus twenty Canaanite cities to Hiram. This was the first land concession known to history, and it was directly precipitated by the exploitation of the cedars of Lebanon.

The Romans, again, saw cedar wood as an essential raw material with which to build their navies. The diminishing supply prompted Hadrian, emperor between AD 117 and 138, to initiate the first conservation legislation by rendering the northern portion of the Lebanon mountains as a forest reserve to ensure a supply of ship timber for the Roman Empire. Hadrian actually placed stones at its boundaries with an inscription which when translated reads, "Boundary of the Forest of the Emperor Hadrian Augustus: Four Tree Species Reserved". Today these stones are left standing in their original positions, but sadly now on a barren deserted mountain-side.

Smelting involved another early extensive use for wood and the first metal to be smelted was copper. It is usually found in the Earth's crust as an ore and must first be heated to yield the pure metal. The technique of smelting was probably first noticed accidentally—perhaps a wind-blown fire produced enough heat to separate copper metal from its ore—but it meant that coppersmiths turned to the forests for charcoal wood to fuel their furnaces. When copper is alloyed with tin, it forms bronze, which is much harder than copper and so was used to make sharp daggers, saws and axes, allowing more forests to be cleared for farmland. But the materials needed to make bronze—wood for charcoal and copper and tin ores—were rarely found in the same locality, making bronze a valuable commodity.

It needed more skill and higher temperatures to smelt iron, which had to be hammered while still white hot and plunged into cold water while red hot to produce a hard cutting edge, but because iron ore was abundant and easy to find, it gradually became a substitute for bronze. It was used in implements to replace many of the older stone and wooden digging implements and, because it was harder, it was better for tools used to cut down large trees.

The Iron Age culture was present in the Celtic communities throughout Eurasia. It developed in the area north of the Alps and spread through northern Europe to Germany

Before 10,000 BC all the people of the world lived in small hunting and gathering communities (left). But this way of life changed with the development of civilizations in the great river valleys of the world. The map (below) shows the ancient metal-working sites. The knowledge of smelting spread from its nucleus in the Middle East to the other civilizations that were developing simultaneously in India and China.

Since wood was the only energy source, it was used in large amounts throughout Eurasia to fuel the furnaces, thus drastically depleting the world's forests at an early stage.

In contrast, the Indians of the south-western USA had less incentive to discover the art of smelting; it was not necessary for the maintenance of their cultures because they had plenty of "native" or pure copper and gold.

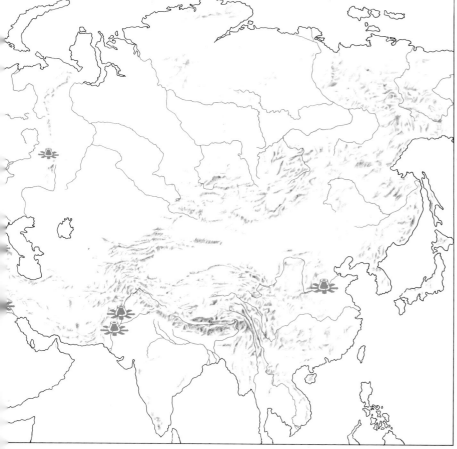

Above *Archaeological remains of a copper smelting site in the Lebanon. Pieces of associated charcoal indicate that cedar wood, imported into the area from 400 miles away, was used to smelt the ore.*

Left *Iron Age furnaces were filled with alternating layers of wood charcoal and ore. Heat from the burning charcoal reduced the ore, allowing soft iron to trickle down and form a puddle at the bottom of the furnace.*

France, Belgium, Britain and Ireland. Before the advent of iron, Eurasia was composed of a huge primeval mixed oak forest that was virtually impenetrable. The new sharp iron axes facilitated clearance of large forest trees and ploughs tipped with iron could cope with the thick clay soils (see pages 32–33).

Amber was another precious commodity of the time. It is a fossilized resin formed from pine trees that once grew on a forested land now covered by the Baltic Sea. Storms and waves washed the amber on to Baltic beaches, where amber hunters would collect and trade it for metal implements.

The Celtic civilization of the temperate primeval forests in Europe and the Maya civilization, thousands of miles away in the tropical rain forests of Central America, flourished simultaneously. Although the two civilizations evolved in different ways, in forests that were different in character, their attitude towards the trees was surprisingly similar. The forest inspired both the Celts and the Mayas with great respect because trees were vital in so many aspects of their everyday life and tree worship was widely practised throughout Europe and Asia Minor. Although no vestige of the magical ceremonies performed in oak groves by Celtic priests, the Druids, have survived, the Mayas have left relics of their religious sanctuaries, some that have only recently been discovered, deep in the high plains of the tropical rain forests of Guatemala.

THE CELTIC CALENDAR

In Celtic times, months were true "moonths", that is, they measured the period of time from one full moon to the next and each month was represented by a tree that was either in season, or flowering at the time. This allowed for thirteen months alternating between twenty-eight or twenty-nine days in length, roughly equivalent to one lunation. The one extra day fell on 23 December, after the winter solstice.

24 December – 20 January
Birch *beth*

21 January – 17 February
Rowan *luis*

18 February – 17 March
Ash *nion*

18 March – 14 April
Alder *fearn*

15 April – 12 May
Willow *saille*

13 May – 9 June
Hawthorn *vath*

10 June – 7 July
Oak *duir*

8 July – 4 August
Holly *tinne*

5 August – 1 September
Hazel *coll*

2 September – 29 September
Vine *muin*

30 September – 27 October
Ivy *gort*

28 October – 24 November
Reed *ngetal*

25 November – 22 December
Elder *ruis*

The Middle Ages

The agricultural practices of the medieval world were not very different from those of the Neolithic era. Although the ancient "scratch" plough was replaced by a heavier and more efficient machine, the political and economic order—feudalism—was very different. About ninety per cent of all the people were farming peasants. They lived within an ordered hierarchical society where life depended upon a careful balance of three competitive resources: arable land, grazing land and the forest. Land cleared of forest could provide extra corn crops, but the forest was needed for many other daily essentials.

The arable land around each village was usually divided into three large fields, and each of these was in turn divided into long narrow strips. The feudal lord took the produce from a third of this land and it was tilled for him by serfs—peasants who were "bound to the soil". The rest might be cultivated by freeholding peasants, or by the serfs for their own use. Beyond the arable land lay marsh, meadow, mountain and forest.

According to his status or the size of his holding a peasant might be allowed to turn a limited number of animals to graze within the forest or on its outskirts, and sometimes open grazing forests of oak stretched right up to the edge of the towns. Here pigs were fattened on acorns, for the oak was then valued as an agricultural fruit-bearing tree and it was not until the advent of the potato in the mid-eighteenth century that the oak became valued primarily for its timber. Ivy stripped from trees and gathered twigs provided the peasant with livestock fodder, and such forest crops as hazel nuts, beech mast and sloes were gathered and stored for human nourishment during the lean winter months.

A privileged peasant might have the right to fish in the forest or to cut turf within it. The gathering of firewood might be permitted "by hook or by crook", that is whatever boughs fell with the aid of a long hooked pole. Wood was necessary in order to build houses (see pages 178–179), boats, tools, carts, wine presses, furniture and even for clogs which served as shoes for the ordinary people. Bees were kept within the forest and their harvest provided not just the only available sweetener—honey—but also the beeswax that was essential for the liturgical candles of medieval Christendom.

Many of the monastic communities of the Middle Ages, particularly those of the austere Benedictines and Cistercians, were set up in remote forested areas because the heavy labour of clearance accorded well with the monastic injunction that "to work is to pray". The renowned Abbey of Clairvaux in France was started up in a rugged forested valley in Champagne where wolves and bandits roamed. With the assistance of local peasants the monks transformed a wilderness into a rich agricultural landscape. Landowners frequently made gifts of forested land to the monks because of their known expertise in clearing it for cultivation, and thus attracting

settlers. Not surprisingly, efficient farming and skilled forest management eventually made the monks prosperous, contradicting the poverty that was supposed to be a hallmark of their lives. The Cistercian landlords of Furness Abbey in England, for example, acted like any other feudal lords, issuing licenses to charcoal burners in their woodlands with heavy fines for infringements.

Charcoal was in increasing demand during the Middle Ages. Apart from its use in the iron forges, it was also required as fuel for such industries as beer brewing. Wood ash was needed as a flux in the glassmaking process, and it was also used in making soap.

These pressures on the forest stimulated the expansion of the practice of coppicing trees in the Middle Ages. Since Roman times it had been noticed that certain broadleaved trees sprouted new shoots from their stumps when cut, and that these shoots grew very rapidly because the fully developed root system of the parent tree nourished them. Thus fuelwood

and fencing, as well as wood for glass and ironworks, came to be largely produced from coppiced trees. Pollarding was another type of coppicing by which the trees were cut above ground instead of at ground level. It was often practised in areas where grazing animals made ordinary coppicing difficult or, because it prolonged the life of a tree, to provide long-lived trees of distinctive shape to mark boundaries.

Such measures were timely because the extent to which medieval industry destroyed the forest is popularly underestimated. In France, for example, only thirty-seven million acres were left covered by forests in 1300—two million acres less than the area under forest there today. Wood was so scarce in Douai in northern France that peasant families could not afford wooden coffins for their dead. Instead a coffin was rented and after the burial ceremony the undertaker would throw the corpse into the earth and retain the valuable coffin for further use.

Gradually each remaining forest was claimed

Above *In an age without sugar, the art of bee-keeping was important. In Russia, it was carried out on a large scale and extensive forests were reserved as bee walks.*

Left *In the medieval world the best hams grew on oak trees, for pigs were fattened on acorns. Oaks were therefore left to grow very old to increase fruit production.*

Below *A 17th-century illustration of Robin Hood who "robbed the rich to help the poor". This medieval outlaw and his "merrie men" operated from within the then large Sherwood Forest. Although such legendary outlaws may never have existed, the popular celebration of him bears witness to the fact that the forest sheltered fugitives from medieval "justice".*

by somebody. The lords, bishops, dukes and court officials of medieval Europe devised elaborate legal codes to enforce their exclusive or delegated enjoyment of the forest's riches. The privileges of bona fide forest workers were strictly defined, however, and sometimes they were abused. The French bishop of Auxerre once crucified one of his foresters for selling his master's pigeons for his own profit, but, by contrast, a thirteenth-century keeper of the Lonsdale forest in England was reprimanded by his lord for depriving lepers of a traditional right to graze their cattle within the forest without paying.

Forest officials checked that no trees were felled, buildings erected or charcoal burned by unauthorized persons and the allocation and payment for grazing facilities were strictly regulated. In addition, the aristocratic preoccupation with the forest as the cover for game worth hunting for meat provided employment for many in the great medieval hunting retinues (see pages 142–143).

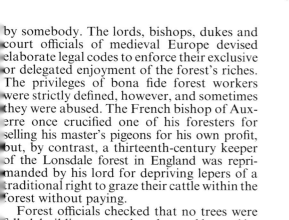

Above *There was a close relationship between woodmanship and carpentry in the Middle Ages. To build a house like this, small 20- to 70-year-old oaks were cut as occasion demanded and worked while still green.*

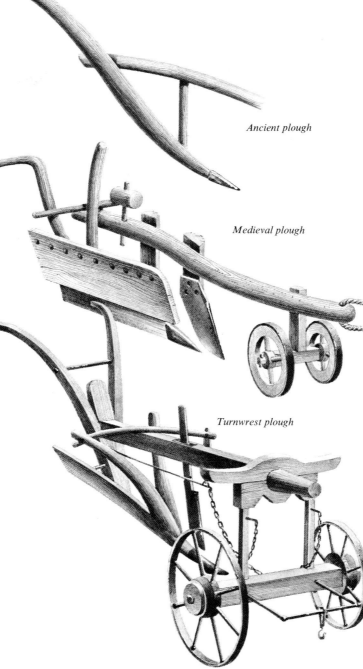

Ancient plough

Medieval plough

Turnwrest plough

THE PLOUGH

Although improved by the addition of an iron tip to the share, the ancient "scratch" plough merely scratched the soil surface and was inadequate for the heavy soils of much of northern Europe. But, as a result of gradual improvements over the centuries, a revolutionary heavy plough came into general use in the 11th century. In its fully developed form (an early Saxon version is illustrated here) it had a coulter to make a vertical cut, a ploughshare to cut under the sod, a mouldboard to turn the sod over and two wheels to make a more even furrow and lighten the work of the ploughman. Apart from turning over the soil more efficiently, this machine created a "ridge and furrow" effect that improved drainage. The eventual replacement of oxen teams by horsepower in many areas further increased its efficiency. The medieval plough stimulated forest clearance and facilitated the cultivation of the rich alluvial lowland soil that had been avoided by early settlers. Plough designs varied according to local geography and information, but owing to the scarcity of iron only the digging parts of the share and coulter were made of metal until the 18th century. The turnwrest plough, which was in use until the 1920s, suited undulating English lowlands because the turnwrest could be adjusted to turn a furrow on either side without turning the whole plough.

Left *Wood became a renewable resource in medieval Europe as a result of the coppicing of trees. The clusters of small shoots springing from the bases of these felled lime trees can be cut after 7 to 20 years. By this time they will have grown to the size of small but extremely useful poles. The stumps will then send forth new shoots, and the process can be continued for a long time. In the Middle Ages coppices yielded wood for charcoal, heating, building and fencing.*

Right *Now an isolated rural craft, hurdle making was once a major forest industry. Coppiced rods are split from end to end and woven into a fence.*

Forests and sea power

Below *Quercus virginiana, a fine ship-building oak from the southern colonies was unappreciated by the English navy because American oak was synonymous with the inferior Quercus alba traded from New England.*

Right *In an age when nations exerted diplomatic pressure for timber, just as they do now for oil, the Baltic trade was jealously watched over by England, France, Holland and Spain. Denmark controlled the Sound, the only safe route for timber ships, while the English navy hovered close by. Mast and planking timber was of particular importance and the precarious nature of the Baltic supply stimulated an interest in the New World's forests.*

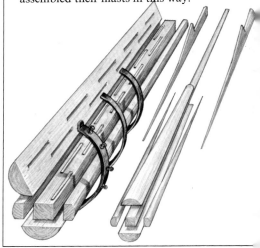

Jarrah   Teak   Mahogany

Oak   African oak   Pine

Timber for the building of ships was one of the earliest resources man found in the forest. Although builders possessed from very early times the necessary skills to make big ships, it was not until the development of maritime warfare in the seventeenth and eighteenth centuries that the forests of northern Europe began to experience yet another pressure to meet this demand. The new onslaught coincided with a period when the forests were beginning to show signs of exhaustion from other causes. Throughout the medieval centuries the increasing population of western Europe encroached steadily on the remaining forested land and claimed it for agriculture. Where iron ore was found in woodland districts, the forests were progressively destroyed to make charcoal, which, before coal was used for the purpose, was employed in vast quantities for smelting.

For many centuries forests were valued primarily for the cover they provided for deer, and therefore the royal pastime of hunting. By the sixteenth century, however, the emphasis had shifted to the trees themselves, which were now coming to be regarded as a national asset. When the invasion of England by the Spanish Armada was being planned, the Spanish ambassador in London was instructed to investigate the possibility of setting fire to the Forest of Dean and so destroying all the ship-building oaks there. The compilation of a census of trees in the New Forest, in southern England in 1608, indicates a realization that the supply was not limitless. For specialist purposes the timber merchants of western Europe were already having to look beyond their own national boundaries.

In ship building special timbers were required for the keel, the curved sides and the mast. For the curved sides, or "compass" timbers, oaks which had grown naturally to the

required shape were preferred to those which had to be shaped by saw, and timber merchants used to send out skilled buyers to scour the countryside for them. They often came from trees standing in isolation. Giant elms were in demand for keels, though the stern post, which held the rudder and which might be as much as forty feet long and twenty-eight inches thick, was normally of oak. For timbers such as this and for the towering masts the western maritime nations turned to the oak and fir forests of central Europe.

There the trees grew in close stands that produced tall, straight trunks with few branches. They grew near great rivers, such as the Vistula and the Oder, down which timber rafts could be floated to the Baltic ports. A huge trade in timber therefore developed between the Baltic and the maritime powers of north-western Europe. Competition was keen and, in time of war, fierce. From 1686 onwards the English sent their fleet into the Baltic time and again to protect their timber trade and more particularly to keep open the narrow straits between Denmark and Sweden.

At the same time, America began to appear as a source of supply for ship-building timbers; the first supply had been shipped from Virginia in 1609. For a first-class ship of the line the mainmast needed a straight trunk with a length of at least 120 feet and a diameter of twenty-seven to thirty inches. New England produced suitable pines in reasonable abundance for a time, but much wasteful felling occurred. To protect suitable trees, commissioners appointed by the Royal Navy explored the forests of New England and eastern Canada and marked the trees with the "Broad Arrow" sign, made by three blows with a marking hatchet, which now came into use for identifying Government forests, and later all Government property.

Above *At times a ship might contain wood from five continents. Teak came from India and Burma, and oak and pine from North America. Mahogany from Central and South America and the Caribbean was also used. There was also a very limited supply of kauri from New Zealand and jarrah from Australia, limited because of the high cost of transporting it. Sierra Leone and the Cape Colony in Africa supplied "African oak", Oldfieldia africana, among other woods.*

COMPOSITE MASTS

One-piece masts could only be constructed from trees with a 27–30 inch diameter at the top. English shipwrights had to re-learn the lost art of composite mast making in 1778 when the New England supply of such trees, which had first begun to arrive regularly after 1653, dried up as a result of the American Revolution. By assembling several pieces of Baltic fir they were able to produce "made" masts to compensate for the absence of giant American pines. But the French, who never acquired a successful transatlantic timber connection, always assembled their masts in this way.

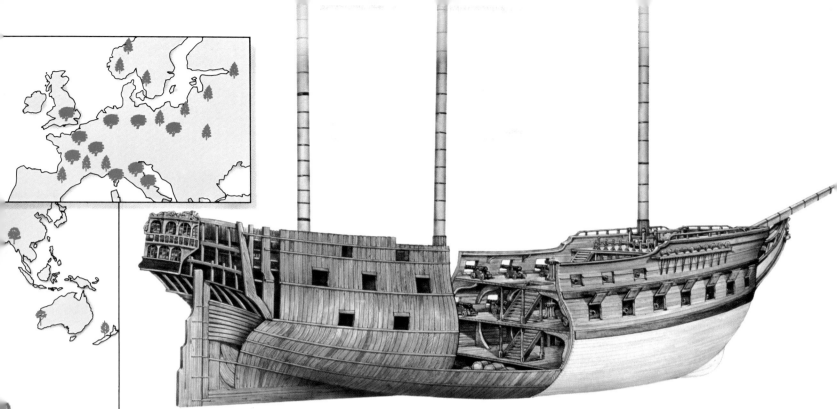

Above England's renowned "wooden walls" were made of ships, such as this classic 74-gun "ship of the line", the Bellona. About 2,600 tons of timber went into the hull alone of a ship of this calibre. The Bellona used about 60 acres of oak trees, and overall such vessels might require 700 large oak trees. For the futtocks, several of which made up each rib, wood naturally grown in the right shape was far stronger than a built-up curve. Contemporary drawings of the parts of ships were done to encourage the gentlemen of England to maintain their oak groves and to plant more to supply the royal dockyards with timber.

Right For the shipwright's craft each tree yielded timber with special properties suitable for different parts of the ship. First, the hedgerow oaks, which were often found growing in isolation and thus displayed more individuality of shape than forest oaks. They were valued for the superior strength of their large and naturally curved timbers, known as great or "compass" timbers. Second, the wood from the forest oaks of continental Europe and North America for stern posts and planking. Third, elm for the planking of warships below the waterline. Fourth, tall American pines, prized for one-piece masts.

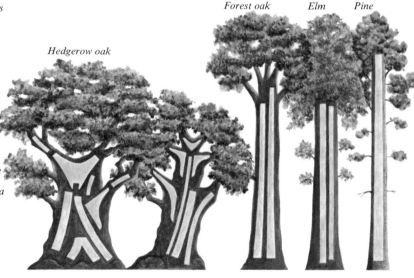

Hedgerow oak Forest oak Elm Pine

Right Turner's romantic depiction of the fighting Téméraire. The oak for this 98-gun ship of the line—the largest vessel for all conditions—came from the Hainault Forest of Essex in England. She was built in 1798 and served as part of Nelson's victorious fleet at the Battle of Trafalgar (1805). When Turner painted her she was being "tugged to her last berth to be broken up, 1838". His painting was a tribute to the passing of the age of sail, but the alternative forms of transport were to be equally demanding in new ways upon the forests of the world.

Despite their reliance on imports for special purposes, the English persisted in preferring their native oak, *Quercus robur*, for the general construction of their ships, maintaining that its slower growth and exposure to Atlantic storms gave it extra strength. Their preference was understandable because much of the Baltic oak was sold before it was properly seasoned. An unreasonable prejudice also developed against American oaks. The Americans had several species of oak, the best of which, *Quercus virginiana* or *virens*, was capable of producing better timber, especially compass timber, than even the English oak. However, the over-astute New England merchants spoiled their trade by passing off an inferior timber from the white oak, *Quercus alba*, to overseas buyers, while retaining the better timbers for their own ships.

Ever on the lookout for new sources of supply, the English authorities discovered in the mid-eighteenth century the potential of the European larch, a quick-maturing species which proved suitable for ship building, and they planted many of these trees in Britain.

When Napoleon's armies were sweeping across Europe and cutting off, one after another, the traditional sources of England's timber supplies, the English authorities sought further supplies from all over the world. In the United States they found and made good use of an excellent conifer, the longleaf pine, *Pinus palustris*, of the southern states. Useful species were also located in West Africa, southern Africa, Australia and New Zealand, but the best of all proved to be Indian teak, which is still highly sought after for present-day ship construction.

By the middle of the nineteenth century the problem of timber supplies for ship building lost its overriding importance as iron steamships superseded the tall-masted sailing ships.

The 18th century

In the blast furnace iron is separated from its ore by smelting. When charcoal was the smelting fuel the iron produced was easily worked and could support stress (wrought iron)

because charcoal absorbed impurities in the ore. Coke derived from coal was a welcome substitute smelting fuel in forest-starved Britain, but the less pure iron produced was not so malleable and far more brittle. Charcoal

Above This painting by Bierstadt of an Indian camp in Kansas captures the natural peace sometimes perceived by settlers as they observed the Indian way of life in the eastern woodlands. From the

forest the Indians had game and wild fruit and vegetables in abundance, as well as fish from the streams. But the second painting shows an attempt to re-create that same kind of tranquility. This

country house is set among carefully planted trees, reflecting the aesthetic attitude of late 18th-century English landowners to the forest and prefiguring developments a century later in the United States.

THE SHAKERS

Refugees from industrial England and religious persecution, the Shakers arrived in the New World in 1774, and were notorious for their ritualistic dancing and

singing and their advocacy of equal rights for women. They built their furniture and sawmills, and a Shaker woman invented the powered chainsaw in 1810.

In the eighteenth century, forests provided the raw material—timber—for almost every industrial activity. Apart from wood's importance as a domestic building material and fuel, it was needed for constructing dockyards and mines. Most crucially, it was still the foundation of the metal industries, because charcoal was required before metal could be extracted from its ore (see pages 192–193).

Until the late eighteenth century ironmaking was a rural industry. Iron was usually smelted in blast furnaces situated within, or on the outskirts of, forests, sometimes near the water that provided power. The charcoal often derived from coppiced woodlands (see pages 32–33), although in parts of Europe the indigenous supplies of timber could no longer keep up with demand. Traditional ironmaking techniques required as much as three tons of charcoal to make one ton of crude iron

and it has been estimated that in forty days, one furnace could level a forest for a radius of more than half a mile.

A substitute for wood became essential. It was in 1709 in Great Britain—where the problem had become particularly acute—that this alternative material was found. At the old ironworks of Coalbrookdale, Abraham Darby was the first person successfully to use coke derived from coal for smelting. The idea of substituting coke for charcoal in smelting had been current for some time, but there were problems. Coking removed less impurities in the mineral ore than charring, and the quality of the iron was inferior. But Darby was able to make coke-blast iron a commercial reality because he used a very clean iron ore and good coking-quality coal that was locally available. In fact the distribution of coking-quality coal was a critical factor in the location and com-

petitive position of ironmaking enterprises in the industrial revolution.

With Darby's technique the industrial revolution in Europe could gather momentum for iron, no longer dependent on vast forests was the ideal material for much of the machinery used in the new industrial processes. But although the forest gained some respite from the charcoal burners, now there would be new demands upon it. The mines, for example, would have to sink deeper for coal to be extracted, and the forest provided pit props, or mine timbers, for which the small regrowth of coppices was well suited.

Something new was happening on the land too. As the population of Europe and Russia increased (estimated to have grown from about 103 million in 1640 to 144 million in 1750), new pressures were put on natural resources because the production of food had to

was therefore still indispensable in the forge, where the impurities were hammered out of coke-blast iron over charcoal fires. It was the invention of the puddling and rolling technique by Henry Cort (1700–1840) that

eventually assured the triumph of the mineral fuel in ironmaking. In the puddling furnace, pig iron was alternately heated and cooled until the wrought iron could be separated out by reason of its higher melting point. After some

preliminary hammering, the rolling mill squeezed out rather than beat out the dross, shaping the iron and turning out an unlimited number of standardized crude shapes, such as bars, beams and rails, for the new industries.

Above With water for power and nearby hills that were once forested for charcoal, Coalbrookdale was a traditional ironmaking site. But the area also had coking-quality coal, which helped Darby to make coke-blast iron successfully in 1709. However, the first stage in the revolution in ironmaking was completed only with the invention of the puddling and rolling process (above right).

Left Since ancient times, water was harnessed to grind corn and it also powered the first factories in the north of England. But by then the millwrights were using iron instead of wood to construct the strong wheels needed to convert the downward force of falling water into a rotary motion.

Right The Elizabeth Furnace in Virginia, which at its peak consumed 600 bushels of charcoal a day, ceased operating as late as the 1880s. The remains of such historic iron furnaces are scattered throughout the forests of the east and mid-west United States. The abundance of forested land in America meant that Darby's charcoal-saving smelting technique could be comfortably ignored for longer than in Britain. Likewise, France and Germany continued to use considerable quantities of smelting charcoal until well into the 19th century. The travelling farmer, Arthur Young (1741–1820), noticed with surprise that French cartwheels were still being made entirely out of wood when in Britain they were more usually iron-shod.

become more efficient. To facilitate new tillage and drainage techniques, a pattern of farm management emerged to displace the old feudal system. The common lands in England, which included areas of wooded country, were fenced off to make larger farms. Marginal smallholders migrated to the growing industrial centres because those common resources, which had once been a substantial part of their subsistence, were removed.

The industrial revolution precipitated a change of attitude towards the forest on the part of those gentlemen who were buying more and more forested land. In the eighteenth century, when the ship-building timber crisis was at its height, a man of wealth saw in afforestation a desirable long-term investment. But with growing industrialization, he was more inclined to put his money, or give his land, to enterprises such as mining that pro-

mised quicker returns. Therefore in England forested land became valued for its scenic beauty and as a sporting amenity, serving as a cover for game. In central Europe, however, forested land continued to be appreciated both for timber production and as a cover for game, thus pioneering the first true multiple use of the forest on a large scale.

Such contemplative feelings towards the forest were not shared by early English-speaking settlers in North America, however. They regarded their unruly surroundings primarily as an obstacle. Until the aftermath of the War of Independence, when the pressure of a growing population stimulated the first push westwards into the plains and mountains beyond the Allegheny-Appalachian Mountains (see pages 144–145), they consolidated their hold on the eastern seaboard.

Many of the settlers were fleeing from the

new alien conditions of industrializing parts of Europe. The Shakers, for example, who arrived in New York State in 1774 and had eighteen communities stretching from Maine to Kentucky by the 1840s, were millhands and mechanics from England's industrial Manchester. Possibly in reaction against the machine age that had started in their homeland, they esteemed craft skill. From local forests the Shakers were able to build their own dwellings, furniture that is admired and even copied today for its efficiency and simplicity of design, and even sawmills.

The forest-bound pioneers quickly became skilled woodsmen. Apart from the immediate value of wooden cabins to live in and stockades to defend themselves and their livestock, American carpenters matched the elegance of Georgian architecture—achieved in Europe with brick and stone—by using wood.

The 19th century

Below left *Towering over old-fashioned wooden neighbours, the iron-hulled Great Eastern (1858) steams away. She was employed to lay the first telegraphic cable between Britain and the continent of North America.*

Below *In the 19th century cheap consumer durables and new foods, such as bananas and cocoa, improved standards of living, while advertising and packaging developed to market such commodities.*

Below *The railway age coincided with mass literacy and publishers met the demand for light reading matter, with magazines designed to be "the ideal size for reading on the train as so many of us like to do".*

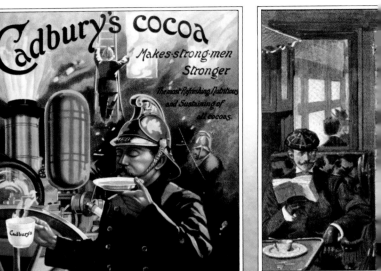

In the nineteenth century the workshops of the world, first Britain, then the United States and other modernizing powers in Europe, began to search for the raw materials necessary to maintain the pace of their accelerating industrialization. There was an unprecedented exploitation of the Earth's natural resources. Minerals, timber, cotton and rubber were widely sought, and a simultaneous push to corner new markets for resulting commodities, such as cheap clothing and bicycles, occurred. Nothing symbolized this age of expansion more than the railroads, the development of which started in Britain in the 1830s, spreading around the globe from there.

Although it is recognized that the railroads were large consumers of iron and steel, it is not often realized that they had an equally momentous impact on the forest. For purposes ranging from the construction of platforms to the provision of fuel, the railroads devoured timber, but the largest single use was for crossties, or sleepers.

In Europe the shortage of forested land by this time meant that coal was the most important fuel, and metal and concrete were used wherever possible for crossties. But in the United States, which was relatively undeveloped at the time, the high cost of transportation and labour and the abundance of forests meant that wood was, and still is, used routinely for crossties. In India the railroads were started in the mid-1850s, and quite soon most of the accessible teak and sal forests had been logged to provide sleepers for the lines as they linked up the subcontinent.

The history of railroad consumption of timber is closely paralleled by the communications industries. Where the railroads went, the telegraph often followed. In India, however, there were difficulties because hungry elephants, mistaking the poles for trees, were inclined to uproot them. In the United States the telegraph and the new railroad mail system of 1834 became catalysts for an evolving popular press catering for the newly literate masses. With the aid of rapid transport and

the telegraph, news could travel quickly, and the very nature of railroad travel created a demand for "half-hour" passenger literature.

In the last quarter of the nineteenth century the whole publishing industry rapidly expanded. Like the growth of railroads, this had a direct impact on the forests. Technologically, for example, the invention of a process in the early 1850s whereby paper could be made from pulpwood instead of increasingly scarce traditional raw materials, such as rags, meant that for the first time the forest became the main source of raw material for the paper industry. It also meant that cheap paper could be produced for periodicals and newspapers. Socially, the spread of education was the change most responsible for the creation of a new mass market for literature with a corresponding growth in demand for paper and its feedstock, pulpwood.

The forest and its by-products played an integral role in this epoch when countless new inventions and commodities, from postage stamps to rubber bands, revolutionized life. And the railroads symbolize the role of the forest during these changes, not simply because they were vast consumers of timber, but because they also gave access to new forested regions and the products of these regions.

At the height of the rubber boom between 1870 and 1911, the rubber barons considered that the precious substance—"black gold"— controlled by them could be less hazardously and more cheaply transported by rail from the Amazon rain forest down to ocean-going ships at their capital, Manaus.

Accordingly, the Madeira-Mamoré railroad was started in 1873. But the first workers on this railroad, Americans, found to their horror that whereas three expert axemen had been able to clear a three-foot path for about 1,450 yards in a day in the "Wild West", it took a day just to clear 300 yards through the rain forest, and even then it was luck if there were no casualties to disease or wild animals.

The development of the railways coincided with a growth in forestry consciousness in the

United States. Towards the close of the century many Americans began to worry lest their forests were about to disappear in smoke, under rails or down mine shafts. President Theodore Roosevelt expressed this mood when he said: "The railroads must have ties . . . The miner must have timber . . . If the present rate of forest destruction is allowed to continue with nothing to offset it, a timber famine in the future is inevitable."

Happily, although such fears were timely, they were unduly pessimistic. The forest's regenerative powers were underestimated and, as mechanization of agriculture made flat land the most valuable for farming, more rugged and inaccessible land was given over profitably to forestry. In addition, the timber consumers themselves took action, because although they were not always ardent conservationists, they knew that their future lay with a growing, surviving forest.

In India the question of ensuring railroad supplies actually stimulated the first official Woods and Forests Department, set up specifically to manage India's forests as a renewable resource. And the papermakers pioneered modern forestry principles, by which they could simultaneously improve the environment and ensure their supplies. Thus, the combined response of the public, foresters and consumers resulted in the situation today where the United States has 75 per cent of the forested land it had in Columbus's time.

TRESTLE CONSTRUCTION

In 1896 there were about 2,000 miles of timber trestle bridges in the USA, but iron, steel and earthworks were increasingly used, as more became known about traffic volume and other design factors.

Railway building reflected the twin processes of industrialization in the modernizing countries and the opening up of underdeveloped parts of the world to provide new markets in addition to essential raw materials.

WORLD RAILWAY MILEAGE PER DECADE			
	Europe	USA	Rest of the world
1840–50	13,000	7,000	—
1850–60	17,000	24,000	1,000
1860–70	31,000	24,000	7,000
1870–80	39,000	51,000	12,000

Below *As a result of the great wealth generated by rubber from the jungle, the Brazilian city of Manaus was transformed into a gaslit boomtown and adorned in 1896 with the most magnificent opera house in the world.*

ight Northern Pacific Railroad workers in the USA's Washington Territory in 1886. The ough-hewn crossties and he timber trestle spanning he ravine were probably made from local timber. The ties were usually cut in winter. It was considered that when they were laid in spring they would be half-seasoned or dry enough to resist decay.

The birth of forestry

THE BILTMORE ESTATE

Until the late nineteenth century forestry as a practised science did not exist in the United States, although it was already 200 years old in parts of Europe, notably Germany. In Europe foresters were often encouraged and employed by aristocrats who were aware of the many benefits of managed estates that could simultaneously produce timber, house game for hunting and provide beautiful settings for their houses. George W. Vanderbilt, a self-made American aristocrat, wanted such an estate, and in 1889 he employed Gifford Pinchot, the father of American forestry, as forester to his 7,000-acre estate at Biltmore, in North Carolina.

Biltmore was already partly wooded. Pinchot immediately had trees planted to make attractive borders for estate roads and to conceal bare and eroding slopes, as well as improving and managing the truly forested areas of the estate. When Pinchot left Vanderbilt's service, a German forester named Dr Schenck took over his work with the help of several assistants who worked with him in return for their training as foresters. It was this arrangement that led to the setting up of the Biltmore Forest School in 1898, the first school of forestry in the United States.

Because of its successful management along multi-use principles Biltmore is still beautiful as well as being a productive forest today.

Unlike all the other creatures that lived in the great forests of the Earth, man, with his early discovery of the deadly weapon fire and the lesser one, the axe, fought the forest to gain advantages over it and over all the other creatures. His wish to settle in one place, grow crops and graze animals required destruction of the forest, but for centuries the forest supplied in plenty, so vast was it and so apparently inexhaustible.

That this permanence of supply was an illusion gradually began to dawn upon the Europeans and, as private landowning increased in medieval times, woodlands were established to provide a regular income from sales of timber, to supply firewood and materials for the feudal tenants and, incidentally, sporting preserves. This was the origin of the systematic management of woodlands as a renewable resource, when the timber cut each year was equal to that grown by the still standing trees during that year.

Such practices could, in theory, provide a permanent supply of timber. But as populations increased and technology advanced, man's tendency to gather in increasingly large centres—the great industrial cities of the nineteenth century—resulted in the demand for timber becoming insatiable. Millions of people needed housing; huge factories were built to supply the wants of a self-generating technology; coal, the fount of all power needed in the factories, could only be extracted from underground if the mines were supported by wooden pit props; and the paper needed for the dissemination of knowledge could only be made by pulping millions of trees.

Left *Gifford Pinchot (1865–1946) was the first professional American forester. He was trained in Europe and in 1898, after service at Biltmore, he became chief of the newly created United States Forest Service. A passionate conservationist, he influenced the conservation policies of Theodore Roosevelt.*

Right *Sir William Schlich (1840–1925) was trained as a forester in his native Germany. With Dr Brandis he pioneered the scientific administration of India's forests and he was later head of Britain's first forestry school.*

Such an onslaught on the forest could not continue. Either new forests in other parts of the world had to be harvested or those forests that had been felled had to be replanted. In fact, both solutions were attempted side by side. Total exploitation gave way to exploitation in far-off and sparsely populated lands, and the science of forestry, the growing of trees as crops of timber, responded to the new situation by becoming more sophisticated.

Europe, the cradle of the industrial revolution, with Great Britain as its centre, looked to the far north of its own continent and to North America, for in both places the coniferous forests were vast and seemingly endless. Yet, in northern Europe, so slowly did the trees grow in that inhospitable climate that natural replacement could not begin to match

the demand. And in North America, so rapidly did the population increase, even the much quicker-growing and much larger trees could not meet the twin demands being made upon them.

The world looked to the European nations that had pioneered the science of forestry—Germany and France—to provide the expertise needed to regenerate the land stripped of trees and to ensure good management of those forests still standing. Pinchot, the father of the United States Forest Service, was trained in Nancy, France; and Brandis and Schlich came from Germany to set up forest services in the ever-expanding British Empire. Even the British, masters of the sea and able to import timber from far and wide, began to take an interest in commercial plantations, although

the paucity of native trees in their islands obliged them to look overseas for species that would grow more quickly than their oaks and beeches if the supply was to come on stream in time to beat the shortage.

Despite great efforts on the part of foresters to husband their woodlands, man's fecundity and his technological advances to build industry caused him to range farther and farther afield for his vital timber supplies. Hitherto untouched tropical forests were entered and increased clearances for agriculture and fuelwood ravaged them on an enormous scale, with all the tragic aftermath of progressive erosion, soil deterioration and the loss of wildlife habitats that had followed the earlier plunder in the temperate regions, but on a vaster and more devastating scale. Naked exploitation had to stop and the role of the forester had to be re-appraised.

Although the chief objective of the forester remains the growing of timber, the forest, which in effect means woodlands together with associated land and water, must now be managed for the benefit of mankind. For, since no country has unlimited land and conflict between competing interests over it, namely watershed and erosion protection, wildlife conservation and recreation, must be avoided, a high degree of sophistication in forest management is necessary. The modern forester must operate in an increasingly complex world and be mindful of the constraints imposed by ecology, economics and politics.

All over the world now national parks, national forests, nature reserves, forest reserves and conservation areas are being set

Above *Like many European landowners, Monsieur de Bensarade, a poet connected with the court of Louis XIV of France and the owner of this estate, knew the aesthetic and certain economic advantages of forested land, especially in wartime when shipbuilders relied on them for timber.*

Left *Modern techniques can guarantee healthy trees for many uses, but the primarily economic concerns of 19th-century foresters have been reinforced by today's ecological consciousness.*

up, usually under the auspices of the national governments, in which to a greater or lesser degree all the benefits of trees and tree cover are combined. Within them both natural forests and man-made plantations, as well as forest regenerated naturally with help from man, can co-exist. Timber is grown and harvested but in such a way that the amount felled is equal to the amount grown in a given time. The felled areas, limited in extent to prevent unreasonable disturbance to the local environment, are restocked with trees either by encouraging natural regeneration, by re-seeding by hand or from the air, or by planting, often in the latter case by using plants with qualities superior to those in the previous crop (see pages 50–51).

Wildernesses can be left in inaccessible places and at the same time access for recreation to the managed areas can be facilitated by the forest roads needed for forest operations. Felling need not take place where landslides or avalanches threaten, nor in watersheds, where tree cover is essential to the gradual seepage of silt-free water into lakes and reservoirs. Where specialized habitats are essential for rare creatures forest management can ensure no drastic change in the tree cover. Indeed, the aim must be to try and re-create something of the multiple use and equilibrium of the forest that it enjoyed when man was just another forest creature. If man can discipline himself, and if technology is used to good effect, we might just manage to grow enough timber and at the same time preserve the forest for our fellow creatures and ourselves.

The wilderness movement

Left *The Lower Falls of the Yellowstone River was painted by the artist Thomas Moran, who was also one of North America's earliest successful conservationists. It was Moran's series of views of the area that encouraged the United States government to establish Yellowstone as the nation's first national park in 1872. Since this time Yellowstone Park, with its cascades, its forests and its wildlife, has been preserved as a wilderness area so that the region today (below) still possesses the unaltered raw, natural beauty that was portrayed by Moran.*

Concern over the disappearance of woods and forests and their native wildlife has never been greater than it is at present. This awareness is timely because, for centuries, man has been taking and using the resources offered by the natural forest without fully realizing the consequences of their indiscriminate removal.

It was the technological advances of the Neolithic epoch, 10,000 years ago, that first stimulated the gradual clearance of much of Europe's natural forest as agricultural economies were developed and populations increased dramatically.

Elsewhere in the world deforestation began much later. In North America, the natural forest cover remained virtually untouched until the sixteenth century. When Europeans first arrived they found dense forests in pure, or nearly pure, stands still covering large areas of the country. It was said that at this time a squirrel could travel from the Atlantic coast to the Mississippi without ever having to touch the ground.

But as the newly arrived immigrants poured into the continent and as the pressures of population in the east pushed farmers farther and farther west, vast areas of forest were felled and countless numbers of wildlife destroyed as the ground was cleared, drained and ploughed to grow crops.

Fortunately in North America this process of deforestation was arrested in time and the continent now possesses much of its original forest cover. But other areas of the world where the same sorry story has been repeated, have not been so fortunate. When the first Polynesians arrived in New Zealand about a thousand years ago, rich evergreen forests extended to the coasts, and it has been estimated that about seventy-five per cent of the land area of sixty-six-million acres was forested at that time. This was down to around sixty-six per cent when Captain James Cook reached New Zealand in 1769 and is now only fourteen million acres and a good deal of that is mountain forest. Very little remains of the native lowland forest of New Zealand as this was the first to be cleared for farming.

EUROPE'S BISON

The European bison, *Bison bonasus*, at one time ranged widely throughout the deciduous woodlands of Europe. By the early 1900s, however, continual deforestation and centuries of hunting by man had virtually eliminated the species. The one remaining wild herd was in the Bialowieza Forest, which had been a hunting preserve of the Polish kings for more than 800 years. But even this herd, which numbered 737 head of bison in 1914, did not survive the First World War. The only Bialowieza animals that remained were those that had previously been donated to zoological gardens elsewhere in Europe, and the descendants of specimens presented to the Duke of Hochberg in 1876. Fortunately, a new Bialowieza herd was created from these sources in 1952 and the forest is now, once again, a reserve for the species.

In more recent years the focus of concern has shifted to the tropical rain forests of South America, Central Africa, South East Asia and Indonesia. The felling of tropical rain forests is now the world's most serious single conservation problem, and only three extensive areas survive—in the Amazon River basin in South America, the Congo River basin in Equatorial Africa, and in the Malay Archipelago in South East Asia. The exact rate of deforestation is debatable, but there is fairly general agreement that these forests are disappearing alarmingly fast. The problems that may arise from their removal are many and varied. Tropical rain forests are particularly important in terms of preventing soil erosion (particularly in relation to watershed protection) and flooding, in buffering variations in climate and in providing for recreation and tourism. If they could be managed on a sustained-yield basis, combining controlled felling with regeneration programmes, they could also provide a continual source of forest products. Most importantly, however, they are reservoirs of genetic diversity, extremely rich in plant and animal species. It has been claimed that some of these species pass into extinction every day.

The removal of indigenous forests, and their wildlife, whether they be rain forests in the tropics or temperate broadleaved forests, is a serious and world-wide problem. Fortunately, in recent years, foresters and conservationists alike have become more aware of the difficulties and their concern is now better co-ordinated and more scientifically based than it was even fifteen or twenty years ago.

There are two major ways in which the conservation problem is now being, and must continue to be, tackled; first, by establishing national parks and wildlife reserves and second, by incorporating conservation policies into the management programmes of national and also, wherever possible, privately owned commercial forests.

National parks and reserves are areas that are designed as wildernesses and are put aside to be used exclusively for the preservation of the native flora and fauna. Normally no commercial activity is permitted. These areas are left to grow wild so that the ever-changing pattern of species dominance continues unchecked, with as little human interference as possible. There are also nature reserves that are "managed" to a limited extent so that the ecological cycle can be deliberately maintained at a certain point, in order to retain a suitable habitat for rare animals or plants.

National parks and wildlife reserves have now been established in both temperate and, more recently, tropical forested regions throughout the world. But only a limited area of the world's forests can be set aside exclusively for the conservation of wildlife. Mankind has many other simultaneous demands to make of the forest resource. Timber production, mining, animal grazing and watershed protection are all essential functions of the forest and it is only practical that, for most of the forested regions of the world, conservation must be integrated into modern commercial forestry programmes.

The first large-scale and successful attempt to incorporate forest conservation with commercial productivity in North America was initiated by Gifford Pinchot with the support of President Theodore Roosevelt. Pinchot was responsible for the creation of the US Forest Service in 1905, and under his guidance a number of national forests were established. He instituted the policy of sustained-yield forestry and created the concept of "multiple use" of the forest, whereby one forested area could successfully serve several different functions simultaneously.

Today, national forests throughout the world, and indeed many privately owned commercial forests use forest management principles based on the pioneer work of Gifford Pinchot. Sustained-yield production has halted deforestation in several countries, and in countries such as New Zealand massive replantation programmes have created a net increase in the areas that are forested.

But although conservation of forest areas has been successfully achieved in many parts of the world, conservation of the indigenous wildlife, until recently, has not achieved a similarly widespread success.

One of the main reasons is that when native forests have been felled, they have often been replaced by exotic, fast-growing tree species that can provide the forester with a quick and therefore economic return for his investment. In New Zealand, for example, where some of the largest contiguous man-made forests have been planted, huge areas that were once clothed with native evergreen forest are now a vast expanse of Monterey pine, a North American species. This pine has also been used extensively for re-forestation in Australia, South Africa and Chile. In many parts of Europe native broadleaved woodlands have been replaced with coniferous species, and in Brazil extensive areas have been replanted with introduced hardwoods such as gmelina and various species of eucalyptus. From the conservation point of view, the great drawback to plantations of exotic species is that they do not always provide a suitable habitat for the flora and fauna characteristic of the original native forest of an area.

Today, however, foresters have begun to realize the importance of preserving native wildlife habitats within the forest and have altered their forestry programmes to better achieve these ends. The importance of diversity of tree species and forest structure is now better understood. It is also realized that a number of large old trees should be allowed to stand in the forest and that some fallen trees should be allowed to remain and decay on the forest floor as these provide homes for many different species of wildlife that cannot survive in a "tidy" environment.

The commercial forest can never fulfil the role of the wilderness reserves, but with co-operation between forester and conservationist, the various functions required of the world's forests may be simultaneously achieved; timber and minerals produced, recreational facilities provided and many of the species of animals and plants that live in the forest protected against the very real threat of extinction within the next few decades.

THE LYREBIRD

The superb lyrebird, *Menura superba*, is just one of the many distinctive and dramatic species of wildlife that are unique to the Australian continent. But this native of the southern eucalyptus and temperate rain forests, was at one time in danger of total extinction. For many years male lyrebirds were ruthlessly hunted and shot in their thousands to satisfy the enormous popular demand for their magnificent tail feathers. At the beginning of the twentieth century, however, government legislation was drawn up to protect the species. Illegal poaching continued for several years, but eventually legal action and public enlightenment reduced trade to a trickle. Between 1934 and 1949 eleven pairs of lyrebirds were released in the Tasmanian National Park, where they are flourishing and the future of the species is now assured.

The natural threats

Below Wind can help
maintain the natural forest
by blowing down old and
diseased trees to make way
for the young ones.
Excessive damage,
however, as in this German
forest, can have a
destructive impact.

The forest is an association of living things existing in finely balanced harmony and, as such, it is particularly vulnerable to threats to its integrity both from without and within. Damage to even one of its many entities can set off a destructive chain reaction.

The greatest of these threats is uncontrolled fire. Engendered by lightning strikes, or the careless activities of man, during dry weather, a fire can devastate vast areas of the forest. At worst a long-term disaster befalls the forest. Then, centuries of development into a balanced association are wiped out in an instant. The charred and lifeless landscape takes decades to struggle back to greenery and half a century may elapse before the tree cover is replaced (see pages 46–47).

Flooding, too, can have a catastrophic impact on the forest. Floods can kill all vegetation and drive out the forest creatures before eventually destroying the trees, although in some instances if the water is shallow, they may be replaced by other species specially adapted to growing with their roots submerged. Flood damage is particularly disastrous if the deluge is prolonged or even permanent such as after an earthquake or the damming activities of beavers. The most damaging feature of flooding, however, is probably the occasional but repeated inundation which gradually renders a forest incapable of sustaining the balanced associations that are its very being, thus reducing it to a watery wilderness.

Conversely, drought can also be a threat. Failure of the monsoon rains in the Tropics or even a succession of dry summers in temperate climates set off a chain of events that can result in widespread mortality among young trees and accelerating debility in the old ones, causing a change in the species composition and thus in the balance of the forest.

In some parts of the world hurricanes and gales can cut swathes through the forest and if they are not speedily refilled by re-growth before the next tempest strikes, the gaps become progressively enlarged. Winds have a part to play in the natural life of a forest by bringing down old trees and making space for the younger generation, but when they are of such force as to fell trees of all ages they threaten the forest as a whole.

These external threats, often widespread and devastating, can be accompanied by, and may even be the indirect cause of, internal threats. A natural re-seeding in a fire-devastated area can result in a new forest composed almost entirely of just one tree species, and each species has its own pests—insect, fungus, and virus—which attack it alone. Hence, if conditions of climate or situation, such as a severe windfall, favour the reproduction of one of these pests, it has an unlimited and unchecked opportunity to spread throughout the forest. This threat to monoculture, uncommon in the natural forest, is very real in man-made plantations. But even in a balanced forest with a natural mixture of tree species, insects and fungal pests can fall

upon one of them with dire results. This is particularly true of those insects with a remarkable capacity for suddenly exploding into vast populations. Each species has a preferred food—some destroying seeds, some chewing leaves or sucking sap, yet others eating buds. They can even carry fungal infection from tree to tree with fatal consequences.

Fungal infection can spread from root to root, regardless of species, thereby entering the base of the trunks, killing and felling the trees. Fungal infection may also be carried by wind action, as happens with rusts, which cause defoliation and death to the trees. Bacteria enter the trees through natural wounds and set up fatal cankers.

Nor are the trees immune to attack from fellow plants. Climbers such as honeysuckles, clematis and vines can, by coiling round young trees, restrict and deform their growth or, by spreading over the crowns, smother them. Even large trees on which strangling-fig seeds have been dropped by birds, can find

themselves at first hemmed in by the trailing aerial roots of the figs and subsequently smothered as these roots penetrate the earth, expand and join up to form a huge trunk around their hapless host.

Some birds and other animals, especially those mammals whose populations from time to time reach epidemic proportions, such as voles, can cause extensive damage to trees. Voles attack the roots and the shoots of tree seedlings, and bark around the base of saplings, killing them in huge numbers. Mice, pigeons and many other seed-eating birds can eat whole crops of seed. Deer, rabbits, hares and other herbivores, especially in hard winters when snow covers all else, eat seedlings and strip the bark from saplings, killing them or, at very best, severely retarding growth. Grey squirrels, introduced into Britain from America where they do little damage, have become a serious pest to beech and sycamore, stripping the bark from young trees and from the upper branches of old ones with fierce

INSECT DAMAGE

By chewing leaves, sucking sap, eating buds, shoots and seeds, or acting as carriers for fungal, bacterial or virus diseases, insects can attack the forest in many ways. Under certain conditions, such as climatic changes or a reduction in natural predators, there is often a sudden explosion of insect populations that can wreak havoc in forests dominated by a single tree species. The insect may increase its population size until it eats itself out of its own food supply. Eventually the population decreases and allows the tree species to re-establish itself. These cyclical attacks may occur at regular intervals throughout the life of the forest. In north-east America the spruce bud worm (right) is attacking and destroying spruce forests at a rate of hundreds of thousands of acres per year. Foresters planning regeneration schemes are being forced to favour species other than spruce, so this insect is having both a direct and indirect effect on the forest structure.

In recent years the elms of Europe have been decimated by Dutch elm disease. This fungal disease, reintroduced from North America in exported logs, is transferred from tree to tree by an insect—the elm-bark beetle.

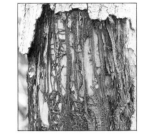

Right *Mycelium of honey fungus on an oak tree. It attacks the roots of living trees, and can eventually ring the whole trunk.*

Below *Beavers chisel at riverside trees to build their dams. Such dams can flood low-lying land many miles up river, "drowning" vast numbers of trees.*

Below *Hungry elephants push over trees to feed on foliage. One can eat a quarter ton of food per day.*

Above *Climbing plants may constrict tree trunks or smother the crown and compete for sunlight.*

abandon. Beavers, constant in their urge to build dams in the coniferous forests of North America and Eurasia, chisel through whole stands of trees; and elephants, deprived of their usual food plants by drought, push over large trees to reach the leaves and have thereby deforested large areas of East Africa.

For the most part the internal threat to the forest is localized, even confined to small groups of trees or to individuals. Nevertheless, taken over a forest as a whole, it causes a significant decrease in the number of trees. If for local reasons the cause, be it animal, fungal or whatever, is exaggerated beyond that containable within the normal balance of nature, serious and even irreparable damage, comparable to that resulting from fire and tempest, can result. Indeed, most natural threats to the forest, although stemming from a natural chain of events, can be greatly worsened by the activities of man, who himself often provides the conditions whereby these natural catastrophes can strike.

Forest fire

Below *From some small
beginning, perhaps as a
tiny spark in the leaf
litter, fire is let loose in
the forest. As terrified
animals flee the
conflagration, the flames,
fanned by currents of air
from below, shoot*

*upwards. From the fiery
tree-tops sparks and
burning debris rise into the
air to start fresh fires
elsewhere. Immediate
action is vital because a
forest fire can spread with
devastating speed—as fast
as ten miles per hour.*

For millions of years the forests have lived
with natural fire threats such as those arising
from lightning or volcanic activity, and in some
cases evolution has accepted the challenge
and become so positively adapted to the fire
danger that certain trees actually benefit
from it. Such natural fires normally start high
up and burn slowly downhill, and they have
probably never been responsible for serious
deforestation, although lightning fires in the
western United States often denude tracts of
several thousand acres. But, today, man-
made fires account for ninety per cent of all
wildfires and because they usually start in the
accessible lower part of the forest, they are
potentially much more devastative. This kind
of fire accounts for the loss of more than four
million acres of trees each year in the United
States alone.

There are three basic forms of forest fire.
Ground fires burn organic material beneath
the forest floor; surface fires consume the
leaves, twigs and other forest debris as well as
low vegetation such as grass; crown fires burn
through the tops of trees, setting fire to fuels
from the ground up to the top of the canopy. It
is these crown fires that are the most destructive of all, because once they take hold they
throw burning embers on to dry fuels, possibly miles away from the main fire, and spread
the fire until it becomes uncontrollable.

Fire-fighters aim to break what is called the
"fire triangle", the three conditions needed to
produce fire—fuel, oxygen and heat. If any
one of these is removed, combustion cannot
take place. Fuels are anything burnable from
grass and dead leaves to tree stumps; heat can
come from matches, a camp fire or the sparks
flying from machinery; and oxygen, which
constitutes about twenty-one per cent of the
atmosphere, is usually available in sufficient
quantities to support a fire. Fire can, however,
be smothered by throwing enough soil on to it
to shut off the oxygen supply.

In seasons or periods of high fire danger
spotter aircraft are constantly in the air, some
now equipped with infra-red sensors that can
detect "hot-spots" through cloud and at
night. Once a fire is reported it is important to
try to contain it as soon as possible. Fire-
fighting crews are on constant alert, ready to
arrive at the scene of a fire within minutes or a
few hours. In regions inaccessible by road
trained "fire-jumpers" may parachute into
the area or helicopters may hover close to the
fire, while fire-fighters climb down ropes
suspended from the helicopter—a technique
known as "rappelling".

Meanwhile, from an operations room the
pre-planned strategy takes account of the
occurrences of natural barriers to fire—lakes,
rivers, ridges and open land—as well as man-
made fire-breaks in the area. The operations
room supervises the tactical movement of
men, fire appliances and planes to vital points
as the situation develops.

The fire is shepherded towards a barrier,
advantage might be taken of a change of
wind, or a back-fire might be initiated to meet

the on-coming flames to widen the fire line and deprive them of further fuel. Bulldozers may be brought in along with water-containing fire trucks. Specially equipped aircraft can "bomb" the fire with water and fire-retardant chemicals, either by releasing it from plastic containers within the aircraft or by using seaplanes, which can fill their floats with water as they touch the surface.

When the last flames have been quenched a smouldering, black landscape is left. The final mop-up may require days or weeks after the fire is brought under control and declared finally "out". A new forest grows up of fire-climax species—those trees which can take immediate advantage of the disaster. In the north-west United States, for example, such a species is the Douglas fir, and where these trees are now dominant a great fire must have occurred hundreds of years ago. But now, beneath them, the western hemlocks—the true climax species—have shaded out their off-spring and will take over from them afresh

unless fire again sweeps through the forest.

Although wildfire is a destructive force in the forest, both aesthetically and commercially, fire at the right time and in the right place—"prescribed burning"—is an essential tool for land management. Fire risk can be reduced by the periodic burning of accumulated fuels. This is necessary, in part, to offset the success of forest fire protection, because with fewer surface fires the build-up of debris becomes so great that should a fire take hold it would be catastrophic.

As a management tool, prescribed fires can also be used for insect and disease control and for selective species control, because undesirable hardwood species are less resistant to fire than the commercially desirable species of conifer. An added bonus to this form of management is that it helps to keep the hardwoods as young individuals so that essential browse for all kinds of animal wildlife, such as moose and white-tailed deer, is maintained and many endangered species are thereby conserved.

Above *A fire-fighting team at work in France. Armed with shovels, these men are digging up leaf litter beneath the ferns. By creating an earthy barricade of forest floor litter they are attempting* *to cut off the fire by arresting progress along its anticipated wind-directed path. Sometimes bulldozers, able to take up gigantic scoops of earth, are used to create such breaks.*

Above *In Canada and the USA fire-fighting methods are sophisticated because of a fire's potential scale. This aircraft is "bombing" foliage with fire-retardant chemicals to slow the blaze and allow access.*

Below *The aftermath of a fire in a Canadian spruce forest. Nature's regenerative work is already visible, as healthy spruce seedlings spring up beside their cruelly scorched parents.*

The human threats

Man and the forest have always enjoyed an ambivalent relationship. Man the hunter dwelled in the forest, was part of it, and relied upon it for his food and shelter. But man the agriculturist, as he subsequently became, while still relying on it for part of his food and for timber to build his houses, cut and burned great slices of it to make fields. The more sophisticated his implements became, the larger were the areas he laid bare until, as in Britain, a country once entirely clothed in forest, only some five per cent of the whole remained under trees.

Yet, in fighting the forest and subduing it, man was at the same time destroying something that was vital to his well-being. Successive Mediterranean civilizations took their toll of the forests bordering the sea, and continued to lay bare the land by the grazing of great herds of sheep and goats until vast areas became arid deserts. Because the need for fuel and timber never lessened, the arcs of destruction were continually extended.

Early settlers on the North American continent found boundless forests that supplied their every need. However, they also seemed fit to meet the needs of Europe, especially as the industrial revolution gained pace, drawing into its maw rail ties, pit props and building timber from the decimated forests. In less than two centuries there was little virgin timber left in North America and all eyes turned towards the tropical forests. Then the assault fell upon them, becoming farther flung each year until few remain untouched. The forests of the world are now in retreat as man, who through medical science has conquered most of his diseases, becomes disastrously numerous and demands so much wood for fuel, shelter and an infinite variety of other needs that the slowly regenerating trees can no longer cope.

In Europe and America the introduction of wood substitutes—steel for building and plastics for many other uses—as well as the readily available coal and oil for fuel, eventually gave the forests some respite, although the huge increase in the demand for wood pulp for papermaking initially negated this trend to some extent. But the demand for fuelwood in Asia, Africa and South America, where ninety per cent of the world's people live, has never lessened. Indeed, the volume of wood burned as fuel has been estimated as equivalent to thirty million barrels of oil a day. In some areas, particularly in Nepal and India, the fuel shortage is already acute. In Kathmandu firewood is more expensive than kerosine and the mountain forests are retreating before the firewood cutters, leaving steep hillsides open to landslides and disaster.

In India some 400 million tons of cow dung are burned each year, as the only fuel available where once firewood could be cut, depriving the fields of a much needed fertilizer and causing an accelerating degradation of the now almost treeless land. Elsewhere in the world, if populations continue to increase, similar crises cannot be delayed for long, as the price of oil continues to rise beyond the means of most of the people. In some regions the time taken to gather firewood has increased by a factor of eight in one generation.

This threat to the forests is caused by a scramble for a sheer necessity, but other threats stem from less urgent requirements. Preference, born of fashion, for the timber of just a few tree species among the thousands which make up the tropical forests has resulted in wasteful, piecemeal exploitation—often in countries that are unable to sustain their economies in any other way. Huge areas are desecrated in a search for suitable logs, leaving a scarred, degraded forest, which is often cleared by burning to assist further penetration. In this way some countries have lost up to eighty per cent of their forests, followed by floods, erosion and a general degradation of the land.

In Amazonia, in the last few years, not far short of half a million acres of rain forest have been felled on either side of the new highways criss-crossing the country to provide land for agriculture which has already proved to be of doubtful viability. Only an environmental disaster can result. Add to the effect of this ecological short-sightedness the indifference of many countries to the damage caused to trees by air pollution from cars and factories, plus the devastating effect of the fuelwood crisis and it becomes apparent that only a world-wide solution can alleviate the crisis.

But man's ingenuity, if it is used wisely, as with the use of chemicals in forestry and agriculture, and not perverted, as is now so horribly possible with defoliation liquids and other developments in military technology, and if it can be accompanied by a decrease in population, could arrest this process. Forest reserves in which all felling is controlled and the natural balance is maintained can be extended or started up in areas where populations are not too great.

Plantations of fast-growing tree species, such as eucalyptus and pines, many of which prosper on degraded soils and even in semi-desert, are being set up. Strains of trees capable of growing more quickly than others, or thriving better in certain climates than those that grew there naturally, are now selected by scientific tree breeding. If all these things, and more, including pest control, are combined with good management and an awareness of the threat facing the world's forests, man himself might turn the tide.

It is ironic that already in the most highly developed industrial countries of the world, the area under man-made forests is actively growing. This is partly due to the realization that the forests will continue to serve industrial needs only if they are wisely managed. But the nations of the Tropics are also developing an appreciation of the forest's importance in their economies, in this instance as support for agriculture.

In addition, there is the encouragement of the forest being developed as a valuable recreational facility, and as a means of enhancing our environment and making this world a more pleasant place to live in.

Above *In war the human threat to the forest can manifest itself most irrevocably. From the First World War onwards, chemicals, which in peacetime are a valuable and important tool in forest management, were enlisted in wartime destruction of the environment.*

Left *The building of the Trans-Amazonian highway permitted the entry of slash and burn farmers whose crops failed after only 2 years, with devastating consequences for the region.*

Right *A windbreak is planted in southern Tunisia to arrest the process of desertification. The value of afforestation in rehabilitating degraded land, aiding water catchment and providing shelter is now appreciated.*

Below *The sad results of slash and burn agriculture on the forest's fragile soil—a wasted, unproductive landscape. Such practices have had a disastrous impact on the tropical rain forests.*

Above *In these days of political preoccupation with oil it may come as a surprise to learn that wood is still the main source of energy for half the world's* population. *Indeed, firewood is the forest's main product in terms of consumption and demand. Here, fuelwood is unloaded from a dhow on the Nile.*

Right *Animal grazing contributed to the desertification of parts of India. Dried dung, a potential fertilizer, must be used as fuel.*

Future forests

What will the forests of the future be like, and what will they be used for? In endeavouring to answer this question certain background facts are very pertinent. First, world timber consumption will increase, possibly by as much as eighty per cent by the end of this century. Second, the tropical moist forests have to date contributed very little to global timber supplies, perhaps only about ten per cent, but this situation is likely to change. It has been estimated that by the year 2000 demand for tropical hardwoods will reach more than 40,000 million board feet annually.

It seems clear that silviculture will have to be much more widely and intensively practised than is the case at present, but this can take place only within the constraints imposed by ecology, economics and politics. The Food and Agriculture Organization of the United Nations classes some 10,000 million acres of the world's land area as forest, of which around sixty per cent is productive in the commercial sense, and the total area increases each year. Harvesting of the tropical forests will depend on the desired objectives. These are likely to be increasing the quantity and quality of resources demanded by human populations and trade and industry, and they may be achieved by modification or even by complete transformations of these ecosystems, as has already taken place in various parts of the world.

In regions with a marked dry season, simplification of the forest ecosystems by transforming them into tree plantations has yielded positive results, particularly since the climatic régime allows close control of pests, diseases and other factors. The humid Tropics on the other hand present some difficult problems. To meet future requirements man will have to become even more of a tree farmer than he is at present, and he must advance the science of wise management in order to produce a sustained yield. Sustained yield has to be related not only to the growth rate of the tree, but also to a range of environmental factors.

In Europe there is a 300-year tradition of silviculture, but forestry as a science is only about half that age. Despite all that has been learned there is a need for much more intensive research, particularly since experience in temperate areas is of only limited application in the Tropics. For sustained yield purposes, tropical forests will require more sophisticated management than temperate forests.

More research is required, for example, on the effects of the destruction of tropical forests; on the ecology, biology and physiology of the species to be introduced; on the genetic improvement of nursery stock and seed (including provenance trials, progeny testing, clone isolations to produce large numbers of identical offspring, and hybridization); silvicultural practices (for example planting, spacing and the use of fertilizers); pests and diseases; on the development of hardy species that give good volume and quality production for specific site conditions; and not least on the economic aspects (see pages 166–167).

Research along these lines is already in progress, but there are many gaps. In Europe and the United States research into broadleaved species lags well behind that on conifers. Difficulties encountered and failures experienced in the regeneration of natural tropical forests caused foresters to neglect research and to direct their efforts towards the complete replacement of native forests by forest plantations. Present efforts at improving regular yields from native tropical forests will need to be extended.

A good example of the type of successful research that will be necessary concerns the obeche tree, *Triplochiton scleroxylon*, of West Africa, a source of highly marketable timber. The tree's erratic seed production and the unpredictable formation of its seed-bearing fruits made proper planting programmes impossible. Research by British and Nigerian scientists has led to a whole new range of propagation techniques applicable not only to the obeche tree, but to most other tropical trees also. Not only is this tree recovering in six countries in West Africa, it may also be introduced into Asia and Latin America to help reverse the relentless trend of degradation of the tropical forests there.

The fact that many species, when introduced into areas where they are not native, show greatly enhanced growth characteristics has been the basis of much plantation forestry. Large areas of sitka spruce, *Picea sitchensis*, and lodgepole pine, *Pinus contorta*, from North America have been planted in Europe; the Monterey pine, *P. radiata*, from California has been planted on such a scale in New Zealand that that country now has some of the largest man-made forests in the world. One of the biggest exercises of this kind anywhere in the world is the Jari River Project in Brazil where nearly three million acres have been cleared of virgin forest. Within this area 123,500 acres alone have been planted with *Gmelina arborea*, *Eucalyptus deglupta* and *Pinus caribea*. In the extremely complex business of the conversion of various broadleaved tropical forests into managed plantation forests, the use of computer models simulating the management plans is likely to make a major contribution to the decision-making process. Forest plantations covered 198 million acres in the Tropics in 1965 and will probably have doubled in extent by 1985.

Forest management in the future will have to accord increasing consideration to aspects other than exploitation for pulpwood or timber alone. The role of forests for wildlife management is one aspect that comes to mind. Then there is the question of the contribution that forests could make to the energy situation, for they have considerable potential for producing energy and chemical feedstocks (see pages 216–217). If, for example, it is assumed that the annual above-ground growth of the world's forests is thirteen billion tons, of which half is economically exploitable, then one million megawatts of electricity could be produced from wood on a sustained yield basis.

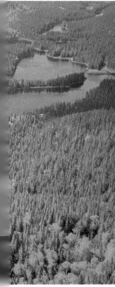

Above *An encouraging sign for the future, the Jari Project in Brazil has taken advantage of the fact that many trees show greatly enhanced growth characteristics when introduced to areas where they are not native. By this scheme large areas of unproductive natural rain forest have been replaced, as here, by plantations of Caribbean pine.*

Left *Given present demands on world forest resources it is not inconceivable that in the future the only surviving natural forests will be those protected as national parks or those, such as this untouched Canadian forest, in topographical situations that make their maintenance for watershed protection essential.*

TOMORROW'S TREES

As the genetic mysteries of the forest become more understandable, they become more controllable and the challenge posed by the ever increasing demand on the forest resource from the forest product industries can be met. Economically, the best trees are fast-growing and disease-resistant with straight trunks. Forest research has shown that hereditary factors, as much as environmental factors, are crucial to the development of such trees, and by controlled pollination more of them can be bred.

When a tree's female "flowers" open they will accept pollen blown from any tree of the same species. But if the flowers are protected in pollen- but not air-proof polythene covers while they are receptive, pollen from male parent trees capable of passing on desirable characteristics, can be introduced via a modified "puffer" syringe (right), which carries the pollen on to the female "flowers".

CONIFEROUS FORESTS

. . . These trees—these forests of trees—so enchain the sense of the grand and so enchant the sense of the beautiful that I linger on the theme and am loth to depart. Forests in which you cannot ride a horse—in which you cannot possibly recover game you have shot without the help of a good retriever—forests into which you cannot see, and which are almost dark under a bright midday sun—such forests, containing firs, cedars, pine, spruce and hemlock, envelop Puget Sound and cover a large part of Washington Territory, surpassing the woods of all the rest of the globe in the size, quantity and quality of the timber.

SAMUEL WILKESON *Notes on Puget Sound* 1869

The ecosystem

Right *A huge expanse of spruce, fir and pine trees stretches through the sub-polar latitudes across the northern hemisphere. The distribution of coniferous trees is also associated with great mountain ranges.*

Far right *In the north the distribution of pine trees is limited by extreme cold, and although man has extended their southern distribution, their natural limit is checked by low rainfall or high temperatures.*

The great coniferous forests of the world are found in high latitudes fringing the treeless arctic tundra, below perpetual snows on great mountain ranges or on drought-prone hill-sides in lower latitudes. And the world's most valuable timberlands are found in these vast but generally inaccessible evergreen forests.

More than half of the coniferous forests are in Asia, stretching across Siberia, through China and Korea to the Bering Straits, with smaller but important areas in the Himalayas and in much of upland Japan. In Europe they occur extensively in Scandinavia and along the Baltic coasts, and in more restricted areas of the Alps, the Vosges and the Carpathians. In North America they stretch across the full width of the north from Alaska to Quebec, down the Pacific coast from Alaska to Califor-nia, and eastwards up into the Rockies.

By far the most spectacular coniferous for-ests, in terms of size and variety of tree species, are those in the Pacific coastal regions of Brit-ish Columbia and the north-west United States, where moist, mild conditions are far removed from the rigours of the high moun-tains and the circumpolar belt. Here, seldom subjected to snow or frost, and with their roots in deep alluvial soil, the trees grow im-mensely tall and massive in bulk, often ex-ceeding 300 feet in height and more than thirty feet in circumference.

Within this forest zone itself there are well-defined sub-zones in which certain tree spe-cies, conditioned to local climatic influences, maintain their own local dominance. The coastal redwoods, their distribution closely correlated to the incidence of sea fogs and a high humidity, form large tracts of heavily timbered forest in a coastal strip in northern California, for example, and the Douglas fir maintains complete supremacy in a huge domain because forest fires favour its regen-eration above all else.

The mountain forests of north-west Amer-ica, sandwiched between the coastal belt and the sub-alpine zones on the mountain ranges, are composed mostly of fire-resistant species; those with immensely thick bark, which pro-tects them from flames and heat, and those with massive or tough cones, which need fire to open them and release the seeds. Many of these trees, mostly pines and the giant Sierra redwoods, grow to great sizes and are well able to survive prolonged summer drought (see pages 72–73).

In the vast tracts of boreal forest that ring the northern polar regions the growing season is but three or four short months, albeit with long days and occasional high temperatures, and the winter is intensely cold and long. Water is locked solidly in the ground and the land is blanketed in thick snow.

To survive at all, let alone grow and enjoy the long-term dominance, which they do, the conifers must have adaptations to resist drought, low temperatures and damage from snow and wind. Their slender, tapering habit ensures protection from the latter, and the long-lived, narrow leaves (needles), coated

Above *Popularly associated with forests of spruce and fir, the moose's preferred habitat is those relatively clear, boggy areas where willow, aspen and birch trees flourish. They are adept at tapping food resources that are inaccessible to other animals. Typically, this moose has waded into a thawed lake in order to browse upon waterlilies.*

Left *A "drunken forest" is created when the top-soil freezes in winter and pushes against tree trunks so that they lean over, sometimes even cracking under the strain. In summer the soil thaws and forms lakes in hollows gouged out by previous glaciers. The trees are left perched on an unstable mo of slowly decomposing vegetation.*

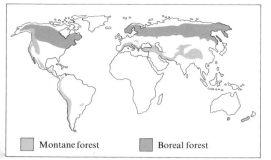

Montane forest Boreal forest

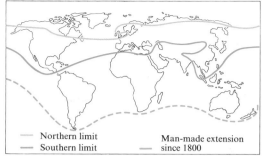

— Northern limit
— Southern limit
— Man-made extension since 1800

THE ACID FOREST FLOOR

SUCCESSION

Where the mature forest of spruce, pine and fir trees has been cut to the ground by natural fires or logging,

aspens, willows, alders and birches colonize the cleared patch first because of the advantage of light,

wind-borne seeds. Gradually, however, the conifers spring up again from the latent seeds and

shoots that survived the fire. They naturally grow taller than the broadleaves and regain dominance.

Sundews (above) *and pitcher plants* (below) *trap insects to compensate for the lack of nitrates in lakeside soils.*

Above *The plantations of pine species that thrive in the rich soil of the southern states of the USA—the*

wood basket of the world—supply the modern pulpwood industry. Pines are remarkably resilient

and adaptable conifers and in optimum conditions such as these they are fast growing and easy to manage.

Subsoil of weathered parental rock
Yellow-brown with a clayey texture
Reddish-brown due to re-deposition of leached minerals, especially iron
Light-leached sandy layer
Dark humus-rich layer
Decomposing organic humus
Leaves and surface debris

The layer of dead leaves, twigs and cones littering the coniferous forest floor eventually decays into a black humus. This is a slow process because decomposing bacteria cannot operate easily in the continual coldness of the northern and mountainous areas. The typical soil, called "podsol", is distinguished by its well-defined layers, maintained because earthworms and other soil-mixing fauna cannot do their usual jobs. The humus forms weak acids that percolate down with rain-water and vital minerals are therefore leached out of the earth. This results in a hard sterile sand, which causes a water-logged top-soil and prevents tree roots from penetrating deep down for their nutrients.

To compensate for this situation conifer tree roots have a symbiotic relationship with a mycorrhizal fungus (*above right*) that provides the tree roots with nutrients in return for carbohydrates. Recent research has shown that these fungi can increase the growth rate of pine seedlings by 50 per cent.

with wax and impregnated with resins, prevent excessive transpiration. The one exception is the deciduous larch which manages to flourish in conditions too severe even for evergreens, casting its needles as temperatures plummet, yet somehow managing to spring into life again as soon as spring returns.

It is the very fact that the leaves of most coniferous trees remain on the branch so long, thus losing nitrogen and other elements by leaching, in combination with the low temperatures, that results in another feature of the coniferous forest—a mass of undecomposed acid litter beneath the trees. Also, because conifer needles are on the whole unpalatable to birds and animals there is no input of nutrients to the soil from their waste products. There might well therefore seem to be danger of the soil running out of vital properties altogether, but this is to a large measure prevented by a remarkable relationship between the roots of conifers and a group of fungi called mycorrhiza, without which pine trees cannot

survive. These fungi populate the coniferous forest's litter and ensure that mineral elements are transferred directly to the host trees before they can be leached downwards out of reach.

In essence the sub-alpine forests are subjected to the same kind of extreme conditions as the boreal, but with a longer growing season and more intense sunlight. The trees, which are of the same genera and even the same species, often reach greater dimensions, although their general habit and needle sizes are very similar.

In the Mediterranean basin and in parts of California, with generally warm, wet winters and hot, dry summers, cedars, pines, cypresses and junipers with short, heavily waxed, resinous leaves and tough, wiry branches, contend with severe summer droughts and form extensive local forests.

In the southern hemisphere coniferous forests are rare and scattered. On the Andean mountain slopes of Chile, thinly covered with poor, dry, rocky soils, Chile pines, *Araucaria*

araucana, form extensive but rather open forests. While in New Zealand some fine remanent stands of kauri pines, *Agathis australis*, show how impressive these forests must have been. In New Zealand too, and in South Africa, podocarp species still form isolated forest stands (see pages 68–69).

The forests of the southern states and of the Pacific seaboard in the United States, which provide vast quantities of timber and pulpwood, grow on rich soils. But the extensive, and relatively inaccessible, coniferous forests of the world are found at high latitudes or high altitudes where the weather is cold. Their trees are the direct inheritors of the poor, shallow rocky soils left by the retreating glaciers at the end of the Ice Ages. They have become so well adapted to the conditions in which they now live that they are unlikely to suffer any challenge to their supremacy from the more advanced broadleaved trees that meet with them on the southern and lowland boundaries of their domain.

The trees

Cedars
Cedar of Lebanon *Cedrus libani*

The cedar of Lebanon has, like the other two true cedars, a magnificent trunk and a flat-topped crown. It grows to a height of 70–100 ft and its lower branches sometimes sweep the ground with distinctive "plates" of foliage, but the branch tips are level, unlike those of the Deodar cedar, C. deodara, which droop, or those of the Atlas cedar, C. atlantica, which ascend. Cedar needles are similar in shape and attachment to those of the larches, but they are evergreen and stiffer. The barrel-shaped cones develop from bud-like female flowers at shoot tips and take 2 years to grow, disintegrating on the tree.

Pines
Lodgepole pine *Pinus contorta*

The hundred or so species of pine have a natural range from the Equator to the Arctic Circle. When young, pines are generally conical in form but may develop wider tops in maturity. Pine leaves form long needles that are set in groups of 2, 3 or 5, each group enclosed in a small sheath. The number of needles is constant for each species and is a major identifying characteristic. The lodgepole, for example, has needles in sets of 2. Occasionally bushy, it can grow to 80 ft. The hard and woody cones vary greatly in size and shape, and are formed of radially set scales.

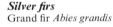

Silver firs
Grand fir *Abies grandis*

The silver firs consist of 50 species and have very straight trunks. The grand fir is so called because it can reach a height of 250 ft, and it grows so rapidly when young that it is a valued plantation tree. Silver firs take their name from the lines of silver stomata on the undersides of the leaves. The needles are generally short and flat and set singly along the branch, leaving circular scars when they fall. The cones are characteristically upright and disintegrate while still on the tree.

Spruces
Norway spruce *Picea abies*

The Norway spruce is typical of the spruce family. Spruces grow symmetrically and have solid dense crowns and trunks that are often buttressed. Although not as tall as some other species, Norway spruces can grow up to 200 ft. Spruces are identifiable by their needles, which are set on small pegs that come away with the needle if it is pulled from a twig. The male flowers produce so much yellow pollen that the forest floor is often littered with it and the female flowers, once fertilized and developing into cones, bend under their own weight. The Norway spruce has the longest cones of any spruce species.

Compared with the number of broadleaved tree species, the conifers are relatively few—only some 570 species—but they comprise some of the most extensive forests in the world and are the most important source of timber.

Nearly one-fifth of all the conifers belong to the true pines, *Pinus*, which form extensive forests in the colder, drier zones of the northern hemisphere, as well as in some areas of high summer temperatures and low rainfall farther south. In the Eurasian high-latitude forests, Scots pine, *Pinus sylvestris*, and Siberian pine, *P. sibirica*, dominate vast areas from Scandinavia east to the Bering Straits; and in North America, the home of the majority of the world's pines, western white pine, *P. monticola*, lodgepole pine, *P. contorta*, Jack pine, *P. banksiana*, red pine, *P. resinosa*, and eastern white pine, *P. strobus*, are important components in the forests that stretch from Alaska across to eastern Canada.

In the forests on the Cascade Mountains and the Sierras, where dry conditions and high summer temperatures prevail, the world's two largest pines, the sugar pine, *P. lambertiana*, and western yellow pine, *P. ponderosa*, are accompanied by numerous others of the same genus at various altitudes up to the tree line, as well as a host of other conifers.

In the United States, south-east of the Great Plains, there are four major species of hard yellow pine—lobolly, slash, short-leaf and long-leaf—that dominate a band of temperate pineland. Although they are among the more resinous pines, these species have a wide range of commercial uses (see pages 132–133).

In the European Alps the Arolla pine, *P. cembra*, shares the upper forest limit with larches, and in the Himalayas two species, the Chir pine, *P. roxburghii*, and the Bhutan pine, *P. wallichiana*, dominate forests between 5,000 and 10,000 feet in the drier areas.

The true firs, much less numerous than the pines and immediately recognizable by their upright cones like candles on a Christmas tree, occur on the better soils in the northern forests. The Siberian fir, *Abies sibirica*, ranges from Scandinavia into northern Russia, being replaced by the eastern Siberian fir, *A. nephrolepsis*, in China and beyond, while in central and eastern Canada the balsam fir, *A. balsamea*, is widespread. In the Alps the European silver fir, *A. alba*, often forms nearly pure forests, and in the Himalayas two firs are among the dominant trees in some of the middle altitude forests—the pindrow fir, *A. pindrow*, and the Himalayan fir, *A. spectabilis*. But the finest of the firs are found in the coastal

and middle mountain forests of north-west America, with the huge grand fir, *A. grandis*, noble fir, *A. procera*, and Pacific silver fir, *A. amabilis*, mostly on the lower ground, and the red fir, *A. magnifica*, together with the alpine fir, *A. lasiocarpa*, which occur at higher altitudes in the forest.

The spruces, with their pendulous cones are represented by the Norway spruce, *Picea abies*, and the Siberian spruce, *P. obovata*, in the northern forests of the Eurasian zone, and by white spruce, *P. glauca*, and black spruce, *P. mariana*, in the Alaskan and Canadian forests, while the great sitka spruce, *P. sitchensis*—the largest of the genus—forms pure stands in the coastal forest of Alaska and British Columbia and is a companion of the greatest timber tree among conifers, the Douglas fir, *Pseudotsuga menziesii*. Two other noteworthy species here are the red cedar, *Thuya plicata*, and the western hemlock, *Tsuga heterophylla*.

The larches, too, are important components of the coniferous forest. The Siberian larch, *Larix sibirica*, and the Dahurian larch, *L. dahurica*, extend up to the timber line in Asia, while in the Alaska–Canada zone the tamarack, *L. laricina*, covers large areas bordering the tree line. In the Rockies and

Larches
European larch *Larix europaea*

Larches are deciduous conifers with straight trunks and symmetrical, narrow, conical crowns. The branches usually turn up at the tips and very old open-grown larch trees often have massive low branches. The most commonly planted species, the European larch has distinctive straw-coloured twigs, ridged, with short "spur-shoots" carrying the clusters of 20–30 soft needles that are characteristic of all larches. Larch leaves change colour throughout the year, from a brilliant emerald green in May to a light orange colour in autumn. The barrel-shaped cones have tightly adpressed scales.

Douglas Firs
Pseudotsuga menziesii

The Douglas firs are remarkable for their stupendous heights—regularly reaching 250 ft—and are identifiable by a few simple features of their foliage. Like silver firs, the single needles tear away to leave round scars. The brown scaly, tapering buds resemble beech buds, but are much thinner. The yellow male flowers open in May and the female flowers on the branch tips look like green shoots and ripen rapidly, being initially green and egg-shaped, later brown and pendulous. Inside each scale there is a 3-pointed bract which is unique to the Douglas firs.

Hemlocks
Western hemlock *Tsuga heterophylla*

Nine species belong to this small genus and they are all originally native to western North America, eastern Asia and the Himalayas. The hemlocks are very beautiful and are often planted as ornamentals, but the western hemlock is also a valuable timber tree and can reach heights of more than 200 ft. Hemlocks can be identified by their flat needles, which, unusually, are of variable length and part on each side of the shoots. The egg-shaped cones are small but numerous, emerging from bud-like flowers at the shoot tips and ripening by autumn through green to lilac-purple, then brown.

CONIFER CHARACTERISTICS

The most distinctive stamp of coniferous trees is the foliage, which, in most of them, consists of small needle-like leaves that persist for several years, except in the case of the larches and a few others that are deciduous. These needles are either borne on ordinary long shoots, as in the yews, spruces and Douglas firs, or they are restricted to special dwarf shoots, each bearing a number of needles. In the pines the numbers vary according to species, but in the cedars and larches they are very numerous and are borne in tufts. In these last two genera, however, the needles are not entirely confined to dwarf shoots. During the first season's growth they also occur on the long shoots and the bases of the needles often fuse with the stem. After the leaves have fallen they persist, leaving small pegs and therefore very rough twigs. A different appearance characterizes the red cedars and cypresses because their minute leaves are almost completely fused with the stem and have a flat scale-like appearance. Seven of the most common coniferous genera are illustrated on the left.

Below A dense congregation of mature conifers. Their simple design—straight trunks with an almost geometrical, branching habit—make them ideal trees for timber production.

Cascades the largest of the larches, the western larch, *L. occidentalis*, overtops its fir and spruce companions; and in the European mountains the European larch, *L. europaea*, shares the alpine forests with Arolla pines.

There are other conifers of limited distribution that are of great interest. These include the coastal redwoods, *Sequoia sempervirens*, the Sierra redwoods, *Sequoiadendron giganteum*, the southern deciduous swamp cypresses, *Taxodium distichum*, and the three true cedars. The cedar of Lebanon, *Cedrus libani*, is, in fact, most numerous in the Taurus Mountains; the Atlas cedar, *C. atlantica*, is found in the North African mountains, and the deodar, *C. deodara*, in the Himalayas.

In the southern hemisphere, where conifers are scarce and the forests much less extensive, the monkey-puzzle tree, *Araucaria araucana*, forms sparse forests high in the Chilean Andes, and the Parana pine, *A. angustifolia*, is an important timber tree of Brazil. In New Zealand the huge kauri pines, *Agathis australis*, are now protected from a nearly fatal exploitation. In the remnants of the once extensive indigenous forests of South Africa the yellowoods, *Podocarpus falcatus* and *P. latifolius*, still raise their broad crowns above the other surrounding trees.

The northern winter

Below *The only visible animals in this wintry scene in Yellowstone National Park are deer and geese. But beneath the snow and in warm nooks and crannies among the trees a host of other creatures survive the cold.*

Winter in the northern coniferous forests is long and severe, with snow lying for up to six months and icy winds at −40°C (−40°F) buffeting the trees. But the forest, by the shelter that it gives, mitigates some of the winter weather's worst effects upon its animal population, and the thick snow insulates the life beneath it from the bitter cold. Winter, however, is still a hard time for the wildlife, much of which moves south to the less cold temperate forests, just as the animals of the tundra themselves move south into the forests.

Food is scarce, so the animals that winter here must, to survive, avoid competition with each other. Capercaillies and blue grouse eat conifer needles, beavers the bark of fallen trees, elks the brushwood, and the caribou moss and lichens—no species competes with the other. Lemmings and voles retreat beneath the snow, into a world of their own penetrated only by the stoats, or ermine, in search of prey, and mainly live on the young buds of rushes and other vegetation similarly protected by the snow. And the insectivorous shrews find grubs, pupae and worms.

Above ground the wolves collect in packs to hunt the deer, their numbers ensuring success in the chase. The lynxes and the wolverines spring from the trees on unsuspecting hares and birds, and the landbound foxes must dig out the lemmings or outrun the snowshoe rabbit across the powdery snow. The squirrels escape competition by collecting and storing nuts and fruits in the time of autumn plenty to call upon when they awake from partial hibernation. But the chipmunk goes one better by feeding voraciously when food is plentiful, storing it in accumulated fat and then sinking into a torpor that may last for six to eight months before spring and fresh supplies become available. And the bears, heedless of all other creatures but man, emerge occasionally from their warm dens, to scratch up roots, moss and ants with their powerful claws.

The birds, although more mobile than other creatures, have an especially hard time, and only those with the most marked adaptations can winter in the coniferous forests. Apart from those that can eat conifer needles, there are the crossbills with beaks specially built for tweeking out the seeds from fir-cones and the nutcrackers whose powerful bills can rip the cones from the trees and tear them to pieces. The eagles and hawks, keen-eyed in the clear crisp air, spot the slightest movement and snatch up any small bird or animal temporarily off-guard in its feverish hunt for food in the all too short day. And the owls, on silent pinions, surprise any forest creatures prolonging their foraging into the long night.

The reduction in competition for the limited food supplies aids animals and birds living in these forests during the harsh winter, but they also need special physical attributes to ensure their survival. Some, such as the foxes, hares and stoats, not only develop thicker fur, as do all the mammals, but their fur turns white in the winter to make them less visible in the snowy landscape. The hares also

Above *Wolves are feared by the animals of the forest, perhaps even more than the lynx. When hunting they cover long distances and encircle their* prey, which is usually the weakest member of a herd of deer or caribou. As winter progresses the wolves move deeper into the forest.

Above *The lynx, Felis lynx, is a solitary hunter, moving silently and stealthily through the snow—its main prey is the snowshoe rabbit. The size* of the snowshoe rabbit population fluctuates in ten-year cycles, which in turn has a direct effect on the number of lynxes that survive in the forest.

Life is a struggle for all forms of life in the northern winter. The only animals that manage to survive are the ones that have evolved specific adaptations, which enable them to withstand the long spell of cold harsh conditions. Some of these adaptations are illustrated below.

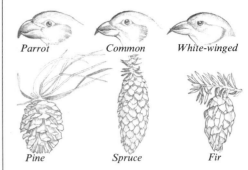

Parrot   *Common*   *White-winged*

Pine   *Spruce*   *Fir*

The three species of crossbill have their mandibles crossed at the tip so that they can extract seeds from the tree cones. Each beak is adapted to the kind of cone each species prefers to feed on.

Shrews, voles and lemmings remain active and warm in tunnels between the soil and snow. They subsist on larvae, which they dig out of the ground, as well as the buds of rushes and other vegetation.

In summer the snowshoe rabbit or varying hare, Lepus americanus, has a reddish-brown coat (above). When the temperature falls and day length shortens it changes into snowy white.

The snowshoe rabbit in winter. It takes its name from the hairy mats that it grows on the soles of its broad feet to enable it to distribute its weight on the soft powdery snow, and thus move more easily.

develop thicker pads on their feet to help them more effectively flee their enemies across the powdery snow. Lynx kittens retain their milk teeth for up to nine months, and because they cannot kill a hare even at that age, they remain in a family group throughout the first winter, totally dependent on their mother for survival.

Bears, which mate in early summer when their food is plentiful and their physical condition good, have their period of gestation prolonged well beyond that which would normally occur in an animal of their size. The egg cells, after mating, do not develop into young animals straightaway. After reaching the earliest stages of differentation they remain dormant for several months, before becoming attached to the wall of the uterus and growing normally. This is known as delayed implantation and it ensures that the cubs are born in the warm den in late winter and will be ready to emerge into the world when the spring and better weather arrive.

So, as winter clamps down on life in the coniferous forest survival is the order of the day; not through multiplication as in the summer breeding season, but through the maintenance of sufficient numbers to ensure that breeding can take place next season.

The trees, which cannot move, close down their metabolism to a minimum against the cold in their crowns and the frozen water round their roots. The animals, birds and insects must either move or make themselves capable of finding food where others cannot find it, or in such a way that others cannot emulate them. Thus in the winter forest which may seem lifeless, nature is actually engaged in the highly successful enterprise of ensuring, by many remarkable specialities, that a huge area of the Earth's surface retains a caretaker resident population of wildlife despite the drawn-out uncongenial conditions.

Summer respite

Below *Canada geese join the avian throng that pours north from the Tropics to spend a brief summer in the boreal forest. A population of geese will return year after year to the same marshy, riverside breeding ground.*

Below *The damp summer provides ideal breeding conditions for mosquitoes. Their eggs are laid in pools of water, where, entrapped in ice, they may remain all winter until, released by the summer thaw, the larvae emerge.*

Bottom *Pine saw-fly larvae, like the many other insects, rapidly complete their life-cycle during the short summer period. Although a boon to insect-eating animals, they are a serious pest to the forester.*

The boreal forest, that broad belt of coniferous trees that encircles the Earth in the higher latitudes of the northern hemisphere, is, in its cold isolation, one of the least disturbed wild-life habitats in the world.

This very isolation, combined with a summer, albeit brief but with almost constant daylight, attracts vast hordes of birds. Many of them travel thousands of miles to breed in safe seclusion and in circumstances of material plenty. And with no night-time darkness to halt photosynthesis, plants and trees grow rapidly and unimpeded, insects proliferate upon them and elsewhere in unbelievable millions, and every other creature multiplies; each provides food for the next link along the lengthening food chain. No curtain of night falls to divide one scene from the next and these frenetic survival activities proceed uninterrupted.

As the days lengthen the tree buds swell and cast their brown, paper-thin scales upon the soil and shrinking snow patches. In the clearings the furry buds of the willows sprout golden, dusty stamens. Birch catkins become pendulous among the opening leaves, and through the quickly thawing soil the flowering plants thrust their stems, the dryas carpeting the drier patches with eight-petalled white flowers, while gentians, orchids and saxifrage add blues and pinks in their turn.

The resident forest dwellers, which have spent the winter in hibernation or in a single-minded search for food, submit to a fresh and

Below *In summer the northern goshawk migrates from the temperate regions of the northern hemisphere to the boreal forests of the far north. Here, it establishes itself as the topmost link in the forest's food chain,* *preying on the burgeoning population of small birds and mammals. The goshawk builds its nest and raises its young in the northern forests, taking advantage of the food supply presented by the proliferating wildlife.*

powerful urge brought on by the increasing food supply and the strengthening sun. Blue grouse, capercaillies, crossbills, nutcrackers, owls and hawks all set about building nests. The woodchucks awaken from an eight-month hibernation and forage feverishly to replace lost fat before breeding. The voles and shrews emerge from beneath the snow blanket that has protected them and their food from excessive winter cold to multiply and supply their predators with food. Bears, their deep sleep interrupted by the birth of their young, come out of their lairs to wander far and wide in search of their omniverous diet. And the lynxes, with young to feed, welcome the seasonal increase of the snowshoe rabbit.

Of all the creatures of the forest none multiply to such an extent as the insects, each with two or three stages in its life-cycle. The eggs and pupae that have lain hidden in bark crevices and beneath the snow in twigs and leaf litter, hatch or burst open. Caterpillars swarm over their food plants; butterflies and moths emerge in their adult splendour, adding colour to the quickly changing scene. Mosquitoes and midges swarm in humming clouds; ants build up tall mounds of dead needles to house their queen and her populous offspring. As one phase in a life-cycle follows another, a myriad creeping, crawling, hopping, flying insect creatures fill the forest and the gaping beaks of hungry nestlings. Partly in an effort to avoid the irritating swarms of insects, the moose spends much of its summer browsing on aquatic vegetation in the forest lakes and rivers.

Flocks of redpolls, bramblings and other finches, which moved south in the autumn to live on the seeds and nuts of the deciduous woodland, spread northwards to rear their young on the glut of insects. Fieldfares, red-wings and other thrushes, fresh from warmer wintering in the south, return to their birth places to raise another generation. Non-resident owls and hawks move in to prey on the increasing population of young creatures, and small, insect-eating warblers, many of which had crossed the Equator to find food enough in the winter, spread in a huge flood through the forest, filling it with song. Overhead in the never-quite-dark skies the honking and trumpeting of wild geese and swans and the shrill cries of wading birds tell of great hordes winging their way to safe breeding grounds in the far north tundra.

This influx of birdlife is perhaps the most remarkable of all the events marking the summer respite in the coniferous forests of the north. It would be less spectacular, however, without the areas of swamp and of broad-leaved trees, such as willow, birch and aspen, which occur here and there throughout the forest where fires, caused by lightning, have cleared away the conifers. These trees, with their tiny, wind-borne seeds, spread rapidly into these pockets and can dominate them for up to 150 years before the conifers can re-assert themselves. It is in these areas of massed scrub, dense with their summer leaves, that most of the birds find their food and shelter.

In the mountain forests, where day-length is the same as in the surrounding lowlands and is often much shorter than in northern latitudes, the change from winter to summer is much less dramatic and the influx of birds and animals much less extensive.

Some birds, which spend the winter lower down the mountains, move up and are followed by their predators as migrants arrive from the south and put pressure on the food supply. The deer that wintered in the valleys climb up to new pastures, bringing with them the lynxes and the cougars. But in general there is much less movement, just a seasonal increase in the resident creatures accompanied by a slight vertical shift in their spheres of activity. To some extent this less marked change in seasonal activity is caused by a much smaller increase in the insect populations.

In northern latitudes the cool temperatures, the slow decomposition of the forest floor and the evenness of the terrain result in damp ground conditions that are ideal for the reproduction of a host of different insects throughout summer. In the mountain forests, however, where drainage is good and temperatures are high, drought conditions that inhibit many insects are much more likely. So the mass of mosquitoes, gnats and midges that need water for stages in their life-cycle is absent and the insectivorous birds must rely on the relatively few insects that live on conifers and their accompanying shrubs and herbs.

The taiga

The circumpolar high-latitude forest of the northern hemisphere—the taiga—stretches almost without interruption across the great continents of Eurasia and America. The taiga forms one of the most widespread forest zones in the world and includes the largest forest of all, the Siberian forest, which extends for an area greater than that of the entire United States of America.

The taiga as a whole is dominated by species of spruce, pine, fir and larch, and although both the Eurasian and American zones are similar in structure, they contain different species of the same tree types. Changes in the tree components are in great measure due to differences in the soils; the pines generally preferring the lighter sandier kinds and the spruces the heavier.

Within these mainly coniferous forests the large and small areas cleared by fires, wind and human activity (for in the more southerly parts much of the world's industrial softwood is grown) are initially recolonized by broad-leaved species such as willows, birches, aspens and alders. These reservoirs of broadleaves are an important food source for birds, insects and other animals.

The climatic conditions in taiga forests are severe and the growing season is very short, barely more than three months. The mean annual temperature varies between 2–6°C (36–42°F) with possible extremes ranging from −50°C (−58°F) to 50°C (122°F), with rain and snowfall totalling only eight to ten inches, evenly distributed during the year. These conditions, together with such a short season when growth is possible, seriously retard the development of the trees. On the northern limits, bordering upon the tundra, trees of great age remain small, stunted and gnarled. Some of the Siberian pines and larches have as many as sixty annual rings to an inch of radial growth on the trunk. With a high proportion of dead wood in their make-up, they are festooned with moss and lichens. On the southern limits of the forest, where it blends into the temperate woodlands, the trees can assume much larger sizes.

Beneath the trees, on a bed of accumulated acid litter, grows a great variety of ericaceous shrubs and ground plants. These include the bearberry, crowberry and bilberry, as well as a host of other species of differing families, all producing berries to provide food for the greatly increased summer wildlife population, which streams up from the south as the days lengthen. And on the rocks in the swamps, and on the trees themselves, a great variety of club-mosses and lichens prosper in profusion.

Human habitations in the taiga are few and far between, usually trading stations that handle fur pelts and other merchandize and, in Siberia, small towns along the Trans-Siberian Railway. Still being constructed along a 3,000-mile route north of Lake Baykal, the new Trans-Siberian railway is opening up the taiga for mining and timber extraction. In addition, many of the animals in the forest are commercially valuable.

Above *Bald eagles, the national bird of the USA, are increasingly rare. Although protected in their range they are now plentiful only in Alaska.*

Below *The Eurasian eagle owl hunts by night, taking over the daytime role of eagles and hawks. It can kill young deer, foxes and capercaillies.*

If the human population of the taiga is increasing, the resident birds and animals remain relatively few and they are specially adapted to severe conditions. Well able to survive on sparse diets of lichens and mosses herds of musk-ox and caribou range throughout the northern limits of the forests in Canada and Alaska; and family parties of moose graze the swampy areas in the forests farther south. In Eurasia reindeer and elk fill the same niches respectively; and in all the forests ferocious wolverines, protected by a special snow-shedding fur, are ravenous predators and aggressive scavengers. Despite being little more than three feet long, wolverines are capable of killing a young deer or, more often, driving a wolf or bear from its kill and staying with the carcass until the lot is eaten—hence their second name—glutton.

Bears too, adapted to semi-hibernation in the cold, dark days, roam through the taiga. The largest carnivore is the lynx, a predatory scourge on the arctic hares. This animal, to-

Below *The northern taiga is dominated by species of spruce mixed with deciduous hardwoods, forming an open-canopied forest rather like parkland. Peat-filled glacier-scoured hollows interrupt its density at frequent intervals.*

Right *Within the lakes and watercourses of the taiga beavers set about changing the landscape, building dams to form ponds and flood pastures and low-lying land. In the middle of the pond, the beaver builds a lodge, or house. Lodges*

gether with another of their predators, the arctic fox, changes its summer, reddish coat to a pure white one in the winter. Confined to the lakes and watercourses within the taiga are beavers, musk rats, otters and mink.

Many of the resident birds are those that feed on conifer seeds. Nutcrackers are particularly numerous in the Siberian "cedar" areas and crossbills and pine grosbeaks, as well as other species, such as grouse and ptarmigan, relish the berries on the heather-like plants. Preying upon all these, and upon the periodically exploding populations of lemmings and voles, are the hawks by day and the owls by night. And with the summer and its perpetual daylight, hosts of birds come into the forest, flying north into solitude and an ample food supply of swarming insects. Warblers, waders, ducks and geese fill the forest and its bogs and lakes with new life for a brief three months, departing south again before snow and frost sparkle once more in the brief sunshine of the northern winter.

vary in shape and size and usually consist of a living room, a food store for the winter, and a sleeping area. Beavers are widespread throughout North America and are recovering their numbers in Europe and Asia.

Lodge
Dam
Food store
Entrance
Entrance

Below Brown bears feed in preparation for their winter sleep. In autumn they eat the numerous berries furnished by the taiga's undergrowth. They then hibernate in large hollow trees or under the roots of fallen ones.

LAKE BAYKAL

Deep within the Siberian taiga, Lake Baykal is the deepest landlocked freshwater lake in the world. Its clear, oxygen-rich water houses unique fish such as the Comephoridae family, whose young are born live, and the endemic Baykal seal.

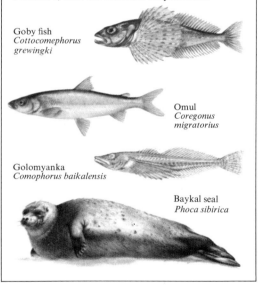

Goby fish
Cottocomephorus grewingki

Omul
Coregonus migratorius

Golomyanka
Comophorus baikalensis

Baykal seal
Phoca sibirica

THE EURASIAN AND AMERICAN TREE SPECIES

Both the Eurasian and American zones of the taiga are similar in structure, but contain different species of the same tree genera. Norway spruce, Picea abies, dominates the Eurasian section of the forest in Scandinavia, but farther east, through Finland and into Russia, Scots pine, Pinus sylvestris, takes over. It gradually gives way to Siberian fir, Abies sibirica, and Siberian and Dahurian larches, Larix sibirica and L. gmelini, as well as, on the lower ground, the Siberian pine, Pinus sibirica, often referred to as Siberian cedar. The seeds of this latter pine are articles of food esteemed by both man and birds. In the North American section—east of the Bering Straits—where the variety of species is greater, the same west-east change in the dominant species occurs. Lodgepole pine, Pinus contorta var murrayana, and alpine fir, Abies lasiocarpa, with black spruce, Picea mariana, in the west, gradually give way to eastern larch or tamarack, Larix laricina, white spruce, Picea glauca, balsam fir, Abies balsamea, and jack pine, Pinus banksiana.

Below The Trans-Siberian Railway is opening up the virgin territories of the taiga and already there are signs of an ecological imbalance as a result of the project. Apart from excessive logging, the removal of layers of insulating mosses for use as a domestic fuel by the construction workers means that large patches of the permafrost melt and this leads to flooding in some regions.

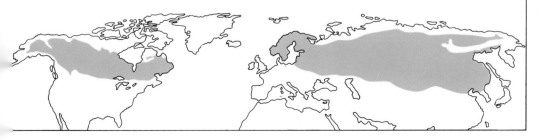

Forest frontiers

Below *Growing in a no-man's-land between the tundra and the forest proper are scattered stands of stunted trees struggling for survival in the shallow soil. Here, it may take a seedling 25 years to reach a height of 2 ft.*

Although conifers are well adapted to withstand low temperatures and harsh conditions, there are extremes beyond these which even they cannot tolerate, be they in northerly-latitude polar regions or at high altitudes in the mountain ranges. When conditions provide only thirty days with average temperatures of 10°C (50°F), and a cold season lasting eight months, the conifers are unable to prosper, and tundra vegetation takes over.

The first indication that conditions are becoming unfavourable to tree growth is a thinning of the forest, with trees occurring in scattered groups on the higher ground. These patches of trees become more and more widespread and smaller in extent the farther north they are growing until only isolated pockets of forest remain, with the trees becoming progressively more stunted and malformed. In these northerly latitudes the zone of stunted trees, the northern zone of which marks the limits of tree growth, may be several hundred miles wide, but in the mountains the corre-

sponding zone of struggling trees lessening in size and vigour is relatively narrow.

The factors that limit tree growth in both polar and alpine forests are basically the same—short summers, long winters and a growing season of little more than three months at best. In this short period the young needles fail to reach maturity and do not attain the thickness and hardness required to withstand the winter, which in the polar regions brings strong, drying, intensely cold winds and in the alpine areas rapid evaporation by intense sunlight that is even stronger in spring. The needles drop off prematurely and stunting results. Beneath a covering of snow such damage cannot occur and this accounts for isolated groups of trees beyond the tree line where the topography allows a deep and thick accumulation of snow.

Another factor limiting tree growth, particularly in the polar regions, is that conditions rarely favour the production of viable seeds. Even those produced after a succession of at

least two favourable summers are either swept away across the frozen snow by the wind or fail to germinate and prosper in the generally unsuitable medium of mosses and lichen beneath the trees. If a seedling does succeed in taking root, it may take at least twenty-five years to become taller than the surrounding herbaceous plants, adding little more than half an inch to its height each short summer.

So great are the distances over which the northerly latitude tree line extends it would be wrong to assume that the climate was uniform throughout, or even that the tree line itself remains at a constant latitude. Where there is an oceanic influence, in areas such as north west Canada and Alaska for example, there is a relatively small range of temperature between winter and summer. But in the continental areas of central and eastern Canada and Siberia a span of something like 82°C (180°F) can occur in extreme cases, with summer temperatures as high as 29°C (85°F) and as low as −71°C (−95°F) in winter.

Below *Ptarmigans clothed
in their winter plumage
seek the shelter of an
isolated copse. They feed
on buds and tree twigs, and
excavate burrows in the
snow for shelter. When the
snow melts they moult and
assume a brown plumage.*

Middle *As the snow melts
the caribou of North
America and reindeer of
Europe migrate to new
feeding grounds. On their
return trek to the tundra,
they browse on mosses and
lichens as they pass through
the forest outskirts.*

These climatic differences result in a variation in the tree species growing along the tree line. In North America only one species, the white spruce, *Picea glauca*, is found along the whole line from the Bering Straits to Newfoundland. But the black spruce, *Picea mariana*, is almost as widespread geographically although it does not extend quite so far west and is found mainly on poorer soils than its white relative. In central and eastern areas, Balsam fir, *Abies balsamea*, jack pine, *Pinus banksiana*, and tamarack, *Larix laricina*, join with the spruces in increasing numbers.

In Europe, Norway spruce, *Picea abies*, and Siberian spruce, *Picea obovata*, are the western tree-line species, with Siberian fir, *Abies sibirica*, Siberian pine, *Pinus sibirica*, and Siberian larch, *Larix sibirica*, in central and eastern areas, the latter being replaced by the dominant Dahurian larch, *Larix dahurica*, in eastern Siberia.

In the mountains of north-west America and Colorado the tree line is generally at about 12,000 feet with Englemann's spruce, *Picea engelmannii*, as the dominant tree in the north. Alpine fir, *Abies lasiocarpa*, grows farther south and the uppermost trees grow in isolated groups on rocky elevations where the winter snow is never very deep and thus melts away quite quickly in early spring.

Whereas in the American mountains completely natural conditions still prevail, in the European Alps a thousand years of human interference in the shape of summer pasturage in the alpine belt has greatly altered the upper forest limit. The check to natural regeneration occasioned by this practice has brought the actual tree line down 300–500 feet lower than it would be under natural conditions, which would normally be about 6,500 feet. At the tree line Arolla pine, *Pinus cembra*, and European larch, *Larix europaea*, are the most commonly encountered species.

In the Himalayas, although the main tree-line species tend to be birch, *Betula utilis*, and rhododendron species, some coniferous trees are present at around 13,500 feet including Himalayan fir, *Abies spectabilis*, and juniper, *Juniperus wallichiana*.

The tree line in the mountains is so close to the warm, more luxuriant forests lower down, that the alpine zone tends to have fewer specialized animals and birds than the polar region tree-line area. There the arctic fox and the snowy owl are winter visitors from the far north tundra, seeking some shelter in the groups of struggling trees; and the summer-visiting birds will tarry briefly in the stunted forest as they move north and south on their annual migrations.

For the most part the tree line is a meeting place, not only of trees and tundra but also of truly polar animals and those that inhabit the boreal forests, the latter moving north to enjoy the continuous daylight of the short summer and the increased food supply it engenders, the former moving south as the bitter cold and perpetual darkness of a severe winter restricts their feeding activities.

Above *The snowy owl is a native of the
tundra, feeding primarily on lemmings
and arctic hares. When the populations of
their prey dramatically crash every 4 or 5
years the snowy owl moves to the forest
south of its usual wintering range.*

Right *Spruce and pine trees, rooted in the
shallow soil among rocks, cling to the
mountain-side at an elevation of 10,000 ft.*

Mountain forests

Coniferous trees in the boreal, or northern forests, have developed many ingenious adaptations to enable them to resist low temperatures, snow, wind and periods of drought. Their narrow, conical habit, the needle-like, wax-coated leaves and the evergreen ability to take immediate advantage of favourable conditions serve them just as well in the montane forests, which occur in all the great mountain ranges of the world. On the Rockies, the Cascades and the Sierra Nevada in North America, the Alps and the Carpathians in Europe, the Hindu Kush and the great Himalayan Range in Asia, mountain-sides are clad in tiers of conifers, each species adapted to its own altitude and conditions. In the southern hemisphere conifers such as the araucarias form special montane forests (see pages 68–69).

The vertical zonation of the montane forests, with no more than a few hundred feet from one zone to the next, makes it much simpler for animals to make seasonal migrations in search of fresh feeding grounds. Deer move up from their winter quarters in the valleys to the higher zones; chamois climb above the tree line as the snows melt; and monkeys, after wintering in the foothill forests, move up into the mountains as their food trees blossom and fruit in stages up through the forest. Both resident and migratory birds, too, move up through the zones as feed becomes progressively available.

For centuries hardy, independent people have lived in the montane forest. It surrounds their alpine meadows and high summer pastures giving shelter from cold winds. It stands as a barrier above their villages against the avalanche of winter-accumulated snow, and it binds the soil with its roots to the steeply sloping hillsides, preventing landslides. The consequences of widespread felling of these forests or, as is happening in the Himalayas, the gradual destruction by overgrazing and fuelwood cutting can be devastating. Heavy rain over a protracted period, as with the monsoon in the Himalayas, soaking the unprotected soil, results in catastrophic landslides tearing away whole mountain-sides; and the spring thaw in the Alps can set a mass of snow hurtling down a bare mountain to engulf whole villages.

So man has more than a special interest in these forests, superb in their grandeur as they cloak the world's greatest mountain ranges. Without the protection they give to the most vulnerable parts of the world's surface, floods and erosion would soon render vast areas of the lowlands too hazardous for habitation.

The Rockies, the Cascades and the Sierra Nevada of North America run from north to south, and the spread of latitude covered is something close to sixty degrees. Since the area covered is so vast, the number of tree species making up these montane forests is great. In the northern part of the Rockies the Douglas firs and black cottonwoods of the valley bottoms give way to aspen, lodgepole pine and western white pine in the transitional zone at about 3,500 feet. These are themselves

replaced by Englemann's spruce and white spruce in the sub-alpine regions.

Farther south, although Douglas fir, together with several oak species, still dominate the lower levels, the transitional zone include such trees as western yellow pine and wester larch, with mountain hemlock and white barked pine joining Englemann's spruce an sub-alpine fir at elevations around 6,000 fee and farther up to the tree line. Farther sout still, where the rainfall is much less, evergree oaks and digger pine in the transitional zon are replaced by incense cedar, sugar pine an western yellow pine at around 4,000 feet, wit Jeffrey pine and red fir coming in at 8,000 fee or so. On the exposed tops, at 10,000–12,00 feet, are the ancient bristlecone pines (se pages 72–73). In the extreme south, pinyo pine and junipers—chiefly *Juniperus mono sperma*—form forests in the dry foothills.

In the European Alps and Carpathians tha run from west to east and cover barely fou degrees of latitude, the tree species are fewe

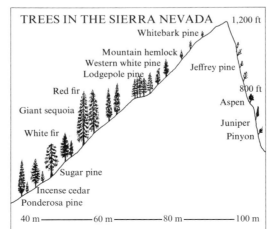

TREES IN THE SIERRA NEVADA

1,200 ft

Whitebark pine

Mountain hemlock
Western white pine
Lodgepole pine
Jeffrey pine

Red fir
800 ft

Giant sequoia
Aspen

White fir
Juniper
Pinyon

Sugar pine

Incense cedar
Ponderosa pine

40 m ——— 60 m ——— 80 m ——— 100 m

From a windswept peak in the Sierra Nevada variations in climate according to altitude can be observed from the successive bands of conifers, each composed of a different species, strung out along the mountain-side.

Below *Montane forests are able to withstand the harshest of environments. Here, hardy alpine firs grip the slopes of Hurricane Ridge at altitudes between 6,000–7,000 ft in the Olympic National Park, north-west United States.*

Below *Being cold-blooded, the alpine salamander, Salamandra atra, is glossy black to absorb any available heat.*

Above *Tiers of conifers, their roots binding the soil against landslides, cling to steep cliffs in the Kulu region of the Himalayas.*

Above *Showy blossoms of moss campion seem to sprout directly from the rocks. Water is derived from the melted glaciers* *that run into rock crevices and dissolve minerals to form a nourishing brew to sustain the plant roots as they cling to their rocky bed.*

Right *Chamois, goats and sheep are well adapted to rugged mountain terrain. Chamois hoofs are like rubber suction pads, enabling them to climb almost vertical rock faces.*

Below *Sturdy mountain trees protect the valleys from hurtling waves of snow after an avalanche.*

nd the variation in zone altitudes is scarcely erceptible. As the broadleaved species phase ut at around 4,000 feet, spruce, silver fir and rch begin to dominate, and the Arolla pines ecome increasingly numerous up to the mber line at 6,000 feet.

The montane forests of the Hindu Kush nd the Himalayas also form a narrow west to ast belt, covering little more than two degrees f latitude, on the foothills of the gigantic ange between the eternal snows of the north nd the plains of the south. Although these orests stretch for some 2,000 miles the number of co-dominant coniferous tree species is ot very great. Just as at the lower levels in the ierra Nevada, which are at about the same titude so, in the Himalayas evergreen oaks nd, in the west, Chir pines form a transitional one, thinning out as they are gradually displaced by deodar at around 6,000 feet. Then imalayan fir and morinda spruce with hododendron undergrowth take over and erge into scrub at about 11,500 feet.

Southern hemisphere conifers

Below left Quteniqua
yellowood, Podocarpus
falcatus, *in the Tsitsikama
forest of the southern cape
of South Africa. Growing
to 180 ft, the yellowoods
once formed extensive
forests but now only occur
in scattered pockets.*

DISTRIBUTION

Agathis

Araucarias

Podocarps

Cypresses

Above The distribution of
*the major coniferous
families—kauris, podocarps
and araucarias—
occurring in the southern*
*hemisphere. Most of the
species are found on the
high plateaux and
mountains throughout the
different continents.*

Although the southern hemisphere has vastly fewer coniferous tree species than the north—there are no pines, firs, spruces, true cedars or cypresses—all the southern lands have forests, or remnants of forests, in which there is a considerable coniferous element among the dominant trees. These trees differ in leaf form from those in the north and, with very few exceptions, are much smaller in stature.

In South America one of the most important timber trees is the Parana pine, or candelabra tree, *Araucaria angustifolia*, which grows in considerable forests in the hilly country of Parana Province in southern Brazil, and also extends into Argentina. Found mostly at between 2,000 and 4,000 feet, it grows fast in youth, eventually reaching a height of some 150 feet, with a clean, straight, cylindrical trunk carrying a candelabra-like, flat-topped crown of upturned branches. Another araucaria, much better known outside its native land, the monkey-puzzle, or Chile pine, *A. araucana*, forms scattered forests at high elevations in the Chilean and Argentinian Andes. These prickly trees of reptilian appearance, standing up to a hundred feet tall, loom large in the swirling mists with their great trunks clad in elephant hide-like bark.

Also from the Chilean Andes is the Chilean cedar, *Austrocedrus chilensis*, a close relative of the North American incense cedar. Smaller than the monkey-puzzle, for it rarely exceeds eighty feet in height, it is a tree of the narrow forest belt intermediate between the southern beech, *Nothofagus* spp., forest of the lower, west-facing Andean slopes and the arid uplands farther east, maintaining its foothold in the beech forests by its ability to grow in very dry situations. Those trees at the lower altitudes have good, straight trunks and crowns

of flattened scale-like leaves, green in colour, while those at the higher elevations around 4,000 feet are stunted, stubbornly clinging to the rocky hillsides.

An élite of the South American conifers is the Patagonian cedar, *Fitzroya cupressoides*, which occurs in the forests of the southern Andes on steep slopes and in boggy places where the southern beeches cannot prosper, pushing through the canopy to form pure stands. In days gone by the range of this tree extended down to sea-level, where in 1833, on Chiloe Island, Captain Fitzroy and Charles Darwin of HMS *Beagle* saw specimens up to 130 feet in circumference. In longevity the Patagonian cedar rivals the Sierra redwoods of North America, and its timber, little seen outside its native country, is very similar in structure and quality to that of the coastal redwoods (see pages 72–73).

In South Africa yellowoods, *Podocarpus falcatus*, are scattered components of the once extensive indigenous forests that now occur in isolated pockets from Cape Province north to Zululand and the Transvaal. They are giant trees up to 180 feet tall with huge trunks clad in grey flaky bark and supporting crowns of stiff, narrow, leathery, yellowish-green leaves, held well above and spreading over the general canopy of the forest, with vines and creepers trailing from the outspread branches down to the forest floor. Three other lesser podocarps are also present in the forest, and in the Drakensberg upland areas the cypress pines, *Widdringtonia* spp., cypress-like as the name implies, but unique as a genus to southern and tropical Africa, grow spreading and rugged on slopes, ridges and in gullies. The best of them are some seventy feet tall.

Australia's conifers are few in number compared with her wealth of eucalyptus and other broadleaved trees. Nevertheless, in the semitropical rain forests of the eastern seaboard where a great assemblage of plants flourish—including three hundred tree species with climbers and epiphytes—a luxuriant forest community very different from that of the neighbouring eucalyptus forests is found and here the giant coniferous trees predominate. In the coastal rain forest of Queensland and northern New South Wales the South Queensland kauri, *Agathis robusta* is a dominant tree—up to 140 feet tall with a heavily branched crown, supported by a fine trunk of very little taper, spreading around its scarcely less stately but more scattered neighbours. These include two species of araucaria: the bunya pine, *Araucaria bidwillii*, and the hoop pine, *A. cunninghami* both fine trees adding their prickly leaved crowns to the mosaic of the forest canopy.

Farther inland, where the climate becomes progressively drier, in scattered locations right across the continent to Western Australia, the white cypress pine, *Callitris hugeli* a relatively small tree up to sixty feet tall with thin feathery foliage, forms occasional pure stands but is more usually a component of the mixed eucalyptus forest (see page 152–153). Unsurpassed in resisting termite attack, it is an invaluable timber source.

In Tasmania a distant relative of the California redwoods, the King William pine *Athrotaxis selaginoides*, occurs in the mountain forests up to 3,000 feet, often multiforked with a short, buttressed trunk. Lower down in the cool, temperate rain forest the Huon pine, *Dacrydium franklinii*, a cypress-like tree with scaly leaves, and the celery topped pine, *Phyllocladus aspleniifolium*, with

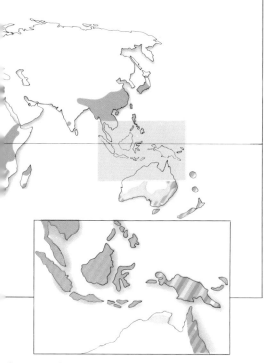

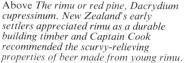

Above *The rimu or red pine, Dacrydium cupressinum. New Zealand's early settlers appreciated rimu as a durable building timber and Captain Cook recommended the scurvy-relieving properties of beer made from young rimu.*

flattened branches that perform as leaves, give the conifers a worthy place in the mainly beech and eucalyptus forest.

Not only is the kauri, *Agathis australis*, the noblest of New Zealand's trees, it is also the best known of the southern hemisphere conifers and is held in as much repute in its native country as the redwoods are in America. In North Island, where they are now confined to limited areas, the biggest of these trees, with their massive, scarcely tapering trunks fifty feet in circumference and often sixty feet clear of branches, support huge spreading crowns up to 150 feet tall. They stand spaced out in the mixed forest like pillars supporting a great green roof formed by many tree species. Most are evergreen hardwoods, but there are some conifers, such as the totara, *Podocarpus totara*, rimu, *Dacrydium cupressinum*, and miro, *Podocarpus ferrugineus*, and all are hosts to ferns and creepers in a luxuriant green cathedral. Although the kauris are confined to the North Island, other conifers are also found in the evergreen broadleaved forests of South Island. These include two more podocarps, kahikatea, *Podocarpus dacrydioides*, and matai, *P. spicatus*.

One of the most superbly symmetrical and elegant of the southern hemisphere conifers, indeed of all the conifers, is the Norfolk Island pine, *Araucaria heterophylla*, native to that island in the Pacific. Because of the almost mathematical precision with which it spaces out its whorls of identically shaped branches bearing upswept flattened leaves, it is extensively planted in subtropical countries as one of the tallest and most stately of the ornamental trees. With their quite different, pale green short-needled juvenile foliage, young trees are popular garden plants the world over.

Left *Captain Fitzroy, who with Charles Darwin discovered the Patagonian cedar, Fitzroya cupressoides, which subsequently took its scientific name from the captain himself.*

Above *Sometimes achieving a height of 70 ft, the cypress pine, Widdringtonia nodiflora, grows on the rugged slopes of southern and tropical African mountains and is a coniferous genus unique to Africa.*

The Olympic Rain Forest

Below left *Branches of the Olympic Rain Forest trees are draped with club-mosses and their barks are typically covered with lichen. Creepers, toadstools and ferns flourish in the underworld's perpetual dampness.*

Below *Hollows in the river banks are often overhung by exposed roots of trees, providing perfect homes for otters. This pair of Canadian otters, Lutra canadensis, are waiting on a branch just above their den or holt.*

The Olympic Rain Forest, clothing the wet west side of the Olympic Peninsula in Washington State of the north-west United States, is the only rain forest growing in the northern hemisphere. The trees are immense and the vegetation is exceedingly lush; a spectacular festooning of the trees with pale green, stringy moss is its fantastic trademark. To enter it is to enter a hushed, damp world where no dry twig snaps, no dry leaf rustles and hardly a square inch of soil is left unoccupied by plants.

Beside mossy stumps the three-leaved wake robin pushes through mats of delicate wood sorrel, and the wiry stems of the vanilla leaf bow to shed drops of moisture. On the stumps and rocks licorice ferns sprout whorls of saw-toothed fronds. In the mottled shadows the devil's club stands armed with cruel yellow spines from the base of its crooked, twisting stem anchored in the soft, damp earth to the veins of its maple-like leaves. Above are the trees: the big-leaved maples with ferns sprouting where two trunks divide in water-holding

dichotomy and the vine maple spreading and ready to tint the forest red as autumn approaches. Here, too, are the giant Douglas firs, hemlocks, Sitka spruce and red cedars, their lower branches festooned with mosses, their lofty crowns tapering 300 feet up towards the heavens.

Here and there, where a giant tree has fallen, shafts of high-noon sunlight stab through to the forest floor, slanting between the great columns of timber, the beams cutting through the steaming atmosphere. Time stands still, as it has for centuries. Man remains an insignificant intruder upon an aged and ageless forest scene.

An abundant rainfall of 145 inches falls annually. It is dropped by water-laden clouds sweeping in from the Pacific Ocean and forced upwards by the Olympic Mountains. The temperature is kept above freezing all winter and rarely exceeds 29°C (85°F) in summer because of the proximity of the ocean. The three deep, glaciated valleys on the western

slopes of the mountains enjoy ideal conditions for tree growth. There is nothing to stop this growth except old age: humid conditions keep fires to a minimum and only freak gales can break the defences of massed tall trees. With such lofty trees, space beneath them is so vast that light and air can filter through, and yet so well protected as to be an immense natural greenhouse in which dry summer spells and winter frosts have no effect.

Regeneration of the rain forest is a never-ending process. When, after half a millennium or more of silent vigil, an old tree falls naturally from age or decay, or is toppled in a gale, it crashes down amidst its fellows to cut a swathe through which the sun's rays can illuminate the dim green scene. Within a year or two mosses cover the huge trunk, and into this ever damp spongy bed fall the seeds of surrounding trees, high above the competing ground flora. Soon the log is covered with a mass of seedlings, their roots searching downwards for the soil. Some, the few, find it and

Left *The forest floor provides a perfect and varied diet for total vegetarians such as this Olympic marmot, Marmota olympus. They also collect some of the plant and grass stems to build their warm dens.*

Left *The azure-winged Steller's jay, Cyanocitta stelleri, buries tree seeds, particularly those of the Douglas fir, and saves them for winter. It thus redistributes many tree species throughout the Olympic Rain Forest.*

Left *Huge translucent tree slugs such as this 6 in banana slug, Ariolimax columbianus, enjoy the humid environment of the Olympic Rain Forest. They thrive on the abundance of mosses and algae hanging from the branches.*

Above *A large area of the Olympic Rain Forest was set aside in 1909 as a refuge for the Roosevelt elk. It was at one time in danger of being hunted to extinction because of the popularity of the elk's-tooth charm. By browsing among the undergrowth it prevents the forest floor from becoming too dense.*

Right *A special feature of the Olympic Rain Forest is the peculiar alignment of its trees. New seedlings grow on the decomposing logs of trees felled by the winter gales that sweep down the valleys. These "nursery" logs eventually rot away, leaving a stately row of naturally colonnaded trees.*

prosper, others, the many, do not and die. Eventually a colonnade of young trees hugs the log, their embracing roots arching over it as they grip the earth on either side. Some logs rot and disappear, leaving a line of trees standing as if planted by a careful prehistoric forester. Other logs, such as those of red cedar, rot so slowly, if at all, that giant successors sit astride them for centuries.

Woven into the space between the half-inch club-moss wrapping a decaying twig on the forest floor and the thrusting shoot that tops the tallest spruce is a population of animals. All these creatures are dependent one upon another and upon their environment: insects, reptiles, amphibians, birds and mammals. Yet the silence is uncanny and the urge to remain silent is overwhelming. The distant hammering of a pileated woodpecker in search of wood-boring insects, the *kip-kip* of a little brown winter-wren questing spiders among the sword-ferns, the monotonous musical trill of the finch-like junco from the salmon-berry

bush, the croak of a raven and the cackle of a jay, all seem like intrusions upon the silence of the cathedral-like scene. But life abounds though hushed and hidden. The great Roosevelt elk and the smaller black-tailed deer find winter browsing and cover in plenty, cougars find seclusion for their lairs, black bears and otters find fish enough in the forest streams; and a multitude of smaller animals, such as Douglas squirrels, jumping mice and shrews, live each in its appointed niche and according to its needs in harmonious equilibrium.

If the whole fantastic scene is what arrests the visitor, it is the size and number of the trees which impress. The old specimens, sometimes but a few feet apart, stand with their massive trunks free of all branches for 150 feet and more, straight with little taper and as much as ten feet in diameter. So tall are the trees that only by their bark can one species be told from another: the scaly surface of the Sitka spruce, the deeply furrowed pillars of the Douglas fir, the shallow-fissured grey of the hemlock and

the thin, stringy cladding of the red cedar. And, as most of the trees eventually reach their maximum dimensions in this arboreal paradise, the truly immense volume of timber standing on the ground is breath-taking; as much as 840,000 board feet on every acre.

This very excellence of timber growth was the cause of the greatest threat to the forest—the energy of the loggers of old. But since 1938, when the Olympic National Park was established to protect the rain forest, the threat has diminished. Now this uniquely entrancing association of giant trees and the plethora of plants and creatures that live beneath them is protected from depredation but remains accessible to those who wish to experience its magic. The Quinault, Queets and Hoh valleys can now all be entered by paved or gravel roads, leading to camp sites from where self-guiding nature trails penetrate the vastness of these timeless wild places, demonstrating that human recreation and forest preservation can work hand in hand.

The oldest and tallest trees

Below left *A dense grove of coast redwoods, Sequoia sempervirens, the tallest trees in the world. They do not live as long as the giant sequoias, Sequoiadendron giganteum. Both trees are named after the Cherokee chief Sequoyah.*

Below *The record-holding General Sherman Tree, Sequoiadendron giganteum. A selection of its vital statistics—272 ft tall with a maximum base diameter of 36.5 ft— demonstrate this giant's unequalled grandeur.*

Since the dawn of history man has been inspired by the towering heights of trees and awed by the massive sizes to which they grow and the great ages to which they can live.

Some species, mainly conifers, have within their make-up an urge to grow ever upwards. In others the tendency is to spread their branches, supporting them on massive trunks. Yet other genera, having lost their capacity to evolve and expand their distribution, have gradually aged in contracting areas of a once much larger range. These trees are very old.

The tallest trees in the world are the coast redwoods, *Sequoia sempervirens*. This species has a limited range in the sea-fog-prone belt thirty miles wide along the Pacific Coast of North America, stretching south from Oregon down to Monterey County in California. It is on the alluvial flats, where the rivers emerge from the coastal mountains, that the redwoods reach their maximum development. Many of the old trees exceed 300 feet in height and as much as forty feet in circumference. The redwoods can do this because they are able to benefit from the annual floods, which deposit richly fertile silt round their trunks, by growing a new root system at the required new level. Other competing species cannot and are eventually killed by the engulfing silt, leaving the redwoods not only unencumbered but invigorated by fresh fertility.

On such a flat in Tall Trees Grove in Redwood Creek, east of the town of Orick in northern California, is the world's tallest tree. Its great, red, tapering trunk stretches through the feathery crown to the phenomenal height of 368 feet with a circumference of forty-four feet, and an estimated age of 600 years— comparatively youthful compared with some veteran redwoods. The oldest redwood so far proved by a ring count was 2,200 years old and this tallest tree stands in a group of other redwoods, which are scarcely less tall, on the edge of the creek in California that has nurtured them for half a millennium.

To the east of these redwoods, 6,000 t

,000 feet up the western slopes of the Sierra Nevada, in isolated groups, and again in a narrow belt some 250 miles long, grow the giant sequoias of Sierra redwoods, *Sequoiadendron giganteum*, the world's largest trees in terms of sheer volume. Their colossal trunks, buttressed at their bases by huge bulging roots, can be more than 100 feet in circumference and nearly 300 feet tall. Towering russet columns with as much as 600,000 board feet of timber in each, a whole tree can weigh more than 1,000 tons. The General Sherman Tree, named after the famous general of the Civil War, is 102 feet in circumference less than five feet from the ground and 272 feet tall; and the McKinley Tree, named after the US president of that name, although of less circumference, is 291 feet tall. Ring counts on felled Sierra redwoods have shown ages up to 3,200 years, but some of the largest standing specimens are probably much older, even as much as 4,000 years.

As do the coast redwoods with their ability to grow new root systems, so do the giant sequoias enjoy a unique attribute which ensures longevity—bark up to two feet thick, fire resistant and capable of protecting the vital parts of the tree against the worst damage that forest fire can do.

The record for age almost certainly goes to the bristlecone pines, *Pinus aristata*, which grow scattered in the most desolate, high ridges of the Rocky Mountains in south-west California, Nevada, Utah, Arizona, New Mexico and Colorado. There they have retreated, having lost as a species their power to evolve and to expand their range, and thus to compete with other trees. They survive as gnarled, misshapen ancients, rarely more than thirty feet tall, at altitudes between 8,000–10,000 feet above sea-level. A tree felled on Wheeler Ridge was found to contain 4,900 annual rings of growth. The oldest known living specimen, the Methuselah Tree, growing in the White Mountains of California at 9,500 feet elevation, is 4,600 years old, and

the current record holder of all living things.

Whereas there is no doubt that the coast redwoods are generally the tallest trees, the giant sequoias the largest and the bristlecone pines the oldest, individual specimens of other species are known to have been of exceptional dimensions. The Douglas firs, *Pseudotsuga menziesii*, another conifer with an extensive range in north-west America and such a valuable timber tree that all but one of the best stands have long since been felled, once may well have been the tallest trees. Records show, and the memories of old men confirm, that there were some gigantic Douglas firs in the sheltered Lynn Valley, near Vancouver in Canada, at the turn of the century. The tallest recorded specimen among them was felled in 1902. This tree was 415 feet tall and had a circumference of forty-five feet.

Nor are conifers the only trees which can reach these staggering heights. A broadleaved species, the Australian mountain ash, *Eucalyptus regnans*, which has a limited distribution in southern Victoria and Tasmania and grows in deep mountain valleys, rivals the conifers. A specimen at Gippsland, Victoria, supposedly measured 417 feet tall when felled. The tallest one still standing is 338 feet tall. A planted tree in Western Australia, it is the tallest broadleaved tree in the world.

The Sierra redwoods may be the most massive trees, but an exceptional specimen of the Mexican cypress, *Taxodium mucronatum*, a close relative of the bald cypress, *Taxodium distichum*, of the Florida Everglades, is the world's "fattest" tree. Known as El Gigante, it grows at Tule, Mexico, and is 115 feet in circumference, although only 140 feet tall.

The once great forests where the giant trees grow were logged and exploited to such an extent in the last century that the very conditions which nourished their growth have altered. But now, isolated in protected groves and national parks, they are safe from further exploitation and will perhaps survive for many more centuries.

Deer

Of all forest creatures the deer are perhaps the most fascinating. Their timid, secretive ways, born of millennia of persecution by a host of predators, including hunting by man for meat and antler trophies, make them difficult to see; but the thrill of glimpsing these graceful creatures is a forest joy that never lessens with each repetition

In the northern forests, stretching round the world from North America to Japan, deer are the main browsing animals and their most conspicuous feature is the antlers of the males. These are branches of exposed bone that are shed each autumn and grow again each spring, increasing in size and the number of "points" with the age of the animal.

As the new antlers of all deer species grow they are encased in an outer coating of skin, or "velvet", which carries the blood stream necessary for growth but which eventually dries up and falls off. This velvet is considered to be an aphrodisiac in China and Japan, and the farming of red deer for this crop is widespread in New Zealand, where this species was introduced by the early settlers and where it thrives to the point of being a serious pest.

The deer that inhabits the northerly fringes of the North American coniferous forests is the caribou (the name is derived from a Micmac Indian word meaning shoveller, because of the way the animal digs in the snow with its clumsy-looking large hoofs in search of food) and its subspecies in Eurasia is the reindeer. As a species the reindeer probably originated in North America and found its way to Asia and Europe by migrating across the Bering Straits.

Semi-domesticated by the nomad Lapps of Finland, Sweden and the USSR, the reindeer stands about three feet high at the shoulder. Both sexes bear antlers (the only deer which do) of remarkable appearance, emerging from just behind the eyes, parallel to the ground before rising and spreading. Their powerful long legs are adapted to carry them on migrations through the snow. Although they spend the summer grazing herbage such as flowers and shoots in the far northern tundra, they make long journeys south (up to 700 miles in North America) to the fringes of the coniferous forest. There they mate and find shelter, feed on mosses, lichens and tree bark among the trees, and return north again to the tundra in spring.

During these migrations, when vast numbers herd together, the reindeer follow trails used by countless generations over the centuries, running the gauntlet of man and wolves as well as scavengers such as arctic foxes, wolverines and predatory birds. The Lapps, too, must move with their herds, which they crop for meat, milk and hides.

Entirely confined to the forest, albeit to the northern fringes in summer, is the moose, or elk as it is called in Eurasia. The largest of the deer, it stands over six feet high at the shoulder and weighs half a ton. The immense, flattened antlers of the bull, weighing over fifty pounds and spreading six feet across, and its huge

DISTRIBUTION OF DEER SPECIES

Many species of deer have representatives in Europe, Asia and North America. Although recognized as belonging to the same species some deer have acquired common names that differ between the two continents. The North American moose is identical with the elk that roams the forests of Europe and Asia. The wapiti, or elk as it is called in the USA, is the equivalent of the European red deer, while the Asian wapiti is very similar to both in its general features. Similarly, the caribou of the tundra region of North America has a counterpart in the European reindeer, which probably found its way to Asia and Europe across the Bering Strait land bridge.

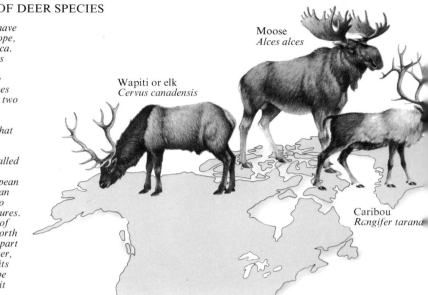

Moose
Alces alces

Wapiti or elk
Cervus canadensis

Caribou
Rangifer taranda

"Roman" nose with the pendulous upper lip give this great beast a haughty and commanding look as it bulldozes its bulk through the forest undergrowth. The bulls roam alone, except in the September breeding season, as do the cows with their calves, requiring a large territory over which they browse. In summer they wade in the lakes and marshes, browsing on the aquatic plants as well as on the saplings of willows, birches and aspens, stocking up for the winter when, even to survive, each animal must find four to five tons of vegetable matter in the snowbound forest, much of it by stripping the bark from trees.

Inhabiting the more southerly deciduous forests as well as the transitional zones bordering the coniferous in both the American and Eurasian continents, is the red deer, or wapiti as it is called in North America. It is a large animal, the stag standing four feet at the shoulder and weighing as much as four hundred pounds, but the hinds are markedly smaller. These deer are essentially forest creatures, feeding on grass, leaves and shoots and, in season, on acorns and beech nuts, although where forests have been cleared, as in Great Britain, they have become adapted to grazing in open country. Here they collect in herds of one hundred or more, but in the forest they are much less gregarious and consort in quite small groups.

In eastern Asia, where deer probably originated and where there are many indigenous species, the Japanese sika resembles a smaller version of the red deer and is indeed believed to be the stock from which red deer arose. It lives in herds in the deep forests of Japan and Manchuria, and it has become naturalized in Europe, where it breeds with the red deer to form a hybrid species.

Not found in North America but widespread in the northern forests of Eurasia is the much smaller roe deer. The buck, with its short, sharp-pointed antlers, stands little more than two feet high at the shoulder, and

the does are even smaller. They are not gregarious; a buck and two or three does with their young may be found together in summer, but they split up as winter approaches. They spend most of their time in the security of the woods, browsing on herbs and tree shoots, emerging into the fields and forest clearings at night to graze. In Great Britain their numbers have increased enormously during the last three or four decades, especially where conifer plantations have replaced open moorland. In areas where their natural enemies are few, and there is no control by hunting, they can do considerable damage to the forest both from browsing on seedling trees and from rubbing their antlers on the bark of saplings.

The most abundant and widespread deer in North America, and one which occupies somewhat the same ecological niche as the roe deer, is the white-tailed or Virginian deer. It shares some of the northern forests with the wapiti but extends much farther south, right into tropical Central America. When these deer are alarmed their tails stand up to show their white undersides as conspicuous signals of danger, hence the name.

The fallow deer is common in the forests of central Europe. In Great Britain it is best known as park deer, but it is found feral, or wild, in some forests. It is a beautiful creature halfway in size between the red deer and the roe. The buck has large, flattened antlers and both sexes retain the spotted coat in adulthood. All other truly forest deer, except the Indian cheetal, lose the spots which all fawns have at birth and which probably have some survival role in the forest. Apart from those (perhaps the majority) that graze as semi-domesticated large herds on the grasses beneath the open-grown trees of deer parks, the fallow deer is essentially a woodland creature. It browses on leaves and twigs, standing on its hind legs to reach acorns and other tree fruit, and the spotted coat acts as excellent camouflage in the dappled sunlight of the forest.

Elk
Alces alces

Reindeer
Rangifer tarandus

d deer
rvus elaphus

bove *White-tailed deer, Odocoileus virginianus, are the ost typical New World deer species. Clearance of the rests of the eastern USA left a congenial habitat and ey are more numerous now than before white settlement.*

Above *Alaskan moose bulls, Alces alces gigas, compete for a mate during the September mating season. The largest member of the deer family and the second largest herbivore in the USA, the Alaskan moose is well adapted* to its environment. Long legs provide mobility and speed and the sharp front hoofs can inflict deadly kicks. With its drooping nose and sensitive hearing, it is easily alerted to the presence of enemies such as wolves or bears.

bove *Familiar in the parks of Europe, fallow deer, ama dama, are now only truly wild in Mediterranean untries. If alarmed, a fallow deer bounds away with its il raised to expose a white underside.*

REINDEER MIGRATION

In spring, reindeer, Rangifer tarandus, leave the forest where lichen is increasingly scarce to search for summer pasture. They are guided along their natural route by nomadic Lapp herdsmen who, in effect, control the migration. The trek takes at least two weeks, often longer because many calves are dropped in May, and there must be a halt for a few days. Once wild, the reindeer herds were domesticated by the Lapps in their modern history. A quarter of the Lapp language's vocabulary concerns reindeer and their breeding.

The trade in furs

Man has used animal skins for warm clothing ever since he ventured from the year-long warmth of his original African homeland to experience the violent vicissitudes of northern climates. Animal skins were the obvious choice of clothing: the northern forests teemed with creatures that bore thick coats of fur to protect them against the bitter winter cold. It is not known exactly when furs came to be regarded as prestige commodities, but the Chinese are said to have esteemed them as long ago as 1500 BC. They were also prized in the Greek and Roman empires; the standard bearer of a Roman legion, for example, was uniformed in a wolf's skin.

As civilization declined in Europe with the onset of the Dark Ages, trading in furs was one of the few commercial activities to continue. The Vikings opened up routes deep into Russia and established a trading post at Novgorod. The northern forests were, and still are, the most prized fur-trapping regions because a harsh climate encourages the growth of dense, rich, winter coats on fur-bearing animals. In cold climates pelts have longer and more lustrous fur with thinner, more supple skin. In warm climates the fur is more coarse and the skin thicker.

The early medieval fur trade was therefore centred on the Baltic towns that imported skins from the northern forests. Once again, fur came to be used as a badge of rank. In the Byzantine Empire ermine, the white winter coat of the stoat, was considered a royal fur and was also much used by senior Latin clergy in Italy, where its colour symbolized purity.

Various laws were enacted to restrict to the nobility the use of scarce but fashionable furs such as sable, ermine, squirrel and marten. These laws served to emphasize one of the fur trade's most enduring characteristics, that for centuries furs have been worn as much for style as they have for warmth. The pelts of otter, cat, ermine and fox were widely used during this time, although they were not highly regarded and were cheaper than wool cloth. The skins of bears, badgers and wolves were also used, although they were not usually hunted for this purpose.

The extensive use of fur produced a notable reduction in the numbers of some fur-bearing species as the human population increased. Scarcity made fur even more valuable and this provided a considerable incentive for the exploitation of the forests of newly discovered North America, which were found to be teeming with desirable animals. The English settlers along America's eastern seaboard were not primarily concerned with furs but even casual exploitation soon caused the extermination of the sea mink and a dramatic reduction of other species.

Unlike the English, the French made the fur trade their chief economic concern in their American possessions. This led to a remarkable and rapid exploration of the north. As the French *coureurs de bois* worked west, Russian Cossack fur traders—*pronyshleniki*—arrived off the west coast in the mid-eighteenth century and went eastwards in search of blue and arctic foxes, Alaska seal, otter and sea otter.

One of the greatest spurs to exploration of the continent was the continual search for beaver. During the eighteenth and nineteenth centuries no European gentleman felt dressed in public without a beaver hat and the beaver population was relentlessly pursued across the forests and rivers of North America.

In the course of this search, the mountain men—white American trappers—explored and opened up the unknown west of North America. By the end of the eighteenth century the population of wolves, grizzly bears, otters, pine martens, fishers and wolverines south of Canada had been drastically reduced and other species had to be considered by the fur trade. Opossum, muskrat and skunk, along with other fur-bearing animals, began to be trapped and sold to an ever-hungry market.

This depletion of wildstock and the con

Left *From the time of the first settlement of the northern regions of North America the main commercial concern in the area was the Hudson Bay Company. Chartered in 1670, it represented England's interests and exported furs to England. Many of the furs handled by the trading posts were acquired from Indian trappers, who exchanged them for goods such as axes and liquor and with whom the Company tried to maintain harmonious relations. But white trappers quickly learned Indian ways of surviving in the harsh environment that was so suitable for fur-bearing animals. They learned that the waterways afforded the best way of travelling through the forested north and adopted Indian dugout and birchbark canoes, as well as snowshoes.*

Right *Sable pelts have been consistently in demand from the fashion industry, reflected in this elegant 19th-century lady's outfit. But the sable, Mustela zibellina, has suffered by being hunted almost to extinction. Sable farming is now carried out in the Soviet Union, but it is suspected that breeders there have difficulties in keeping this nervous highly strung animal in captivity.*

tinuing demand for furs of all kinds led to the first large-scale attempts at fur farming. Breeders soon realized the potential of fur farms for developing exotically coloured furs such as silver fox, a mutation of the red fox, but one that is rarely found in the wild. By 1930, 65,000 ranched silver fox pelts were being produced every year in response to the fashionable demand for long-haired furs.

In the 1940s and 1950s short-haired furs became fashionable and ranched mink came into its own. Every year, production of ranched mink increases to keep pace with demand and in 1978 more than twenty-three million pelts were produced on ranches. Chinchilla, sable and nutria have also been farmed, but attempts to ranch the marten or the lynx or beaver have not met with success.

Ranching has never promised to provide all the fur for which there is a demand. Many fur-bearing animals, including those that are ranched, are also trapped or hunted in the wild. The majority of these furs are still obtained from the forests of the northern hemisphere. North America's forests provide fox, wolf, beaver, raccoon, lynx, coyote, bobcat and squirrel. The once numerous species of fur-bearing animals native to European forests, however, have been greatly reduced by centuries of hunting and forest-felling and most European wild furs are produced from the relatively large tracts of forest remaining in Scandinavia and eastern Europe. Hunted species include muskrat, wolf and squirrel. Russian forests, however, are still a rich source of furs such as squirrel, muskrat, ermine, sable, red fox, white fox, lynx, marten, wolf and wild cat.

The fur market has always been affected by fashion, and in many cases sheer rarity provides a fashion value. This has ominous implications for the survival of endangered species. It should be borne in mind, however, that while the fur trade has contributed to the depletion of many wild species, the most dangerous threat to most of them comes from the spread of human population and pollution. In any event, increasing government sensitivity and consumer concern may help to keep rare animals from slaughter for fashionable clothing. In the USSR trapping is a government monopoly and it appears to be satisfactorily controlled, while most of Canada has adopted a strict licensing system for trappers. In the United States, which is the world's greatest producer and consumer of furs, most states have pushed through legislation to conserve threatened species and most wild animal populations have made remarkable recoveries, sometimes exceeding their original numbers.

THE MINK FARM

Fur farming has been carried out for centuries but it was not until the nineteenth century that the demand for furs encouraged serious research into the breeding of fur-bearing animals in captivity. The prestigious mink, which is native to the forests of North America, has been farmed on a large scale since 1930. The fur varies in colour from a lustrous brown to a red-brown, although other mutant colours (pearl mink below) have been developed in a profitable response to the whims of fashion.

Above *In the northern forests the stoat's red-brown coat changes to white with a black tip on its tail. This ermine coat has been esteemed in the fur trade for centuries and still commands the highest prices.*

Left *Beavers live in the forest watercourses of North America and are still the most financially important animal for Canada's fur industry. But today they are more threatened by river pollution than by trapping.*

Above *A modern fur trapper displays his wares, which are being dried in the sun in preparation for the raw fur market. This "mixed bag" includes skunk, raccoon, weasel, beaver, wolf and muskrat pelts.*

TROPICAL FORESTS

... The sombre shade, scarce illuminated by a
single direct ray, even of the tropical sun, the
enormous size and height of the trees, most of
which rise like huge columns a hundred feet or
more without throwing out a single branch, the
strange buttresses around the bases of some, the
spiny or furrowed stems of others, the curious
and even extraordinary creepers and climbers
which wind round them, hanging in long festoons
from branch to branch, sometimes curling and
twisting on the ground like great serpents, then
mounting to the very tops of the trees, thence
throwing down roots and fibres which hang
waving in the air, or twisting round each other,
form ropes and cables of every variety of size.

ALFRED RUSSEL WALLACE *Narrative of Travels on the Amazon and
the Rio Negro* 1905

The ecosystem

Tropical rain forests form a dense evergreen girdle round the Equator, thriving in a stable climate of constant rainfall and even temperature. There are no seasons and temperature changes from day to night are greater than those from day to day. Within this warm, wet, humid environment a forest has evolved that harbours an immense richness and diversity of plant and animal life.

The nature of the tropical forest ecosystems changes with rainfall, and moving farther from the Equator, north or south towards the Tropics of Cancer and Capricorn, they take on a partially deciduous character to cope with up to three months of low rainfall. But in the rain forest proper more vegetation is packed into one acre than anywhere else on the Earth. Dense and overlapping canopies of vegetation absorb as much of the precious sunlight as they can, making the interior so dark that small plants cannot live on the floor.

The giant trees are the kings of the forest as they emerge majestically through the canopy. Below them the young giants await their chance to achieve greatness and they are accompanied by the fruit trees, palms and ferns that will never touch the canopy no matter how many years they grow. Animals of all kinds live and feed at different levels and each has its particular niche and part to play in maintaining the world's richest ecosystem.

It needs a helicopter ride to see the "real forest"—an undulating canopy festooned with multicoloured flowers and humming with the frenetic activity of birds and insects. The canopy is criss-crossed by myriad vines, called rattans, which stretch across the forest like Christmas decorations, binding together neighbouring trees to add stability when strong winds blow. With their own roots in the ground these thin-stemmed woody plants coil around the trunks of the large trees for additional support. Some species of fig are not grateful for the help which they receive and they so encircle their hosts that the latter are eventually deprived of sunlight by the overpowering parasite and die in the embrace.

Here are found the epiphytes, such as the orchids and bromeliads, that flower in the canopy like the vines, but are entirely dependent on the trees for support. Their roots are meshed into a spider's web and dangle beneath the canopy waiting to collect any dead plant or animal matter falling from above. Some bromeliads (in the same family as the pineapple) have little water tanks in the bases of their flowers so that they do not dry out in the intense heat (see pages 100–101).

With this host of living things one would expect to see the forest floor littered with the decaying remains of trees or the skeletons of animals. Not so, however, because when a tree dies and falls to the ground it is pounced upon by termites who break down the wood at an incredible rate. A single leaf can be carried away by an army of ants or pulled down into the soil by earthworms.

Fungi complete the cleaning process, even to the point of living full time in termite nests.

Their tentacles intertwine with the tree roots spread just below the forest floor. They suck in any nutrients no longer needed by members of the forest community just deceased and return them to the living plants. In the upside-down world of the tropical rain forest most of the fertility of the land is stored in the vegetation and not in the soil. Millions of plant roots and the armies of ants and termites recycle the nutrients so efficiently that few of these nutrients actually reach the soil.

It is always the growing season in the humid Tropics and at any one time there is bound to be at least one tree species flowering. With no spring snowdrops or autumn leaf fall to guide them, local people use the annual flowering cycle as a calendar. In a forest where life has carried on much the same for millions of years the trees are of a lazy disposition and may not bother to bear any fruit for a couple of years at a time. This is important as it has a critical

effect on the natural regeneration of a forest after logging. Much forestry research is being directed to understanding the regeneration process and how it can be accelerated by land preparation and planting.

Animals are vital in pollination and seed dispersal. Some trees may only be pollinated by a specific insect. Others might rely on bats feeding upon the nectar of a number of tree species as each one comes into flower throughout the year. If, for example, two of these tree species were to be felled for timber, a two-month gap in the bats' food supply would ensue. If the bats disappeared as a result of this, other trees might not be able to continue to bear fruit and propagate. It is these complex ecological relationships that present a challenge to the forester, but if managed wisely the tropical forests could become as important a source of fibre and timber as the coniferous forests of the northern hemisphere.

Below *A gap in this Australian rain forest's canopy allows sunlight to reach the lower levels, where ferns, shrubs and herbaceous plants proliferate.*

Below right *An aerial view of a West African rain forest's dense green canopy. The tall, scattered emergent trees can be seen spiking through here and there.*

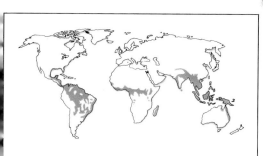

Height in feet

115 —

90 —

60 —

15 —

5 —

Above *Tropical rain forests occur where rainfall exceeds 80 or 90in per year. Farther from the Equator they become semi-deciduous, usually with one or more "dry seasons". They lie in four main geographical regions: Central and South America, Africa and Madagascar, South and South East Asia, New Guinea and Australia.*

Right *Five layers of vegetation are traditionally identified in tropical rain forests. The emergent trees occupy the top storey. The canopy of densely packed trees is beneath them and below it the tree crowns are narrower. Farther down are shrubs and young trees, and on the ground herbs. Such layers are not always distinct, however, and some may be absent.*

NUTRIENT CYCLING

In the tropical rain forest most of the mineral nutrients are not held in the soil. When a plant or animal dies, soil fungi, the micorrhiza, quickly break down the dead organic litter and transfer it to the living cells of plant roots. This rapid recycling allows few minerals to be leached out of the soil by the high rainfall. Nutrient distribution in a northern coniferous forest and a tropical rain forest is shown below.

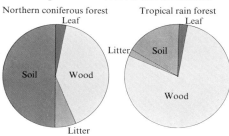

Northern coniferous forest
Leaf
Litter
Soil
Wood
Litter

Tropical rain forest
Leaf
Soil
Wood

Prospective farmers in Brazil have discovered that, despite the lushness of the rain forest's vegetation, the soil is not fertile. Because the soil minerals are used up by crop plants and unprotected ground is quickly leached by high rainfall, the quality of crops diminishes rapidly after only two years. The farmer then has to move on and clear another area, leaving a wasteland (below). Encroaching agriculture and population pressures are the cause of eighty per cent of forest destruction in the Tropics.

The trees

Below *Thin or waterlogged rain forest soils allow only shallow roots, which in many dominant trees thicken on their upper sides to form buttresses; these are unaccountably rare outside tropical rain forests.*

Below *The sharp spines on the trunk of this Bolivian "thicket" tree evolved to deter animals from climbing up to the high canopy which they must reach in order to exploit the abundant supplies of nuts and fruits.*

One can travel for miles in a northern forest and encounter only four or five species of trees, but in a tropical rain forest there are usually at least twenty, and often as many as 700 different species to the acre. There are more than 2,500 different species of tall trees in Malaysia alone.

Yet these different tree species show remarkably similar characteristics, which bear no relation to their botanical classification. The wing-like buttresses that surround the taller trees is one of the most obvious and striking features. These buttresses may reach thirty feet up the trunk and extend even farther along the ground, tapering towards their outer limits. Their exact function is still unexplained, but it seems likely that they provide essential support for the tallest trees seeking stability in the rain forest's shallow soil. Stilt roots are often found on smaller trees, springing from the main trunk and looping gracefully to their anchorage in the soil.

Although buttresses and stilt roots add bulk, the trees are remarkably narrow-stemmed for their height, zooming upwards to the canopy like sleek rockets on a launching pad. The bark is generally smooth and very thin and light in colour, although it appears paler due to a covering of white lichens. Naturally, there are exceptions to the rule and some trees have almost black bark, while in tropical forests with dry climates some trees have thorny nodes on their trunks.

The rather monotonous look of the rain forest is in part due to the same dark green leathery leaves sported by most trees and shrubs, and it has been said that "the nor

botanical observer may easily be excused for supposing that the forest was predominantly composed of species of laurel".

Leaves of many tropical trees have evolved a drip-tip and it is thought that the purpose of these tips is to drain water from the leaf surface . This appears to confer two advantages. First, a thin film of water on the surface would reflect light and reduce the rate of photosynthesis—not advisable in the gloom of the crowded forest. Second, in the regions where there is high humidity and little wind, moisture on the leaves reduces transpiration, thus affecting the uptake of the rather scarce essential minerals from the soil (see pages 80–81). Another common feature of tree leaves is the presence of pulvini, or joints, on the leaf stem. These are movable and allow the leaf to adjust its position in relation to light.

Contrasting with the sombre green of mature leaves are some trees that have juvenile leaves which unfold from their buds entirely lacking in chlorophyll. They are often bright red in colour, but blue, purple and white leaves have also been recorded. Not only are they brightly coloured, but for some days after extending to their full size they hang limply as if wilted, only becoming fully green when they are stiff and fully erect. Young twigs of some trees also act in this way, but rather than this being due to a shortage of water, the leaves and shoots expand so quickly that there is a lack of mechanical tissues to support them. The brilliance of the leaf colour makes a fine display in place of the flowers that are usually inconspicuous and whitish or grey.

Flowers and fruits of the tropical rain forest trees have fewer common characteristics, but there are peculiarities of interest. The most remarkable is that of cauliflory—the formation of flowers or fruit on leafless woody stems. More than a thousand species exhibit cauliflory and they are almost exclusively lower storey trees. These are frequently pollinated by bats, a method unknown in temperate and cold lands, and the conspicuousness may be to aid identification by the bats who fly at night. The strange shape, unattractive colouring and often foul smell and taste of many tropical fruits may also serve to attract these bats.

The seed dispersal mechanism varies between tree types. In the secondary forest all the new young trees have efficient dispersal by wind, or animals such as birds and bats, and so can rapidly colonize any earth that is bared by agriculture or logging. In the primary forest, however, wind and animal dispersal is less common, and some trees seem to have no efficient adaptation at all. Wind dispersal may be present in the upper storeys, but in the lower storeys it is entirely absent and the seeds tend to be large and heavy and drop to the foot of the parent tree where they may be dispersed by animals, or even by water, as with the dipterocarp species of the Malayan forest (see pages 88–89).

Heavy large seeds are an advantage to tall trees, ensuring they reach the ground and avoid lodging in the branches of trees below and providing the seedling with an ample supply of food so it can establish itself in the relative darkness of the forest floor. But heavy seeds often restrict the spread of some species and it has been suggested that those that dominate a lowland habitat are unable to colonize steep slopes because the seeds roll downhill.

The large diversity of species, and the inability of many of the species to distribute themselves effectively, is one of the reasons why a few trees of one species are present within one acre of logging concession. Every tree felled has to provide a wood that is saleable on the world timber market and even today the number of commercial species is relatively small. Some West African rain forests may have been logged ten times as more of the species they contain become acceptable to the timber trade. Their most famous wood is mahogany, *Khaya ivorensis*, which is very dense and referred to as a heavy tropical hardwood.

Tropical hardwoods of all kinds have become much more sought after in recent decades as the hardwood forests of Europe and North America have been replaced by young tree plantations. The dipterocarps of South East Asia, a family of no less than 385 species of giant trees, have become increasingly popular. All these trees provide similar kinds of wood, which are lighter and easier to work than the heavier cabinet timbers, such as mahogany, and they are known as light tropical hardwoods (see pages 162–163).

Because their woods are so similar, different species are grouped together. When a timber merchant purchases "red meranti" he knows that it could come from a whole number of *Shorea* spp. but he can be confident that the properties of the wood will lie between certain limits of tolerance. Species grouping means that more trees can be felled from an area of forest and so logging becomes more profitable.

The Americas

Tropical rain forest

Moist deciduous forest

Montane forest

Left *The American rain forests include the great Amazonian "hyleia", stretching from the Andes to the Guyanas in the east. High rainfall also sustains similar forests through Colombia and northwards to Central America, as well as a block in the Brazilian Highlands.*

Right *The tamandua is an arboreal anteater, climbing high in Cecropia trees with the help of its prehensile tail. It claws open ant nests, then inserts its narrow snout and laps up the disturbed ants with a long sticky tongue.*

Below *Dusk falls over the Amazon as it flows calmly to its rendezvous with the Atlantic Ocean, where the discharge of water extends for 300 miles into the sea. The river provides habitat, food and breeding grounds for thousands of insects, fish and birds whose activity is almost undiminished during the warm tropical nights.*

South America houses the greatest continuous rain forest in the world, accounting for half of all moist tropical forests. The region is so dominated by the great Amazon river and its tributaries that at certain times of the year it is impossible to tell where the river ends and the forest begins. At any one time up to two-thirds of the world's fresh water may be found in the more than two million square miles of the Amazon basin, and the volume of water that eventually surges into the Atlantic is one-fifth of all water discharged into the oceans by the world's rivers.

An astonishing assortment of the world's rare and fascinating wildlife matches the awesome size of the forest and power of the rivers. Here abide up to one million species of plants—a third of the world's flowering plants—more than half of the species of birds, and the rivers and forest teem with so many fish and insects that they have never been fully identified and classified.

Despite this great diversity and number of animals, few are densely distributed and many are nocturnal. The daytime visitor to the forest will see little. As in all rain forests most of the activity is high up in the canopy where the trees flower, the lianas leaf and the epiphytic orchids and bromeliads display their outrageously coloured blooms. It is here that the troops of acrobatic New World monkeys advertise their extravert skills, contrasting with the sloth that, living up to its name, makes funereal progress through the branches of food trees such as *Cecropia*.

Most of the birds live here too, rarely moving from their home range and nature has endowed them with the short wide wings essential for manoeuvring within the restricted areas between the branches and tree trunks.

Below *These toy-like short-horned grasshopper nymphs (Acrididae) are poorly camouflaged, their bright colours deliberately advertising their* unpalatability to deter predators. Some insects— nymphalid and papilionid butterflies, for example—if not poisonous themselves, often mimic the heliconiid *butterflies, which are. The Lichenochrus nymph adopts the alternative strategy of true camouflage, by successfully posing as a lichen.*

RUBBER AND RICE

Henry Wickham, right, inspired by the successful transplantation of cinchona—quinine—from South America to South East Asia, decided on a similar scheme for the rubber tree, Hevea brasiliensis, to ensure a regular supply for the expanding European industry. Seeds were taken to London and those that germinated were sent on to be planted in South East Asia, where the extensive plantations ultimately displaced the economic importance of wild rubber collected in South America. Almost one hundred years later Daniel Ludwig reversed the story by introducing non-native selected strains of rice into South America. Melting snows in the Andes regularly swell the Amazon, carrying down rich alluvial soil, which is ideal for this crop.

They range in size from the huge-billed toucan that feeds on fruit to the tiny nectar-sipping humming-birds that skip from flower to flower with vibrating wings. Above the canopy swifts skim the surface, taking insects on the wing, while the fearsome harpy eagle patrols the skies ready to plunge into tree-tops to take reptiles, birds and even monkeys.

In comparison there are few land mammals and they tend to be small and rather shy. There are some deer but the browsing and grazing habit has, to some extent, been taken on by rodents such as the paca and agouti. Family groups of capybaras, despite their unflattering description "a rat as large as a pig", live peacefully on the river banks. Other strange Amazonian creatures are the solitary anteaters, the tapirs, the vampire bat and the only marsupials found outside Australia, which include the common opossum that ranges northwards to the United States, and the only aquatic marsupial, the yapok.

To match the wealth of animal and plant species the Amazon region has paid economic dividends since the discovery of the New World. The Spanish discovered mahogany, *Swietenia mahogani*, in Cuba, and later in Brazil, and began to ship it home in the second half of the sixteenth century. Its strength, resistance to dry rot and dimensional stability make it much superior to oak, and it was quickly put to use in building many of the ships which sailed to England in the Spanish Armada of 1588. Ease of working, and the warm brown colour of matured wood, made it the cabinet timber *par excellence*. But the Amazon saga really began with the rubber boom in the late nineteenth century, when people poured into the area to tap rubber and "get rich quick" (see pages 38–39 and 198–199).

Recent efforts to harvest the wealth of the forest have taken a more ordered and informed approach. Daniel K. Ludwig's Jari Project has involved the replacement of a large area of natural forest by plantations of fast-growing gmelina and pine. When harvested the wood will be converted into pulp by mills, built in Japan and floated thousands of miles to the River Jari (see pages 50–51). Although this is the latest chapter in the Amazon story it is still the rivers that mould the economy and culture of local people.

They have traditionally lived beside a river and shaped their activities to fit in with its rhythms, cultivating crops on land whose fertility is regularly replenished by silt deposited by the annual flood. In the flood season river dwellers fell trees from the seasonal swamplands, floating them to the river where they are exchanged for food. Sixty per cent of Amazon timber is still harvested in this way.

Yet while more than eighty per cent of Brazil's forests lie in the Amazon region only a tenth of national roundwood production, and less than a third of all sawn timber is extracted from it. Four-fifths of the Amazon forests are on land that is never flooded, but they are rarely logged because transport is difficult and expensive—hauling logs long distances by road is not economic.

Even the construction in the 1970s, at great expense, of a massive new network of highways through the forest helped little because logging is impossible during the rainy season from January to July. At this time the justly famed Trans-Amazonian highway, which stretches for 3,380 miles in an attempt to promote farming (an aim that proved disastrous, see pages 80–81) and give access to mineral and timber resources, becomes impassable.

Africa

The rain forests of Africa are considerably less extensive than those of South America and Indo-Malaysia, and the two main blocks—one in West and one in Central Africa—are similar in species composition to each other, although in the west there is very little aseasonal rain forest. There is also a fringe of forest on the east coast of Madagascar, an island which, because of its ancient separation from the mainland of Africa, houses unique plant and animal species. Madagascar's flora and fauna are free to occupy the niches from which potential competitors have been excluded.

In the wetter parts of the forest red iron-wood, *Lophira alata*, niangon, *Tarrietia utilis*, makore, *Mimusops*, and *Guarea* species characterize the middle and upper storeys. Below them shrubby euphorbias and palms occupy a twilight zone and this merges into a relatively sparse ground storey. Some species of aromatic herbs, such as *Costus engleriana*, grow on the poorly lit forest floor, which is otherwise remarkable for the almost complete absence of grasses, although species of bamboo are found in wetter places.

The sparseness of the ground vegetation is matched by, and largely explains, the few ground-living animals in the depths of the forest. Many more are found high up in the tree canopies or at the forest fringes, either with more open woodland, or on river banks, where reasonable light penetration and the virtual non-seasonal climate allows trees, lianas and other epiphytes to leaf profusely, providing food for primary consumers—herbivores—who in turn are preyed upon by secondary consumers—carnivores.

Squirrels and monkeys climb through the leaves of the upper canopy, enjoying the abundant supplies of insects, nuts, fruit and tender leaves, relatively untroubled by the carnivorous cat-like civets and genets, which feed mainly on birds. Birds are occasionally preyed upon by monkeys, but have more to fear from snakes. Weaver birds construct spherical nests at the outer edges of tree crowns and design the entrance to each nest in the form of a two-foot-long pendent tube to discourage snakes.

Among the 400 species of birds in the rain forest are the excellent mimic the grey parrot and the touracos, some of them brilliantly attired in green and red feathers. The red feathers yield a red dye, turacin. Many of these birds are poor fliers that travel swiftly from tree to tree by running along branches and interconnecting lianas. A lack of flying ability is no great handicap as the vegetation in the upper levels is so dense that the birds, always to be heard but more difficult to see, can easily hop from tree to tree without needing to fly around.

The forest floor is quieter: African forest antelopes are solitary creatures, and include the shy, exquisite duikers that "duik" or dive into the undergrowth when alarmed, and feed at night on leaves and fruit. The giant forest hogs frequent the swampier parts and charge at intruders without warning.

The forest buffalo and forest elephant are the largest rain forest animals, although they

Below *The okapi was first discovered by scientists in 1900. A solitary half-deer, half-zebra-like animal, it is related to the giraffe and lives deep in the Zaïre forest. It feeds on leaves that it has stripped from low branches with its prehensile tongue.*

Right *The rain forests of Africa occur in two main blocks—one along the south coast of West Africa and one centred on the Zaïre river basin. There is also a fringe of forest on the east coast of Madagascar, with a distinctive flora and fauna.*

■ Tropical rain forest
▨ Moist deciduous forest
☐ Montane forest

Below *The hippopotamus derives its name from the Greek for river horse. It was common in lakes and rivers throughout Africa, but is now restricted to inland waters between the Upper Nile and the Zambesi rivers. Weighing up to four tons, they are too clumsy to spend much time on land and they emerge from the swampy water only at night to feed on nearby vegetation. Egrets rid their backs of parasites and warn them of danger.*

MADAGASCAR: ISLAND SANCTUARY

Forests cover about a quarter of Madagascar and lie mostly on the east coast of the island, benefiting from the heavy rain deposited by the trade winds, while the island's western forests are drier and more open. Because of its ancient isolation Madagascar houses a distinctive collection of birds and animals, many of them not found elsewhere. The tenrecs, lemurs and many other species owe their survival and diversity to the early separation of their island home from mainland Africa because it allowed them to occupy many uncontested niches.

The white-breasted and brown mesites, although they have wings, are both flightless birds of the forest. The kiwis of New Zealand have also survived the loss of flight, perhaps because of the similar early isolation of their islands. The insectivorous tenrecs vary in appearance from the spiny *Echinops* to the tiny mouse-like *Microgale*. The mole-like *Oryzoctes hova* has poor eyesight and hearing, and it burrows deep underground with its strong claws, filling a niche elsewhere occupied by the true moles. Of the civets, the fossa, a voracious carnivore, preys on small rodents, birds and lemurs; it adopts the role of absent small wild cats. The sifaka (below) is one of the arboreal lemurs, a group of primitive primates numbering some twenty species, which survives only in Madagascar, free of competition from the African monkeys and apes, competitors whose arrival would surely have signalled their end.

much smaller than their relations of the open savannah. The elephants form extended family groups a hundred strong and wander through the shrubs, eating fruit and leaves as well as roots and tubers that they dig up. They rarely move far from water, drinking tens of gallons each day and taking baths to cool themselves. The continuous punkah—fanning—movement of enormous ears, up to six feet long by five feet across is the most important method of heat loss. The forest elephant population is falling fast, due to the activity of poachers and partly because they are such voracious and destructive feeders that they destroy their own forest habitat.

Many animals are hunted by the hunting and gathering population of the Ituri forest, which covers some 20,000 square miles in the north-eastern part of the Central African rain forest. Known because of their comparatively short stature as pygmies, these people have long-standing intimate knowledge of local forest resources, and consequent skills leave them with surplus meat and honey, which they trade for vegetable crops with neighbouring Bantu farmers who superstitiously avoid the forest (see pages 112–113). The unfamiliarity of this population with the outside world and their vulnerability to harsh sunlight and disease necessitate the conservation of these forests unless they are to perish.

The main agent of destruction of the African forests has been the changing climate. Geological evidence such as plant remains and fossil soils and elephant fossils as far north as Algeria and Morocco indicate the end of the last pluvial or wet period about 6,000 years ago. Since that time the forests have shrunk drastically, with the simultaneous advance of arid desert. The blistering Sahara once enjoyed reasonable rainfall and supported populations of people and animals, vividly depicted in the prehistoric rock paintings of elephants, buffalos and even hippopotamuses. It was not until the nineteenth century that man had a serious effect on the forest, extracting valuable hardwoods, among them the African mahoganies, *Khaya* spp., obeche, *Triplochiton scleroxylon*, and the prestigious and highly sought-after ebonies, *Diospyrus* spp.

The wealth of timber species in the rain forests of West Africa has brought about the disappearance of large tracts of forest, but clearance for farming has accounted for the destruction of even greater forested areas. The inaccessibility of the Central African forests and the near self-sufficiency of many forest tribes have tended to reduce the rate at which trees have been harvested. In Zaïre, a country with considerable mineral deposits, the vast forest reserves are of little national economic importance. Finally, the physical geography of the African continent alone compared with the island formations of South East Asia is partially responsible for the less systematic realization of timber resources in Africa. Today the brunt of world demand for tropical hardwoods is met by South East Asia, but this is likely to change in the future.

Indo-Malaysia

Below *The Indian tiger betrays its cool Siberian origins, escaping the heat of the day immersed in a soothing forest swamp. A lack of large arboreal animals obliges tigers, often 9 ft long, to live and hunt on the ground.*

Right *The Indian, Sumatran and Javan rhinoceroses survive in fractions of their former ranges. They have been ruthlessly hunted for their horns, which, powdered down, have reputed aphrodisiac properties.*

Above *Dipterocarp trees in the Haranutigala forest of southern Sri Lanka are bathed in the bright even light diffused through the monsoon cloud cover. Dipterocarps also dominate the moister aseasonal forests of Malaysia and Borneo.*

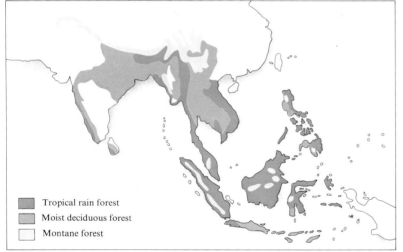

Left *The rain forests of Indo-Malaysia are extraordinarily complex, with literally hundreds of tree species—many of them dipterocarps—in loose mixed stands. Thousands of orchids and creepers contribute to this diversity, but in the drier moist deciduous and montane forests the ephiphytic element is less evident.*

- Tropical rain forest
- Moist deciduous forest
- Montane forest

The Indo-Malaysian region comprises the Indian subcontinent and the land east and south to the tip of the Malaysian peninsula, and Sumatra, Java, Borneo and the Philippines, as well as countless thousands of uninhabited islands. The rain forests of Indo-Malaysia are probably the richest in the world in terms of tree species and as a tropical hardwood resource. Peninsular Malaysia and Singapore have 8,000 or so species of seed plants compared to the meagre 1,450 of the much greater area of the British Isles; the great floristic wealth of Borneo is domonstrated by the presence of approximately 270 species belonging to the dipterocarp family alone.

A great number of related species, all members of the dipterocarp family, which is so named because of the two wings that each fruit bears, stand very close to each other in Indo-Malaysian rain forests. They dominate the forests in this region, both as upper canopy trees and as emergents, although legumes such as *Dialium* and *Koompassia*

occasionally break the dipterocarps' near monopoly of the upper layers.

The close co-existence of so many related species is perhaps surprising; similar species make similar demands on the environment and may compete so intensely with each other that some disappear altogether. The continuing diversification of species within the dipterocarp and other families may be in part due to the long climatic stability of the region, but another plausible suggestion assigns an important role to the activities of herbivorous animal predators.

Because the dipterocarps have relatively poor seed dispersal the majority of young seedlings grow up under the parent, and present predators with a highly localized and abundant food supply. Thus the population number of any single tree species is kept down. This allows other species to grow nearby and so discourages the formation of pure stands of a single species. Plant distribution in the community is, therefore, largely determined by the

activities of insects and other animals that live there; in turn the plants exert a reciproca[l] influence on the distribution of the animals.

Extraordinary disguises and efforts at mim[icry] icry occur in a wide range of insects. Bus[h] crickets and leaf grasshoppers resemble leave[s] in every stage of growth and decay. The blac[k] and white mottled crab spider blends perfectl[y] into the background of its own white silk web[,] similar in colour to a spot of bird excrement[.] The small tortoise beetles, enclosed in thei[r] transparent cases, have higher aesthetic pre[-] tensions, catching the light like brilliant jewel[s] to resemble flashing drops of rain-water.

The Indo-Malaysian ant plants, *Myrme[-] codia*, *Hydnophytum* and *Dischidia*, provid[e] ants with living space in return fo[r] protection—the resident ants attack all in[-] truders. Other plants have developed different defence; they produce unpalatabl[e] chemical compounds—alkaloids, tannins an[d] resins—that can only be de-toxified by one o[r] two predators. Fig trees, *Ficus* spp, illustrat[e]

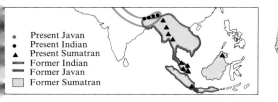

- • Present Javan
- • Present Indian
- ▲ Present Sumatran
- — Former Indian
- — Former Javan
- ▢ Former Sumatran

Indian

Sumatran

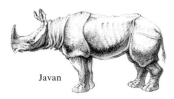

Javan

KRAKATOA

The cataclysmic eruption of Krakatoa in 1883 completely altered the topography of the islands and effectively destroyed all life, giving future ecologists the opportunity to study the gradual re-establishment of vegetation and wildlife.

Within three years, thirty-four species of plants including blue-green algae, mosses and ferns—all with light wind-dispersed spores—had established themselves. Other early arrivals were four orchids—they also have light wind-dispersed seeds—and *Cocos nucifera*, whose seed, the coconut, while very heavy is resistant to seawater, and germinates on the beach once it has been watered by fresh rain-water. *Cyrtandra*, a rare Javan forest species, initially spread widely before being displaced by young forest dominants. Increasingly lush vegetation has favoured an ever expanding animal population now numbering more than 600 species including lizards, crocodiles, pythons, rats, bats and many birds. Such a succession of plants and animals heralds the regeneration of forests, which, if undisturbed, will once again return.

another aspect of co-evolution. They bear numerous small unisexual male, female and gall flowers organized to provide breeding and mating chambers for agaonid wasps whose larvae feed on the nutritious ovary walls; the male wasps die after they have fertilized the females, who are dusted with pollen as they leave, on their way to a new breeding site where the female flowers will be pollinated.

A great variety of mammals—elephants, rhinoceroses, tapirs, wild pigs, tigers, leopards, the marbled cats and numerous primates—is another characteristic of the Indo-Malaysian rain forest. Tigers, preferring to feed upon crested and bearded pigs, deer and antelopes, enjoy undisputed freedom in the jungle. Unmolested by other animals, they seek out the thickest, shadiest and sometimes swampy areas of the forest, where they can lie up during the heat of the day. The marbled cat is much smaller and lighter than the leopards and tigers, and is well adapted to an acrobatic arboreal existence—it is agile enough to catch

birds, small rats and squirrels as they scamper and hop through the upper foliage.

The Malayan tapir, up to eight feet long, is well adapted to life in the dappled light of the forest floor with its curiously elegant *art deco* black-white-black coat. If threatened, it retreats to and submerges itself in the nearest river. Sadly, most of these animals, notably tigers and rhinoceroses, are becoming increasingly rare, either because they are hunted or simply because their natural habitats in the forests are beginning to disappear.

For a long time, village traditions ensured sensitive unobtrusive agricultural practice; the nomadic Penans of Borneo still rely on wild sago palms for their staple starch food and thatching material, moving from one palm grove to the next when necessary. Another Bornean people, the Ibans, are shifting cultivators who clear and farm small areas of forest, moving on when the land is exhausted or overrun by weeds. Shifting cultivators predominate in many tropical regions, and are

being steadily integrated into the cash economy by growing rubber trees.

Loggers, attracted by the high density of commercial timber trees, particularly dipterocarps—red merantis (*Shorea*) and yellow and white varieties (*Anisoptera*) for export, and teak mainly for domestic consumption—are as yet tapping only a small proportion of the millions of acres of forest in Malaysia and Indonesia, but this trade earned the region nearly one and a half billion dollars in 1979. The area as a whole supplies more than eighty per cent of the tropical hardwoods and ninety per cent of the world's natural rubber, also dominating the world market in palm oil, which is used extensively in the manufacture of soap and detergents.

Estimates give the natural forests of peninsular Malaysia and Sumatra about ten years before they are exhausted if destruction continues at the present rate, an indication of the potential disruption of the delicate equilibrium between man and forest.

Australasia

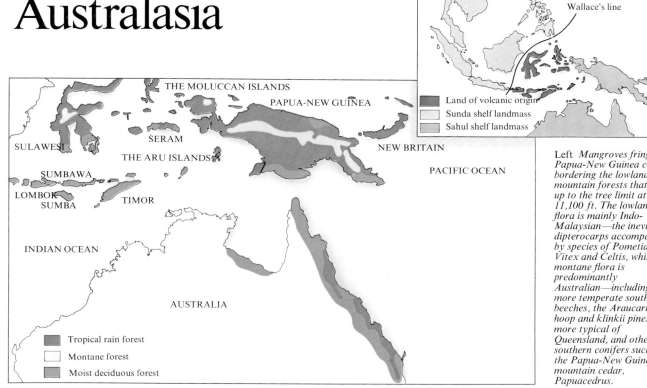

THE MOLUCCAN ISLANDS
PAPUA-NEW GUINEA
SULAWESI
SERAM
NEW BRITAIN
THE ARU ISLANDS
PACIFIC OCEAN
SUMBAWA
LOMBOK
SUMBA
TIMOR
INDIAN OCEAN
AUSTRALIA

Wallace's line

Land of volcanic origin
Sunda shelf landmass
Sahul shelf landmass

Tropical rain forest
Montane forest
Moist deciduous forest

Left *Observations on the natural history of the Malay Archipelago encouraged Wallace to make his own contribution to the development of the theory of evolution by natural selection. From the distribution of species in the area, Wallace concluded that lower water levels in the past created land bridges between the Asian mainland, Sumatra, Java and Borneo on one side and Australia and Papua-New Guinea on the other, but maintained the separation of Indo-Malaysia and Australasia. The Wallace line marks the limit of the Indo-Malaysian continent. The distribution of marsupials and flightless birds with respect to the line is remarkable: they are confined to Australasia. The largest mammal in Papua-New Guinea, the tree kangaroo (right), is well adapted to arboreal life with its fine tail and shortened hindlegs, bouncing irrepressibly along branches. It can leap to the ground from 40 ft, but may prefer to descend sedately, tail first.*

Left *Mangroves fringe the Papua-New Guinea coasts, bordering the lowland and mountain forests that run up to the tree limit at 11,100 ft. The lowland flora is mainly Indo-Malaysian—the inevitable dipterocarps accompanied by species of Pometia, Vitex and Celtis, while the montane flora is predominantly Australian—including the more temperate southern beeches, the Araucarian hoop and klinkii pines, more typical of Queensland, and other southern conifers such as the Papua-New Guinea mountain cedar, Papuacedrus.*

The Australasian region includes Australia, Tasmania, Papua-New Guinea and New Zealand, and a wealth of islands stretching from New Britain to Fiji, east and south into the Pacific, as well as Timor, the Moluccan Islands and Lombok dotting the Indian Ocean north and west towards mainland Asia.

The region has its own peculiar plant and animal communities, quite different from those of the Indo-Malaysian region to the north. The floras and faunas of the adjacent Australasian and Indo-Malaysian regions meet in the middle islands of Indonesia, but remain quite distinct from each other because the islands on which they live lie on two different continental shelves—Sunda in the north-west and Sahul in the south-east—separated by deep marine trenches.

The Australasian tropical rain forests are concentrated in two areas, on the Queensland coast of Australia and in Papua-New Guinea. The size and the climate of Papua-New Guinea permit almost complete cover of the island by one of the most extensive tropical rain forests (both evergreen and semi-evergreen) in the world.

Papua-New Guinea is perhaps the poor relation of Borneo botanically, but it has its own special collection of trees. These include Asian dipterocarps mixed with Australian eucalypts and casuarinas. The giant dipterocarps, which grow in profusion in Borneo, are rarer in Papua-New Guinea, mainly because their seed dispersal and reproductive capacity are fairly poor. Papua-New Guinea lies on a different continental shelf from Borneo and the few dipterocarps that have successfully negotiated the journey, among them *Anisoptera*, *Hopea* and *Vatica*, must give way to *Canarium*, *Eugenia* and *Lithocarpus*.

Papua-New Guinea's position, just south of the Equator, is attested by the absence of pines, though the island is richer in conifers than any other in the archipelago. Forests

contain the essentially southern hemisphere conifers *Agathis*, *Dacrydium*, *Podocarpus*, *Phyllocladus*, *Araucaria* and *Papuacedrus*. In the Far East the last two are found only in Papua-New Guinea. Conifers occur as belts in the lower montane forests, while *Agathis* and *Podocarpus* can be found scattered throughout the lowland rain forests.

Since most animals disperse across water less easily than plants, the Australasian fauna is more characteristic of the region than the flora. Papua-New Guinea and Australia remain the bastions of the pouched marsupials, unbreached by the placental mammals so successful everywhere else.

The divergence of animals on the neighbour-islands of Bali, on the Indo-Malaysian side, and Lombok, on the Australian side, greatly impressed Alfred Russel Wallace during his eight-year tour of the Malay Archipelago. In 1858, he composed his ideas on the origin of species by natural selection into a report which he sent to Darwin in England, a move which encouraged Darwin to publish *On the Origin of Species* in 1859, much earlier than he had intended. Wallace and Darwin differed, however, over human evolution and the significance of colour differences in male and female birds.

Many birds enjoy the forests of Papua-New Guinea and more species are found there than in Borneo, among them the beautiful birds of paradise. The combinations of startling and subdued colours, and the way in which each bird seems to be individually hand-coloured and sculpted, defy easy description. Papua-New Guinea is the home for nearly all of the forty or so species, with the remainder being found in Australia, New Zealand and the Moluccan Islands.

The birds of paradise, like the magical birdwing butterflies with wing spans of almost a foot, have become prey for hunters. A trader can receive up to 1,000 dollars for a single

Above *The cassowary, a giant flightless bird of the tropical Australian rain forests, feeds mainly on fallen fruit. If disturbed, it flees through the undergrowth at 30 miles an hour, head down, hurdling obstacles, or crashing regardless through those it cannot jump.*

Right *Muddy creeks permeate the warm tropical lowland forests covering most of Papua-New Guinea. Forested creek and river banks, where light penetrates to the forest floor, present impenetrable green barriers with exceptionally thick undergrowth—so obviously absent from the deeper interior. 100 million years ago the forests were largely composed of the now rare Araucarias and Agathis—conifers with poor dispersal that then faced less competition from the more recently evolved flowering trees.*

CROCODILE FARMING

Crocodile farms have been started by the Papua-New Guinea Government both to meet the demand for the skins and ostensibly to reduce the danger of extinction. Unfortunately, crocodiles bred in captivity are often grown-up *hatchlings from eggs collected in the wild. The argument that crocodile farms can be used for re-stocking rivers can therefore not be taken too seriously. The skin trade earned Papua-New Guinea more than $1,000,000 in 1977.*

butterfly, and in 1978, 2,000 skins of birds of paradise were exported from Indonesia every month, many of them smuggled out of Papua-New Guinea.

The other spectacular bird of Papua-New Guinea is the cassowary. There are three species and they are protected and prized by the Highlanders as status symbols. If there should be an intertribal dispute, the parties involved hold a cassowary race—that is, they parade their cassowaries and the richer man, judged by the number of his birds, is the winner.

The Australian rain forests occupy a coastal belt in the north-east state of Queensland, but their original area has been halved by timber extraction and clearing for dairying and the growing of sugar cane and maize. The first white settlers arrived in Queensland in 1873 and in the course of a year logging parties cut down more than ninety million board feet of red cedar, *Toona australis*.

These forests are only semi-evergreen and are less luxuriant than the Papua-New Guinea forest, although they also house the cassowary and the cuddly, woolly cuscus with its protruding eyes and tiny ears. Other forest dwellers include the tree kangaroo with sharp claws and foot pads that enable it to cling to branches, and the striped possum.

Although a few isolated groups of hunter-gatherers live deep in the Papua-New Guinea forests, most of the population practises shifting cultivation on grassland in valleys surrounded by rain forest. Of the 251 species of plants utilized for food only seventeen per cent are cultivated, while sixty-three per cent are gathered from the forest, savannah or grassland. The degree of dependence on the forest, and the extent to which it permeates the national culture is probably unique. The traditional lifestyles of the Papua-New Guinea people encourage them to resist the destruction of their forests but the future of Australia's rain forests is less assured.

The cloud forest

Blankets of cloud and mist permanently swathe many of the mountains of the Tropics, blotting out the summits of the smaller mountains and forming a foggy circle around the middle altitudes of the larger ones. Although this misty covering enhances the mystery and magnificence of tropical mountains, it does nothing to make life pleasant. Even when the sun shines, there is an all-pervading dampness in the atmosphere.

This transformation, from the hot humidity of the lowlands to the cooler dampness of the tropical mountain slopes, is accompanied by a change in the vegetation; a decrease in the stature of the trees, a reduction in leaf size and increased leatheriness of leaf-texture. The buttressed giants of the lowland rain forest are rarely found in forests more than a few hundred feet above sea-level.

The cloud cover also particularly favours the growth of epiphytes, which, because of the saturated atmosphere, do not face the problem of desiccation. Vascular epiphytes, such as bromeliads and orchids, cover the trees of the middle altitudes and then mosses and bryophytes become more common towards the upper limit of the forest, where they often hang in festoons from the branches and form deep cushions on the forest floor.

By the time the upper limit of tree growth is approached, at around 11,500 feet, the trees are gnarled and stunted, forming a thick, closed, evergreen canopy only a few feet high. These stunted forests are often called elfin woodlands because of their diminutive stature.

Many of the mountain forest trees are furnished with aerial roots which descend from the branches into the soil, perhaps to augment their nutrient supply. A few of the trees, particularly the palms and pandans, have stilt roots extending obliquely from the trunks and these serve specifically as extra support for the trees in the loose mountain soil.

The complete sequence of mountain vegetation, from lowland rain forest to cloud forest to alpine meadow to permanent snow, may be found in all three tropical regions. In the Far East, the mountain forests form a huge archipelago of disconnected "islands", some separated by sea, others by intervening lowlands. The world's largest continuous area of mountain forest is also found in these regions, in the highlands of Papua–New Guinea.

In Africa, as in Asia, most of the mountain forests are distributed like a string of islands, running the length of the eastern part of the continent, and with outliers in West Africa, for example on Mount Cameroun. In the New World, there are island-like forests in the Antillean mountains and Guyana Highlands, and continuous areas in the sierras of Central America and the Andes of South America.

The Guyana Highlands are an exceptional group of ancient mountains rising out of the lowlands of Venezuela, Brazil and Guyana, between the Amazon and Orinoco river valleys. These mountains are flat-topped and vertical-sided, and the highest of them, Mount Roraima, stands in all three countries. The

Left The steep Guyana Highland mountains rise from the lowlands of Brazil, Venezuela and Guyana between the Amazon and Orinoco river valleys. High plateaux support a stunted vegetation, rich in endemic species that have evolved in isolation for millions of years. Lower down, the slopes are clothed in forest frequently bathed in cloud. In the dank slime forests on Mt. Roraima, the trees and the ground are coated with thick layers of dark mucilag

Below The Chocó mountains in Colombia are wreathed in cloud at 6,600 ft. Above this height, the forests are exposed to brilliant sunlight; the vegetation here is adapted to the lower humidity and greater extremes of temperature.

poor soils of these plateaux support a scrubby vegetation, but one that is rich in endemic species that have evolved in complete isolation for many millions of years.

Tropical mountain forests, wherever they are in the world, show great similarity to each other, not only in their structural zonation, but also in the kinds of plants that they support. The genus *Podocarpus*—one of the conifers—occurs in the Far East, Africa and the Americas, always at relatively high altitudes, although in the southern temperate zone it occurs in the lowlands. The heather family, Ericaceae, are well represented towards the upper limit of most wet tropical mountains, mostly as shrubs and sometimes as epiphytes. Despite these similarities, however, the actual species of such genera and families are usually different from those found in the temperate regions and, moreover, are usually unique, if not to individual mountains or ranges, then to one or other of the tropical continents.

Neither the flora nor the fauna of mountain forests is as diverse as that of the lowlands, possibly because of the mountain forests' smaller total area and poorer conditions for growth. Slower plant-growth rates result in less food, which ultimately results in fewer animals. Most of the arthropods, birds and reptiles of the lowland forests are absent from the mountains, although many species of mammal are found over a wide range of altitudes.

In the Virunga Volcanoes in eastern Zaïre, for example, gorillas and elephants range from the lowlands to more than 9,000 feet into the mountains. Both of these species consume the leaves of a wide variety of herbs, shrubs and trees, but they are particularly partial to young bamboo shoots, which they root from the groves of bamboo that grow at the higher altitudes. In Malaya warm-blooded plant-eaters such as gibbons and tapirs are found both in the lowlands and in the mountains.

There is a long history of human activity in the mountain forests. The forests of the African mountains, have, until quite recently, been relatively undisturbed, although now there is increasing pressure from settlers and small farmers. In New Guinea, however, the mountain forests have been inhabited by tribal peoples for many thousands of years. And because these natural forests and woodlands regenerate slowly after clearing for cultivation, especially in densely populated areas, the extent of the natural vegetation has been considerably reduced.

In the Andes of Peru, it was the Incas who cleared large areas of upper montane forest and elfin woodlands in order to graze llamas and alpacas and to cultivate potatoes and other indigenous crops. And today, modern logging practices are also having serious consequences for large tracts of montane forests throughout the world; erosion of the soil, following the removal of trees, renders the land unusable and delays natural regeneration of forest. If this continues only the inaccessible forests on the most precipitous slopes are likely to survive.

Right *The Andean condor, Vultur gryphus, is one of the world's largest flying birds, with a 12 ft wingspan. It soars high above the mountain-sides, able to detect slight movement of live prey with its keen eyesight.*

Below *The lush greenery of these forests at 10,800 ft in Ecuador thrives in the cool, damp mountain air. Sufficient light penetrates the relatively thin upper canopy to allow creepers to leaf before they reach the tree-tops. These leafy creepers and the thick, springy ground cover of moss are a characteristic of tropical mountain forests and absent from lowland forests.*

Seasonal forests

Below *In Kenya a seasonal drought dries out the isolated patches of open acacia woodland and imparts seasonality to all plant growth. The dying back of ground vegetation and scarcity of water oblige zebras and wildebeest to seek new feeding grounds. Trees anticipate the end of the dry season, bursting into leaf well before the rains start; similarly, many animals arrive prematurely on wet ground, sensing the imminent growth of grass.*

With increasing distance from the Equator rainfall becomes seasonal and forests must withstand progressively more unfavourable dry seasons, during which time the low availability of water is compounded by high temperatures. Where the dry season lasts more than two and a half months, tropical rain forests are gradually replaced by forests, woodlands and savannahs dominated by plants adapted to seasonal drought. There is a progressive shift from the evergreen to the deciduous habit, initially in the upper and emergent strata, and then in the lower strata as the severity and length of the dry season mount. Combinations of the length and severity of the dry season, soil conditions and the effects of fire, man and animals give a variety of seasonal forests which includes the semi-evergreen deciduous and thorn forests.

The semi-evergreen seasonal forests—the *cerradao* of Brazil, the "dry evergreen" in West Africa and the wetter monsoon forests of Indo-Malaysia are distinguished from the tropical rain forest by the lesser stature of the tallest trees, often clothed in relatively thick bark, and with less extensive buttressing. Many trees flower in the dry season and the blaze of colour is accentuated by the leaflessness that permits a denser ground cover. Epiphytes are the most obvious casualties of the dry air of the upper layers, although lianas remain relatively unaffected.

The monsoon forests of Indo-Malaysia may be typified by the moist teak, *Tectona grandis*, forests of Thailand and Burma and the sal

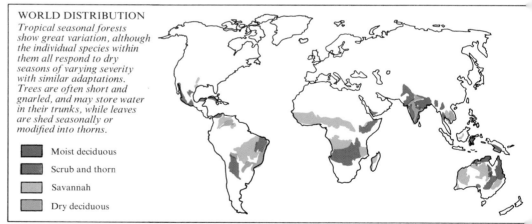

WORLD DISTRIBUTION

Tropical seasonal forests show great variation, although the individual species within them all respond to dry seasons of varying severity with similar adaptations. Trees are often short and gnarled, and may store water in their trunks, while leaves are shed seasonally or modified into thorns.

- Moist deciduous
- Scrub and thorn
- Savannah
- Dry deciduous

forests of India. One of the common deciduous trees is the leguminous pyinkado, *Xylia xylocarpa*, which is associated with teak in the drier areas. Where attempts at conservation have been made by reducing grazing and the occurrence of fires, the fire-resistant teak is displaced by evergreen rain forest saplings and this suggests that the distribution of teak is not determined by climate.

The deciduous trees shed their leaves in the first month of the dry season, and the new leaves appear well before the onset of the rains; a temperature cue rather than direct moisture availability is probably significant.

The deciduous seasonal forests are found where the dry season is more prolonged (five months) and severe. They occur in the rain

shadow areas of the West Indies, Central America and Brazil, Africa and the drier area of monsoonal India, Burma and Thailand Generally, they have two distinct tree storey the upper mainly deciduous and discontinuou and the lower evergreen and continuous. Th crowns of the emergent trees are flat-toppe in contrast to the more conical crowns those in the wet monsoon forests. Lianas an epiphytes are almost entirely absent, and gra cover is significant only in Africa.

In Africa the seasonal forests extend fro Angola to Tanzania and northwards to th Sudan and also cover much of West Afric The local name given to the forest in Tanzan is *miombo*: most of the trees are quite short only fifty feet—and spread their flat tops

SEASONAL RAINFALL AND WINDS

seasons in the tropical and subtropical regions are defined primarily by the pattern of rainfall during the year. Comparison of summer and winter seasons shows that the rainfall over Indo-Malaysia is heavily concentrated in the summer months, while the winter is relatively dry. In Central America, too, there is a dry winter and a wet summer. In both cases, the pattern of rainfall is determined by the direction of the prevailing winds.

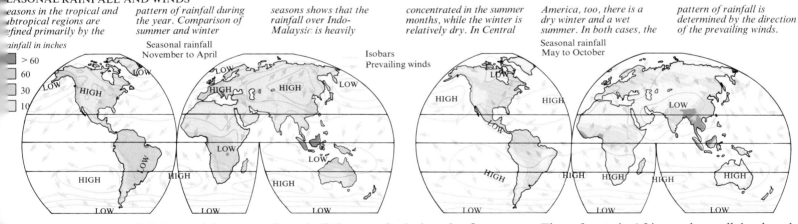

Rainfall in inches
- > 60
- 60
- 30
- 10

Seasonal rainfall November to April

Isobars
Prevailing winds

Seasonal rainfall May to October

have a canopy cover of sixty to eighty per cent. Droughts are prolonged and may be absolute—lasting for perhaps seven months—and this leads to a marked seasonal contrast in appearance. Deprived of rain, the trees shed their leaves, herbs and grasses die back and the whole forest takes on a barren, brown, almost lifeless appearance, with the grey stems of the miombo trees shimmering in the intense heat. New leaves predict the onset of the rains, which revive the whole landscape with reds, pinks, salmon and coppery hues.

A typical miombo tree, and one that is locally important for its timber, is *Pterocarpus angolensis*. After germination, the *Pterocarpus* seedling soon develops a large tap root and an extensive root system, while above ground there is little growth during the first year. Each year the aerial shoot dies back at the end of the rainy season, and the plant relies on the food stored underground in the tap root for rapid elongation the following season. After about seven years the *Pterocarpus* sapling finally overtops the grasses.

The thorn forests or *caatinga* of north-east Brazil cannot depend on regular rain either in or out of season; deciduousness is inadequate as the main water-conserving adaptation; most of the trees have reduced leaves in the form of spines or thorns. The general layer of thorny scrubs is dotted with swollen *Cavanillesia* bottle trees, cacti and xerophytic—dry-adapted—palms, and ground cover is composed largely of cacti and terrestrial bromeliads.

Thorn forests in Africa are less well developed, the similar environmental conditions supporting the baobab tree, *Adansonia digitata*—one individual was estimated to contain 25,000 gallons of water in its trunk—and scattered thorn acacias in stretches of grassland.

There are marked global differences in the character of vegetation of seasonal tropical areas. Indo-Malaysia is inundated regularly by the monsoon rains each year and enjoys more rain than comparable vegetation areas in Africa and South America. In Africa, the junction between evergreen rain forest and open tree savannah is relatively sharp, which may be largely due to a long history of grazing, not practised so much in South America, where the transition is more gradual.

The mangrove swamps

MANGROVE ZONATION

In the mangrove swamps there is a distinct zonation of tree types, each genus taking up its position according to its tolerance to submersion by the sea. The pioneer species, Avicennia and Sonneratia, push up roots just below the low water level and begin to catch the silt. Behind them, species of Rhizophora colonize the newly won mud, throwing out arching roots to consolidate the gains and build the land higher. Farther landward, taller Bruguiera trees stand close to each other in wide belts, giving way to the smaller Ceriops that grow in thickets, often along creek banks. The landward fringe commonly contains many different species, including Xylocarpus, Bruguiera and Rhizophora. These trees border on the tropical forest, a proximity that encourages epiphytic Dendrobium orchids to extend their normal range.

Avicennia

Rhizophora

This mangrove formation occurs on the Queensland coast of north-east Australia. Local rainfall and soil drainage conditions largely determine the species composition of a mangrove swamp and the

Bruguiera

distinctiveness of the zone. Each zone, characterized by a dominant tree species houses its own fauna. Algae, oysters and barnacles attach themselves to Avicennia pneumatophores in the seaward zone, where they

Down where the tropical forest meets river estuaries and the sea coast there exists a strange world halfway between land and water. Behind protective coral reefs battalions of trees advance out to sea, dedicated to regaining at least some of the land that is eroded each year. These complex but well-ordered warrior forests of salt-tolerant trees are better known as mangrove swamps.

To survive in a hostile environment, where oxygen is lacking from the soil and high salt concentrations make water uptake difficult, the native mangrove trees have evolved unique survival mechanisms. Modified roots or pneumatophores, visible above the mud at low tide, absorb oxygen from the air and transport it to the buried roots. The leaves are succulent, a common form in plants subjected to water stress, and they are capable of secreting the excess salt. The salt is washed away by rain or it is simply dissolved in the perpetually humid atmosphere.

The differing ability of each tree genus to withstand regular inundation by the incoming tide is reflected in the successive zones of mangrove tree types. In South East Asia, for example, the first line of trees is composed of pioneer species of *Sonneratia*. Without air their roots would suffocate, so they push up ranks of little tubes above the surface of the water. These tubes funnel back life-giving oxygen to the roots as they struggle to establish a firm and ever-expanding grip on what was once the ocean floor.

Once the pioneer species have claimed their rights over new territory, and the tangled mass of vegetation has trapped silt from the sea, the level of the land slowly rises and creates a home for the larger trees, usually species of

Tropical forest

Ceriops   *Mixed landward zone*

can be assured of a regular
bathing. In the Rhizophora
and Bruguiera zones,
vegetarian crabs scuttle
about, while the very
energetic mud lobster digs
up high mounds of earth in
the dense thickets of
Ceriops.

Below *The aerial roots of
Sonneratia mangroves are
exposed at low tide and
permit underwater
breathing in thick mud.
Seaward mangroves resist
the wave action's weak-
ening of their hold and
removal of nutritious soil.*

Above *Spoonbills and
ibises frequent tropical
swamps. Spoonbills are
lethargic during the day,
stirring themselves in the
evening to sweep the water
with their flat bills to catch
small crustaceans.*

Below *Mudskippers
conserve water efficiently
with their tight-fitting gill
covers and survive happily
in the intertidal zone,
where they are distributed
according to their feeding
and breeding habits.*

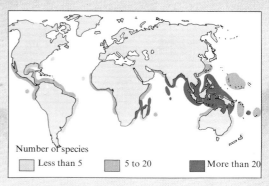

Number of species
☐ Less than 5   ☐ 5 to 20   ☐ More than 20

Above *Mangroves grow in
river estuaries or on
sheltered coasts. The
formations in South East
Asia and parts of West
Africa are richer in species
than those of East Africa
and the Americas.*

Below *Rhizophora seeds
germinate before leaving
the parent plant, ready to
take root and establish
themselves on landing in
the mud before they can be
washed away by the
shifting tide.*

Rhizophora. These do not send up timid peri-
scopes for air; instead they have large stilt
roots that sprout from the trunk and branches, providing support in the shifting silt and
acting as a giant sieve to build the land higher
still. Behind them lies a zone of *Brugueira* spp.
Unable to withstand long periods of inundation, they throw out "knee roots" that curl
in and out of the water like roller coasters.

The land behind mangrove swamps is regularly flooded at times of high water throughout the year and therefore remains a brack-
ish swamp. Here, the Nipa palm is found
extensively throughout South East Asia. It is
used by local people for thatching and the
edible seeds are harvested. Farther inland
begins the forest proper.

Yet this succession can only be a general-
ization much modified by local conditions: it
may be determined by the first species to
throw its seeds on to the muddy banks, and in
many areas it has been destroyed and exploited by man. Along the west coast of Africa
many mangroves have been converted to
paddy-fields for rice-growing, while others
have been reduced to pitiful remnants by over-
cutting for firewood. Mangrove forests also
provide raw materials for papermaking, tannin and charcoal manufacture, as well as dyes
and preservatives for fishing nets. Some
mangrove woods are much prized for building
in Arab lands and the heavy tandawood from
Rhizophora mangle, which does not float in
water, is transported from Africa to Europe
for use in building piers and other marine
constructions (see pages 178–179).

The animal life in mangrove swamps reflects the mixed habitat of land and sea; the
land animals move seawards and the high
humidity and shelter from the burning sun
has created the ideal place for marine life migrating inland. Indeed, it was in the coastal
swamps that perhaps the most crucial advance in the evolution of life on Earth took
place. Some 350 million years ago bony fishes
dragged themselves out of the sea for the
first time and learned how to live on land.
From them evolved the amphibians, the reptiles, and eventually the human race.

Still today, mudskippers can be found,
stretched out on the mud well above the waterline, now the only fishes able to live both
on land and in the water. They move very
nimbly by using muscular front fins as limbs
and feed on insects and small animals. One
species even climbs trees to escape from the
incoming tide. Some crabs have also followed
the ancient fish on to land. They do not possess lungs but still breathe using gills encased
in compartments flooded with water. Like
tending an aquarium, the crabs oxygenate
their own water supply.

When the tide is low, wild pigs and monkeys
descend to feed on the shore. The crab-eating
macaque spends much of its time seeking
crabs in the shallows, tearing them apart and
feeding on the soft flesh. In the canopies of
trees that are never flooded, proboscis monkeys may be found feeding on the leaves of
Sonneratia caseolaris. Iguanas patrol the
mangrove branches. Parrots and pigeons find
protected night-time roosts and migrant
birds, such as cormorants, ospreys and kingfishers, nest there during winter. Reptiles and
amphibians have found refuge here too. Sea
snakes hunt in the waters, sea-going crocodiles bask on the mud flats, and crab-eating
frogs search the salty waters for prey.

The bamboo forests

Bamboo is the common name given to the species of tree-like and shrubby woody grasses that abound, from sea-level to the snow-line, in tropical and subtropical regions. The many different species of bamboo are particularly numerous in southern Asia and in South East Asia, from where the word "bamboo" is said to have originated—derived from a Malay word conveying the distinctive sound made by bamboo when it burns.

The hollow, aerial, neatly sectioned culms, or stems, produced by bamboo plants spring from stout prolific rootstocks and the bamboo thickets found in the favourable moist sites of tropical forests often establish themselves at the expense of all other plants. They form one of the most impenetrable natural barriers known, for not only do the stems of most tropical species grow very close together, but the heavy impregnation of silica in bamboo wood dulls the sharpest cutting edge of any tool used to open a path.

The density of growth achieved by bamboo varies widely and the many different species can be divided into two broad categories—monopodial and sympodial—depending upon their density, or clumping habits. Monopodial bamboos develop long, thin, fast-growing rhizomes that run underground, sometimes for several feet, before they develop new stem buds. These species, most common in dry subtropical regions, produce the widely spaced tree-like stems that are typical of Japanese bamboo groves. Sympodial bamboos tend to develop short stubby rhizomes and new stem buds grow close to the parent stem, producing the dense clumps of bamboo commonly found in wet tropical areas.

The luxuriance of bamboo growth is effected almost entirely by vegetative growth. In many species, flowering occurs only after several years of prolific sprouting from the rootstocks and is often followed by the death of the flowering stems, with regeneration from the seedlings and yet more vegetative shoots. This flowering is such a rare occurrence in some species that it only takes place every sixty to one hundred and twenty years. Because of this, and because it often occurs in response to a long period of drought, the flowering of these bamboos was at one time interpreted as an ill omen, although the seeds of certain species that flower in times of drought have provided a vital source of famine food for rice-impoverished people.

Many species of bamboo grow to more than sixty feet in height, and the tallest bamboo, an Indo-Malaysian species, *Dendrocalamus giganteus* can have stems 120 feet tall. These stems emerge as pointed shoots from the plant's massive old food-storage roots and they push skywards in serried ranks, growing at a rate of three feet each day (nearly one and a half inches every hour) to form great shiny green clumps. This bamboo, and many other of the larger species, often form considerable areas of dense, impenetrable, high forest, while the smaller kinds, equally and formidably dense, remain as undergrowth to the trees.

It is perhaps not surprising that such a quick-growing and successful plant as the bamboo should serve many human needs as a source of food, fibres, medicines and building materials (see pages 206–207). But it also serves some of the world's rarest animals.

The giant panda has little cause to leave the abundant food supplies of its habitat in the bamboo forests of western China. It feeds strictly on the leaves, shoots and stalks of dwarf species of the *Bambusa* and *Dendrocalamus* genera, which are found throughout its range of habitat. Giant pandas have developed powerful teeth for chewing this tough and fibrous food, and their forefeet have specially modified pads that assist in clasping slender objects such as bamboos. Unlike true bears, they do not hibernate, but during very cold weather they have been known to make dens or nests from broken pieces of bamboo.

One observer of the animal, puzzled at the purpose of a bamboo nest set on top of a large flat stump in the opening of the bamboo forests, was informed by local inhabitants that it was constructed by panda mothers who retired to it when bringing forth their young. The bamboo forests have afforded invaluable shelter to this unique and increasingly scarce mammal, and are the sole element of its exclusive vegetarian diet. Now this food supply

Below *The giant panda inhabits the dense bamboo forests that clothe the eastern slopes of the mountains bordering western Szechwan in China. It feeds almost exclusively on the leaves, stalks and shoots of* bamboo *and its digestive system has been highly adapted to cope with this rough and fibrous food. Local farmers, however, have reported the animal's predilection for honey, which it steals from beehives in the area.*

Right *The open ranks of this Japanese bamboo grove typify the growth habits of subtropical bamboos. These monopodial species form widely spaced stems that are connected to the parent stem by rhizomes.*

Above *The intermediate egret is found in wet marshy regions of South* East Asia, tropical Australia and southern Africa. The tall leafy *stands of bamboo that also favour these areas are ideal breeding places.*

s threatened by drought and the panda is faced with a fight for survival.

Bamboo is also a major source of food for mountain gorillas inhabiting the bamboo and montane forests of eastern Zaïre. An important part of their diet is made up of the young shoots of local bamboo species.

In both Asia and Africa animal species have developed a lifestyle that relies heavily on bamboo as a source of food. It is therefore surprising, and perhaps only an accident of animal distribution, that no creature has evolved to take exclusive advantage of the enormous wealth of bamboos that are found in tropical South America.

Right *The largest of all the primates, the mountain gorilla, ranges the bamboo and montane forests of Central Africa. The gorilla is essentially a ground-dwelling creature and the delicate young shoots of alpine bamboo, which sprout from the forest floor, form an important and highly relished part of its diet. But perhaps a more important function of the bamboo forest is that it gives the animal some shelter from its only enemy, man.*

Plant adaptations

Although large trees constitute the framework of the rain forest, they are outnumbered by many species of smaller trees, shrubs, herbs, vines and lianas. These other life forms have evolved a remarkable array of adaptations to cope with the associated problems of obtaining adequate light, nutrients and water to grow and reproduce successfully in the face of the massive demand of the large forest trees for the same resources.

The sunlit gaps created by falling trees allow a range of shade-intolerant herbs and fast-growing trees to establish themselves. These are the pioneers, and all of them exhibit some form of specialization for the colonization of gaps. Such plant species as *Macaranga* tend to have small seeds, "cheap" to produce and easily dispersed, sometimes by birds or bats. Although these plants attain full size quite rapidly, they are gradually overtopped and shaded out by the young forest giants growing to refill the canopy.

Epiphytes—plants that grow on other plants without parasitizing them—may be found at all levels in the forest, but are especially abundant in the canopy. In the rain forests of South America, bromeliads are conspicuous members of the epiphytic community. Each plant appears as a series of concentric rosettes of leaves, forming a number of receptacles or "tanks" that hold water. Suspended above the ground, these tanks are miniature freshwater ecosystems and may contain up to a gallon of water in which mosquitoes and tree frogs can breed.

Orchids are common epiphytes throughout the Tropics and they survive by storing water in thick fleshy stems and leaves, and also in fleshy aerial roots. The roots are covered with a specialized tissue, the velamen, which together with an impermeable exodermis, effectively prevents the escape of water by evaporation. Root development in epiphytic orchids is often tremendous, forming a tangled mat in which organic debris builds up. Nutrients may be derived from this and rainwater flowing down the tree trunk. Combined with aroids, ferns and mosses, these aerial roots often obscure the host tree from view.

The "strangler" figs have evolved a clever compromise in their quest for light and nutrients. Their seeds, deposited by fruit-eating birds in the crotch of a branch or an epiphytic clump in the canopy, germinate epiphytically. The young plants send down roots, eventually forming a solid cylinder of roots around the host tree; the fig is soon an impressive tree, its crown shading out the host, which gradually dies due to competition for light, rather than by strangulation, as is often thought. The mature fig thus stands unsupported alongside normal forest trees, having obeyed the laws of gravity by growing down rather than up.

The leaves of rain forest trees are often encrusted with a covering of very small

Left *This South American turtle staircase liana has been carried up to the sunlit canopy by successive generations of trees, so escaping the dark forest floor without having to build strong supportive tissue.*

epiphytes—mosses, liverworts, lichens and algae—properly known as epiphylls. Although the light reaching the leaf surface is therefore reduced, the lichens and blue-green algae may indirectly assist the host by fixing atmospheric nitrogen, which can then enter the tight nutrient cycle of the forest.

The *Myrmecodias* of South East Asia are small epiphytes that have evolved, in common with a number of other tropical plants, a close relationship with ants, upon whom they partially rely for their nutrient supply. The plant shelters the ants in a large tuber riddled with passages and chambers. Ants transport dead insects and debris back to the tuber where, with the help of fungi, they decay and some of the nutrients made available in this way can be absorbed by the plant.

Some plants have dispensed altogether with light and parasitize others for their photosynthetic products. The pale vegetative parts of *Rafflesia arnoldii*, a Sumatran rain forest plant, are entirely subterranean, penetrating the roots of forest trees. This species sports a gigantic mottled red flower, nearly three feet across, and emits a pungent smell of rotting flesh to attract carrion flies that unwittingly transport pollen from one flower to the next. Guidance relying on the sense of smell is a particularly suitable strategy for the plant on the dark forest floor.

South American passifloras—climbing passion flowers—produce nectar, both deep in the flower for pollinating bees or hummingbirds, and at nectaries on petioles, stems and leaves to retain the services of aggressive ants and wasps that discourage herbivores. The leaves of *Passifloras* are eaten by the larvae of *Heliconius* butterflies, of which there are about forty-five species; each of these species lays eggs on only a few specific species of *Passiflora*, identified by their leaf shape.

The 400 species of *Passiflora* have evolved a wide range of leaf shapes, it has been suggested, in response to this herbivore pressure; but the powers of recognition of the *Heli-conius* butterflies have evolved just as rapidly. Some *Passiflora* species produce nodules on their leaves, resembling the eggs of *Heliconius*; this is a further defence mechanism, because a female *Heliconius* will not lay eggs on a leaf that has already been used. Only two *Passiflora* species appear to have won the evolutionary race against *Heliconius*, one by evolving hairs on the leaf surface that are lethal to the caterpillars, and the other with a toxic chemical contained in the leaves that is equally deadly.

Our knowledge of the array of ingeniously economical and finely tuned energy-saving adaptations of the plants of the tropical rain forests is still tantalizingly rudimentary. But it is certain that these co-evolved systems, and many others between plants and animals, are so delicately and closely interwoven that their disruption accounts in part for the failure of rain forests to regenerate once destroyed. Hopefully, there is yet time for us to learn more about nature's stratagems in the forest.

PITCHER PLANTS

Above *This epiphytic Vriesia bromeliad germinated high up in the forest canopy, and although it is never short of light, unlike the lianas it has no ready water supply. It solves this problem by developing a water tank, enclosed by leaves joined at the base, in which decaying organic material is caught. This furnishes the plant with a ready supply of nutrients that are taken up by absorptive hairs in the leaf bases.*

Insects, attracted to the pitcher by nectar glands on the underside of the lid and the inner edge of the rim, are tricked into straying downwards by the relatively translucent cells and the shadow cast by the lid, on to the slippery waxy zone. Here they lose their footing and fall into the digestive liquid.

Lid

Transverse rim section

Waxy zone

Nectar gland and duct

Digestive zone

Decaying insect remains

Most of the 60 species of pitcher plant are epiphytic, scrambling up trees as high as 50 ft. Tendrils extend from the leaf midribs and terminate in upright pitchers, adaptations for trapping insects from which minerals are derived.

POLLINATION

The flowers pollinated by birds are usually red or orange, and are often borne in large conspicuous heads as in this *Calliandra*, which is being pollinated by a starthroat humming-bird. The reward in this case is nectar, which is offered in quantities large enough to make a visit to the flower worthwhile, but insufficient to satiate the bird, so ensuring that it visits another flower to effect cross-pollination. The pollen is deposited around the face, head, chest or bill of the bird, depending on the plant species. In the New World, humming-birds are the most important bird pollinators—there are more than 300 species. In the Old World their counterparts, the sunbirds, do not hover while they feed, and other plants provide convenient perches close to the flowers.

It is possible that humming-birds originally pursued fleeing insects to flowers, which then adapted themselves for pollination by birds. Insect pollination is a less recent adaptation, and many believe that the rise of the flowering plants was greatly accelerated by their close association with pollinating insects.

Animal adaptations

In the blocks of rain forest strung around the Tropics there lives an array of animal life to match the wealth of plants. Most, however, live a secretive life and without a special search they go unnoticed unless betrayed by a flash of colour and movement among the foliage, or by far-carrying calls. Many of the lower orders are still unknown to science.

The tropical rain forests have survived with little change of climate for some sixty million years and evolution towards specialization has proceeded unchecked. Animals have become physically adapted for tree life, and competition between them for food has forced the creation of specialized diets. At the same time the pressure of predation favours the development of cunning strategies for defence. In its own little niche an animal survives by its advantage over other species in finding food and shelter and avoiding predators.

The adaptations for tree climbing involve grasping limbs, prehensile tails and often large forward-facing eyes to give the stereoscopic vision necessary for rapid judgement of distances. Many of the primates, for example, have long digits on hands and feet for grasping branches. The digits typically end in blunt nails, but the marmosets have sharp claws for gripping large smooth-barked boughs. Sharp claws are also a feature of the squirrels and cats. In contrast, tree frogs and geckos have pads on their fingers and toes to aid climbing. A prehensile tail for use as an extra limb has been developed by the spider monkeys, the coendou or South American porcupine, the pangolins, the monkey-like marsupial cuscuses and the fruit-eating kinkajou.

Perhaps the strangest of all the arboreal animals are the sloths, which spend their lives hanging upside down by their hook-shaped claws. They eat, sleep, mate and give birth in this position, although they can prop themselves upright against a vertical trunk and are

THE CHAMELEON *Chamaeleo dilepis*

The chameleon's whole structure is adapted to living among forest trees. Its tongue could not operate from ground level; its eyes roll about freely, independent of each other; its feet and tail are perfect for grasping twigs; and its skin can change colour in waves that sweep slowly over its body, enabling it to merge into the background scenery. To scare rivals or territorial trespassers the chameleon can turn crimson and blue, a frightful combination with its bright orange throat.

Above *The chameleon takes on the shape, and even performs irregular trembling movements, to imitate the leaves that surround it.*

Below *The superbly adapted sloth spends much of its life hanging upside down on branches, using hook-shaped claws.*

Right *The cue to change colour may come from the eyes, an emotional stimulus or changing light and temperature conditions, and the response is controlled by nerves or hormones. Colour change is controlled by star-shaped, pigment-bearing cells called melanophores in the skin's lower layers. When the pigment, which is in tiny granules, is distributed throughout the arms of the cell, it excludes light and the skin becomes dark. When the pigment is concentrated in the centre of the cell, light is reflected through the xanthophores that are arranged in stacks and contain an orange pigment, so the skin becomes pale. The silvery white iridophores serve as a background hue for the varying pigment combinations.*

Action of the pituitary gland

Light stimulus on the eye

Skin cells

Melanophore

Suprarenal gland

Epidermis

Xanthoph

Dermis   Iridophores   Melanophores

As the chameleon approaches prey, its tongue shoots out with amazing speed to trap small animals with the sticky substance on the end. It then retracts into its mouth like a spring.

reputed to be strong swimmers. Even their fur is inverted, lying from belly to back so that rain runs off. The coarse grooved hairs are often infested with green algae that no doubt aid camouflage by making the sloth appear like a clump of dead leaves. The fur is also the home of a peculiar moth whose life was a mystery until the recent discovery that its eggs are laid in sloth dung.

As might be expected, the warm, moist environment of the tropical forests, with very little seasonal and diurnal temperature change, is ideal for soft-bodied invertebrates. These include the gaily coloured flatworms (aquatic animals outside the Tropics), which slide over the ground, and many amphibians, such as the thirteen-inch Goliath frog of East Africa—the world's largest frog. Arboreal frogs lay their eggs in cavities in plants or in the bowls of water provided by ephiphytes. Goeldi's tree frog lives in a bromeliad and carries her eggs under a fold of skin on her back until they hatch and drop into the bromeliad cup.

Fruit and flowers are strictly seasonal in temperate regions, but at any time in the Tropics some plant species will always be in flower or fruit. It is therefore possible for birds and mammals specialized in feeding on these to breed all the year round. The plants benefit by pollination of their flowers and dispersal of their seeds and in tropical forests birds and bats join the insects as pollinators. The New World humming-birds are the equivalent of the Old World sunbirds and in both hemispheres they are replaced after nightfall by various bats. Many flowers are modified to attract the pollinators not only by bright colours and scents but by more bizarre lures.

Certain orchids, for example, mimic the shape of the female of a particular bee. The male bee is fooled into attempting to mate with the flowers and so collects and transfers pollen. The *Coryanthes* orchid flowers are "booby traps" that trip bees into a basin of

water. The only way out is through a side tunnel where they collect the pollen.

Another odd relationship is that between plants and ants. Many kinds of ant make their nests in convenient hollow stems, but some plants, such as *Macaranga caladifolia* of Borneo, foster the association by secreting sugary fluids to attract them. The ants, in return, protect the plants from defoliating caterpillars or browsing herbivores. The epiphytic plants benefit by the excreta and plant debris from the ants' nests acting as fertilizers. Fruits are another lure for hungry animals. They are designed to be eaten, attracting birds and mammals by their colours and sweet flesh, so that the seeds are dispersed.

In the bid to survive the attacks of predators the animals of the tropical forests employ two basic strategies apart from the simple expedient of running away. First, they can camouflage themselves by blending into the profusions of green and brown. Some insects carry this to perfection by adopting the shape

of dead leaves or twigs, while the chameleons change colour to match their surroundings. Camouflage is, however, a double-edged weapon because predators can disguise themselves to trap the unwary. There is the crab spider that resembles a bird dropping on a leaf and the praying mantises that are mistaken by butterflies for flowers.

The second stratagem is the opposite of camouflage, through warning coloration an animal advertises the fact that it is dangerous. This is vividly demonstrated by the brilliant arrow-poison frogs, whose skins secrete a powerful nerve poison once used by South American Indians to tip their arrows. A fascinating extension of warning coloration is the way in which harmless animals gain protection by mimicking the colours of harmful species. In Asia there are wasps that advertise their stinging power by striking colouring. They are matched by innocuous crickets, spiders and roaches that fool predators into thinking that they, too, can sting.

Above *The predatory mantis assumes a flower's colour and shape so well that insects search for its nectar. A mistake for which they pay with their lives.*

Right *The arrow-poison frog's skin secretes a powerful nerve poison, but its brilliant coloration serves as a warning device to frighten predators away.*

bove *A large prehensile tail and sharp digging claws nable the pangolin to lead a life in the trees. Having no teeth, it relies on its heavily elongated sticky tongue to rap food—ants and termites.*

MIMICRY FOR SURVIVAL

The most successful animals have evolved adaptations to help them survive in their surroundings. In addition to the many who exploit features resembling the shape and colour of plants in order to camouflage themselves, countless other ingenious strategies are employed by creatures bent on avoiding predators. The spider *Cyclosa tremula* weaves the remains of insects into a replica of itself in its web, serving as a decoy. Some harmless animals succeed in evolving the shape and markings of poisonous or unpalatable animals, as do certain flies, and squirrels in Borneo that resemble notoriously unpalatable tree shrews. Many of the butterflies are particularly expert at deceiving predators. In addition to the confusing markings on its wings and a "false head" on its hind quarters, *Thecla togarna* performs a startling feat at the moment of landing— swinging in the previous direction of flight to misdirect predators.

Above *For protection, harmless flies, such as Milesia vespoides (left), mimic a poisonous wasp, Vespa cincta (right), so that predatory birds who recognize the poisonous wasp features, avoid the fly as well.*

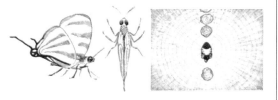

Above *Some butterflies have wing markings that divert attention to an imitation "head"*

Above *Certain spiders manufacture objects into their web to act as deterrent decoy spiders.*

The river community

With one hundred inches or more rain falling each year, it is not surprising that rivers, lakes and swamps are an important feature of tropical rain forests. When a thunderstorm deluges the forest most of the water runs off the ground in trickles and rivulets, which gather into streams that flow into the great rivers. When the rains reach their peak, huge areas of lowland forest become inundated. For man these watercourses can be a barrier to travel or a most valuable highway through the forest, but for forest animals they represent a welcome clearing and a source of food and water.

Sunlight can penetrate to the forest floor, and along the banks a dense, luxuriant undergrowth springs up. Fig trees and other fruiting plants thrive in abundance to become a particular attraction. Monkeys, fruit pigeons, hornbills, toucans, bulbuls and many others, according to geographical locality, gather to strip the trees. And even fishes benefit. Figs from the tangkol tree of Borneo fall into the water and are snapped up by several fishes, one catfish being particularly attracted to and feeding on this fruit.

A wonderful array of huge, kaleidoscopic butterflies gathers along the water's edge. Flocks of birdwings, morphos, swallow-tails and milkweeds probe the bank-side sand and mud with their long tubular tongues. They are seeking vital salts that are lacking from their diet of nectar. The salts come from seepage water oozing out of the bank or from the urine and droppings of animals that have drunk at the water's edge. If the mud is hard, the butterflies secrete fluid through the tongue to dissolve the salts and then drink it. When Alfred Russel Wallace discovered Rajah Brooke's birdwing in Borneo he noticed that only males were present. The same was found to be true for other butterflies and it is now known that the females stay aloft in the trees. Presumably the more active males have a greater need for salts.

Around lakes and in the quieter corners and

Above *The largest of all living snakes is the anaconda which haunts the pools of the Amazon basin. It usually preys on fish, throwing tight coils around its victims, but it also attacks larger animals such as this caiman at the water's edge.*

Left *A dead piranha fish has many uses among the Indians of the Amazon basin. The teeth make perfect barbs for poison darts, piercing the wound to let the curare poison enter the prey. The saw-like jaws are used as scissors, and among some tribes Western scissors are known as piranhas.*

THE ELECTRIC EEL

Nervous electricity is a characteristic of all higher animals but some genera of freshwater electric fish, such as *Gymnarchus* and *Mormyrus*, have adapted it to serve specific functions. They use electricity for communication and navigation in the dimly lit muddy waters. The African catfish, *Malapterurus*, and the Amazonian eel, *Electrophorus*, use electricity as a powerful weapon. A mature eel can emit pulses of 600 volts—enough to stun a horse.

The electricity-producing organs in the eel take up four-fifths of its elongated body and consist of three distinct groups of fibres, shown above right. They are actually modified muscles in which the contractile tissue has been replaced by motor end-plates that respond to nervous stimulation in exactly the same way as an ordinary muscle does. They are almost immune to their own electric shocks because their nervous system is embedded in a thick layer of fat. Nevertheless, as eels mature they become blind, possibly as a result of repeated electric discharges. Another attribute of these eels is that they breathe and must, therefore, rise to the surface every fifteen minutes or so.

Main organ   Organ of Sachs

Organ of Hunter

Right *The main electricity-producing organ consists of rows of about 10,000 electric cells. Stacked in groups of 70 columns, orientated in the same direction and arranged in series, they act like a battery. A nerve impulse from the brain to the tail triggers off a response, each single cell producing 150 millivolts. Within the fish the current flows from the tail to the head, but in the water it flows from head to tail to complete the circuit.*

An electric field is continuously generated to act as a locatory device.

When prey is located, the eel switches on the main electric organ.

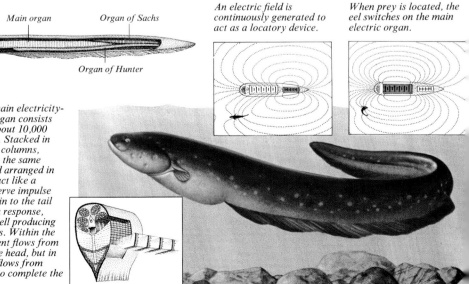

backwaters of rivers, water plants and the small animals living on them are an important food supply. This is the hunting ground of herons and egrets, darters, kingfishers, the osprey and fish eagle. Peculiar to the river banks and swampy woods of tropical America is the poorly known sunbittern, which feeds in a heron-like posture, standing still as a sentinel then spearing its prey with a lightning jab. It has a spectacular display, fanning its wings and tail to look like "a sun darkly glowing in a sunset-tinted sky". Even less well known are the finfoots of South America, Africa and South East Asia. They are most secretive and, unusually for water birds, take to the land when disturbed. The sharp claws and stiff tail feathers of the finfoots are an aid for clambering through the forest undergrowth.

The best known amphibious mammal of the tropical forest's waterways is the hippopotamus. These bulky creatures spend the day in water and emerge at night to feed, but they are not so much forest animals because they feed mainly on grasses. The pygmy hippopotamus of Sierra Leone and Liberia lives by forest streams and is less aquatic than its larger relative *Hippopotamus amphibius*. In South America, the capybara, the largest of all rodents, is the equivalent of the hippo, although it will feed on aquatic plants. It shares the hippo's grace when swimming, despite the unwieldy build, and has the eyes, ears and nose on top of the head so its senses are fully alert when all but fully submerged. For bulk, the hippo's rivals are the manatees of American and West African rivers, and the tapirs of South America and South East Asia—heavy pig-like animals that live in swampy forests.

Tropical rivers abound with fish, a number of which have strange habits. Some catfish migrate overland and the freshwater butterfly fish flaps its fins in flight over West African pools. Fish form the main food for a variety of amphibious and aquatic predators. Apart from the birds other fish-eating predators

live in the tropical forests. Asia has a fishing cat that scoops its prey out of the water from a riverside perch. South America has fishing bats and there are several fishing owls in the Old World forests. The unique South American yapok, or water opossum, is a marsupial that eats fish and other aquatic animals. Its pouch can be closed by a ring of muscle to make a waterproof nursery. Otters also abound, although the giant otter of Brazil is now seriously endangered. There are even freshwater dolphins: the bouto and bufeo of the Amazonian river system and the sousa of the Cameroon river. The boutu was said to come ashore for affairs with young girls—a convenient excuse for irregular pregnancies.

Snakes, among them the giant anaconda of South America and the python of India, also haunt the rivers and swamps. It is difficult to judge the size of a large snake but there are few authentic reports for any longer than thirty-five feet and reports of man-eating are very rare and usually circumstantial. A truly aquatic snake is the South East Asian fishing snake. Well camouflaged to hide among water plants, it can also close its nostrils while swimming underwater.

The crocodiles are the super-predators of the fresh waters. During the day they spend much of their time basking on the bank or on sandbars, waiting until twilight for their main hunting effort. Some, such as the slender-snouted gharial of India and the New Guinea crocodile, are exclusively fish-eaters, but others take a variety of food. In general baby crocodiles eat insects and other small animals. The largest can take warm-blooded prey, however, although they adapt to a diet of fish as they grow up. Animals coming to the waterside to drink are knocked over with a blow from the tail or seized in the jaws and dragged under. Man-eating can occur in restricted areas but excessive hunting has sadly depleted the size of most populations and of individual crocodiles, so this threat is dwindling.

THE HOATZIN

Strangest of all the waterside birds is the Amazonian hoatzin. The young chicks clamber through the branches with the aid of two claws on each wing, rather like the prehistoric *Archaeopteryx*, which must have led a similar kind of life to the hoatzin, living among the trees on leaves, flowers and fruit. The hoatzin's food is crushed in its crop, situated near the base of the neck, rather than in the muscular gizzard as in other birds. A well-fed hoatzin is top heavy and flops onto its horn-padded breast.

Hoatzin

Young hoatzin's wing claws

Archaeopteryx

Above *Jacanas or lily trotters appear to walk on the surface of the water but actually pace over sparse water plants on their impossibly long toes, using the plants as if they were stepping stones.*

THE MANATEE

Nicknamed "Christopher Columbus's mermaids" because of their habit of suckling and nursing their young in an upright posture, the manatee, *Trichechus inunguis*, feeds on water hyacinths. Sometimes they rise out of the water to eat bank-side plants.

LUNGFISH AND AESTIVATION

In evolutionary terms the most ancient of all of the living freshwater fish, lungfish were abundant aeons ago but today only three neo-tropical species exist. The Australian, *Neoceratodus*, is the largest (being five feet long); *Lepidosiren*, or mud siren, inhabits the Amazon and its tributaries; and *Protopterus*,

below, is indigenous to Africa. They live in warm muddy waters that can be as hot as 38°C (100°F) and almost devoid of oxygen. They must rise to the surface at intervals to breathe because if deprived of air they die. If their murky swamps dry up, they burrow into the mud and become dormant.

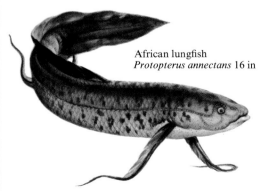

African lungfish
Protopterus annectans 16 in

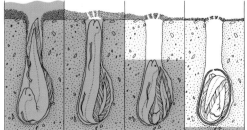

Above *Protopterus retreats as the water table falls. Subsisting on accumulated fat and* *breathing trapped oxygen, it secretes a cocoon and becomes torpid. If put in water it revives.*

The forest at night

Below *Unfortunately, the main threat to this species of ochre-yellow ocelot, Leopardus pardalis, has been the human demand for its fur. Asleep all day, ocelots emerge at twilight and hunt in pairs, preying on small mammals.*

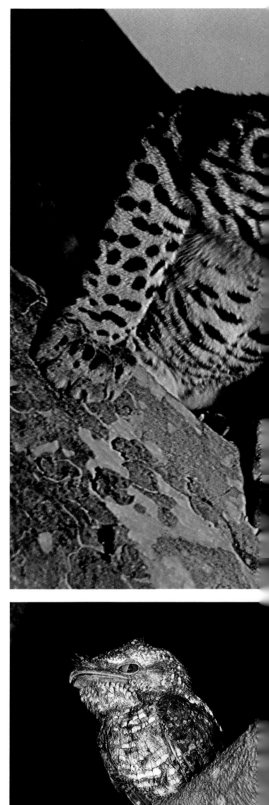

Darkness comes quickly at the end of the tropical day and as dusk deepens the wildlife abroad in the forest undergoes a radical change. Those animals that have been active during the day, especially the birds and monkeys, make for their resting places. Human beings are as diurnal as their closest relatives, the monkeys and apes (with the exception of the nocturnal South American night monkey), and sunset sees the end of the day's labour and a retreat from the night's predators, be they tigers or mosquitoes. While the day-feeding animals retire the nocturnal animals emerge, perhaps to enjoy basking in the sun's last rays before setting out to feed.

From the security of an encampment, the striking difference between day and night life is the animal calls. In the density of the forest foliage sound is a better medium for communication than sight, so many forest animals advertise their whereabouts vocally. This is even more necessary at night and, as the choruses of parrots and monkeys die down, new refrains spring up from cicadas, frogs, tree hyraxes, fruit bats and, in Madagascar, the many lemurs.

With the onset of night the bursts of activity from nocturnal animals mirror the similar bustle at dawn from diurnal animals. There is a peak of feeding activity as stomachs are filled after the day's sleep. This dies away as hunger is satisfied, and some animals are considered to be crepuscular, or active at twilight, rather than nocturnal or diurnal. Self-advertisement reaches a crescendo after dusk and is dominated by the cicadas and amphibians in monotonous choruses which can drive to distraction.

Cicadas are plant-sucking bugs, not related to the grasshoppers and crickets that share their ability to sing. The shrill song that may be heard for more than a mile is the male cicada's advertisement, and it is produced by the rapid vibration of a membrane which pops in and out in the same way as a tin lid can be made to "click". Each species has its own signature tune and entomologists can identify cicadas by their song as ornithologists identify birds. The same holds for the frogs whose chorus changes through the night as different species join in and drop out.

Nocturnal life is a secondary development in evolutionary terms, but the pressure of adaptation is such that any unoccupied way of life soon attracts colonists. A forest that was empty and silent during the hours of darkness would be unthinkable, especially in the Tropics where conditions are equable at night.

There were two basic pressures to encourage animals to change their life-cycles and become active at night. They could "escape" into the night to avoid competition for living space and food, and they could avoid predation. Evading predation must have been short-lived, however, because owls, cats and other predators followed their prey into the darkness. Competition was, therefore, a more potent force and within the nocturnal habitat there has been evolution and differentiation

into ways of life often paralleling those seen during the day. Marked parallels can be seen between the diurnal hawks and the nocturnal owls, the diurnal fruit- and insect-eating birds and the nocturnal bats, and the geckoes, which have both diurnal and nocturnal representatives.

The full extent of this parallelism is being appreciated as more zoologists investigate the forests at night. A nocturnal animal can often be tracked down by its eye-glow, which is due to the mirror-like structure of the tapetum behind the sensory tissue of the retina. When a faint light strikes and penetrates the retina it is reflected back to double the stimulation. The beam of a head-lamp or a torch held at head level is reflected back by the tapetum so that the animal's eyes appear to glow. The eyes of cats, dogs, lemurs, lorises and bush-babies show up pink or pale green and tiny pairs of lights show where hunting spiders are lurking.

An intrinsic source of light is possessed by several beetles, notably the glow-worms and fireflies, but tropical click beetles also show a bright light. One American click beetle has two white lights at the front of the body and a reddish one on the abdomen, hence its local name of "Ford bug". The fireflies are responsible for most impressive light displays. They gather along the banks of tropical rivers by the million and flash in perfect synchrony for hour after hour.

Bats' echo location is adequate for high-speed navigation but competition from the birds with their accurate visual system has kept the bats nocturnal. Within this domain they have been remarkably successful. Because of the difficulty of observation, the importance of the bats is often not appreciated. There are hundreds of species in tropical forests, some of which roost and feed in huge flocks, and they have developed many ways of life. Apart from the familiar insect-eaters, there are the fruit bats or flying foxes, which have better vision and poorer echo location than other bats. They eat flowers and pollen as well as fruit, and some sip nectar. At dusk they take over from the many fruit- and nectar-eating birds. Other bats are carnivores, eating mice, lizards, birds, fish, other bats and even scorpions. No bat is a herbivore and the vampire is unique as a blood drinker.

By contrast, few birds have invaded tropical forests at night. The only competition that insectivorous bats face is from the nightjar and frogmouth family, and some of the owls. The owls are the most successful of night birds in terms of variety and adaptation. Their muffled plumage and sensitive eyes and ears make them very efficient hunters, but the bat hawk, one of the kites, hunts bats and swifts in the half light of dusk. The peculiar oil-bird, or guacharo, of northern South America and Trinidad, is the only nocturnal fruit-eating bird and it is related to the nightjars. It eats the fruit of palms and other trees, and retires into caves by day. To find its way to the ledges at the back of deep caves the oil-bird employs a form of echo location.

Above *When the grotesque nocturnal Papuan frogmouth, Podargus papuensis, opens its huge* colourful mouth it resembles a bright flower on a tree branch and insects are lured inside.

Right *Bats obtain a detailed picture of their surroundings from their reflected high-pitched sound waves. When an insect prey looms near to this little brown bat, Myotis lucifugus, it drops the pitch to locate it.*

Far right *Phyllostomus hastatus, an Old World horseshoe bat, has nose leaves that act as horns to focus its sounds into a sharp beam. Sweeping back and forth, it scans the surroundings up to a radius of 50 ft.*

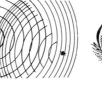

Below *At twilight the flying foxes, Pteropus seychellensis, fly off in search of fruit trees. The large eyes suggest that they depend on vision rather than a sonar sense. During the day they sleep, hanging upside-down.*

Above *Lucernuta, a luminous beetle in its larval stage, aptly called a firefly.*

Left *The light-producing organ's structure. The photocytes, stacked into rosettes and interconnected with nerves, contain the enzyme luciferin, which produces light when activated by nervous impulses.*

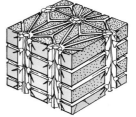

bove *The python, hondropython viridis, has ivities on either side of its out which are lined with* specially designed cells that can detect minute changes in radiant heat, thus guiding the snake unerringly to warm-blooded prey, up to 4 ft away, in the pitch darkness of the forest at night.

Above *In full cry the giant tree frog, Hyla maxima, is dwarfed by the balloon-like vocal sac which amplifies* the vibrations of its vocal chords. Giant tree frogs also have excellent hearing and the loud nightly calls of the males appeal to females of the same species and make them amenable to mating.

Fliers and gliders

It is a great advantage for an arboreal animal to be able to jump from one tree to the next without descending to the ground. This saves time and the animal avoids running the gauntlet of predators. Expert leapers include tree frogs, squirrels and many primates.

The basic requirements for leaping are powerful back legs for springing, a tenacious grip when landing and good eyesight for judging distances. The next stage is to increase the leaping range by adding wings. The leapers now become gliders and they can roam farther in search of food.

Gliders cannot achieve speeds of more than nine miles per hour and would make easy targets had they not largely adopted a crepuscular or nocturnal habit; the difficulties of seeing the way clearly through the gathering shadows are outweighed by the protection gained from fast, day-flying birds of prey.

The initial development of the gliding habit may have been a response not just to greater predator pressure, but also to higher water levels, and the success of gliders may be measured by their numbers and diversity.

Faced with the problem of developing flight surfaces reptiles, amphibians and mammals have arrived at several different solutions; most of them can be seen in the forests of South East Asia and they are an excellent example of evolution finding several means to the same end. Common features of the gliding animals are flaps or membranes of skin to provide the wing surface, and a long bushy tail for control. The flying snake and the flying frog are exceptional in that they have neither.

One of the commonest gliders in the South East Asian rain forest is the flying lizard or flying dragon, of which there are more than a dozen species. As with all these animals, flying is a misnomer because flying lizards are in reality gliders. They must descend to the ground to lay their eggs in the soil. The flying gecko, however, has overcome this problem by gluing its eggs to tree trunks. The gecko's "wings" consist of a flap of skin running around the body, most apparent on the belly and as a scalloped fringe decorating the tail. Webbing between the digits also increases the effective flight surface.

Four kinds of mammals have taken up gliding. The flying phalangers are marsupials living mainly in the eucalyptus forests of eastern Australia, but one—the sugar glider—extends north to New Guinea. As with other gliding mammals, the phalangers have a flap of skin, the patagium, which is stretched between fore- and hindlegs. Early zoologists mistook them for the very similar flying squirrels, of which there are nearly forty species; two of them North American and the rest South East Asian, one of them ranging across to Sweden.

In the larger species the patagium is strengthened by a rod of cartilage attached to the wrist, and is equipped with muscles to alter its tension to control the glide. Flying squirrels can turn around and return to the point of take-off and they are reported to ride air currents, covering several miles before landing. The moment they do land, they run round the tree trunk to position themselves facing downwards, ready for immediate flight from any lurking predator.

The scaly-tails take the place of the flying squirrels in the rain forests of West Africa. They also have a cartilaginous stiffening rod, but the web of skin is extended from the hindlimbs to the tail, as it is in the colugo, or flying lemur (a bad name: again, it does not fly and it is not a lemur). The colugo lives in South East Asia and rivals the flying squirrels in gliding prowess. The female does not build a nest but carries her baby everywhere. When resting, she hangs from the underside of a branch, providing the baby with a comfortable ready-made hammock.

The true fliers—the insects, bats and birds—very probably began as gliders who had the good fortune to develop wings that could be harnessed to powerful muscles. True flight has enabled some of them to explore fully the forest's three-dimensional structure.

The forest habitat offers the flying and gliding animals one resource not available elsewhere—a continuous supply of fruit and flowers. And they take full advantage of it. The canopy is the home of a multitude of colourful fruit-eating and nectar-supping species. Many of the birds are not strong fliers, but their rounded wings give manoeuvrability. Here, in the canopy, are the flashy humming-birds (duller coloured ones live at lower levels), the fruit pigeons, parrots, birds of paradise, toucans, hornbills, tanagers and cotingas.

The outsize bills of the toucans and hornbills may be for reaching out to fruit hanging from the tips of slender twigs, but this does not explain why they should be so ornate. The casque on the bill of the helmeted hornbill has been its downfall. It has a thin sheath of ivory called ho-ting by the Chinese, who prize it highly for decorative snuff bottles. Hornbills particularly have been victimized for their enormous bills, used in Malaysia in attractive ear ornaments and by certain African tribes in scarification rituals.

An abundance of food allows the males of the fruit-eating birds to lead an easy life and frees them from family duties. These are left to the drab-feathered females while the males expend their energies in elaborate courtship. They gather at traditional sites, called courts or arenas, where they flaunt their brilliant plumages at each other and promiscuously seek to attract mates. The birds of paradise carry this to extremes by indulging in a riot of evolution as they become bedecked in elaborate plumes, sprays and epaulettes. They were first brought to Europe early in the sixteenth century by the survivors of Magellan's expedition to South America, and the Court of Spain was so impressed that it decided such birds could have come only from Paradise. So fantastic are some of the plumages that naturalists examining specimens imported for the nineteenth-century feather trade were convinced that they were fakes, the manufacture of artificial plumes then being a common trick

Right *The flying squirrel is an accomplished glider, although it has a less extensive flying membrane than the colugo and the scaly-tails. Pushing off primarily with its back legs, the flying squirrel balances itself by spreading its legs to stretch the flying membrane to its maximum: it then uses its thick bushy tail as an airbrake to bring it into a vertical attitude—in effect a stalling position—before making a gentle, controlled "four-point" landing on a tree trunk. There are nearly 40 species of flying squirrel and they vary in size from the 5½-inch-long pygmy flying squirrel of Borneo to the 4-foot-long giant flying squirrel, a richly coloured cat-sized creature which is found all over South East Asia.*

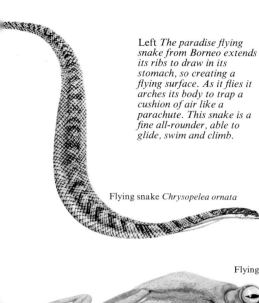

Left *The paradise flying snake from Borneo extends its ribs to draw in its stomach, so creating a flying surface. As it flies it arches its body to trap a cushion of air like a parachute. This snake is a fine all-rounder, able to glide, swim and climb.*

Flying snake *Chrysopelea ornata*

Ribs when motionless

Ribs extended in flight

Flying frog *Rhacophorus nigropalmatus*

Left *The Borneo flying frog has long extensively webbed toes and slightly fringed forelimbs that give it considerable buoyancy while gliding. In mid-air it assumes a rigid posture quite unknown in terrestrial frogs.*

ight *The flying gecko's ain lifting surfaces are rapped around the belly ke an outgrown aistcoat, until the gecko ves off a tree. Air essure then forces them en, converting the gecko to a rather inefficient glider.*

Flying gecko *Pytchozoon kuhli*

Above *Despite their very different coloured plumage these Eclectus parrots (male left, female right) belong to the same species; differences are quite common as male birds are often highly coloured, having to win their future mate by fine bright performances.*

Left *The Malaysian flying lizard lives on tree trunks. It glides on flaps of skin supported by extended hinged ribs. As the lizard launches itself, the ribs swing out, tautening like an open umbrella. Because of their graceful flight and brightly coloured wings, these lizards have been mistaken for butterflies.*

HO-TING AND HEAD-DRESSES

The casque of the helmeted hornbill, valued for its thin ivory sheath known as *ho-ting*, has been decorated with peacock feathers and worked into a fine carving by 19th-century Chinese craftsmen (*below*). In Papua–New Guinea birds are also hunted for their brilliantly coloured plumage, displayed in this extravagant head-dress (*right*) made from bird of paradise feathers.

Primates

The human species is one of the few primates to have taken to living on the ground, and this makes observation of our arboreal relatives rather difficult. Most observers are rewarded only with tantalizing glimpses of creatures high up in the foliage. Shaking branches and chattering calls, accompanied sometimes by a shower of half-eaten fruit and the flash of a body as a monkey leaps across a gap in the canopy, may be the only signs of activity.

Primates exploit the three-dimensional structure of the forest to its full extent. Troops of shy gorillas amble along the African forest floor—following the senior male, who may be six feet tall and weigh 450 pounds—climbing only to find a perch for the night, or if danger threatens. Spider monkeys enjoy the dizzy heights of the tree-tops in the South American jungle, complacent in the security conferred by a fifth limb, the extraordinarily sensitive and strong prehensile tail, which can either support them as they eat, hanging upside down, or be used to reach for nuts and small edible fruits while they hold on with their hands and feet.

The variety of primates, from the small five-inch-tall tarsier to the massive gorilla, is evidence of their adaptability and their capacity for taking any habitat offered to them, often by dividing it up to avoid direct competition. Prosimians, based mainly in Madagascar, move freely through the forests during the day. The mysterious aye-aye operates at night, however, relying on its fine senses of smell and hearing to locate insects under tree bark before hooking them with its incredibly long middle finger.

The absence of prosimians in South America has encouraged the douroucouli to acquire the nocturnal habit, which frees it from the need to match the acrobatic one-upmanship of the spider and woolly monkeys. The douroucouli's niche is occupied during the day by prosimian-like marmosets. In South East Asia, the canopy is the home of brachiating gibbons that swing confidently arm over arm from branch to branch in carefree ease, bridging gaps with prodigious jumps.

A little lower, in the middle storeys, the orang-utan travels using hands and feet with equal facility. Although it is a dexterous climber, the mature orang-utan, weighing perhaps 200 pounds, is too heavy to leap well and it crosses gaps between the tree crowns by seesawing the branch it is on until it can reach across and grab a branch from a neighbouring tree. Clearly, the means of locomotion is important in determining the distribution of primates.

The division of food resources is another aspect of the adaptability of primates. The African equatorial forests provide separate niches for five prosimians. The potto and the needle-clawed monkey feed side by side in the foliage, eating fruit and gums respectively. The angwantibo, the potto's lorisine relative, lives lower down and hunts insects, while its companion, Allen's bush-baby, enjoys fruit. Above them, Demidoff's bush-baby threads its way through lianas and leaves, also in search of fruit. The catholic tastes of primates result in considerable habitat overlap between species. Different species also co-operate with each other in giving general alarm calls on spotting a common enemy, such as the African crowned eagle.

The orang-utan, whose name means "man of the forest" in Malay, is the largest of the arboreal primates. It lives in a relatively even environment and is a solitary animal, moving only a few hundred yards a day to satisfy its hunger. In contrast, chimpanzees of the Ugandan forests search in large troops for ripening fruit, calling to each other to share particularly large finds.

Monkeys also find safety in numbers in defending their territory. In the dense foliage, sound is the most effective medium of communication, and threats bandied across boundaries ring through the forest as each troop proclaims its sovereignty.

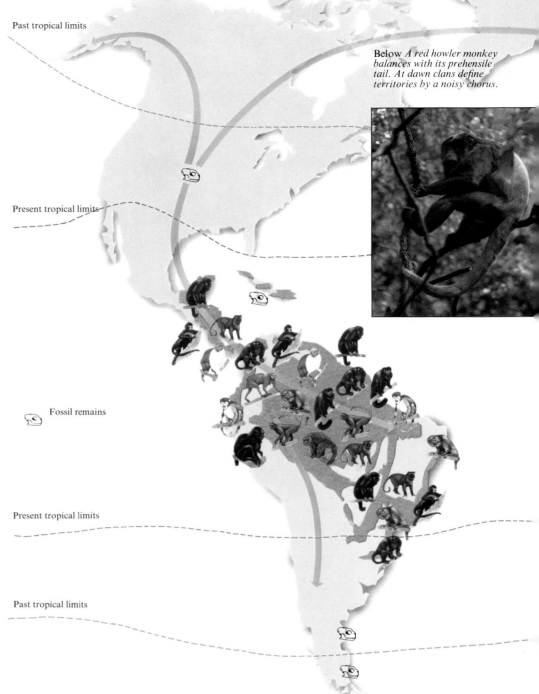

Past tropical limits

Present tropical limits

Fossil remains

Present tropical limits

Past tropical limits

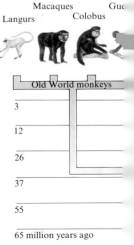

Below *A red howler monkey balances with its prehensile tail. At dawn clans define territories by a noisy chorus.*

CLASSIFICATION

This chart considers only the tropical forest primates. The primates are divided into four groups: the Old World monkeys, the apes, the New World monkeys and the prosimians. These groups and the extinct insectivore stem are all descended from a common stock. The prosimians evolved some 55 million years ago and it was not for another 20 million years that the true monkeys and apes emerged as groups with their own distinctive characteristics. Resemblances between tropical primates are due not only to shared ancestry but also to adaptations to similar environments.

Langurs Macaques Colobus Gue

Old World monkeys

3

12

26

37

55

65 million years ago

Above *The orang-utan is too bulky for life in the high canopy, although it climbs happily to pick fruit and raid wild bees' nests for honey.*

Above *The tiny tarsier is an agile jumper and its outsize eyes adapt it well to a nocturnal habit.*

bove *The ring-tail lemur fills niche left empty by the olation of Madagascar from ainland Africa.*

THE DISTRIBUTION OF PRIMATES

The primates have long been associated with the tropical forests. A wider distribution of primates, indicated by fossil finds, corresponds with the previous greater width of the tropical and subtropical belts.

The primates dispersed from their evolutionary birth place, thought to be in North America, crossing land bridges eastwards into Europe and west and south into Asia. Another land bridge linking Europe to Africa facilitated the colonization of Africa. North and South America were not at this time joined to each other, and migration south across the gap may have taken place by precarious rafting on floating masses of vegetation.

About forty million years ago, a drop in world temperature and the increasingly dry climate heralded a gradual shrinking of forests from the cooling polar regions to their present limits. This contraction forced the majority of primates into simultaneous retreat, committed as they were to arboreal life in the protective warmth of the forest.

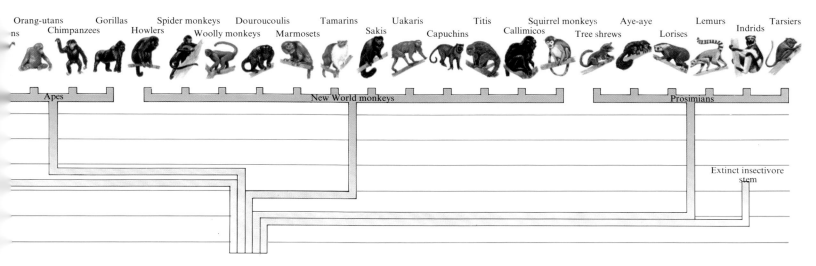

Orang-utans Gorillas Spider monkeys Douroucoulis Tamarins Uakaris Titis Squirrel monkeys Aye-aye Lemurs Tarsiers
ns Chimpanzees Howlers Woolly monkeys Marmosets Sakis Capuchins Callimicos Tree shrews Lorises Indrids

Apes New World monkeys Prosimians

Extinct insectivore stem

Forest people

Below *Men of the Baka tribe prepare to collect wild honey in the dark interior of their homeland in a Central African forest. They survive through an intimate knowledge of their environment. The honey is more easily* *extracted, for example, because they first wrap a special bark in leaves and haul it up the tree to the hive. The leaf parcel is then ignited and smoke issuing from the bark acts as a drug to tranquillize the bees.*

The people that live within the tropical rain forest have varying relationships with its mysterious and untameable nature. Some of them respect and worship the delicately balanced ecological system of their dark forest world; others have life-styles that involve cutting the forest back to create fields for their crops; and some attempt to harvest or destroy it.

Among those who live in harmony with the forest are the Baka people of Central Africa, known, because of their comparatively short stature, as pygmies. They still lead a traditional nomadic life, hunting and gathering in the forest for most of the year and living in semi-permanent camps set alongside their neighbours the Bantu, who are villager-agriculturists, for the rest. In exchange for Bantu-grown bananas, macabo and manioc—food that is not nutritionally essential but is greatly enjoyed—the Baka provide the meat and honey that they have collected from the forest. In addition, they assist the Bantu in their daily battle against the forest; seen by them as a fast-moving enemy, constantly threatening to overgrow their crops.

It is precisely the repetitive nature of the work involved to combat the daily growth of the forest that makes the Baka such poor and uninterested cultivators. Theirs is a philosophy of immediate return based on luck, knowledge of the forest and a great deal of skill. Daubed with a red dye, known as *ngélé*, from a tree *Pterocarpus soyauxii*, they hunt for game, which ranges from small animals such as duiker antelope to larger game such as elephant, pig and gorilla. Their economy is based on disposable commodities that can be obtained, manufactured and discarded instantly. Musical instruments, ropes, baskets for collecting fruits or honey, the materials for their leaf shelters and medicines can all be obtained from their surroundings.

By contrast, the Birhor of the Chota Nagpur plateau of central India—whose name in their own dialect means "the men of the jungle"—were also originally a hunting and gathering people, but they no longer survive with the same degree of self-sufficiency in their forest as the pygmies do in Africa. The Birhor trade such forest products as rope,

wooden vessels, honey and wax for rice an other grains at intertribal markets. The grains subsidize what would otherwise be a inadequate diet from the forest, where th game has been depleted.

The transition from a passive hunting an gathering relationship with the forest to on where it is transformed, tamed and used f agriculture must have spanned many thou sands of years. The Senoi Semai of centr Malaya represent the remnants of a very a cient population who are thought to have i habited South East Asia before the arrival the Malays and Chinese. They live by sla and burn agriculture, growing mixed crops small fields created in the rain forest, and th move to new areas after one or two years wh their land becomes less fertile. The Semai ha names for different kinds of forest growth a the tools necessary to clear each kind.

The forest-dwelling South American I dians, who have extreme reputations f either ferocity or passivity, share three chara teristics. Economically they all survive by combination of hunting, gathering and sla

Right *The shaman, who can be male or female, plays a central role—best described as that of a doctor-priest—in the culture of South American forest people. Believed to be in touch with the spirits, the shaman is familiar with the properties of various plants and uses drugs derived from them to induce a trance-like state whereby an illness can be diagnosed or cured.*

Left *A Baka boy felling a tree. The boys make footholds in the bark and support themselves with a liana harness, which is tied round their waist and the tree trunk. Usually, they learn how to fell trees by practising on trees with ready-made footholds prepared by the older men.*

nd burn horticulture, involving the culti-
ation of cassava (manioc). Socially, they
roup themselves in small village populations
nd culturally they are governed by their
elief in "witch doctors" or shamans who use
allucinogens to diagnose and cure illness.

The shaman may be male or female and is
elieved to be in touch with the spirits. Hal-
icinogens are essential to the trance state in
/hich this contact is made and many differ-
nt local plants supply the drugs. A simple
bacco is used in some areas; *ayahuasa*, a
orest creeper, is used by the Sharanahua
ndians of eastern Peru, the Jivaro of the
cuadorian Amazon and many others, while
atema, made from a local vine, is used by
ie Jivaro and other tribes.

Many South American Indian tribes, such
s the Sharanahua, are now threatened with
xtinction, or are already reduced in numbers
s a result of the destruction of their forests
nd the diseases brought by outsiders. How-
ver, shamanism and the necessary knowledge
f forest products is evident among the slum
wellers of Amazonian cities.

Above *The Baka people's dome-shaped shelters, mongolus, are built in large forest clearings. The stalks of leaves hooked on to a framework of bent saplings form the basic structure. This is then covered with dead leaves to camouflage it against dangerous animals and weighed down with logs for protection against winds.*

Right *A Birhor family in front of a temporary dwelling in the sal forests of Central India. They are nomadic hunter-gatherers and only manage to survive by supplementing their diet with rice, which they receive in exchange for forest products such as bark fibre rope, at intertribal markets. Here, the bartered rice can be seen being parched on a date palm mat.*

Explorers

There is a romantic ring to the word explorer that conjures up a picture of human endurance and enterprise. No unknown area has ever been a place for the weak or fainthearted, but the teeming density of the trackless forest still proves as stern a test as any. Seemingly impenetrable, the dripping trees and tangled undergrowth of the tropical rain forest exude gloomy menace to those who are unfamiliar with them. To the first explorers it was a "green hell": the domain of stinging insects and deadly reptiles—a place where clothes rotted in the humidity or were eaten by ants.

The first Europeans to brave the dangers of the tropical rain forest were driven by lust for its possible riches as much as by any curiosity. In the first half of the fifteenth century, Portuguese captains—inspired by their Prince Henry "the Navigator"—began to sail the west coast of Africa and penetrated far south of the Equator in their search for gold, slaves and the mythical kingdoms. Like most early explorers, the Portuguese penetrated the forest area along the lines of the rivers rather than actually hacking through the vegetation. They achieved much in the cause of mapping Africa but gained little knowledge of the interior because those who entered it, such as Vallarte in 1448 or Diogo Cão in 1485, often never returned. Despite these setbacks and the discomforts of West Africa's fever coast the Portuguese managed, by courtesy of friendly local rulers, to maintain a presence there.

If booty was the magnet for the Portuguese in Africa, it was even more so for the men who first explored the great forests of South America. Wild courage and frenzied cruelties characterized the conquistadores as they struggled to carve their share from the land that had yielded the wealth of the Aztecs and Incas.

The first major penetration of the great rain forests of the Amazon was made by a small party under a tough brutal Spaniard named Francisco de Orellana. They were in search of gold as well as cinnamon trees that would yield a spice highly prized in Europe. Starting in 1541, Orellana completed a nightmarish seventeen-month journey from the Andes to the mouth of the Amazon during which his men sometimes had to live on toads and serpents and constantly fought with the forest Indians. They even claimed to have been attacked by white female warriors like the Amazons of the ancient world, but subsequent expeditions failed to encounter these women, after whom the river was named.

Until the eighteenth century exploitation was the only motive for exploration. But with the Enlightenment a new mood of scientific curiosity led a French mathematician by the name of Charles Marie de la Condamine to sail to South America, charged with the task of making measurements to determine the shape of the Earth. During this eight-year expedition La Condamine encountered rubber, which had been spoken of by Europeans in the seventeenth century, and was the first man to bring it back to Europe. He was followed by a series of distinguished botanists

Above *A passionate scientist and geographer, La Condamine's most famous discovery was the rubber tree, Hevea brasiliensis, which caused a sensation at the time, although it was not to be exploited until later.*

Above *Roosevelt wrote of the forest beside the River of Doubt, now the Rio Roosevelt: "The lofty and matted forest rose like a green wall on either hand . . . looped and twisted vines hung like great ropes."*

Above *Humboldt's raft, equipped with food from the forest. "At each change of place, new forms present themselves to the traveller, who, however, often finds that he cannot reach the blossoms of trees whose leaves and ramifications had previously arrested his attention."*

The Amazon rain forest, one of the greatest challenges to explorers, could at first only be traversed by the rivers. Because of the density of the riverside undergrowth, early impressions of the forest portray it as an unruly jungle, whereas in the interior, where sunlight cannot penetrate, the forest floor is actually bare. From the watercourses, however, early explorers could observe the Amazon's animals coming to drink.

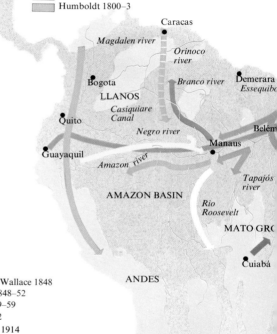

Orellana 1541
La Condamine 1735
Humboldt 1749
Humboldt 1800–3

Caracas
Magdalen river
Orinoco river
Bogota
Branco river
Demerara
LLANOS
Essequibo
Casiquiare Canal
Quito
Negro river
Belém
Guayaquil
Manaus
Amazon river
Tapajós river
AMAZON BASIN
Rio Roosevelt
MATO GRO
ANDES
Cuiabá

Bates and Wallace 1848
Wallace 1848–52
Bates 1849–59
Bates 1852
Roosevelt 1914
Fawcett 1925

Right *Alfred Russel Wallace was an enthusiastic Darwinist who, in the company of Henry Walter Bates, started exploring Amazonia with the aim of "solving the problem of the origin of the species". The teeming virgin forest was, and still is, a naturalist's paradise. Bates's discovery of the phenomenon of mimicry among butterflies (some of his sketches of butterfly species are illustrated below) is now a biological study in itself.*

4.—*Leptalis Theonoë, var. Ega.*

5.—*Leptalis Theonoë, var. Ega.*

6.—*Leptalis Theonoë, var. Ega.*

7.—*Leptalis Theonoë, var. St. Paulo.*

8.—*Leptalis Theonoë, var. Ega.*

9.—*Leptalis Theonoë, var. St. Paulo.*

6a.—*Ithomia Illinissa.*

Above *"Inviting my friendly natives to my aid, we buckled on to the two largest canoes while the weaker Wanguana cut a road through the forest." Where the Congo was too difficult to navigate H. M. Stanley continued his exploration of the region through the forest.*

Right *Today explorers tend to be more interested in lost peoples than in lost cities, but the dangers remain the same. Michael Rockefeller never returned from an anthropological expedition he undertook to the Ismat people in Papua-New Guinea in 1961.*

Right *Colonel Fawcett bids adieu to Brazilian "camaradas" at Dead Horse Camp, the farthest recorded point in his expedition into the Mato Grosso. He was probably murdered by Indians.*

who were despatched by the Spanish authorities. Father Mutis, the naturalist who set out in 1760, obtained *Aristolochia*—the snakebite remedy—and saw *Cinchona*, the tree whose bark yields quinine (see pages 212–213). He, and others, were to be succeeded by two of the greatest names in the history of exploration—Humboldt and Darwin.

From 1799 to 1803 Friedrich Heinrich Alexander, Baron von Humboldt, always accompanied by the French physician and botanist Aimé Bonpland, explored South America in an odyssey of thousands of miles through uncharted territory. His interests extended to every scientific discipline from geology to zoology, and anthropology to meteorology. He confirmed the existence of a link between the drainage of the Orinoco and the Amazon and studied the plant and animal life with such care and detail that it took him twenty-one years to collate all the observations and data he collected.

The great Humboldt was swiftly followed by Charles Darwin, the most towering figure among natural historians. In 1832, on his famous voyage to the Galápagos Islands, which was to establish his belief in the evolution of species, Darwin made many stays on the South American mainland and observed: "The noise of the insects is so loud that it may be heard . . . several hundred yards from the shore; yet within the recesses of the forest a universal silence appears to reign."

The inspiration provided by Humboldt and Darwin firmly set forest exploration on a scientific path. Throughout the nineteenth century men from all walks of life, from the German Prince Maximilian of Wied-Neuwied to the humble English brewery clerk Henry Walter Bates, made collections of tens of thousands of specimens of flora and fauna. This activity cost some explorers—such as the Frenchman Jules Crevaux—their lives. Among the explorers of the African forest the ruthless hard-driving American journalist Henry Morton Stanley, who accomplished a hazardous voyage up the Congo, was an exception amid scientists because he was a straightforward publicist.

The twentieth century has provided its share of the courageous and the curious who have ventured into danger and hardship behind the dense green curtain. Perhaps the most remarkable was former US president and "rugged individualist" Theodore Roosevelt, whose exploration party lost two of its members in 1914 along the River of Doubt in South America. Indeed, tragedy has never been far away for the explorer. Even the greatest and most experienced explorers who penetrated such forests faced it. The knowledgeable English surveyor Percy Fawcett disappeared with his entire expedition in 1925 as he searched for a lost city deep in the Amazonian hinterland. Michael Rockefeller, son of the former New York State governor, was in all probability killed in Papua-New Guinea while undertaking an anthropological investigation to the Ismat people in 1961.

The rain forest dilemma

Below *One-fifth of all the water discharged into the oceans flows from the Amazon into the Atlantic and its basin and, at any one time, the Amazon basin holds two-thirds of the world's fresh water. The area stays so wet only because the same water that is transpired by the forest falls again as rain. If the forest were felled an ecosystem of exceptional diversity would be lost to us, the global water cycle severely affected and Amazonia might be a deser*

Just as the North American forests seemed endless to the early settlers, so the tropical rain forests appeared vast, impenetrable and inexhaustible. It was not until the problems of disease and transport were solved in the nineteenth century that man made an impact on the quality and extent of these forests.

As the world population increased and land and natural economic resources became more scarce, the rain forests came under increasing pressure. Today the rain forests are undoubtedly retreating, whether it is ranchers in the Amazon, shifting agriculturists and loggers in South East Asia, or encroaching deserts in Africa. It has been estimated that every year more than thirty-seven million acres are cut down—an area of forest as big as a football field disappears every second.

In recent years there has been much debate, argument and counter-argument regarding the future of the tropical forests. Much of this has centred on the role of the forests in the global ecology and their place in the world cycles of oxygen, carbon and water.

As the forests grew larger and more complex over millions of years, they took carbon dioxide out of the air and gave back the oxygen that we now breathe. In return, they stored the carbon in their trunks, roots, branches and leaves. About two-thirds of all the oxygen produced on Earth comes from land vegetation and one-third comes from the tropical forests.

But they only produce as much oxygen as they consume, for, because they are climax ecosystems, they do not need to accumulate any more carbon. The loss of these forests would therefore have a negligible effect on the atmosphere's oxygen content. In fact, if these forests are cut down and there is regrowth of young natural or planted trees, the production of atmospheric oxygen will increase.

But there is another side to the coin. When such forests are felled at least half of the wood contained within them is burned as fuel or in slash and burn agriculture. The carbon that was once locked up in the forests is converted into carbon dioxide in the atmosphere. Carbon dioxide acts like a gigantic insulation jacket, storing the heat from the Earth that would otherwise escape into space. Over the last twenty years the level of carbon dioxide in the atmosphere has grown by five per cent as a result of the burning of wood and fossil fuels such as coal and oil. One theory suggests that if this trend continues, the world will become warmer, the polar ice caps will melt, and cities such as London and Washington D.C. will be submerged as ocean levels rise.

Alternatively, it is argued that as more particulate matter from human activity, and natural phenomena such as volcanic eruptions, enters the atmosphere, so less heat from the Sun is able to penetrate and so th temperature will fall. Both theories are un confirmed but both need serious consideration

The tropical rain forests are also at th centre of another major natural cycle—that c water. The Amazon alone discharges into th Atlantic one-fifth of all water discharged int the oceans, and its basin contains at any on time two-thirds of all the world's fresh wate The disappearance of the Amazon rain fore could not only have untold consequences fc the global water cycle, it could also caus considerable climatic changes. Since th Amazon basin only stays so wet because th same water is transpired by the forest an then falls again as rain, the loss of those fo ests could possibly turn this huge region into much drier place. Even on a smaller scale so erosion and leaching of the soil are majc consequences of unplanned logging.

If it were possible to throw a fence aroun the tropical forests in order to conserve the as the world's air conditioner and water co troller, there would be little conflict. But mo tropical forests lie in developing countrie

Below *Partly as a result of the modern realization of the immense economic and ecological importance of the long-term health of the rain forest, there is now an increasing interest among the tropical nations in its conservation.*

Governments can take the initiative, exemplified by the creation of the Quezon National Forest Park in the Philippines, by developing the forest as a recreational facility, which, incidentally, also provides a tourist attraction.

Above The wild plants of the tropical rain forests present a genetic bank on which scientists can draw. Agriculturists can breed new strains of food crops and new medicines are being discovered regularly. The rosy periwinkle contains alkaloids capable of curing some forms of cancer.

whose cash economies are dependent on the forest and its products. It is unfair to expect these countries to forgo their economic development in deference to predictions of global disaster while the reality of everyday poverty and hunger still exist.

It is unlikely, however, that the rain forests could ever be destroyed totally. They have remarkable powers of regeneration and re-colonization, as farmers who fight a daily battle to keep their fields and crops free of weeds will testify. Vegetation of some kind springs up, but a secondary forest of low-grade commercial timbers will not provide economic returns comparable with those from the hardwoods, such as mahogany and ebony, that exist in the primary forest.

The failure of farming schemes in Brazil (see pages 80–81) and the success of the Jari project, where fast-growing pines were planted on sites occupied by natural forests (see pages 50–51), have shown that care and adequate research must be realized before any major project is undertaken to attempt sustainable ways of simultaneously harvesting wood and food from the forest. Forestry is not incompatible with food production; the latest research in agroforestry has shown that it may be far more economical in the future to pro-

duce both food and wood at the same time, modelling our cultivation system on the way in which the natural forest survives in these hot and humid areas.

Besides their role as food and timber producers these forests have yet another, albeit passive, role. They contain so many different species of plant that they may still house new plants of economic importance, such as the rosy periwinkle, *Vinca rosea*, which contains alkaloids capable of curing some forms of cancer. Rubber was just one plant that was snatched from the ragged confusion of the Amazon rain forest and has since become the kingpin of the economy of South East Asia. Many more may remain to be discovered.

The tropical rain forests also act as a gene bank that is an insurance policy for world agriculture. Cultivated plants may fall prey to pests and diseases that make it imperative to breed a new variety. Plant breeders often must return to the forest to find a wild variety so that resistant strains can be bred.

The governments of Costa Rica and Sarawak have already laid down firm conservation policies, but throughout the rain forest regions such policies, whereby forest conservation is integrated with timber production and agriculture, need to be extended.

TEMPERATE WOODLANDS

. . . Palpable spring indeed, or the indications of it. . . . The sibilant murmur of a pretty stiff breeze now and then through the trees. Then a poor little dead leaf, long frost-bound, whirls from somewhere up aloft in one wild escaped freedom-spree in space and sunlight, and then dashes down to the waters, which hold it closely and soon drown it out of sight. The bushes and trees are yet bare, but the beeches have their wrinkled yellow leaves of last season's foliage largely left, frequent cedars and pines yet green, and the grass not without proofs of coming fulness. And over all a wonderfully fine dome of clear blue, the play of light coming and going, and great fleeces of white clouds swimming so silently.

WALT WHITMAN *The Gates Opening* 1891–92

The ecosystem

Because the temperate forests grow in the moist and moderate climate that is especially favourable to man and his agricultural pursuits, the woodlands of the northern hemisphere have been profoundly changed by the establishment of permanent clearings for settlements and farming. Even in relatively recently settled North America little undisturbed temperate deciduous forest remains; but from what is left their original character can be pieced together.

The original world-wide distribution of the temperate woodlands is beyond doubt, however. They ranged over the greater part of central and western Europe north of the Alps and the Pyrenees, and eastwards across Russia in a belt between the northern coniferous forests and the southern steppes, dying out towards the Urals. They re-appeared in the Amur region, in parts of central China and in Japan. In North America they were best developed on either side of the Appalachians, between the Atlantic Coast and the Mississippi River and north to the Great Lakes.

It is somewhat puzzling why deciduous temperate forests are so widely distributed in the northern hemisphere, for areas in the southern hemisphere that enjoy a similar climate are dominated by temperate evergreen trees. Perhaps in the distant past the broadleaved trees, during their spread into the northern regions, may have developed the deciduous habit due to a prolonged period of seasonal drought.

The climatic conditions under which these temperate forests flourish vary considerably in terms of mean annual temperatures and the seasonality of rainfall and day length. Despite this their structure is remarkably similar, for although the variety of species is wide, the same genera are often found world-wide.

Large trees such as oaks and beeches form the canopy with lesser trees such as maples and birches in a secondary layer, beneath which dogwoods, hawthorns and hollies shade a ground flora of remarkable diversity and a soil nurtured by the seasonal leaf fall. The trees in these forests are mainly deciduous. They divest themselves of their leaves during the winter period when cold would damage them and when wind, by resistance from this foliage, would break the branches or even fell whole trees. In addition, they store their next year's leaves and flowers in well-protected buds.

The North American and east Asian forests contain a great many more species than those in Europe and west Asia. This is probably due, at least as far as North America is concerned, to the orientation of the main mountain ranges. In North America they run north–south and in Europe east–west. It would therefore have been much simpler for trees migrating north after the last glaciation to move up the valleys in America than to cross the mountain ranges as they had to in Europe (see pages 26–27).

There are so many species in North America that three main climax types of forest can be recognized. In the north the American beech, *Fagus grandifolia*, and the sugar maple, *Acer saccharum*, tend to dominate in mixture with some coniferous species; in the southeast various oaks, such as chestnut oak, *Quercus montana*, and white oak, *Q. alba*, are the main dominants. Farther west, red oak, *Q. borealis*, and black oak, *Q. velutina*, are found in mixture with shagbark hickory, *Carya ovata*, and other members of that genus.

In Europe the species mix is much less varied but the same genera generally predominate. The two oaks, *Quercus robur* and *Q. petraea*, the two beeches, *Fagus sylvatica* and *F. orientalis*, sycamore, *Acer pseudoplatanus*, and birch, *Betula pendula*, are the main trees. In Asia the same genera appear with oaks such as *Quercus dentata* and *Q. mongolica*, beeches such as *Fagus japonica* and *F. longipetiolata* and birches including *Betula ermanii*.

Around the world these forests, so similar in character, have seen man multiply and encroach upon them; for not only are the soils beneath them—built up over aeons of time—particularly suitable for agriculture, but the timber produced by their greatest trees is paramount in those qualities of strength and beauty of texture that civilized communities have always sought. No wonder that these forests have witnessed so much clearance, while at the same time being celebrated in all the human cultures that have benefited from them for thousands of years.

Right A profile of a typical deciduous forest in North Carolina, eastern United States. The trees form a vertical pattern. The upper strata—mainly oaks, hickories and some pines—reach a height of 100ft or more, dominating the community by their shading effect (below). Beneath these dominants there is a layer of smaller shade-tolerant trees, typically oaks, maples and dogwoods, and below these, only a few feet above the ground, is a layer of shrubby junipers and arrow-woods with herbaceous flowering plants growing between them. Saplings of either the dominant or understorey species may appear in any of the lower strata, passing through on their way to maturity. The ground is often covered with mosses and lichens.

WORLD DISTRIBUTION

The principal temperate deciduous forests are found in eastern Europe, North America and Asia. The warm temperate forests are found also on the eastern sides of the continents, but in lower latitudes, where there is a Mediterranean climate, broadleaved evergreen trees flourish. It is therefore thought that the deciduous habit may have been developed as a response to a prolonged drought in the north millions of years ago.

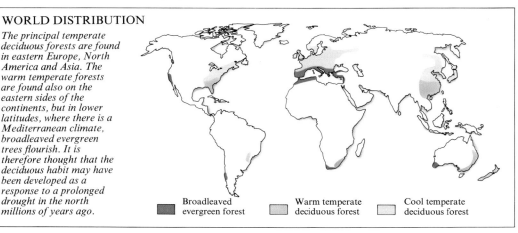

Broadleaved evergreen forest

Warm temperate deciduous forest

Cool temperate deciduous forest

Above *Tree roots penetrate deep to collect minerals and nutrients. Every autumn leaves fall to the ground, forming a thick layer of debris and providing food and shelter for small animals, fungi and bacteria. The bacteria and fungi decompose the litter layer into dark organic humus, thus replenishing the soil with the vital nutrients used up by the trees. The soil also contains earthworms and insects, which maintain fertility by aerating and mixing the humus and soil.*

The trees

Of all the many thousands of tree species found in the temperate forests of the northern hemisphere the oaks are probably the best known. Although there are hundreds of oaks, *Quercus* spp., each with aberrations as to size and exact shape, these trees have one constant feature—the bearing of egg-shaped nuts, or acorns, borne in cups covered with scales.

Some species, the red oaks of north-east America for example, turn a glorious scarlet in autumn; others, such as the European oaks, are more modest in their autumn tints but superb in their timber quality and immensely long-lived. They are the dominant trees of the great deciduous forests of western and central Europe wherever the soil is deep and fertile.

On drier soils, and usually on those with a high lime content, beech trees, *Fagus* spp., often form pure forests. Although some eight different species are found in the beech forests from North America to Japan, the differences between them are small. All are stately trees with broad, flat, bright green leaves that turn a rich golden-brown in autumn, leaving the smooth grey trunks standing in a russet forest floor almost bereft of all other plants, so thick is the summer canopy. The timber of the beeches is smooth-grained and easily worked for turnery, flooring and many other uses.

The twenty-six hornbeam species, *Carpinus* spp., often accompany the beeches, although the hornbeam is a slightly smaller tree with thicker oval, toothed-margined leaves and with winged fruits borne in bunches. The most noticeable feature of these trees, however, is the deeply fluted trunk, often oval in section, containing a very hard wood once used for cogs and gears in old watermills.

The ashes, *Fraxinus* spp., of which there are more than sixty species, are as large as the oaks and beeches and better formed as timber trees. All of them have large, compound leaves that emerge from the very conspicuous black-brown buds late in spring and fall early in autumn. The purple flowers come out before the leaves, giving way to bunches of winged seeds, or "keys", that hang on the tree all winter. The ash is usually found in rather open forest and on fertile soils with a considerable lime content. Their rough-barked pale grey trunks contain a tough elastic timber used for making hockey sticks, tool handles and, at one time, for the spokes of horse-drawn carriage wheels.

Rarely forming pure or dominant stands, but more often scattered in the forest, are the eighteen species of elm, *Ulmus* spp. They are large trees with lop-sided, oval, rather rough leaves and they bear winged seeds in great profusion, although many species reproduce themselves mainly from root suckers. When leafless, the crowns have an almost smoky appearance, so dense and fine are the twigs at the branch ends. The timber in the often bristle-spattered trunks is very durable in damp conditions and is used for coffins and outside coverings for buildings as well as for the manufacture of furniture.

On the northern fringes of the temperate forests, where they merge with the coniferous belt, a large assortment of willows, *Salix* spp., poplars, *Populus* spp., and birches, *Betula* spp., cover large areas. Most willows are small trees, often only shrubs and sometimes sprawling dwarfs, associated with the damper parts of the forest and near rivers.

The poplars, particularly the aspens, *P. tremula* and *P. tremuloides*, mingle with the conifers and early in their life often fare better than their coniferous rivals in the high latitudes. Usually found growing along watercourses and in marshy areas, some of the poplars develop into large trees, especially the black cottonwood, *P. trichocarpa*, of northwest America and the black poplar, *P. nigra*, of Europe. Their white, rather soft timber, not suitable for large timbers or planks, is used for pulping and for making matches.

Except for the dwarf species in the coniferous zone the birches are graceful trees. Most of them support white paper-like bark flecked with black patches, and the crowns of slender, cascading twigs combine to give these trees a uniquely colourful and elegant appearance in the drab winter of the temperate forests.

The maples, *Acer* spp., are of great economic importance and very numerous in the forests of eastern North America, where they provide most of the spectacular colours in autumn, and in Asia, where their leaf forms and bark colourings are strikingly varied. In Europe, however, there are only three species in the temperate forests.

The silver maple, *A. saccharinum*, and the big-leaf maple, *A. macrophyllum*, of North America are large, spreading trees. The sugar maple, *A. saccharum*, is tapped for maple syrup. The hardy and wind-firm sycamore, *A. pseudoplatanus*, of Europe—perhaps the largest of all maples—grows in exposed places where few other trees thrive, producing an excellent fine-grained white timber. The snake-barked maple, *A. hersii*, and the paper-barked maple, *A. griseum*, of eastern Asia add colour to the forest with their special displays. The downy maple, *A. palmatum*, of Japan, with its multiplicity of leaf forms and colours, has

Oaks
English oak *Quercus robur*
There are more than 800 oak species, some deciduous, some evergreen and all varying in size and shape. North American species are divided into red oaks and black oaks.

Maples
Sugar maple *Acer saccharum*
The maples comprise a genus of more than 200 species distributed through North America, Europe and Asia. The sugar maple leaves take on brilliant red and yellow tints in autumn.

Beeches
Common beech *Fagus sylvatica*
Eight species of beech occur in the temperate woodlands. They prefer dry limy soils and usually form fairly dense stands. The common beech frequently reaches a height of more than 100 ft.

Hornbeams
European hornbeam *Carpinus betulus*
There are 26 species of hornbeam, ranging in height from the 100 ft European hornbeam to the American hornbeam, C. caroliniana, at 40 ft. They have deeply fluted trunks and often grow with beeches.

Poplars
Eastern cottonwood *Populus delto*
Like their close relatives the willow, and birches, the poplars are found in the northern parts of the temperate woodlands, frequently mingled with conifers.

brought the distinction of this genus to many gardens in the temperate world.

Most of the trees mentioned serve the forest and its wildlife in their own particular ways, but man is also served by them. Some are simply beautiful, others provide timber and yet others, while doing these things, also supply food. The cherries, *Prunus* spp., bedecked with springtime blossom on the forest edges, bear palatable fruit before colouring in autumn, like the maples, and carry a sweet-scented timber in their smooth red trunks. The chestnuts, *Castanea* spp., produce sweet, edible (when cooked) nuts held in prickly burrs amongst the canopy's long, toothed leaves. And the walnuts, *Juglans* spp., are bearers of both a beautifully marked, valuable timber and a much esteemed nut, convoluted and brain-like encased in a shell wrapped round with green, fleshy pith. Hickories, *Carya* spp., are closely related to the walnuts and many, such as the pecan, *C. illinoensis*, produce edible nuts. The timber from the twenty-two or so species is similar to that of ash and is also used for purposes where a combination of strength and elasticity is required. Confined to North America and China, hickories form extensive climax forests with oaks.

Asia, too, has a great variety of temperate trees, including some in the Far East that closely resemble those in north-east America; these are not found in the intervening European and Asian zones. But be the species numerous or few, the associations of genera are similar, if not identical. This gives at once a sameness and a diversity which, combined with the changing scene as the seasons progress, makes these woodlands some of the most attractive in the world.

Southern magnolia
Magnolia grandiflora
Although many of the 35 species of magnolia are grown as ornamental trees all over the world, the southern magnolia forms climax forests in its natural range in the south-east United States. Like nearly all the other magnolias it has unusually large flowers and leaves. Magnolias can grow to 100 ft with trunks 15 ft in diameter.

Left *Because they thrive on chalky calcareous soils, the beeches can dominate temperate woodlands where other trees would fail. Moreover, the shade cast by the dense layers of flat foliage of a congregation of beech trees allows no light to penetrate for ground-dwelling plants, such as brambles or fungi, to grow.*

imes
mall-leaved lime *Tilia cordata* nown as limes in Europe and sswoods in the USA, there are) species of this genus in the rthern hemisphere.

Elms
American elm *Ulmus americana* There are about 20 elm species and they are found west of the Rockies and south of the Himalayas. They appear scattered through the forest rather than forming dense stands.

Birches
Paper birch *Betula papyrifera* Forty species of these short-lived trees and shrubs are found on the forest edge in poor soils in Europe, North America, China and Japan. All the birches have male and female catkins on the same tree.

Ashes
Green ash *Fraxinus pensylvanica* There are more than 60 species of ash and they have a world-wide distribution. They form fairly open stands in the forest and, like the beeches, prefer a chalky soil.

Hickories
Pignut hickory *Carya glabra* The hickories comprise a genus of 20 species and are related to the wingnuts and walnuts. They are found only in China and North America, where they form extensive climax forests with the oaks.

Winter

"The forest is dead. Long live the forest" could well be the cry as winter grips the temperate woodlands. The once leafy trees are mere skeletons; the once green and colourful forest floor is carpeted with myriad dead brown leaves. No insect hums, no bird sings, only the sighing of the wind in the tree-tops keeps silence at bay. Yet even leafless trees give considerable shelter from cold wind and frost and life is there, hidden and protected, waiting for the return of spring.

Wrapped in billions of waterproof bud-scales, next year's leaves and flowers lie secure. Beneath the blanket of dead leaves countless seeds lie safely hidden, each containing a tiny living embryo complete with enough food to start into growth. And in the top-soil, where the mice and the shrews have their burrows, all the little lower animals—the worms, the millipedes, the wood-lice—may go on short time as the temperature falls, but they are never really stilled in their work of returning to the soil those substances that were taken from it in the hectic summer.

In labyrinthine burrows beneath the tree roots badgers lie in warm beds of dry grass. They emerge only on warmer nights, the sows already quick with young. Squirrels, warm in their leafy homes wedged high up on tree forks, come down from time to time to take nuts from their carefully hidden caches. The resident woodland birds are there too. Silent and secretive for the most part, they forage in the leaf litter by day, sheltering in holes in trees, in cracks in the bark and in the dense shrub layer during the night.

This lessening of activity is universal throughout the forest as plants and animals take a rest from the feverish activity that attends the accomplishment of their primary objective—the reproduction and survival of the species. But the degree of inactivity during winter varies greatly from plant to plant and from creature to creature.

The leaves of the deciduous trees gradually

LIFE UNDERGROUND

In underground burrows, badgers and foxes remain warm and secure in winter, emerging only to hunt or forage for food. Other animals hibernate for the duration, allowing the winter to pass them by as they sleep. The North American woodchuck finds solace in burrows beneath the tree roots, while the European hedgehog and dormouse build nests of leaves and grass in the leaf litter, sheltered by the trees above. Even cold-blooded toads, snails and many insects seek refuge under stones or beneath fallen trees.

A layer of snow acts as insulation and those creatures beneath it—voles and shrews—dig out the worms, millipedes and woodlice that are continuing their role of breaking down the leaves and twigs divested from the trees and herbs. The herbs have now died back, retreating into the fleshy roots where they have stored up food during spring and summer. The seeds of annual herbs and the countless fruits of the trees lie in the leafy blanket of the forest floor, ready to germinate in spring.

Woodchuck
Marmota monax

European badger
Meles meles

Hedgehog
Erinaceus europaeus

Bank vole
Clethrionomy glareolus

Millipede
Tachypodojul

Common earthworm
Lumbricus terrestris

Purple
tuber

cease to function as food factories and fall to the ground. The twigs are left bare but for the buds set along their length, each containing a growing point and a set of new leaves. Underground in the roots, protected by the leaf litter and humus, and in the trunk wrapped in protective bark, stores of food substances will have been built up. So the trees, having reduced their resistance to the winter wind and the surfaces from which water can evaporate, sleep deeply although poised to burst into life as soon as the days begin to lengthen and the sun's warmth increases again.

The evergreen trees and shrubs—the hollies and the yews—retain most of their leaves, but they too have next year's replacement for foliage worn out by age or damaged in the winter,

together with their flowers, all safely in buds at the bases of the leaf stalks.

The herbs, which throughout the summer have carpeted the forest floor, either retreat below the ground as bulbs or as thick fleshy roots, or they die as winter approaches to leave their seed protected in the leaf litter, ready to give rebirth to the species in spring.

Most of the animals, glad of the protection given by the trees, remain active from their lairs and burrows throughout the winter and some, such as foxes and badgers, even leave the woods to forage for food in the open. A few, however, notably the European hedgehogs, dormice, and the North American woodchuck or groundhog, hibernate. They fall into a profound sleep in previously pre-

pared nests. During this hibernation their metabolism slows down, their body temperature drops and they remain torpid and cold to the touch for weeks on end, maintaining their slight hold on life by a slow absorption of fat accumulated during the summer and autumn plenty. The build-up of fat to an optimum level is a factor that triggers this remarkable life-saving mechanism in mammals and enables them to survive a period when their food supplies are scarce.

The low temperatures of winter reduce the metabolism of most cold-blooded woodland creatures, such as toads, snails and insects, to a level where normal activity is impossible. Some of them, including a few insects, hibernate as adults. This process is not so drastic as in mammals, provided they can find shelter, because their blood temperature is always that of the surrounding air. But most adult insects die leaving their eggs to await better times. In some cases they develop into a larval state and spend the winter as grubs and caterpillars hidden beneath dead bark or underground where they are protected from the weather and from the attentions of predators.

So, as the snowflakes fall and are filtered through the leafless trees to the forest floor, all is quiet and still where life once bubbled over. The footprints of a deer, the dog-like tracks of a fox, the sprinkling of feathers where an owl has seized a small bird may mark the pristine whiteness and show the passage of those larger creatures who must forage to live and who find the long winter night good cover for their hunting activities.

The staccato song of the European mistle thrush, the twittering of titmice, the strident warning notes of the blackbird and the harsh crowing of a pheasant may break the daytime stillness. But life in general is safely stored in the forest warehouse beneath and inside a roof and walls of trees that are neither too dense to exclude such sun as may sometimes shine, nor too sparse to ward off wind and frost.

Left Despite their forlorn and skeletal appearance, these sleeping broadleaved trees will be ready to burst into life again when winter winds and snow cease, and the warmth of spring approaches.

Right This wily red fox, Vulpes vulpes, expert at concealing its tracks, steals across a silent woodland scene with its prey. The unfortunate rabbit will feed the fox's vixen and their young. The red fox enjoys a wide range of food, feeding on insects, berries, snails, mice, frogs and birds, but in winter food is scarcer and hunting skill is at a premium. It is a versatile animal and the only canine to have survived in any number in a wild state over most of Europe. The red fox is also found in North America, Asia and in Africa, north of the Sahara.

Red squirrel
Sciurus vulgaris

Wood mouse
Apodemus sylvaticus

Common shrew
Sorex araneus

Oak
Quercus

Ash
Fraxinus

Hazel
Corylus

Beech
Fagus

Maple
Acer

Toad
Bufo bufo

Common wood-lice
Armadillidium vulgare

Common wood-lice
Porcellio scaber

Wild hyacinth
bulb

Wood anemone
rhizome

Wild arum
corm

Moth
pupae

Truffles
Tuber melanosporum

Spring

As February gives way to March the winter's grip on the forest begins to relax. Beneath the oaks lamb's-tail catkins on the European hazels lengthen and become dusted with golden pollen ready for transfer to the little pink female flowers by the still-icy east winds. At ground level the race is on to use the sun's increasing light and warmth before the trees come into leaf and cast their summer shade. The heart-shaped leaves of the lesser celandine—a member of the poppy family—are followed by their shining yellow flowers.

Patches of leafy herbs set in motion the gradual change from brown to green, and the star-shaped white blossoms of the wood anemones appear in constellations around the old oak trees. Primrose flowers emerge yellow from rosettes of crumpled leaves and just before the tree canopy closes in late April the bluebells flourish in unbroken drifts of blue.

Sunny days in early spring see the rooks at their tree-top nests repairing winter storm damage and pairing up once more amidst a cawing cacophony. Other resident birds, especially those that feed on winter berries and on worms and slugs, which can readily be found once frost has left the ground, start to stake out territories before February is half done. The songs of thrushes and blackbirds ring through the forest on mild evenings, and the nests of the mistle thrush appear as untidy bundles buffeted by gales in the low-down forks of the leafless trees. Blackbirds and song thrushes are not far behind in building their nests, placing them more discreetly in the evergreen ivy on the trees or in holly bushes.

As March draws to a close the first of the summer migrant birds announce their arrival from the warmer southern lands. These harbingers announce the start of an increasing flood of migrant birds that wells into the woodlands as the trees grow greener, all hurrying to find territories, mates and safe places for their nests. Among the first to arrive in Europe is the chiffchaff, which is followed a few days later by the willow warbler. The chiffchaff is earlier because it winters no farther south than the Mediterranean, but the warbler returns to the springtime forest after a winter spent south of the Sahara. From spring until autumn the temperate forest offers a rich and varied habitat for birdlife. The willow warbler conceals its nest in the tangled undergrowth of forest clearings, while other birds, such as the flycatchers, seek holes in trees undiscovered by resident titmice.

As spring advances the woodland rings to a swelling chorus of bird song at dawn as the sun starts to tint the eastern sky. A few sleepy, liquid notes from a robin may be followed by repetitious phrases from a song thrush and the mellow notes of a blackbird, mixed with the cooing of a dove. Soon a score of each will join the chorus in a crescendo in which the piping of a treecreeper, the shivering trill of the wood warbler and the bubbling notes of the blackcap will be lost as individual sounds, each bird proclaiming sovereignty over a patch of woodland where his mate sits protectively on a clutch of new-laid eggs.

On warm evenings the bats emerge from their roosts in cracks and splits in the old trees, briefly breaking their hibernation to flit among the trees in search of early moths. Dog foxes, foraging at night time, return to their

Above *In early spring downy leaves start to break from the swelling buds of a beech twig. Before all the leaves appear windflowers, or wood anemones (left), can brighten the clearings while sunlight penetrates.*

Right *In late April and May, just before all the leaves have come forth and the canopy becomes a dense bright green parasol relatively shade-tolerant flowers, such as bluebells, can flourish and carpet the woodland clearings.*

Right *In spring the magpie, Pica pica, builds a large and elaborate nest at the tops of bushes. Both the male and female engage in building the nest, which is roofed with one or two entrances on the side.*

Left *The woodchuck, or groundhog, emerges in March to feed on grass, insects and small animals in order to double its weight before it hibernates in September. In the United States, 2 February is Groundhog Day, based on the belief that on this day the animal wakes, sees its shadow and returns to sleep for six weeks.*

dens beneath the tree roots. They creep into the woods carrying rabbits or rats for the nursing vixens. Badgers extend their nightly forays along their well-worn tracks to meet the needs of their growing cubs.

As the soil warms up all the little creatures from tiny mites and springtails to worms and slugs, become increasingly active and start to multiply as they set about their work of converting dead plant material into substances that the growing plants and trees require. And as the numbers increase (at peak periods there can be as many as forty million mites and twenty-eight million springtails in one acre of woodland) so does the food available to shrews, moles and birds, stimulating them to reproductive activity.

Meanwhile the trees themselves start to shake off their dormancy. The pointed beech buds swell and cast their papery scales as the bright green, downy leaves unfurl, the golden globe-shaped male flowers hanging on threads among them. The plump oak buds unfold reddish-brown at first, turning dark green as they take on their familiar shape amid the chains of yellow-green male flowers. Everywhere in the forest canopy fresh green awakening life is on the move again. A great surge of sap, channelled into millions of tiny pipe-like vessels, is running up from the spreading, questing tree roots, through the massive trunks to the smallest twigs, drawn by transpiration from the new leaves, and bearing with it chemicals that will meet and mix with those manufactured in the leaves to fuel the summer season growth.

As the tree canopy puts on its mantle of leaves in late spring in an all-enveloping protective umbrella, the insects—those creatures which the migrant birds have come so far to find in plenty—start to display their incredible powers of rapid reproduction. Pupae burst to release butterflies and moths, eggs hatch in millions to spawn a host of wriggling caterpillars, greenfly in sticky masses multiply profusely without the aid of matings. Billions of flying and creeping creatures explode into the forest domain each with a role to play in this, the first, and succeeding acts of the wonderful drama that is woodland life re-created.

BIRD TERRITORIES

Displaying red breast

Intruder arriving from below

Intruder arriving from above

Battle in full flight if threatening behaviour fails

The spring woodland is full of the sounds of birds proclaiming control over their particular territories. The robin uses his red breast as a warning display, but his strategies depend on the intruder's position.

Summer

Below *From June until August tall purple foxgloves hoist their nodding spikes of bell-like flowers in the forest clearings and edges. They are biennial, spending one year building a rosette of leaves to flower in the next.*

Grey squirrel *Sciurus cardinensis*

Blackcap chickadee *Parus atricapillus*

Ladybird and aphids *Coccinella septempunctata* and *Aphis*

Acorn woodpecker *Melanerpes formicivorous*

♀

♂

Oak eggar moth *Lasiocampa quercus*

Nut weevil *Curculio venosus*

Oak hook tip *Drepana binana*

Buff tip *Phalera bucephala*

Moth caterpillars

Stoat *Mustela erminea*

Common treecreeper *Certhia familiaris*

Oak bark beetle *Scolytus intricatus*

Each individual tree of the broadleaved forest is a world of its own, providing innumerable habitats for plant-eating animals. Some, such as the grey squirrel and acorn woodpecker, feed on the fruits of the trees. Smaller animals such as caterpillars bite holes in the leaves as they wander the surface; aphids suck the sap from leaves while others burrow into the soft parts. Ladybirds feed on aphids, wasps and spiders on flies. Many of the larger insects are in turn consumed by the insectivorous birds that crowd the woods in summer to breed. The birds themselves, however, fall victim to such animals as the stoat, or ermine, which raids nests to take eggs or newly hatched young.

Above *In the short summer nights this tawny owl finds food in abundance. Young mice, voles, birds and frogs fall prey to such predators.*

Below *A summer visitor to the North American temperate forests, the yellow warbler nests in small trees, feeding its young on the teeming insect population.*

During the summer months the river of life in the forest rises to full spate, fed by countless rivulets of reproduction as all the creatures submit to the primary urge to perpetuate their species. Each plant and animal, mindful as it were of the threat its enemies pose, aims to ensure its survival by overproduction. The forest is filled with young life, the very excess of some being the salvation of others. One large plant shades out a hundred small ones, one bird devours a hundred seeds, a fox swallows a whole nest of rabbits. Kill or be killed, eat or be eaten, grow upwards or be stunted, is the order of the day.

This struggle for survival is no less ruthless when played out in the forest than elsewhere; indeed, it has many more actors, but the protection which the forest gives ensures that those individuals which do survive, do so with advantage. Even so, the apparent tranqillity of the summer forest scene, where so much beauty accompanies and hides the excesses of "tooth and claw", is somewhat illusory.

There is no more drawn-out struggle for survival than that among the trees themselves. For centuries, perhaps, they have added to their stature. Each summer the seedling trees overtop annual herbs and shrubs in their struggle for light, and then expand their crowns in gaps left by fallen forebears. Each year, in a span of maturity unmatched by other living things, they bear countless seeds. Around one mature oak tree, which over the centuries must have cast millions of acorns on the forest floor, there is room for but one other as a final replacement.

Yet each summer there will be many seedling oaks and a collection of saplings of varying ages and sizes. The numbers of each group decrease as the size and age increase, due to competition from their own kind and other

plants as well as to predation by plant-eating animals. But this inexorably drawn-out struggle leaves us with a forest of outstanding beauty. The great trunks of the dominant trees stand well spaced and interspersed with co-dominants of other species. Beneath them all, layers of younger trees of varying heights down to shrubs and herbs, provide a series of protected horizontal summer habitats.

From the leaves in the crowns of the tallest trees down to the smallest plants on the forest floor, each layer supports a mass of creatures all bent upon raising families. Hungry millions of leaf-eating caterpillars, hatched from eggs overwintered on the twigs, spread out among the new leaves to the delight of the leaf warblers and titmice, which run a constant daylight service from the canopy to their clamouring young below. The larvae of beetles and wood-boring insects hatch beneath the loose bark of dead trees and are sought out by woodpeckers, nuthatches and treecreepers as they run up and down the trunks.

Squirrels descend from their lofty nests, or dreys, to seize eggs and even nestlings from the less well-hidden nests. Butterflies in glorious array, newly released from their pupae, flit across the clearings in search of mates and their special food plants on which to lay eggs. Deer fawns lie still in the thickets, safe in their spotted camouflage.

As the short night descends a silence settles on the forest. The hum of insects, the songs and warning cries of nesting birds, the shrill clamour of hungry nestlings fade away. Sounds become occasional and loud in their isolation. Owls call to one another, swooping from their nesting holes to snatch up woodmice. Fox cubs play in mock anger at the mouth of their earths, awaiting the dawn return of their parents and a meal of young

rabbit or fat pigeon squab. The forest floor rustles as mice and shrews, feeling safer in the darkness and with young to feed, prey upon lesser creatures and the shoots and seeds of the quickly growing plants. Some are fated to be preyed upon themselves and never return to their young, who are then easy prey to insects and the microscopic creatures of the soil—thus returning whence they indirectly came.

As summer advances, competition in the struggle to achieve maturity increases. Hosts of young animals are cast upon their own resources with nothing more than instinct to protect them until luck and experience establish them as adults. The vast majority succumb to hunger or predation; only the fittest survive. The forest claims the rest as a forfeit for its part in ensuring the survival of the countless species that dwell in its protection.

But even this drastic thinning out during summer's latter days is not enough to maintain the balance. Young birds of many insect-eating species, preceded by their parents and drawn by an inborn urge, fly south to warmer climes and surer food supplies; perilous journeys which many fail to finish.

Meanwhile, among the plants on the forest floor, one group has succeeded another with its floral displays. Bluebells, anemones, primroses and arum lilies all flowered before the trees were in full leaf. They set their seeds and withered as the forget-me-nots in large blue patches, the pink willow-herbs and foxgloves and the yellow archangels added spots of colour to the sombre greens of the sedge tussocks, the woodland grasses and the tangled mass of brambles. From these flowers, visited and fertilized by woodland insects in search of pollen and nectar, or by the wafting summer breezes, fruits and seeds will follow in the profusion that marks summer in the forest.

Autumn

Quiet cold days when frost rims the leaves and glistens white on the woodland grasses, crisping the leaf litter. Damp days when the patter of raindrops on the dying leaves masks all other sounds. Windy days when the trees creak and groan as they sway in unison. This is autumn, a melancholy season. The wasteful harvest of young creatures, shoots and seeds has been gathered, yet the gathering has ensured the survival of the species.

Now fully grown and confirmed in their dominance over the forest, the trees burst into glorious colour before lapsing into the naked dormancy necessary for winter survival. The crowns cannot support the huge burden of leaves during winter gales nor can roots anchored in frozen ground supply the water which the leaves would exhale.

As autumn approaches corky barriers start to insert themselves at the junction of the leaf stalks and the twigs, gradually cutting off the flow of sap until the leaves wither and drop off. At the same time the destruction of chlorophyll in the leaves accelerates so that the green colour is masked by the yellow, red and purple dyes that are manufactured from residual foodstuffs in the leaves.

These autumn colours and their intensity vary from tree to tree and are most marked in the maples, whose leaves vary from lemon yellow to intense crimson, and in the beeches

TOADSTOOLS AND MUSHROOMS

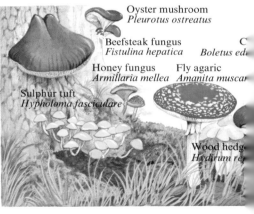

Oyster mushroom
Pleurotus ostreatus

Beefsteak fungus   C
Fistulina hepatica   *Boletus ed*

Honey fungus   Fly agaric
Armillaria mellea   *Amanita muscar*

Sulphur tuft
Hypholoma fasciculare

Wood hedg
Hydnum re

Left *Autumn glory in a North American woodland. As the green chlorophyll breaks down in the leaves, brilliant dyes are made from residual food.*

Below *Late autumn fros encrust the fruits of a wil rose that will become essential food for the woodland birds in the winter months to come.*

which turn a deep red-brown. There is no more spectacular display of natural colouring than in the deciduous forests of eastern North America. There in the fall the maples and the oaks "set fire" to great expanses of wooded country. In Europe, too, as the low evening sun lights up the burnished copper canopy of the beechwoods, the scene is no less eagerly anticipated despite the winter rigours to come.

Within the forest, as the year draws to its close, the autumn dampness and the increased accumulation of debris provide ideal conditions for fungal growth. On the leaf litter, round dead stumps, in cracks in huge trees and on dead twigs they appear. Some are mushroom-like and of brilliant reds and blues; others grow out as brackets on the trunks of trees; and yet others ring tree stumps in layered masses. But even if the fruiting bodies are conspicuous in some species, the spreading networks of mycelia of these and countless others are hidden beneath the ground, behind the bark of trees or in the very wood of the trunks.

One subterranean group of fungi of the genus *Tuber* spreads among the roots of forest trees, each kind associated with a particular species of tree. They form irregular spherical growths, some white, some black, known as truffles. The best of these gastronomical delicacies are found in beechwoods. In great demand, they are keenly sought by dogs, pigs and even goats trained to recognize their strong scent and indicate where, beneath the leaf litter, they are hidden.

As the trees slowly divest themselves of their many-coloured leaves, the squirrels are busy collecting and burying nuts and acorns in little stores for future use. Mice, too, bury seeds and berries against leaner times, while the European hedgehogs and dormice and the North American woodchuck store up their food in body fat before lapsing into a dormant, hibernating state. Around the badgers' dens the old bedding of leaves and dried grass lies scattered, replaced by new material taken down for winter use.

The migrant birds have gone, leaving the lessening food supply with fewer demands upon it. The resident birds, moulted and in fresh feather, no longer consort in pairs but forage singly, except for those such as the titmice, or chickadees, still ranging through the forest feeding and twittering incessantly.

This preparation throughout the forest for the winter season, this storing of food and fat, is greatly helped by the fruitfulness of the trees and shrubs. Acorns, once green and shiny, fade with a touch of brown and drop noisily to the ground; beech nuts, released by the opening husks, fall like huge rain-drops; ash keys, reluctant to fall until winter is well advanced, hang in bundles on bare branches; sycamore seeds, spiralling down on papery wings, are scattered far and wide. The wild cherries lost their fruit to the blackbirds in late summer, but the red rose hips, which will not be touched until times are very bleak, vie with the pink spindle berries, the scarlet fruit bunches of the honeysuckle and the green hazel nuts in frilly cups in brightening up a sombre scene.

As the autumn gales tear the last leaves from the trees, sending them whirling in spirals round the trunks, and the frost picks the last of the fruits, only the dark greens of the evergreens remain to relieve the greys and browns. Here and there yews and holly bushes, or ivy clothing an old tree, break the sameness of the scene, becoming like blocks of dormitory flats for roosting birds.

A robin may let fall a gentle snatch of song, the cock and the hen marking out their separate winter territories; a wren may sing suddenly and shrilly atop an old tree stump; a shrieking blackbird may dive for cover. An owl may hoot as the lengthening night falls, or a dog fox may answer his vixen's eerie call with a short, sharp bark. But few other sounds will mark the final scene before the curtain of winter drops. Nature's overt work is done, silence is the most telling accompaniment to the hidden preparations which presage life reborn as the cycle of the seasons turns on.

The fruiting bodies of fungi appear at different times of the year, according to the species, but in general those of the larger fungi appear in the autumn months. Below are illustrated some European woodland fungi.

Common ink cap
Coprinus atramentarius

Parasol mushroom
Lepiota procera

Devil's boletus
Boletus satanas

Death cap
Amanita phalloides

Chanterelle
Cantharellus cibarius

Earth star
Geastrum triplex

Pear-shaped puffball
Lycoperdon pyriforme

Right *The eastern chipmunk of North America only hibernates in particularly cold winters. They can then be observed carrying food in their cheek pouches to underground nests.*

Below *The European common dormouse is the smallest member of the rodent family. Hazel nuts are its preferred diet and it often lives in hazel trees or blackberry bushes in deciduous woodlands. When the temperature drops in late autumn dormice hibernate in spherical nests made of grass, leaves and moss.*

TRUFFLES

Truffles are underground fungi that have been prized since Roman times. The truffle of commerce flourishes in the chalky soils of the open deciduous woodlands of the Périgord region in France. Truffles often occur at depths of a foot, so dogs and pigs are trained to detect the scent emitted by the fruiting bodies in autumn. About one-third of the truffle crop is exported and the industry is so esteemed that the French Government has undertaken the planting of oaks in thinly wooded truffle areas.

Temperate pinelands

Pine trees are common in the northern coniferous forests but it is the forests of the temperate and subtropical climates that contain the greater diversity of species and also exhibit better growth rates. These temperate pinelands, where pine trees are grown commercially, have assumed great economic importance.

In North America these species of pine are known collectively as the southern pines. The southern pines are comprised of several trees including four primary species; loblolly, *Pinus taeda*, slash, *P. elliottii*, longleaf, *P. palustris*, and shortleaf, *P. echinata*, and other relatively minor species, such as pond pine, *P. serotina*, sand pine, *P. clausa*, and Virginia pine, *P. virginiana*. The natural distribution of these pines covers an area from New Jersey to southern Florida and westward into east Texas, but commercially the most important part of this region is an eleven-state area in the south.

Various factors go into making the southern United States such an important forestry area, not the least of which are climatic conditions and soils and topography that favour rapid growth. Additionally, the south was heavily farmed from colonial times to the Civil War period, and many of the abandoned plantations and exhausted farmlands of that era, even through the 1920s, reverted to pine forests. Some of this abandoned land was also planted by the state during the depression years of the 1930s and as part of large-scale soil conservation programmes which were undertaken after the Second World War. These plantations and the older, and more common, naturally seeded forests formed the basis for the development of the south's forest products industry.

The white pines are another important group of temperate conifers in North America's timber economy. Eastern white pine, *P. strobus*, which ranges from south-eastern Canada and the north-eastern United States southward to the Appalachian Mountains of northern Georgia, is a tree that, for many years, was used as the primary building material in the north-east. There are five other white pines native to the western United States, but of these the most important commercial species are sugar pine, *P. lambertiana*, and western white pine, *P. monticola*. The wood of these two western trees closely resembles that of eastern white pine in its structure and properties and is used for similar purposes.

Two relatives of eastern white pine, which occur more than 12,000 miles to the south in the highlands of Mexico and Central America, are Chiapas pine, *P. strobus* var *chiapensis*, and Mexican white pine, *P. ayacahuite*. The existence of these three widely separated tree populations, combined with the fact that several other white pines are found in Asia and Europe, is proof of the pines' migrations, which occurred in past geological times.

The most widely distributed pine in the world, Scots pine, *P. sylvestris*, grows throughout northern Eurasia, from Scotland across Russia to the Sea of Okhotsk, and southward into Turkey and Greece. Geological evidence indicates that Scots pine migrated from North America across Greenland into northern Europe. During the Tertiary glaciation period, it was able to survive the harsh climate in refuge areas untouched by the glaciers because of the resistance it has to cold weather. No doubt, this characteristic is also a major reason for its wide present-day distribution.

This extensive occurrence has made Scots pine one of the most widely used timber species throughout Europe and northern Asia, where it is highly valued for construction purposes, pulp and paper manufacturing and a multitude of other products. It is also one of the most intensively studied pines in the world and foresters are continuing to improve the qualities and utilization potential of this tree.

Three other pines of considerable commercial importance in southern Europe and the Mediterranean region are black pine, *P. nigra*, Aleppo pine, *P. halepensis*, and French maritime pine, *P. pinaster*. Unlike Scots pine, which was hindered in its southward migration by the Alps, the predecessors of Aleppo, French maritime, and black pines trans-migrated from eastern Asia into the area presently occupied by the Mediterranean Sea. The most widely occurring of these three species, Aleppo pine is found throughout the entire Mediterranean region at elevations ranging from near sea level in Greece and Israel up to 5,000 feet in Morocco.

There are various pine species in eastern and south-eastern Asia which derived from the original distribution centre in north-east Asia. Several of these species such as Korean pine, *P. koraiensis*, Japanese white pine, *P. pentaphylla*, Japanese red pine, *P. densiflora* in the north, and the tropical Khasia pine, *P. khasya*, and Merkus pine, *P. merkusii*, are used extensively for the manufacture of wood products in Asia. However, one species that was important in ancient China was Masson pine, *P. massoniana*.

This tree originally occupied an area that extended throughout the highly populated section of central and southern China, but it and its habitat were so intensively exploited that today very few remnants of this important

Above *Masson pines, Pinus massoniana, growing in White Cloud Mountain Park in the Canton region of China. Although these pines are found over a vast geographical area, which encompasses more than ten provinces and a great variety of climatic and soil conditions, there appears to be no adaptive variations.*

Right *Stone (or umbrella) pines, Pinus pinea, growing in Portugal. This Mediterranean pine grows as far east as Turkey, but man has modified the Mediterranean region so much over the centuries that it is impossible to recognize the areas where such pines are native or where they have been planted. Its large seeds are edible.*

tree still exist. Attempts are being made to improve the quality of Masson pine and to re-establish forests of this tree, but many years of hard work will be needed before it will regain its former stature in the Chinese economy.

Pines are not native to the southern hemisphere, and foresters have been actively engaged for many years in introducing these useful trees into that part of the world (see pages 54–55). Many examples of successful introductions, which have formed the basis for flourishing wood products industries, exist, but no discussion would be complete without mentioning the amazing story of radiata pine, *P. radiata*. This tree is native to southern California and Baja California where four small relict populations of this species exist. During the early colonization of California, many seafaring botanists and laymen, who were impressed with the beauty of these picturesque trees, collected and distributed seed of radiata pine for use in gardens and arboreta of the southern hemisphere. The species responded extremely well to its new exotic environment and the growth rates which it exhibited far exceeded any of those for pines in the northern hemisphere. Today radiata pine is grown in extensive plantations in South Africa, Chile, New Zealand and Australia, and it has become the most important commercial timber species of those countries.

Investigations are being continued by foresters following the introduction of pines and other tree species into the southern hemisphere, and many equally impressive stories have already been written regarding other species with similar records. This testing and development of "exotics" is one of the most exciting and dynamic aspects of forestry today.

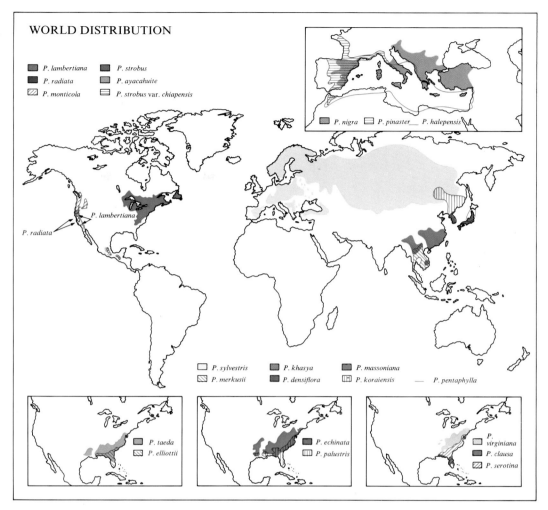

WORLD DISTRIBUTION

- P. lambertiana
- P. radiata
- P. monticola
- P. strobus
- P. ayacahuite
- P. strobus var. chiapensis

- P. nigra
- P. pinaster
- P. halepensis

- P. sylvestris
- P. merkusii
- P. khasya
- P. densiflora
- P. massoniana
- P. koraiensis
- P. pentaphylla

- P. taeda
- P. elliottii

- P. echinata
- P. palustris

- P. virginiana
- P. clausa
- P. serotina

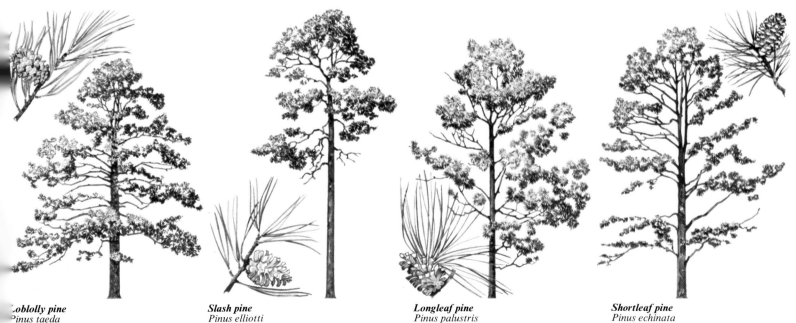

Loblolly pine
Pinus taeda

The principal timber tree in the south-east United States, which reaches more than 120 ft. It has a tendency to prune itself, leaving long clean stems.

Slash pine
Pinus elliotti

Reaching heights of 100 ft, slash pine grows rapidly on the best sites. It is capable of putting on as much as 5 ft in height in a single year.

Longleaf pine
Pinus palustris

A smallish pine, the longleaf is rarely taller than 100 ft or thicker than 3 ft, but it bears the longest (up to 18 in) needles of any pine.

Shortleaf pine
Pinus echinata

With the widest distribution of the southern pines, the shortleaf grows in 22 US states, but it is little used for forestry in other parts of the world.

Evergreen forests

Below The colourful fruit
of the evergreen
strawberry tree often
breaks the green monotony
of large stands of forest.
Its fruit is only just edible
as its specific Latin name
of unedo (I eat but one)
suggests.

Below The encina, or
California live oak,
Quercus agrifolia,
resembles its close relative,
the canyon live oak, in only
occurring in extensive
stands when conditions are
sheltered. Then it can
reach 90 ft in height.

In many parts of the world, particularly in those parts of southern Europe bordering the Mediterranean and in the south-west United States—where the summers are hot and dry and the winters are wet and mild—broadleaved trees have returned to some conifer characteristics to overcome climatic extremes. They are evergreen and their attributes are designed to conserve moisture during hot dry spells. The leaves of these trees are usually small, tough and leathery, and glossy on the upper surfaces, while their trunks are often clad in thick bark to protect the vital growing processes within from excessive dry heat.

Long ago, evergreen trees of this type must have formed extensive forests bordering upon the Mediterranean and on the mountain slopes rising from its shores, as well as in the Iberian Peninsula, but few areas of such forest remain. The pressures of human population, with the ever increasing demand for farm and pasture land, have reduced them to mere thickets with just an odd larger tree standing here and there. Even so, in certain more inaccessible places, such as in the hills of Catalonia in Spain, it is possible to see what the forests must once have looked like.

They were sombre places where the intense midday summer sun was screened from the forest floor by the trees' thick evergreen leaves and where the silent wildlife, glad of a refuge from the heat, was disturbed only by the strident screams of the cicadas. Huge holm oaks, *Quercus ilex*, supported broad crowns of holly-like leaves on their massive, black-barked trunks (a specimen measured in Portugal had a crown spread of sixty-two feet and produced more than twenty-five bushels of acorns each year) and cork oaks, *Q. suber*, were often even larger. Their great trunks were twenty or more feet in circumference and wrapped in corky bark up to a foot thick. This cork was, and still is, harvested at regular intervals without any apparent damage to the

trees (see pages 204–205). Again, in Portugal a cork oak produced more than one and a half tons of bark in 1879 and produced more than two tons just ten years later.

Another tree in these forests would have been the strawberry tree, *Arbutus unedo*, which is smaller than the oaks. It has large shiny leaves, a burnished copper-coloured bark and white urn-shaped flowers that eventually give way to red, edible but unpalatable fleshy fruits. These forests of the past would not always have been composed exclusively of broadleaved evergreen trees, however. Often the stone and maritime pines, *Pinus pinea* and *P. pinaster*, as well as the spire-like Mediterranean cypress, *Cupressus sempervirens*, would have been mixed with them, or even been locally dominant.

Centuries of fires and grazing have reduced the number of these large trees that can be found today. Scrub thickets or maquis—from which the heroic members of the French Resistance in the Second World War derived their name and cover—have replaced much of these forests. But human intervention has brought another tree into these areas—the olive, *Olea europaea*. Probably a native of central Asia, it was imported in ancient times. With their silvery-green leaves on twisted branches and gnarled trunks, they have been cultivated for 2,000 years or more for their fruits and oil, and are now not only a hallmark of these regions but have also formed an important addition to the landscape.

In coastal California, where coniferous species are far more numerous than in Europe and thus have adaptations for almost every habitat, broadleaved evergreen trees rarely comprise forests of any great extent. More often they are confined to canyon bottoms, coves and sheltered depressions. Here evergreen oaks, such as the encinas, *Quercus agrifolia*, and canyon live oaks, *Q. chrysolepis*, form areas of woodland. They can be up to

eighty feet tall with short trunks and wide-spreading crowns, the encinas with numerous great limbs resting on the ground and forming crowns as much as 150 feet across.

But such giants and the woodlands they form are usually surrounded by the pines and other conifers that dominate the forest as a whole. The only really extensive areas of evergreen broadleaved forest are those covered by scrub oak, *Q. dumosa*, a tree which, as its name implies, rarely exceeds thirty feet in height. As in Europe, there is a strawberry tree, and the madrone, *Arbutus menziesii*, is also found among the oaks. It reaches considerable sizes in the wetter north, but is usually stunted in the dry south and its bright reddish-brown bark breaks the dull green monotony.

In the southern hemisphere evergreen broadleaved forests occur in Australia, New Zealand and South America. The trees in Australia, mostly *Eucalyptus* spp., arm themselves against the intensely hot dry summers with the same tough, wax-covered leaves. But in the montane and sub-alpine belt of New Zealand's South Island and in Chile south of the 45th parallel (where the extremes of temperature and rainfall are less severe) evergreen beeches, with small shiny leaves like the oaks, cover extensive areas.

Despite the enormous geographical distances between the two countries, the similarity between the species is remarkable. Rather than hot dry summers or warm wet winters there is uniformly cool weather throughout the year in these southern beech forests. But the black and red beeches of New Zealand, *Nothofagus solandri* and *N. fusca*, just like the antarctic and southern beeches *N. betuloides* and *N. dombeyi*, of Chile, have retained the evergreen habit in this climate which, in the northern hemisphere, would have resulted in trees becoming adapted to the deciduous way of life.

Below *and* bottom
*Southern beeches are
evergreen trees unusually
at home in the temperate
climates of New Zealand
or Tierra del Fuego.
In the northern hemisphere
they are planted for
fast-growing timber.*

THE OLIVE

Olive trees typify those evergreens that have evolved to conserve moisture during long hot periods and whose tough and glossy foliage is usually small. Their thick bark protects the vital growing processes within from excessive heat. The fruit can be eaten green or black but must be allowed to ripen black when used for oil. Olives have provided their valuable fruit since prehistoric times and have become a familiar part of the Mediterranean landscape.

Above *An ancient Greek vase shows olives being harvested with sticks, a method still used today when the finest grades are not required.*

Right *Olive trees, like the ones in this Corfu grove, like dry but deep soil, growing very slowly to reach maximum heights of about 50 ft.*

Swamp and cypress forests

Below *Thriving in the still and stagnant marshy waters, these moss-draped bald cypresses with thickened trunk bases are supported by massive horizontal roots which are submerged below the waterline of the swamp.*

Below *The Everglades are fringed by mangrove communities and dominated by such tree species as the red maple, the water tupelo and the southern cypress. The islands of trees in what is essentially a broad, if slow-moving, river provide an extensive and rich habitat for a wide variety of rare plants and animals.*

The temperate deciduous forests that cover so much of the northern and central parts of the eastern United States gradually merge, from South Carolina southwards to Florida and westwards into Texas, into semi-tropical forests subject to considerable flooding in the summer months. These swamp and cypress forests comprise an exceptionally wide diversity of species. Indeed, in the state of Florida alone more than half of the 3,000 or so North American tree species are indigenous.

Best known of these forest zones is the Florida Everglades—a shallow limestone-floored basin some 4,000 square miles in extent, sloping very slightly southwards. With an annual rainfall of about fifty-five inches, falling mainly between June and October, mean temperatures varying between 17–28°C (63–82°F) and a climate that is largely frost free, a unique landscape has resulted. Low islands, or "hammocks", supporting a profusion of trees are interspersed with shallow water, swamps, grass-covered marshland and groups of swamp cypresses, *Taxodium distichum*—their great, buttressed trunks surrounded by the stagnant water.

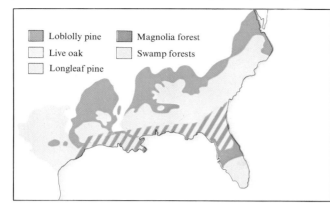

Below *The south-eastern states were once densely forested, forming the bottom tier of the great eastern deciduous forest. To the south of remnants of this forest lies a broad zone of pinelands where slash, long-leaf and loblolly pine rely on frequent fires to secure their hold on the* landscape. *Farther south, hardwoods re-establish their domain, but take on an evergreen character. Sweet bay and evergreen magnolia form the climax forest, along with several species of evergreen, or live, oak. In low-lying regions swamps, bayous and everglades are found.*

Loblolly pine
Live oak
Longleaf pine
Magnolia forest
Swamp forests

Below *A great white heron,* Ardea heroides occidentalis, *stands silently in the swamp forest* water. *It frequents the mangrove tidal areas that fringe the Everglades and is tolerant of seawater.*

ANIMAL LIFE IN THE EVERGLADES

The Everglade watercourses support a multitude of fish, alligators and wading birds such as the spoonbills, egrets and herons. But the hammocks support a greater variety of tropical plants and animals. In spring, songbirds arrive, insects such as zebra butterflies swarm and tree snails crawl along branches.

Brown pelican
Anhinga
Common egret
Roseate spoonbill
Raccoon
Limpkin
Purple gallinule
Green tree frog
Box tortoise
Mississippi alligator
Tree snail
Zebra butterfly

These swamp or bald cypresses—the latter name given them because, unlike most conifers, they are deciduous—are largely unchanged relics of ancient times (see pages [2]0–21), when similar trees covered much of North America and Europe. This may account for the strange adaptation that enables them to thrive even when their roots are entirely and permanently submerged in water.

Vertical "knees" held above the water-level grow from their roots to take in oxygen, which is in short supply in the swamp soil. The trees are therefore able to thrive in a habitat where no serious competitors can grow. Indeed, they have been driven there by their inability to compete with more modern rivals elsewhere. In fact the largest swamp cypresses are found in deep, damp though not swampy soils, but in such sites very little regeneration takes place because swamp cypress seedlings are almost always smothered by the seedlings of more successful species.

The swamp cypress is a long-lived tree that can grow to a great size. A specimen in Tennessee was found to be 1,300 years old, measuring 122 feet in height and 39 feet in circumference. The crown of bright green feathery leaves turns a beautiful foxy brown in autumn and on swampy sites it is often festooned with Spanish moss, hanging in long grey masses that wave in the wind and lend a strange appearance to the forest.

Outside the somewhat specialized habitat of the Everglades, along the Gulf Coast and on the flatlands up the river valleys, especially in the less swampy areas and on the hammocks, the swamp cypresses grow alongside a wealth of other trees. Swamp and water tupelos, *Nyssa sylvatica* and *N. aquatica*, with their glossy green leaves, which turn a deep red in autumn, grow in many areas. Loblolly pines, *Pinus taeda*, with their graceful drooping needles are fast growing in the "loblollies"—moist depressions. Several oaks are found in these forests, of which the most magnificent are the live oaks, *Quercus virginiana*. Like the swamp cypresses, these massive evergreen trees are often festooned with mosses and their short trunks support spreading crowns of glossy leaves. The willow oak, *Q. phellos*, with feathery vivid green leaves, together with laurel oak, *Q. laurifolia*, with wider, lustrous leaves are also common species.

Willows, too, abound especially the coastal plain willow, *Salix caroliniana*, and a true cypress, the Atlantic white cedar, *Chamaecyparis thyoides*, is another conifer common in damp places. But among this profusion of softwoods and hardwoods two palms make a somewhat surprising appearance. These are the tall and graceful royal palm, *Roystonea elata* (confined to the hammocks of the Everglades) and the more widespread and smaller cabbage palmetto, *Sabal palmetto*, both with long clean trunks holding up spreading fronds high in the forest canopy.

So, in these swampy areas, and in the country bordering them, a host of competing trees have found their ecological niches. Some, like the swamp cypresses, are able to thrive in permanently stagnant water. Others, such as the tupelos, survive regular inundations and permanent sub-soil water. Yet others, such as the pines, prefer the relatively drier raised ground bordering the swamps, but are able to compete with seasonal flooding. The whole rich mixture presents a forest of enormous variety and great beauty.

China

China is the third largest country in the world. It occupies nearly four million square miles of land and extends across a huge part of the Eurasian landmass. It has enormous variations in climate, with the most northerly areas on the Siberian border knowing no summer, and the most southerly area, the Nansha Islands, experiencing no winter. And despite a long history of deforestation of the land, the territory still has examples of every one of the world's major native forest types. The woodland communities of China range from tropical rain forests in the south through to temperate broadleaves, with boreal coniferous forests in the far north.

The deciduous broadleaved forests extend in two distinct types—cool temperate to the north and warm temperate to the south of the great Yangtse River valley, although there is considerable mixing of the tree species typical of both in the centre of the zone. To the north, oak forests gradually give way to birch, ash and poplar, with some spruce, larch and pine. In the south, the forest is characterized by the large number of tree species found in it—as many as sixty genera, nearly all of them broadleaved and deciduous. No single tree species is predominant in the composition of this southern forest and the crown layer is shared by a number of tall trees. Indeed, in its complexity of composition and its lack of any single constituent tree it resembles the rain forests of the Tropics, and by its uniqueness can be called the true Chinese forest.

A striking feature of some of these trees is the parallel between those in China and in the south-eastern United States. Despite the many thousands of miles that separate the two countries, the same genera have separate and distinct species, widespread in their respective countries but entirely absent from the vast expanse of countries in between. The stately tulip tree, *Liriodendron tulipifera*, has a slightly less impressive but otherwise very similar sole near-relative *L. chinense* in China. The Kentucky coffee tree, *Gymnocladus dioicus*, with its huge compound leaves and large seeds that were once ground as a coffee substitute, has but one other close relative in the world, the Chinese soap tree, *G. chinense*, whose seeds have saponaceous, or soap-like, properties. This parallel in genera offers great potential for both Chinese and American tree breeders who, by exchanging related germ plasm, may well be able to produce crossbreeds with improved qualities such as disease- and drought-resistance.

Although none of the trees in these forests has been planted as a timber tree outside China's borders, a great many of them are now grown as ornamentals in Europe and North America. Of these perhaps the best known are the deciduous maidenhair tree, *Ginkgo biloba*, of ancient lineage, with its bright green fan-shaped leaves, and the recently discovered dawn redwood, *Metasequoia glyptostroboides*, which, until 1943, was known only from fossil remains. This deciduous conifer, with its delicate, feathery leaves that turn foxy-brown in the autumn, is quick growing and is now widely planted as an ornamental tree.

Among the wealth of trees that have been exported from Chinese forests, to grace the gardens and parks of half the world, are such flowering species as the beautiful magnolias derived from the Yulan, *Magnolia denudata*; the handkerchief tree, *Davidia involucrata*, with large white bracts resembling laundry hanging out to dry; the host of flowering cherries, probably derived from *Prunus serrulata*; and the glorious foxglove tree, *Paulownia tomentosa*, with its masses of violet-coloured bell-shaped flowers. Maples abound too, some with striped snake-like bark and others clad in reddish-brown papery scales, as well as stewartias with smooth creamy-orange trunks. There are also such immensely tall trees as the tree of heaven, *Ailanthus altissima*, which withstands the air pollution of cities.

These forests and those in the other zones were disastrously depleted over the centuries until, in 1949, only some eight per cent (as opposed to Japan's sixty-eight per cent) of the land area was covered in forest. But China claims to have increased this area by four per cent over the last thirty years—a remarkable achievement when one considers that this represents an area larger than the whole of the United Kingdom. Peasants have been encouraged to plant trees round their homes and villages, as well as along roads and waterways, so that what was a treeless waste, ravaged by war and by a vast population hungry for firewood, has been transformed by lines of poplars and other quick-growing trees. In addition, a major task has lately been given renewed impetus—the planting of a 1,800-mile shelterbelt across Northern China, the "Great Green Wall", which when completed will form a windbreak against the persistent cold, dry winds which sweep south-eastwards from the deserts of North West China.

The forest plantation programme, however, has been fraught with difficulties, partly because the competition between the growing of food and timber production remains intense and many plantations have been prematurely felled to increase agricultural land, and partly because lack of research into suitability of species and other aspects of tree planting meant that the most widely planted tree was the most readily available, the south China pine, *Pinus massoniana*, which in fact proved unsuitable for many of the planting sites.

China, however, is bent on reducing her timber shortage both by more scientifically researched planting of more suitable trees mostly conifers, and by facilitating the use and management of existing but remote forests by improving the roads to them. But despite the significant achievements that have been made the task ahead, to increase forest production to control erosion and to continue to feed a vast population, is a monumental one.

MAJOR FOREST TYPES OF CHINA

- Coniferous
- Mixed coniferous and broadleaved deciduous
- Broadleaved deciduous
- Broadleaved evergreen
- Monsoon forest

Despite massive deforestation over the centuries the great landmass of China accommodates examples of all the major forest types: taiga, evergreen broadleaved and monsoon forests. The clear north-south progression of the zones is, however, complicated by the intervention of mountains with their own specific forest types.

FORESTRY AND AGRICULTURE

Before 1949 China's sparse forest cover meant an extremely low timber yield and little protective vegetation for watersheds, sandy tracts and coastal areas. Food production suffered as a result of erosion and impoverishment of soils, lack of soil moisture and a constant reduction in cultivable areas due to shifting sand-dunes and damage by flood and droughts. After 1949, however, a massive programme of reforestation and forest improvement was initiated with immense popular support. This energetic campaign was based on a new understanding of the interdependence of agriculture, forestry, animal husbandry and grazing. The leaves and undergrowth from a forest, for example, provide fodder for animals and this is ultimately an important source of organic manure for agricultural fields. It is claimed that today ten per cent of China is forested. Trees are also planted as coastal windbreaks and as farmland shelterbelts.

Below *The warm temperate forests of China are unlike those of any other region. The tree species are so numerous that no single tree predominates, although most are broadleaved deciduous. They include* oak *(especially to the north of the zone), maple, poplar, Chinese species of the Catalpa tree, boxwood, wingnuts, which are oak-shaped trees with catkins that develop into chains of winged nuts, and the small Chinese sweetgum.*

Left *The ginkgo or maidenhair tree is the oldest of all trees on Earth and has remained unchanged for millions of years. Resistant to pollution, it is ideal for urban planting schemes.*

Above *The handkerchief tree, also known as the dove or ghost tree, is so called because of the two large white bracts surrounding each of its small scented flowers.*

Japan

THE FOREST GARDEN

Traditional Japanese households have for a long time maintained two family altars, one Shinto and one Buddhist. Many temples still stand, their precincts providing refuges for worshippers and trees. A harmony of nature and architecture is created by the proximity of tree and temple, the trees lending an appropriate formal serenity to the scene.

Intense cultivation in much of Japan has lead to the simulation of nature on a small scale—the art of bonsai. Plants originally collected from the wild are now scientifically propagated as miniature trees—the momiji or Japanese maple is a particularly adaptable and popular species.

FOREST TYPES OF JAPAN

From the northern island of Hokkaido to the southern point of Kyushu, the climate changes from the cold temperate to the almost subtropical, and the vegetation changes with it. Mountains that run the length of the islands also affect the vegetation, trapping most of the snow and rain on their eastern flanks. Mixed fir and spruce forests admit a few birch trees in the far north, but concede their dominant role to the beech, Fagus crenata, in the Oshima peninsula in south-west Hokkaido. The higher mountains of Honshu are shared by Abies mariesii and A. veitchii, Maries's fir on the colder eastern

HOKKAIDO

OSHIMA PENINSULA

HONSHU

SHIKOKU

KYUSHU

☐ Coniferous

☐ Mixed coniferous and broadleaved deciduous

☐ Broadleaved deciduous

☐ Broadleaved evergreen

side and Veitch's fir tending to the warmer western side, where there is less snow. Elsewhere, beech, oak, ash and maple trees form a light green cover over shrubby viburnums. In the warm heavily populated southern lowlands, evergreen oaks

survive or have been planted in the few places where the land has not been taken for paddy-fields. Tree plantations managed purely for timber production consist almost entirely of conifers—among them the Japanese cedar and the hinoki cypress.

The islands of Japan lie between 24 and 46 degrees north and 112 to 148 degrees east, and thus enjoy a very wide range of climatic conditions, particularly temperature, and heavy rainfall throughout the year, as well as typhoons in summer and considerable snowfall in winter. Mountains, often with steep and greatly indented profiles, occupy some three-quarters of the land area. Forests, with a great number of tree species—many of them indigenous to Japan—cover more than sixty-eight per cent of the country. And the greater part of them are on the mountain slopes. Few countries in the world have a higher proportion of forested land than Japan.

In the mountains, up to 5,000 feet in central Japan and down to sea-level in the far north, coniferous forests predominate. The main tree species are Hondo and Sakhalin spruce, *Picea jezoensis* and *P. glehnii*, mixed with Maries's and Veitch's firs, *Abies mariesii* and *A. veitchii*, with some hinoki cypress, *Chamaecyparis obtusa*, and larch, *Larix kaempferi*, as well as birch, *Betula ermanii*. Willows and poplars are found along the banks of the rivers in the steep-sided valleys. Mosses and lichens hang from the branches of the trees and cover much of the ground beneath them.

The richest display of Japan's flora is found in the cool temperate deciduous forest zone, which covers much of the largest island, Honshu, and the lower-lying parts of southern Hokkaido. These forests are dominated by beech, *Fagus crenata*, in the higher areas and *F. japonica* in the lower warmer parts. But mixed with the beech is a host of other trees, most of which are deciduous. Oaks, chestnuts, maples, limes and zelkovas, each more numerous than the others in their own favoured habitats, give an extraordinary wealth of variety to the forests; and the presence of some giant conifers such as the Japanese cedar, *Cryptomeria japonica*, and the cypress-

like hiba, *Thuyopsis dolabrata*, often in locally pure stands, make them even more stately and impressive.

The Japanese cedar and the hiba are two of the most important timber trees of Japan. The cedars, clad in reddish bark with long tapering stems exceeding 150 feet in height, form stands rivalling the redwoods in California and live to a great age; some giants being more than 1,000 years old and designated as national monuments. Together with the hiba and three other species, the cedars were chosen for special preservation as long ago as the mid-sixteenth century, when considerable attention was being given to forest management. This edict no doubt accounts for the giant old trees that are still alive today.

Southern Japan, and in particular the islands of Shikoku and Kyushu, was once covered with a warm temperate broadleaved evergreen forest. But, following the introduction of primitive agriculture in ancient times, the forest has largely been converted into rice paddies and farm land. The remnants of these great forests are now found only in the precincts of Buddhist and Shinto temples and on some of the smaller and more remote islands off the coast. Camphor trees, *Cinnamomum camphora*, their evergreen leaves and timber impregnated with aromatic oil, evergreen oaks of the *Cyclobalanopsis* genus, various podocarps and pink-flowered albizzias are some of the trees that once abounded in these historic forests.

Of the huge proportion of Japan covered by forest, man-made forests form thirty-five per cent. The principal trees are Japanese cedar and hinoki cypress, both of which are very adaptable and produce excellent construction timber. Red and black pines, *Pinus densiflora* and *P. thunbergii*, are two other conifers much used. Although coniferous plantations exceed broadleaved plantations by as much as forty

Below *The splendid Japanese cedar occurs in both planted and natural forests in Japan and is one of the very few Japanese trees that has been planted abroad—in the Himalayan foothills of India—to provide timber.*

five to one, oaks such as *Quercus glandulifera* and *Q. acutissima*, as well as the chestnut, *Castanopsis cuspidata*, are also planted on a considerable scale. More than seventy per cent of these forests are owned privately.

With its wealth of tree species and with so much of the country enjoying a climate somewhat similar to western Europe and western North America, it is surprising that so few Japanese trees are planted for timber production beyond their native land. The Japanese larch has been successfully exported and has been planted extensively in Britain since its introduction in 1861, but since 1868, when the country was opened up to foreigners, the influence of Japanese ornamental trees on the gardens of Europe and America has been enormous. Centuries of plant breeding from trees whose natural origin has been lost has produced a host of flowering cherries that colour the streets and gardens of cities red and pink and white each spring with their short-lived profusion of blossom.

The Japanese maple, *Acer palmatum*, has been coaxed by centuries of patient attention into producing more than 200 varieties with differing leaf shapes and colours whose bursting buds in spring and tinted foliage in autumn fill our gardens with rich and varied hues. A bushy type of Japanese cedar, *Cryptomeria japonica* 'elegans', retains its feathery juvenile foliage into old age and slow-growing varieties of the Sawara cypress, *Chamaecyparis pisifera*, range in colour from green through blue to gold. The deciduous katsura tree, *Cercidiphyllum japonicum*, with red buds and neat, round leaves, although a huge timber tree in Japan, remains a small and elegant garden feature elsewhere, while the beautifully symmetrical Veitch's fir, *Abies veitchii*, with its upright purple cones and neatly arranged needles, is one of the most handsome representatives of the genus.

The hunting forests of Europe

Deep inside the limestone hills of south-western France and northern Spain wonderfully lifelike cave paintings of wild animals can be found. These pictures, painted some 15,000 years ago by the hunter-gatherer inhabitants of the region, demonstrate with great clarity the intensity of primitive man's relationship with the animals on which he depended for food. The paintings may have been produced as part of some ritual to ensure the success of the hunt although no one can be sure. They do show, however, that the inhabitants of the huge prehistoric forests were familiar with animals that are no longer found in western Europe and even with species that are now extinct (see pages 26–27).

The hunting of these animals was essential for early man's survival. Their meat provided food and their skins and bones provided clothing and tools. And when, three or four thousand years ago, agriculture was introduced to western Europe and the forest began to be cleared to make room for crops, the hunting habit was not lost. Indeed, hunting has occupied a leading place among human activities throughout the intervening period and

it remains a major leisure activity today, although there is no material need for the bodies of wild animals.

Hunting survived for two reasons. Initially, crops and livestock had to be protected from the ravages of wild animals and the extra meat constituted a welcome supplement to the diet. It is only in the last two or three hundred years that agricultural techniques have allowed for large numbers of domesticated animals to be kept through the winter. Previously, all of a herd except for a small breed stock, would be slaughtered in the autumn and the meat salted or smoked to provide food through the long winter. In these circumstances, the taking of a wild animal in a freezing February might be a matter of survival to a poor peasant.

The second and most enduring reason for hunting's survival was that people actually enjoyed it as a sport. The literature and art of the ancient world shows that the Greeks and Romans, as well as the uncivilized tribes of northern Europe, indulged this passion. The virgin huntress Diana, Artemis to the Greeks, was one of the most popular gods, shown in classical art with bow and arrows, sur-

rounded by hounds and in pursuit of a stag.

But hunting, whether for food or for pleasure, requires a healthy population of wild animals. As fields were extended and a little more forest was cleared each year, the habitat in which the hunter's quarry could reproduce and thrive was eroded.

The tribal societies of the early Middle Ages had defined all free men's rights to the wild creatures of the forests and other uncultivated lands. But, as a more hierarchical and organized society developed, those with power decided that their hunting should be protected. The hunting rights of individuals were emphasized with complex codes of privileges, integral to the feudal system of land tenure. These laws clarified which individuals were entitled to which animals on any particular piece of land. Areas reserved for hunting, or "forests", were also defined and steps were taken to prevent further encroachments by the medieval peasant's plough.

Energetic lords extended their forest privileges, nibbling away at the hunting rights of the peasantry and extending their exclusive hunting territories. If the rule of a king or local

Above *An illustration from a 14th-century manual that describes how to catch stags, wild boars, wild cats, otters, wolves, foxes and badgers—forest animals that were pursued not only for food but also to protect domestic* *livestock and villages. The hunting tradition is still vigorous in France today (right) and whole areas of forest are banned to human entry so that the most favoured animals of the chase can breed in peace.*

noble was weak, cultivated lands would creep into the margins of the forests. William the Conqueror, for example, claimed large areas of England as his personal royal forests and his nobles followed suit when they divided up their individual fiefs.

The laws of these royal forests reflect the feudal concept of the forest as it operated throughout western Europe. Generally, hunting in the forest and the felling of trees were exclusively the rights of the lord of the forest, while certain pasture and gathering rights were granted to the local populations. The forests were certainly not deserted. A whole range of officials—some with honoured positions—were appointed to represent the lord's interests, enforce the forest laws and protect the deer and other game. Minor officials held a few acres of cultivated land within the forest and could pasture a specified number of cattle or sheep in exchange for forestry duties. Peasants on the margins of the forest might have the right to keep geese in the forest or gather hazel nuts or bracken. These rights were jealously guarded and were the object of a constant stream of litigation and petitioning throughout the Middle Ages.

The nobles seem to have taken immense pleasure from their exclusive hunting preserves. A number of illustrated hunting manuals have survived and these give a vivid picture of a cultivated aristocracy at play and of the animals that they hunted. There were three major forms of hunting. Most favoured was the chase where dogs were set on the scent of a stag or boar, and the hunters followed on horseback and finally dispatched the animal with sword or spear. Another method used beaters to drive the game into an ambush where the hunters waited with bow and arrow. Finally, and perhaps most elegantly, there was falconry. In this method, a trained bird of prey would be released to chase larger birds on the wing. Herons were a favourite quarry.

The waning of the Middle Ages did not mean the end of the hunting forests, although forests did become smaller. They also became even more private to the nobles, who by this time owned them rather than merely holding feudal rights to them. Aristocratic enthusiasm for hunting continued unabated throughout the sixteenth, seventeenth and eighteenth cen-

turies and contributed greatly to the preservation of woodland that otherwise would have gone under the plough.

These hunting preserves could well be considered as the first examples of "managed" forests. Timber was only selectively felled from them, the balance of animal species and their habitats were carefully controlled and woodland pathways were constantly cleared to allow passage for the hunt. In fact, hunters throughout the ages to the present day have directly or indirectly worked to preserve the forest and its wildlife.

Even today, hunters can be numbered among conservationists struggling to protect wild animals from the effects of modern farming and indiscriminate, uncontrolled shooting with efficient firearms. In south-western France, for example, where primitive man painted his quarry on cave walls, whole areas of forest are banned to human entry, allowing the animals to breed in peace and the trees and other plants to grow in their natural profusion and diversity. This is just to ensure that a healthy stock of breeding animals is maintained for the modern hunters of the region.

Above *In medieval forests the pheasant ranked far below boar and deer but its status as a game animal increased from the 18th century onwards.*

Below *The keen-eyed hawk's predatory prowess was harnessed in falconry to provide meat, chiefly other birds, for royal and aristocratic tables.*

The forest creeps back

Below *Glowing reports of frontier opportunities were promulgated by land companies eager to sell holdings and were accepted uncritically by would-be owners of a slice of Eden. This idealized picture of the pioneering* *life, entitled The Hunter's Return, was painted by a 19th-century New York artist who had no experience of the deprivations and the grinding manual labour required for a prosperous pioneer settlement.*

Before the arrival of Europeans, North America's vast landscape lay virtually unchanged by the hand of man and thousands of square miles of the land were clothed in dense primeval forest. The Indians who inhabited this rich continent were never very numerous and they satisfied their material needs without changing their environment. Many of the woodland tribes were sophisticated and knowledgeable farmers, but the small forest clearings that they made for their fields of corn and vegetables had little impact upon the vastness of their natural surroundings. Within three hundred years of the arrival of the first white settlers in the east, however, the remorseless progression of Europeans westwards across the continent was to make unimaginable changes.

National aspirations drove the first migrants to the New World: the Spaniards to the south, the English to the eastern seaboard and the French to Canada. But it was the British settlement with its reliance on agriculture that produced the most durable and drastic changes in this virgin territory.

The whole length of the east coast wore a familiar and inviting aspect for European farmers. There were parallels in climate and landscape, forests providing building materials and fuel, and beneath the forest cover there were soil types to which the settlers could accommodate themselves. The forests were felled; large plantation holdings for cotton and tobacco were established in the south with its network of navigable rivers providing easy transport for bulky produce; and small mixed farms were set up in a village pattern in the stony north with its shorter growing season.

For a century and a half after the founding in 1607 of the original British town, Jamestown, European settlement along the coast grew thicker and pressed back to the mountain ridge where rivers flowing from the Appalachians broke in waterfalls that were a temporary obstacle to waterborne transport. But behind this natural barrier the forests of the back country were soon dotted with the log cabins and clearings—"little houses in the woods"—made by pioneer farmers.

For a while this frontier was held and disputed by the French, who were more interested in fur trapping than clearing land for agriculture (see pages 76–77). The only settlements were far-flung forts and trading posts that relied upon Indian trappers for pelts. But destruction of French power by the redcoats in 1763 changed this, for French Canada and all land east of the Mississippi were ceded to Britain and although the British government accepted the rights of the Indians to their lands west of the Allegheny Mountains, the settlers did not. The pioneer farmers moved doggedly westwards and the forests continued to shrink under their impact.

The American War of Independence, which culminated in the defeat of the British by the colonists in 1782, threw off all restraints on expansion and pushed the frontier beyond the

SETTLEMENT OF THE UNITED STATES

The frontiers of North American settlement were gradually pushed westwards as pioneer farmers sought out new land. Then the prairies were reached and trails were established as migrants travelled through these treeless and unalluring regions and headed for the fertile lands of the west coast.

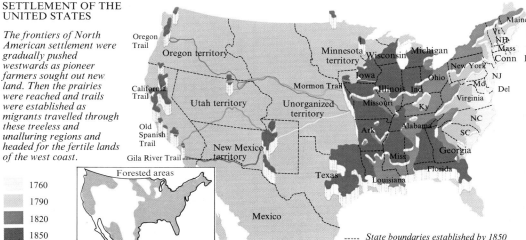

░	1760
▒	1790
▓	1820
█	1850

Forested areas

----- *State boundaries established by 1850*

Mississippi in a breathless rush. A huge change occurred once the cotton gin had given a boost to the plantation economy and the fierce Indian defence of their culture and lands had been broken by a combination of disease, drink and the United States army. In the early nineteenth century mules, ploughs and slaves were poured West in an unending stream and the forest that had clothed the land for a thousand centuries came down virtually in a decade. The eastern and southern states of the United States were established as the farmlands of the New World.

The great prairies and deserts beyond the Mississippi held back the human tide for a while. Until 1830 almost the only Americans who moved on west were the hardy fur trappers or mountain men who plied their lonely trade through the Rockies and penetrated to the west coast.

For a while the great prairies held no lure for farmers because they were treeless. On the frontier the pioneer relied on timber for build-

ing his log cabin, for fuel and for split pos railings so, once the mountain men had dis covered the Oregon trail, westward expansio passed over the prairies as migrants made fo the wooded country of the west coast. Th 1840s and 1850s were the decades of the wago train as settlers left St. Louis to cross th wilderness to the fabled richness of the land i Oregon. It was also the gold rush era as hope ful miners made for the California strikes an to others in Colorado and Nevada.

This haphazard development was onc again consolidated by technical inventio The first transcontinental railway was com pleted in 1869 and it was railways allied to th new steel plough and mechanical reapers an harvesters that made the treeless plains a pract cal place to settle and farm.

Mechanization of agriculture, howeve brought with it further changes. The sma eastern farms rapidly became comparativel uneconomic because their patchwork c rocky, hilly fields was unsuited to mechanize

Below *The crumbling remains of old stone walls mark the site of a long-abandoned New England farm. Mature trees now stand on the once-ploughed land, as they did before the early American settlers wielded their axes.*

New England farmers began to abandon their holdings in the 1850s when the agricultural potential of the prairies was first realized. Since then, New England's forests have been slowly creeping back to rule the landscape again.

Bottom *Many American leisure pursuits today carry on the traditions of frontier life. Log cabins buried in the backwoods make holiday retreats. But the cabins are no longer hacked from the forest; they arrive ready built.*

ploughing and harvesting. Farming families began to move to the prosperous grain-growing regions of the mid-west, farms were abandoned and the forest began to reclaim the land. In the cotton-growing south a similar movement west was taking place, but for different reasons. Continual heavy cropping of cotton and tobacco had exhausted the plantation soils. The useless land was abandoned, planters moved away and the forest crept back. Now these southern pinelands feed the modern forest product industries.

Today much of the North American forest has returned. In the east oaks, maples and hickory flourish amidst the crumbling stone walls that at one time bounded the farms of the earliest settlers. In the southern states, tall stands of pines line the hill terraces that once bore cotton. And, ironically, the one area that the early pioneers did not covet as farmland is now the most productive agricultural region in the United States. Today the prairies are the bread basket of the nation.

ISLAND FORESTS

. . . The mountains or hills are chequered with woods and lawns; some of the hills are wholly covered with flourishing trees; others but thinly and the few that are upon them are small, and the spot of lawns or savannas are rocky and barren, especially to the northward where the country did not afford or produce near the vegetation that it does to the southward, nor where the trees in the woods half so tall and stout. The woods do not produce any great variety of trees; there are only two or three sorts that can be called timber. The largest is the gum tree, which grows all over the country; the wood of this tree is too hard and ponderous for most common uses. The tree which resembles our pines I saw nowhere in perfection but in Botany Bay; this wood, as I have before observed is something of the same nature as American live oak; in short, most of the large trees in this country are of a hard and ponderous nature, and could not be applied to many purposes. Here are several sorts of the palm kind, mangrove, and several other sorts of small trees and shrubs quite unknown to me, besides a very great number of plants hitherto unknown; but these things are wholly out of my way to describe.

CAPTAIN JAMES COOK *Journals* 1770

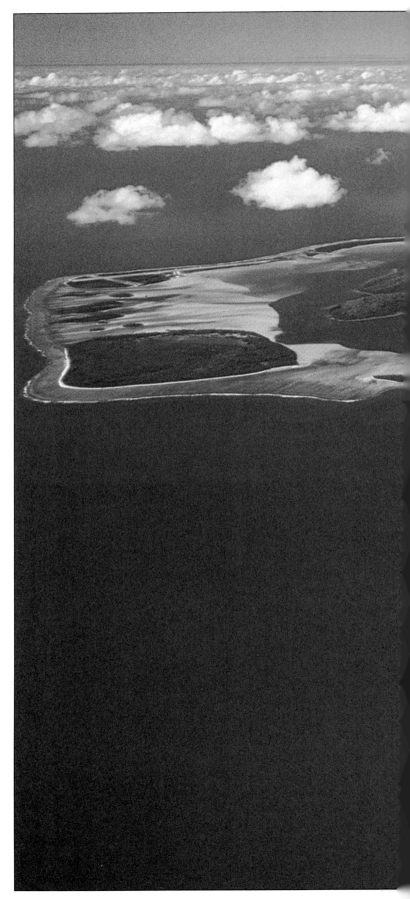

The ecosystem

Below *Species of eucalyptus
dominate the forests of
Australia, except in the
northern tropical area.
The eucalypts have become
adapted to a wide range of
climatic conditions, from
cold alpine to desert.*

ANDESITE LINE

MICRONESIA

PAPUA-
NEW GUINEA

BISMARK
IS.

AUSTRALIA

Left *Nothofagus species—
literally false beeches—are
widely distributed
throughout the southern
hemisphere. They are
important elements in New
Zealand's forests,
providing pulpwood in
some regions and
protection against soil
erosion in other areas.*

Left *Palm trees on the
French Polynesian island
of Moorea. The heavy
fruits are dispersed by
water and the palms easily
colonize the island
beaches. The large size and
heaviness of the fruits
rarely allow palms to
establish themselves
naturally farther inland.*

The flora and fauna of the geographical area
comprising Australia, Papua-New Guinea,
New Zealand and the islands of the south-
west Pacific encircling Australia's north and
north-east seaboards—Timor, the Bismarks,
the Solomons, the New Hebrides and New
Caledonia—show remarkable differences
from those of the islands of the southernmost
part of the Indo-Malaysian region (see pages
90–91 and 154–155).

The huge landmass of Australia has under-
gone great changes of climate for millions of
years. Successive plant communities have
been modified by alternating periods of
drought and flood, heat and cold, and by the
continual arrival of new species. In geologically modern times, the main natural factor
influencing the vegetation has been fire.

Many trees—in particular the eucalypts
that form more than ninety per cent of the
forests—have evolved tough, fire-resistant
leaves and the capsules containing the seed
are woody and do not release their contents
until they have been dried out by fire. Many
eucalypts also respond to fire by sending up
new shoots from their bases. These adaptations allow them to gain ascendency over

Below *Australia, New Zealand and some of the Pacific islands were once part of the supercontinent Gondwanaland. These islands lie on a continental crust characterized by relatively light rocks rich in silicon and aluminium.*

Islands of volcanic origin, such as the Gilberts, are part of the underlying continuous oceanic crust whose rocks are rich in silicon and magnesium. The Andesite line is the boundary between these two crustal types.

GILBERT IS.

POLYNESIA

SOLOMON IS.

MARQUESAS IS.

NEW HEBRIDES IS.

MELANESIA

NEW CALEDONIA

Moorea
Tahiti

NEW ZEALAND

Above *While naturalists marvelled at scientific riches to be found in southern ecosystems, the*

Impressionist painter Paul Gauguin derived inspiration from them. He spent the last decade of his

life on remote Pacific islands and this idyllic image of Tahitian life was painted in the year 1897.

Right *In 1768, some 250 years after Vasco Nuñez de Balboa discovered the Pacific Ocean, James Cook sailed the Endeavour to Tahiti to observe an eclipse of the Sun by the planet Venus. He was accompanied by Joseph Banks leading a small team of natural historians and the botanical finds made on the trip encouraged the participation of natural historians in many similar ventures. Nearly a century later, on the other side of the Pacific, in the Galápagos Islands, Charles Darwin continued this tradition, making many observations concerning the theory of evolution.*

MILES 0   300   600   900   1200

neighbouring trees and, combined with their ability to grow in almost all soil conditions, are responsible for their domination of the Australian flora.

Forests in New Zealand originally developed in the absence of grazing and browsing mammals, in predominantly benevolent conditions of moderate temperature and ample moisture. The New Zealand fossil record shows no traces of dinosaurs, turtles, frogs or mammalian remains and, apart from bats, there are still no native mammals. Large flightless birds were the dominant vertebrates.

The trees are nearly all evergreen, both broadleaved and coniferous (see pages 156–157). During the Tertiary period, about fifty million years ago, New Zealand and the Indo-Malaysian region had a rich flora of palms, yet there are few signs of their existence even in Australia. Fifty per cent of the tree genera in New Zealand are endemic—most of them conifers, twenty-five per cent are shared solely with Australia and twelve per cent solely with South America. These common inheritances suggest a past close connection between New Zealand, Australia, Antarctica and South America.

Among the Pacific islands, too, there are interesting anomalies in the flora. The tropical forests of the Solomon Islands and the Bismark Islands contain markedly fewer tree species—only some sixty, which when adult exceed six feet in circumference—than those of Papua-New Guinea and the Indonesian islands. This relative paucity is probably the consequence of the isolation of the islands by the fragmentation of a previously more extensive Australasian landmass. The eucalypts are poor travellers and have not reached the Pacific islands, most of which were never joined to a greater landmass. On those islands which still retain primary vegetation from sea-level to mountain peaks such as Kolombangara and Vangunu—both in the Solomon Islands group—there is a progressive change in the tree species with elevation. Big-leaved, buttressed trees, 120 to 150 feet tall, sinuous woody climbers and epiphytes are all found at lower elevations, whereas high upon the mountains the trees rarely exceed fifty feet in height and have smaller leaves. Woody climbers are less common and the trees are draped with ferns and mosses.

Vegetation zones are compressed on many

Pacific islands—mossy forests occur at about 2,300 feet; in the mountains of Papua-New Guinea they occur above 7,000 feet. Several tree species found at sea-level in the Santa Cruz islands grow much higher up in the Solomons. Forests throughout the area have been rendered shadows of their former selves by human activities and introduced animals. In Australia, where the forests survived the attentions of grazing kangaroos and browsing arboreal animals, introduced rabbits reached plague proportions and prevented the regeneration of natural forest in many places. In New Zealand, natural forests have been severely modified by imported mammals—deer, possums and rabbits, and the remnants lie mainly in the more inaccessible uplands.

Through long isolation, individual islands have come to have their own exclusive species. The best example of such complete endemism is the narrow distribution of palms in the Pacific—all Hawaiian and New Caledonian palms grow only in those respective islands. Frequently, native trees have failed to meet local needs; North American pines and Australian eucalypts are now the main species in New Zealand's commercial forests.

The trees

Cycads
Lepidozamia hopei

The cycads are a small group of palm-like trees that have changed very little in 280 million years. They have a columnar habit and some grow to a height of 80 ft, bearing enormous cones that can extend to 2 ft in length and weigh as much as 60 lb.

Kauris
Kauri pine *Agathis australis*

The kauri pine is one of the 20 tall evergreen resinous trees belonging to the southern genus Agathis, which is distributed in Polynesia, Australasia and the Philippines. They are large trees—regularly with heights in excess of 200 ft—with massively spreading crowns and a scaly bark.

Palms
Nikau palm *Rhopalostylis sapida*

New Zealand is the southernmost outpost of the palm family, which includes some 4,000 species, and the nikau is their only representative there. Nikaus regenerate profusely, but only under the cover of other trees and never in the open.

Acacias
Koa *Acacia koa*

The magnificent koa tree grows on the mountain-sides of Hawaii. Koa trunks with diameters of 10 ft have been frequently recorded and the tree once provided the Hawaiians with timber of adequate dimensions for large canoes and surfboards.

Many of the tree genera indigenous to this vast southern region are unique to it or are found elsewhere only south of the Equator in South Africa and South America.

The largest group is the eucalypts, a highly adaptable and variable genus of more than 500 species, widely spread over Australia and Tasmania, with some representatives native to many islands of Australasia, but entirely absent from New Zealand. Although eucalypts show a great divergence in form, in general they all bear evergreen, aromatic leaves, differing in shape in the juvenile and adult plants, but always simple and usually with smooth margins; the flowers are fluffy from masses of prominent stamens and the fruits are small woody capsules containing many little black seeds.

The most variable factor apart from size is the appearance of the bark. Some have deeply furrowed, persistent bark, such as the narrow-leaved iron bark, *Eucalyptus creba*; in the red flowering gum, *E. filicifolia*, it is cracked into rectangular pieces. Many have bark persistent at the base but peeling in strips from farther up the trunk and from the branches, and yet in others the whole tree is smooth and shiny, such as the ghost gum, *E. papuana*, one of the species also found in Papua-New Guinea.

Apart from the monumental mountain ash, the Western Australian karri, *E. diversicolor*, the Sydney blue gum, *E. saligna*, and the messmate stringbark, *E. obliqua*, all reach more than 150 feet in height and 20 feet in circumference. The important timber tree jarrah, *E. marginata*, however, does not reach these large dimensions.

Other members of the Myrtaceae family,

which includes the eucalypts and many other aromatic trees in tropical regions, are the brush box, *Tristania conferta*, with eucalyptus-like leaves, glossy green above and dull below; the turpentine, *Syncarpia glomulifera*, has finely matted hairs on the leaf undersides, and the apple box, *Angophora intermedia* has twisted and contorted branches.

In the world-wide Leguminosae family are the acacias or wattles of Australia, even more wide-ranging than the eucalypts and conspicuous in somewhat colourless forests, with their yellow and golden blossoms. Most of them are shrubby in habit. The largest, the hundred-foot blackwood, *Acacia melanoxylon*, yields a beautiful cabinet timber. As in many acacias this tree has feathery leaves when young, replaced by narrow tapering phyllodes (flattened leaf stalks functioning as leaves). The true acacias are absent from New Zealand, where the closely related beautiful flowering kowhai represents the family.

Native to north and east Australia and New Caledonia, but again not to New Zealand, are the graceful sheoaks, the "she" denoting their inferior size to the north temperate oaks, or beefwoods of the Casuarinaceae family. All are evergreen trees with twigs modified into green twitchy needles finely grooved along their length between whorls of minute teeth-like leaves, the whole giving a feathery appearance. Most of the twenty or so species are small trees essentially limited in distribution to a particular habitat. One of the largest is the forest oak, *Casuarina torulosa*, of the cool wet coastal forests of Queensland and New South Wales.

The southern beeches of the genus

Nothofagus, also found in South America, ar most numerous in New Zealand, but they also occur at high altitudes in eastern Australi and in Tasmania as well as high up in the Ne Guinea mountains. They are usually even green trees with small, olive-green leaves, se more closely together on shorter stalks tha those of the northern beeches, *Fagus* spp with the male flowers solitary or at most i twos or threes as opposed to massed bunches The most common species in New Zealand which forms extensive areas of almost pur mountain forest, is the red beech, *Nothofagu fusca*. There is only one species in Tasmani N. cunninghamii, and in Australia the lone re resentative is *N. moorei*, high up in the Divic ing Range, although at one time it may hav had a wider distribution. Unlike Australi which has no true palms, New Zealand ha one, the Nikau palm, *Rhopalostylis sapide* which forms a small tufted tree twenty-fiv feet tall in the lowland forests of North Islanc In Australia, the nearest thing to palms ar the primitive cycads of the *Macrozamia* gent and the liliaceous blackboys of the *Xantho rhoea* genus, whose short black trunk support crowns of shaggy grass-like foliag from which emerge flower stalks that reach height of fifteen feet.

On some of the islands, and on the tropic coasts of Australia, the coconut palm, *Coc nucifera*, has become established or has bee planted. Its wild origin is unknown but ev dence suggests that it came from the ancie Pacific or even from the west coast of Sou America, its huge seeds carried from island island until man realized its value and plante it throughout the tropical world.

Southern beeches
Red beech *Nothofagus fusca*

The red beech belongs to a genus of about 20 species of usually evergreen trees that are native to Australasia and South America. The red beech is one of the four species found in New Zealand and it grows in areas of high rainfall, often to a height of 100 ft.

Eucalypts
Mountain ash *Eucalyptus regnans*

The mountain ash is the tallest broadleaved tree in the world, reaching heights of 200 ft in typical conditions and sometimes more than 350 ft. Its distinctive "stocking" of rough bark at the base of its otherwise smooth white or grey trunk is an identifying feature.

Eucalypts
Snow Gum *Eucalyptus pauciflora*

The snow gums of south-east Australia and Tasmania are the hardiest trees of the region, growing in open forest at the snow line. The timber has little commercial value and the trees are conserved to prevent soil erosion.

Eucalypts
River red gum
Eucalyptus camaldulensis

The river red gum grows in semi-arid areas along watercourses—it is most common along the Murray River—and on flood plains where it forms pure stands. With their reddish timber and thick peeling trunks, the red gums constitute a very distinctive group.

Above *The Norfolk Island pine, Araucaria heterophylla, is native, as its name suggests, to Norfolk Island. It can reach a height of up to 200 ft and has precisely positioned branches. This symmetry has made it popular as an ornamental greenhouse plant throughout the world.*

Right *Tree ferns, such as these Dicksonia, form extensive forests on many of the Pacific islands, growing to great heights in Samoa and New Zealand. They are particularly suited to island life because they are adapted to the moist but cool upland Tropics—conditions often provided by islands.*

Australia

Australia, one of the oldest land entities in the world, was once a vast undulating plain covered with uniform vegetation. But subsequent land movements, glaciations and flooding profoundly modified the climate, and affected the migration and establishment of plant species. Although the main element of the present-day flora—the myrtles, the sheoaks and the wattles—is typically Australian in origin, some species from the Indo-Malaysian region have invaded the northern tropical areas and are still advancing south. Influxes from the south, when Australia was still part of the larger continent of Gondwanaland (see pages 20–21), have brought such species as the southern beech, *Nothofagus*, which is now established in the higher altitude regions of eastern Australia and Tasmania.

Vast areas of Australia, some forty per cent, are desert or semi-desert, supporting grasses and tough drought-resistant shrubs. Only along watercourses and on periodically flooded land can the hardiest trees such as the red river gum, *Eucalyptus camaldulensis*, and the coolabah tree, *E. coolabah*—of *Waltzing Matilda* fame—survive.

Dwarf eucalypts in the mallee scrublands grade into a discontinuous band of open woodland, populated with the lemon-scented gum and the Darwin stringbark, both members of the bloodwood group, so called because of the red gum that oozes from the pockets or "kinos" in the timber.

Closed forests flourish only in the more humid upland and coastal areas of south-west and eastern Australia and Tasmania. Two distinct forest formations are recognized; the more highly developed and complex rain forest in coastal Queensland (see pages 90–91) and the sclerophyll forests, in the areas of lower rainfall. Flat-topped eucalypts and angophoras provide an almost unbroken cover, the underlying sheoaks benefiting from the considerable light that penetrates through the vertically hanging leaves of the upper layers. On the forest floor a multitude of shrubs equipped with small, spiky, leathery leaves soaks up the remaining light.

Typical of the dry sclerophyll forests is the jarrah forest of western Australia, where these valuable timber trees grow either in almost pure stands or mixed with marri, *E. calophylla*. The scribbly gums, such as *E. micrantha*, their smooth grey bark marked with scribbles made by burrowing insect larvae, several species of stringybarked gums, and a few of the deeply furrowed ironbarks and bloodwoods are other species commonly found in the dry sclerophyll forests. Underneath them grow the blackboys, *Xanthorrhoea* species, with their fat dark trunks topped by shaggy masses of foliage, lilies and palm-like *Macrozamia* cycads, all of which are capable of withstanding the frequent fires that devastate the area.

The wet sclerophyll forests of Victoria and Tasmania harbour the magnificent mountain ash, one of the tallest trees in the world, replaced in south-west Australia by the dominant karri gum, while in the eastern forests, *Dicksonia* tree ferns offer a foothold for epiphytes on their massed aerial roots, a feature more associated with the nearby rain forests.

The eucalypts dominate ninety-five per cent of Australia's forests and are almost confined to the sub-continent, where they have become adapted to a wide range of conditions ranging from the desert to the cool temperate. The slender leathery leaves are impregnated with aromatic oils and in many species hang vertically with their edges towards the sun to reduce water loss. The consequent lower incidence of sunlight on the leaves would decrease the rate of photosynthesis had not many eucalypts responded to this ecological constraint by developing photosynthetic cells on both the upper (normal) and lower leaf surfaces.

Eucalypts are also unusual in that the petals fall off early in the opening of the flowers, which derive their colour and form from the bared stamens. Equally attractive are the wattles with their exquisite feathery leaves and multiple fluffy yellow flowers, the silky-oaks similarly handsome of leaf, with orange comb-like flowers, and those graceful ornamental trees the sheoaks.

There are also some valuable softwoods indigenous to the temperate regions of Australia. The fine-leaved *Callitris* cypress pines cover extensive tracts in the drier parts of Queensland and northern New South Wales. The huon pine, the aptly named celery-top pine, and a number of other conifers are found in the Tasmanian forests together with the myrtle beech. These indigenous conifers have been supplemented with extensive plantations

FOREST TYPES

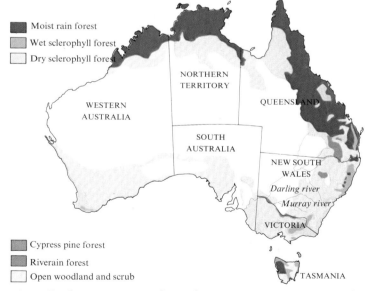

- ■ Moist rain forest
- ▨ Wet sclerophyll forest
- ☐ Dry sclerophyll forest

NORTHERN TERRITORY

WESTERN AUSTRALIA

QUEENSLAND

SOUTH AUSTRALIA

NEW SOUTH WALES

Darling river

Murray river

VICTORIA

- ▨ Cypress pine forest
- ▨ Riverain forest
- ☐ Open woodland and scrub

TASMANIA

Above *Eucalypts dominate all but the wettest rain forests in parts of New South Wales and Queensland. Much eucalyptus forest is distinguishable as either wet or dry sclerophyll forest. Karri, mountain ash and blackbutt gums typify the wet forests, while jarrah, stringybarks and spotted gums are more typical of the drier forests. Annual flooding transforms a few arid areas sufficiently to support river red gums, but these stands lack the grandeur of the true sclerophyll forests. Cypress pines are found throughout Australia but occur in significant stands only in a few places.*

Right *This wild acacia displays delicate, finely divided leaves and massed white-yellow flowers that are not so different from those of its more familiar relative the silver wattle, one of the acacias favoured as an ornamental tree far beyond the limits of its natural range in south-east Australia.*

of exotic species—the Monterey, slash and Mexican pines—to provide softwood timber.

Woodlands and forests, natural and exotic, are inhabited by a rich variety of wildlife, marsupial mammals predominating. The largest of these are the red kangaroo and the grey kangaroo, which is sometimes called the forester because of its partiality for open woodlands. The grey kangaroo is a browser, feeding on leaves and herbage rather than grass, and its future in the wild depends on the survival of its wooded habitat. Most governments protect the species, only allowing shooting permits to certain farmers.

Wombats, opossums, koalas and hosts of other creatures live in and underneath the trees. Little green budgerigars that breed in the mallee congregate in huge colourful flocks as the young develop their flying feathers; crow-like currawongs build untidy stick nests in the eucalyptus; laughing kookaburras lay their eggs in hollow tree limbs and honey-eaters hang their grassy nests near the ends of the sheoaks' drooping branches.

With the possible exception of parts of Tasmania and New Zealand, nowhere else in the world do associations of flora and fauna remotely resemble those of Australia. Fire may sweep through the forests, drought may stunt growth for decades but the ingenuity of evolution has permitted adjustment to these and other adversities posed by the isolation and aridity of much of Australia, yielding more than 500 eucalyptus species alone, and a wonderful variety of marsupials.

Right *Australia has a high proportion of venomous snakes whose poison may be used defensively against predators or offensively to capture prey. This carpet snake is not venomous but relies on its constricting strength to suffocate its victims—mice, rats and small birds. Carpet snakes are adept climbers and often feed and then rest high up in trees. The rat-catching ability of these snakes is exploited by farmers who release them despite their size—they may reach a length of 12 ft—in their barns to reduce the mice and rat populations.*

Left *Australia's fauna is, for the outsider, epitomized by the grey kangaroo. It ranges freely through the open forests of eastern Australia and can cover short distances at more than 25 miles per hour with its long heavy tail acting as a counterbalance to the forward thrust from the powerful hindlegs.*

Right *The kookaburra is one of the best loved birds in Australia and feeds on fish, insects and snakes, which it batters to death on tree branches. Its distinctive maniacal laugh and popular affection for the bird are celebrated in the rhyme: Kookaburra sits in the old gum tree, Merry merry king of the bush is he, Laugh kookaburra laugh Kookaburra, gay your life must be.*

Marsupials

Below *The koala,
Phasolarctos cinereus,
feeds on the leaves of six
species of eucalyptus. It
descends to the ground
only in search of fresh
food, or when there is a
build up of toxins in the
eucalypt leaves.*

Marsupials are distinguished from other mammals by the premature birth of their young and the continuation of their development in the warm shelter of the mother's pouch, attached to her teats. Renowned for their unique method of reproduction, the marsupials also have a peculiar distribution. The American opossums are probably the oldest surviving mammal family, dating back to the Cretaceous period a hundred million years ago. Fossil finds in North America and Europe indicate the wide distribution of marsupials at that time, but the record is too incomplete to reveal their origins and the routes of dispersal.

Marsupials survive today in South and Central America and of the species penetrating North America, one is found as far north as New England, but their most secure home is the ancient continent of Australia. The diversification of the Australian marsupials is a classic example of adaptive radiation—the opportunistic spread of species into a wide variety of niches terrestrial, arboreal, aerial and aquatic, which were previously vacant because of long periods of isolation. Although forests occupy only a small portion of this vast continent, they offer many niches to marsupials, most of whom are nocturnal.

Small mouse-like creatures scurry through bark and leaf litter: these are the marsupial mice which, despite their superficial resemblance to small rodents, are fearless little predators, hunting not only insects, but also small birds, mice, rats and snakes. The brown

marsupial mouse, *Antechinops stuartii*, is a typical species in the eastern forests.

The unique jarrah and karri forests of south-western Australia contain a number of marsupials, among them the beautifully patterned numbat or marsupial anteater, *Myrmecobius fasciatus*. It is one of the four diurnal marsupials and constantly sniffs the ground litter of fallen, rotting branches that are infested with termites. The numbat scratches open the passages hollowed out by the termites and then picks the insects up on a long cylindrical sticky tongue.

In the eastern forests, bandicoots play a similar role on the forest floor and can be detected by rustlings in the undergrowth and disturbed patches of soil; they first dig conical pits with the aid of a specially adapted fingernail on the middle digit of each forefoot, before inserting their distinctive tapering snouts to extract beetle larvae and worms.

The common wombat, *Vombatus arsinus arsinus*, is large—a sturdy, squat but very peaceful animal measuring more than three feet long and weighing more than a hundred pounds. It favours mountain forests, particularly those with large stands of mountain ash, *Eucalyptus regnans*, and constructs great burrow systems where it stays during the day—safe from introduced foxes, wild dogs and the numerous devastating forest fires caused by lightning. It emerges at dusk to consume grasses, bark, roots and fungi.

Ring-tailed opossums and brush-tailed opossums are perfectly adapted to arboreal life. The ring-tail, *Pseudocheirus peregrinus*, has a long prehensile tail with a naked patch on the lower surface that secures a tight grip when climbing. The tail is also used to carry bundles of twigs used to make a large globe-shaped nest. The brush-tailed opossum, *Trichosurus vulpecula*, is one of the most frequently encountered of marsupials. Although a forest animal, it has adapted to suburban sprawl and can be found in city parks in and around Sydney.

In contrast, the koala is not at all common. Its numbers have suffered since the early days of settlement when hundreds of thousands were slaughtered for their fur. Today, several thousand survive under protection in isolated pockets of forest along the east coast.

Banksias, grevillias and baronias are some of the many native shrubs that form a dense understorey beneath the straight limbs of the gum trees and constitute a major source of food for many arboreal marsupials. In this dense undergrowth live pigmy opossums, which resemble the European dormouse in appearance and habits, although they have prehensile—grasping—tails and feed mainly on insects. During the day they sleep in typical dormouse repose, coiled up in a nest of shredded bark. In winter they are torpid and survive in this inactive state by drawing upon reserves of fat stored under the skin and in the tail.

A common feature of the large marsupial family, the Phalangeridae, to which the pigmy opossum belongs, is the opposable first toe of the hindfoot, which functions like a thumb when climbing. More spectacular is the development, in several members, of a gliding membrane or patagium, consisting of a fold of skin along the sides of the body between fore- and hindlimbs. When extended, the surface area of the body is greatly increased—a principle also used by the tropical flying squirrels (see pages 108–109). Three species of *Petaurus*, the squirrel, sugar and yellow-bellied gliders, have bushy tails and well-developed gliding membranes and all three feed on a mixed insect-flower diet.

The largest "flying possum" is the greater glider, *Schoinobates volans*, with a patagium that extends from elbow to knee. When gliding, these animals have been likened to "aerial frying pans" and can easily cover a hundred yards, launching themselves from the top of one gum tree to the base of another. The landing curve is often so low that the animals fall prey to foxes and native cats who pounce on them before they land.

Tasmania, 200 miles south of the mainland across the Bass Strait, with a temperate climate and a high annual rainfall, supports a thick eucalypt forest interspersed with high dense scrub and stands of southern beech, *Nothofagus* spp. These form refuges for marsupials that are rare or extinct on the mainland. The thylacine, a six-foot-long marsupial wolf was the most impressive. Although the last captive specimen died in 1933, numerous unauthenticated sightings suggest that a few pairs may still survive in the wild mountainous districts of the west and south-west.

Left This south-western pygmy opossum, Cercartetus concinnus, preys on insects caught near flowers such as this Banksia. It also feeds on the flower's pollen and nectar, inadvertently pollinating the flowers.

Right The Tasmanian devil, Sarcophilus harrisii, is Australia's version of the scavenging hyena. This heavy-set animal, the size of a small dog, has a disproportionately large head and fearsome teeth. It is a slow shuffling hunter and a tidy eater, securing its prey with long canine teeth and employing shearing teeth to tear up the flesh, before crunching up the bones with its strong molars. The devil now survives only in Tasmania where it feeds on insects, frogs, chickens and lamb and sheep carcasses. The devil is an unusually vocal marsupial, calling in a crescendo of hyena-like screams interrupted by rasping snarls.

REPRODUCTION

This small pink blob being suckled by its mother is unrecognizable as the brush-tailed opossum into which it will develop. The physical immaturity of marsupials at birth—the comparable stage in the placental mammals is the unborn embryo—necessitates a prolonged uninterrupted attachment to the teat. Immediately after birth, marsupial young must make an unaided journey from the mother's cloaca to the teats in a more or less protective pouch. Natural selection operates even at this early stage—the weaker ones either fail to complete the distance, or they arrive in the pouch only to find that all the teats are occupied. This premature existence outside the mother's body restricts the range of marsupials. They are noticeably absent from the polar regions, and only one, the water opossum, *Chironectes minimus*, occupies an aquatic habitat.

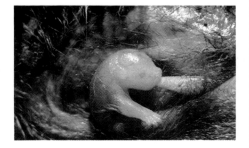

New Zealand

FOREST DISTRIBUTION
*Although isolated in the Pacific, New Zealand's trees
have similarities to those across the ocean. But New
Zealand's varying climate and terrain encourage a
patchwork distribution. Kauri is found in the north, rarely
with beech but more often with the podocarps, rimu and
totara, and the hardwoods, rewarewa and tawari. South of
the kauri, podocarps predominate. The canopy is usually
filled by softwoods over understoreys of the hardwood
kamahi and young northern rata. Extensive forests of the
southern beeches grow in South Island, reflecting the
colder climate, although hard beech favours the
subtropical climate of North Island. The silver beech and
mountain subspecies are common at the timberline, with
red and black beeches in lower warmer regions.*

NORTH
ISLAND

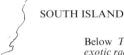

Pure or mixed montane beech stands

Mixed lowland beech stands

Pure or mixed hardwood and softwood stands

Kauri

Exotics

SOUTH ISLAND

Below *The tight ranks of
exotic radiata pines in this
plantation contrast with
the chaotic native
evergreen forest. Although
the pines are only 7 years
old they have already
grown 35 ft tall.*

Above *Captain Cook's first sight of
New Zealand, perhaps: high snow-clad
mountains rising steeply behind densely*
*forested foothills. A naval man, he was
thrilled to discover vast kahikatea trees
with their potential for boat building.*

Aotearoa—the long bright land or the long
white cloud—was first sighted by the Polynesian Maoris 1,000 years ago and they
migrated there in significant numbers 300
years later. Both versions of the name fit; the
two main islands intercept moist winds and
are washed by cool currents. In the extreme
north much rain falls from the "long white
cloud" and the climate here, warm and subtropical, and tolerated by mangrove swamps,
graduates to cold temperate in the far south.

New Zealand has long mountain ridges and
high hills along the west coast of South Island,
with volcanoes in North Island. Rocks are
generally soft, and steep easily erodable slopes
were held in place by previous extensive forests that were free of grazing animals. In their
absence, birds, many of them flightless, from
the small kiwi to the massive moa, could feed
undisturbed on the ground. Land denuded by
natural fires was rapidly reclothed by native
vegetation. Massive forests of huge kauri
mixed with evergreen broadleaves grew in

North Island, while tracts of podocarps, tall
conifers related to the yews, occupied richer
soils throughout the country.

The self-pruning kauris, which yield valuable durable timber, are conifers with round
cones and broadish leaves and they also grow
in Queensland, Indonesia and Fiji. The podocarps, often with yew-like leaves, but sometimes with small scaly cypress-like foliage,
produce fleshy coated fruits, some like small
acorns. These softwoods vary from tall clean-
trunked timber trees to relatively bushy ones,
and of the eight main species—all known by
their Maori names—totara, rimu and kahikatea are the most important. Great war
canoes were once made out of single totara
trees. Podocarps are also found in South
America, Australia, southern Africa, the East
Indies and as far north as Japan.

In the southern hills, kauris were replaced
by small-leaved evergreen beech trees and
these grow in fairly pure communities, some
tall, and others, on the higher tops, stunted.

These southern beeches also grow in Chile,
Argentina and south-west Australia, and they
now form important associations with the
conifers from North Island. The New Zealand
softwood forests are dense and dark green and
only a few flowers, such as the pohutakawa
with its brilliant red blossoms and the delicate
yellow kowhai, relieve the green monotony.
On poor soils the forest faded to low woody
scrub—*Hebes* are common elements of montane evergreen scrubland—and the dry areas
in the eastern lee of the south carried tussocky
grasslands up to the footlands of the long
high-wooded ranges.

The Maoris cleared forest on better soils for
agricultural use, growing sweet potato and
bracken roots, and smoked out rival tribes in
the process. But their casual farming was of
negligible consequence compared with the impact of the white man, the *pakeha*. European
whalers were among the first to realize the
qualities of the native timber, and forests were
soon cleared from the accessible lowlands.

Tui
Prosthemadera novaeseelandiae

Pigeon
Hemiphaga novaeseelandiae

Red crowned parakeet
Cyanoramphus novaeseelandiae

Rifleman
Acanthisitta chloris

Kakapo
Strigops habroptilus

Kiwi
Apteryx australis

Left *This fine Maori carving represents an important ancestor as a victorious warrior. It was fashioned from totara wood by a tohunga or wood carver who would probably have offered a prayer to Tane, god of the forest, before cutting down the tree for it. Particularly fine individual trees, highly valued by local chiefs, were reserved for future use by the imposition of a "tapu" or restriction which might last several generations, and this word has been absorbed into the English language as taboo, for us meaning any general or recognized prohibition.*

Right *The forests still rely on their original tenants, birds, for checking insects, fertilizing flowers and dispersing seeds. Forest-floor insects are hunted by the nocturnal flightless kiwi and others are picked off tree trunks by the dynamic 3 in-long rifleman. The tui, also known as the parson bird because of its "dog collar", feeds with its brush tongue on kowhai and rata nectar, pollinating the flowers in the process. Pigeons, kakapos and parakeets prefer berries, and the seeds they contain are widely dispersed and fertilized by the birds' droppings.*

The 1840s witnessed rapid colonization, and forest trees were felled not only for domestic building—the parliament house in Wellington is of kauri—but also for export, and to free land for farming. It seemed that there would always be plenty of forest.

Introduced domestic stock escaped to the wild. Deer, chamois and Australian opossum imported to provide sport, thrived in the hills, and rabbits overran the drier plains. Where farming had failed on poor soil, the newly introduced European gorse, briar and bramble flourished uncontrollably. In the late nineteenth century, concern for the remaining forest grew. It was realized that the timber resource was not inexhaustible and that the cut-over forest should be regenerated where the land was not needed for farming. The bracken and smoke bush, or *manuka*, areas on the pumice slopes of the North Island volcanoes were widely planted.

Patches of native forest had survived in South Island, but there, as in North Island, conifers imported from North America and Europe were grown successfully; wherever it was tried, except in the far subtropical north and on the poorest southern gravels, the remarkable radiata pine, from the Monterey Peninsula of California, grew far faster and became the most popular species, although Douglas fir has also been successful. This pine reaches a usable size in only a fifth of the time taken by the podocarps, although it yields a coarse knotty timber compared with the slow-grown fine and knot-free native woods.

In the 1940s, surveys identified forests accessible and manageable for timber, and those that protected erodable slopes by aiding water catchment and sheltering farmland. Exotic or non-native tree plantations were accepted as a permanent feature of the landscape and recognized as an asset invaluable to the growing forest products industry.

Today, forested land occupies about a quarter of New Zealand's land surface, compared with almost two-thirds before the arrival of the European settlers. Virtually no kauri is felled—there is little left anyway—and it is regenerating fairly well. The sustaining of podocarp forests is more difficult because the seedlings grow slowly in fierce competition with faster growing shrubs and lesser broad-leaved trees. Where they grow well on good soil the farming lobby clamours for forest clearing; on poor soil they fare less well and here they will be increasingly replaced with the commercially viable pines and Douglas fir.

The southern beeches may have brighter prospects. They occupy high, relatively inaccessible land and the soil is often unsuited to agricultural purposes. Beech forests are protection forests, holding soil on steep slopes loosened by grazing red deer, and to a small extent provide pulpwood.

The dangers of indiscriminate forest clearing, multiplied by the introduction of browsing animals, are receding, as responsible forestry policies are implemented and the survival of the remaining native forests seems assured.

The Pacific islands

Below *Continental Pacific islands such as New Caledonia support a variety of vegetation and wildlife, which is completely absent from tiny, remote coral atolls. This island forest resembles rich mainland forest.*

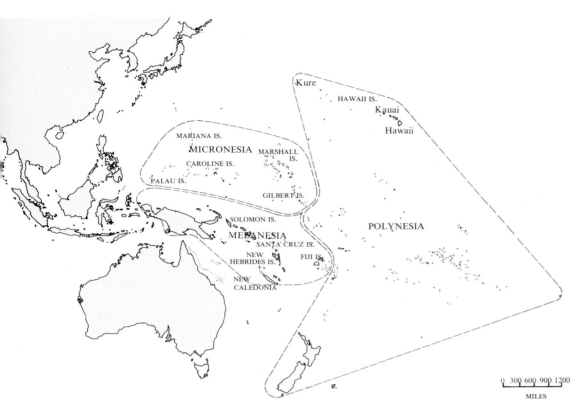

The continental island remnants of Melanesia, in contrast to oceanic islands formed by volcanic processes, provide a relatively stable and benevolent environment for plants and animals. After volcanic activity and uplifting cease altogether, oceanic islands slowly settle back on to the sea floor, their disappearance accelerated by erosion and only slightly delayed by coral formation. The volcanic

Micronesian islands range from the western Mariana, Caroline and Palau islands with a few peaks of 1,000–2,500 ft, to the low coral formations of the Marshall and Gilbert islands farther east, which are similar to many Polynesian islands. The younger Hawaiian Islands are exceptional in that they offer habitats ranging from dry alpine to rain forest.

The Pacific Ocean covers nearly one-third of the Earth's surface, some sixty-four million square miles. Apart from Australia, Papua-New Guinea and New Zealand, the land area is divided between thousands of diverse and widely scattered islands. In the western Pacific the islands are grouped into three divisions known as Melanesia, Micronesia and Polynesia. Of these three island groupings, only Melanesia has extensive forests.

The sea isolates the islands from the mainland masses to varying degrees and acts as a barrier to the free passage of both plant and animal species. Most of the islands are remote and small, and their size compounds the effect of the seawater barrier in reducing the numbers of immigrants.

The islands conform well to the theory of island biogeography, which is based on the observations that small islands usually contain fewer species than large ones, and remote islands contain fewer species than those near a large landmass. Area is the most accurate single guide to the number of species on an island, because it best reflects the diversity of habitats available.

Before the advent of man, particularly the white man, forests probably covered nearly the whole of Melanesia. An important feature of these forests is the abundance of trees with short branches and very large leaves, and the

forests are markedly less tall than similar forests in Malaysia. Tree ferns are well represented—in New Caledonia and the New Hebrides they may reach a hundred feet.

Conifers are located mainly in New Caledonia (forty-four species), with ten species in Fiji, but very few in the New Hebrides and Solomon Islands. Kauri pines occur throughout New Caledonia, the New Hebrides, the Santa Cruz Islands and Fiji, where they dominate the humid closed forest. In New Caledonia, there is only ten per cent forest cover at low altitudes. Large areas of forest exist only in the southern part of the main island, the most characteristic trees again being kauris, which reach 130 feet in height. Several species of *Araucaria* are also distinctive trees of this island. In the New Hebrides, high forest is restricted on most of the islands, especially those densely populated or with active volcanoes. In the humid northern islands, the finest forests occur towards the west on slopes protected from prevailing winds.

In the Solomon Islands tropical rain forests remain the dominant element and freshwater swamp forests are extensive where they occupy coastal plains and low-lying valleys. About sixty species of tall trees have been identified, much fewer than in Malaysian forests but greater than in any other Melanesian archipelago. The compression of vegetation

zones, occurrence of a few montane species in the lowland rain forest and the common incidence of climbers and epiphytes throughout the lowland and mountains are prominent features of the Solomon Islands' rain forests which flourish in the exceptionally wet climate.

The Hawaiian islands were formed by the welling up of hot material through the ocean floor at a "hot spot" just north of Hawaii. Kure at the north-west end of the chain, which appeared about fifteen million years ago, shows signs of decay. Eroded by wind, rain and the incessant pounding of Pacific surf, only a low coral atoll remains. Hawaii itself is barely a million years old and its relative youth is expressed in the two 13,000-foot volcanic peaks of Mauna Loa and Mauna Kilauea. Plants and animals disappear as conditions deteriorate on ageing islands, but further upheavals on the ocean floor will continue to offer them new island habitats.

A striking feature of both plant and animal distribution in the Pacific islands is the presence of species restricted to one or a few islands. Some eighty per cent of the plant species in New Caledonia are endemic, but only fifteen per cent in the New Hebrides. Mammals have had particular difficulty in making long sea journeys and with the exception of a phalanger in the Solomon Islands, the indigenous mammalian fauna of Melanesia

Above *The idyllic palm-fringed island beach is the most evocative and familiar popular image of the Pacific islands. These palms rarely grow naturally far from the sea because the heaviness of the seed prevents the coconut from travelling far.*

Below *Where the land is protected from scouring winds and has not been sterilized by recent lava flows Hawaii's distinctive trees—koa, ti and ohia—can sprout and provide shelter for flittering kamehameha butterflies and honeycreepers.*

represented exclusively by bats, of which the Megachiroptera (flying foxes) are a pronounced element.

New Caledonia, 700 miles off Queensland, Australia, and one of the largest islands in the Pacific, completely lacks mammals and frogs, but there are some snakes and lizards. There are no indigenous amphibia in the New Hebrides, but there are several in the Solomons. The larger islands of Fiji, 1,500 miles northeast of Australia, are true continental remnants and they harbour lizards, skinks and snakes and two species of frogs; they represent the most remote point reached by amphibians in the Pacific. The most interesting lizard is an iguana related to species in the West Indies and the Galápagos Islands.

The replacement of forest in extensive areas by thickets of small trees and climbers is due to the combined influences of natural disasters and human intervention. The arrival of the white man accelerated the harvesting of trees for timber and valuable kauri species are now scarce. Lowland forest areas have been largely replaced by coconut or other plantations, or converted to savannahs. The greatest threat at the present time to the native forest of Melanesia comes from the practice of shifting cultivation, but some forested areas are being placed under protection, and on some islands afforestation has been initiated.

THE FOREST RESOURCE

. . . The productions of vegetation have had a vast influence on the commerce of nations, and have been the great promoters of navigation, as may be seen in the articles of sugar, tea, tobacco, opium, ginseng, betel, paper, etc. As every climate has its peculiar produce, our natural wants bring on a mutual intercourse; so that by means of trade each distant part is supplied with the growth of every latitude. But, without the knowledge of plants and their culture, we must have been content without hips and haws, without enjoying the delicate fruits of India and the salutiferous drugs of Peru.

GILBERT WHITE *The Natural History of Selborne* 1778

World timber: geography

HARDWOODS

Alder, red	Plane, American
Ash, American	Poplar/cottonwood
Basswood	Tupelo
Beech, American	Walnut, American
Birch	Whitewood, Americ
Cherry, American	Minor species
Dogwood	
Elm, American	**SOFTWOODS**
Gum, American red	Cedar
Hackberry	Southern cypress
Hickory, pecan	Douglas fir
Hornbeam, American	Fir, true
hop	Hemlock
Magnolia	Larch
Maple	Pine
Oak	Sequoia
Persimmon	Spruce

Nearly two billion tons of timber are cropped from the forests of the world each year. Almost half of this total harvest is immediately burned as fuel within a few miles of the felling area, but the rest of the crop is destined for commercial uses. Commercial timber is divided into softwoods from coniferous trees and broadleaved hardwoods (see pages 16–17).

The major indigenous softwood forests are found in the northern hemisphere. North America provides mostly white and black spruce, balsam fir and southern pine from the east, and from the west sitka spruce, Douglas fir, western hemlock, red cedar and ponderosa pine. Europe supplies Norway spruce and Scots pine, as well as larch. The montane forests also provide softwood timbers, but these slow-growing trees provide tighter grained knotty woods.

The natural distribution of subtropical softwood trees is relatively limited, but extensive man-made forests of these species, particularly of southern pine and radiata pine, have been established in the southern United States, New Zealand, South America and other subtropical regions. When these forests reach full production in ten to twenty years, they will alter the pattern of softwood supply.

Most commercial softwood species produce faster growing, more uniform trees of smaller diameter than hardwoods. Furthermore, the species variation among the softwoods is relatively small and, even within the natural coniferous forests, large stands of single species occur. These characteristics create ideal cropping conditions that produce far cheaper timber than it is possible to obtain from the hardwood forests.

The hardwood forests of the Tropics produce a far greater range of timbers than the softwood forests. As many as 200 species of trees can be found in one square mile, and there are as many as sixty commercially important tropical hardwood species (see pages 82–83). Because these timbers are generally denser, more durable and are freer of knots than softwood, the tropical forests are particularly valuable sources of heavy construction timbers, such as greenheart and iroko, and woods for fine joinery and veneers, such as mahogany and teak.

The more familiar hardwoods, deciduous species such as oak, beech and elm, are products of the temperate woodlands. European temperate forests provide most of these, as well as quality woods such as walnut. In the United States sugar maple, red oak, black cherry, yellow birch, white ash, black walnut and beech are the major deciduous hardwoods, often mixed with conifers such as larch, "cedar" and white pine. Mediterranean-type evergreen forests bear such trees as the evergreen oak, which is ideal for furniture and floors because the grain is tightly formed by a growing season curtailed by summer drought.

The map, right, shows the internationally important timber-producing regions and the timbers they produce.

CENTRAL AMERICA and the CARIBBEAN

HARDWOODS

Almacigo	Cocobolo	Magnolia	Satinwood,
Andiroba	Cocuswood	Mahoe	West Indian
Angelin	Cordia, American	Mahogany	Simaruba
Aromata	light	Manni	Sterculia
Balata	Courbaril	Mauricif	Tabebuia,
Basralocus	Degame	Nargusta	white
Bois bande	Encens	Petit citron	Teak
Bois gris	Fustic	Pipirie	Tonka
Bois lait	Gommier	Prima vera	Virola, light
Bullhoof	Guayacan	Quaruba	Yokewood
Bustic	Hura	Resolu	
Caconnier rouge	Lancewood	Roble	**SOFTWOODS**
Carapite	Laurier petites	Rosewood,	
Cativo	feuilles	Honduras	Pine, Caribbean
Central American	Laurier poivre	Sabicu	pitch
cedar	Lignum vitae	Saman	Yellowood

SOUTH AMERICA

HARDWOODS

Acapu	Faveiro	Mahogany,	Satiné
Andiroba	Freijo	Brazilian	Simaruba
Angelim pedra	Gonçalo alves	Manbarklak	Snakewood
Arariba	Greenheart	Mandio	Sterculia
Baguacu	Grumixava	Manniballi	Sucupira
Balsa	Guariuba	Massaranduba	Surudan
Baromalli	Hevea	Mora	Tatajuba
Basralocus	Hura	Muiratinga	Tineo
Maracaibo	Imbuia	Olivillo	Tulipwood,
boxwood	Ipê	Pakuri	Brazilian
San Domingo	Itauba	Pau amarelo	Ulmo
boxwood	Jacaranda pardo	Pau marfim	Verawood
Brazilwood	Jatai peba	Pau mulato	Vinhatico
Canafistula	Jequitiba	Peroba rosa	Virola, heavy
Canela	Kabukalli	Peroba, white	Virola, light
Canjerana	Kingwood	Piquia	Wallaba
South American	Kurokai	Purpleheart	
cedar	Chilean laurel	Quaruba	
Ceiba	Licania species	Rauli	**SOFTWOODS**
Cerejeira	Lingue	Rosewood,	
Coigue	Louro inamui	Brazilian	Alerce
Courbaril	Louro pardo	Sajo	Manio
Dukali	Louro, red	Sande	Chile pine
Espavel	Macacauba	Santa-maria	Parana pine

MAJOR FOREST REGIONS

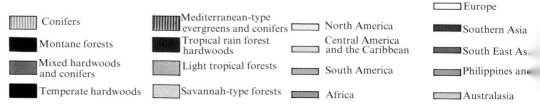

Conifers	Mediterranean-type evergreens and conifers	
Montane forests	Tropical rain forest hardwoods	
Mixed hardwoods and conifers	Light tropical forests	
Temperate hardwoods	Savannah-type forests	

MAJOR TIMBER-PRODUCING REGIONS

North America	Europe	
Central America and the Caribbean	Southern Asia	
South America	South East As	
Africa	Philippines an	
	Australasia	

EUROPE

HARDWOODS

Alder
Ash, European
Beech, European
Birch, European
Boxwood, European
Cherry, European
Horse chestnut

Chestnut, sweet
Elm
Holly, European
Hornbeam, European
Lime, European
Maple, European
Oak

Pear
Plane, European
Poplar
Robinia
Sycamore
Walnut, European
Willow

SOFTWOODS

Cedar
Western red cedar
Cypress, Lawson
Douglas fir
Fir, silver
Larch, European
Larch, Japanese

Pine, Austrian
Pine, Corsican
Pine, lodgepole
Pine, maritime
Pine, Scots
Pine, Siberian yellow
Spruce, Sitka

Spruce, Norway
Thuya
Wellingtonia
Yew

PHILIPPINES AND JAPAN

HARDWOODS

Agaru
Agoho
Ailanthus
Albizia species
Alder, Japanese
Amugis
Apitong
Aranga
Ash, Japanese
Bamboo
Banuyo
Batete
Baticulin
Beech, Japanese
Binggas
Birch, Japanese
Boxwood, Japanese
Calamansanay
Calantas
Cherry, Japanese

Horse chestnut,
  Japanese
Diospyros species
Hopea species
Kaki
Katsura
Keyaki
Kiri
Lanipau
Lauan
Liusin
Malabayabas
Malagai
Mancono
Maple, Japanese
Mengkulang
Merbau
Molave
Narra
Oak, Japanese
Palaquium species
Paldao
Palosapis
Sophora
Tindalo
Willow

SOFTWOODS

Almaciga
Benguet pine
Fir, Japanese
Hemlock
Larch, Japanese
Pine, benguet
Pine, Japanese red
Spruce, Japanese
Sugi

SOUTHERN ASIA

HARDWOODS

Aini
Amari
Amoora
Anan
Anjan
Axlewood
Babul
Benteak
Blackwood, Burma
Bombax, Indian
Bombway, white
Bow wood, Andaman
Boxwood
Bullet wood
Canarium, Indian
Burmese cedar
White cedar
Champak
Chaplash
Chickrassy
Chuglam, black
Chuglam, white
Cinnamon
Cutch
Dhaman
Ebony
Elm, Indian
Eng
Gum, grandis
Gumhar
Gurjun
Haldu
Hollock
Kindal
Kokko
Indian laurel
Lunumidella
Marblewood,
  Andaman
Mesua
Padauk, Andaman
Padauk, Burma
Pali
Panakka
Pterospermum species
Pussur wood
Pyinkado
Pyinma
Rosewood, Indian
Sal
Sandalwood
Satinwood, Ceylon
Siris, black
Siris, white
Sissoo
Teak
Thingadu
Thitka
Tulipwood, Burma
Walnut

SOFTWOODS

Cedar
Chir
Cypress, Himalayan
Fir, Himalayan silver
Juniper, Indian
Pine, blue
Spruce, Himalayan

AFRICA

HARDWOODS

Abura
Afara
Afrormosia
Afzelia
Agba
Akossika
Albizia, west African
Alstonia
Aningeria
Antiaris
Avodiré
Ayan
Banga wanga
Berlinia
Blackwood, African
Boxwood
Bubinga
Camphorwood, African
Canarium, African
Ceiba
Celtis, African
Cordia
Dacryodes species
Dahoma
Danta
Difou
Ebony, African
Ekaba
Ekebergia
Ekki
Ekoune
Erimado
Esia
Gaboon

Gedu nohor
Gheombi
Gmelina
Grevillea
Guarea
Idigbo
Ilomba
Iroko
Izombe
Kanda
Limbali
Loliondo
Longui rouge
Mafu
Mahogany,
  African
Makarati
Makoré
Malacantha
Mansonia
Missanda
Moabi
Mtambara
Mueri
Mugonha
Mugonyone
Muhimbi
Muhuhu
Mukulungu
Muninga
Musizi
Niangon
Niové
African oak

Obeche
Odoko
Ogea
Okan
Okwen
Olive, East African
Omu
Opepe
Ovangkol
Padauk, African
Pillarwood
Poga
Pterygota, African
Rapanea
Sapele
Satinwood, African
Sterculia, brown
Sterculia, yellow
Tchitola
Rhodesian teak
Tetraberlinia
Utile
African walnut
Wenge
Zebrano

SOFTWOODS

Cypress
Pencil cedar, East
  African
Pine, radiata
Podo
Thuya

SOUTH EAST ASIA

HARDWOODS

Amboyna
Bangkirai
Balau, Selangan
Batu, Selangan
Belian
Bintangor
Binuang
Bitis
Canarium, Malaysian
Chengal
Durian
Geronggang
Giam
Jelutong
Kapur
Katon
Kelat
Keledang
Kempas
Keranji
Keruing
Kungkur
Machang
Medang
Melunak
Mempisang
Mengkulang

Meranti
Meranti gerutu
Merawan
Merbau
Merpau
Mersawa and krabak
Nyatoh
Penarahan
Perupok
Pulai
Punah
Ramin
Rengas
Resak
Sepetir
Sepetir, swamp
Sesendok
Simpoh
Teak
Tembusu
Terap
Terentang
White seraya

SOFTWOODS

Kauri, East Indian
Sempilor

AUSTRALASIA

HARDWOODS

Amberoi
Australian white ash
Wau beech
White beech
White birch
Black bean
Blackbutt
Blackwood, Australian
Brush box
Calophyllum species
Campnosperma species
Australian cedar
Celtis species
Cheesewood, PNG
  white
Coachwood
Coconut palm
Endospermum
Erima
Flindersia species
Gum, blue
Gum, Red River
Gum, spotted
Gum, water
Gum, yellow
Hopea species
Ironbark
Jarrah
Kamarere
Karri
Kwila
Labula

Malas
Meliaceae
Northern rata
Nothofagus species
PNG oak
She oak
Silky oak
Tasmanian oak
Palaquium species
Peppermint
Planchonella species
Padauk, Solomons
Spondias
Stringybark
Tallowwood
Taun
Tawa
Tea Tree
Terminalia species
Turpentine
Vitex
New Guinea walnut
Queensland walnut
Wandoo

SOFTWOODS

Araucaria species
Kauri
Celery top pine
Podocarpus species
Rimu

163

World trade

Ninety per cent of all the timber produced is used in the country of origin. Nevertheless about 200 million tons of timber products—softwoods, hardwoods and timber-derived materials such as wood-based panels and pulp—enter the international market each year. This world-wide commodity trade is worth nearly forty billion dollars to the producing and exporting countries, and it is growing each year.

Canada, the United States of America, the Scandinavian countries and the Soviet Union are the world's major producers of softwoods, and because these are highly industrialized nations most of their softwood is processed into sawn boards, wood-based panels or paper pulp before entering trade.

But the world trade in hardwoods presents a different picture. Until ten years ago, most of the world's supply of hardwoods was produced by countries with limited industrial capacity. These producer countries were unable to process much of their timber and a

high proportion of hardwood exports were in the form of unsawn logs. This is gradually changing, however, as developing countries seek to increase the value of their exports. But since timber for some specialized hardwood uses, such as matched panelling, will probably always have to be sawn where the wood is used, it is most unlikely that the log trade will cease altogether.

The industrial capacity of individual nations has a significant effect on patterns of trade in timber products, but the relative cost and availability of labour is an equally important factor in the labour-intensive processes such as plywood production. The soaring cost of labour in many industrialized countries, and the availability of suitable logs, has caused a decline in plywood production in Europe, and a dramatic growth of the industry, particularly the hardwood plywood industry, in the Far East. Today, almost all of the developed nations of the world are net importers of plywood (see pages 174–175).

Below With the exception of South East Asia, the major exporters of timber and timber products are the developed nations of the northern hemisphere, who have large supplies of fast-growing softwoods and the industrial capacity to process the timber. Despite the phenomenal rate of deforestation in Africa and South America, as yet only three of the African nations export

more than 500,000 tons of timber and timber products each year. This is because, first, much of the timber is burned either as fuel or during "slash and burn" land clearance; second, as of yet many of these countries still lack sufficiently developed economies to process their timber; and third, because world markets for costly tropical hardwoods are smaller and more

TIMBER PRODUCTS
% breakdown of national timber trade

- ☐ Other timber products
- Fibreboard
- Veneer sheets
- Particleboard
- Plywood
- Hardwood sawlogs and veneer logs
- Softwood sawlogs and veneer logs
- Pulpwood
- Sawn hardwood
- Sawn softwood

IMPORTS AND EXPORTS (1,000 tons)

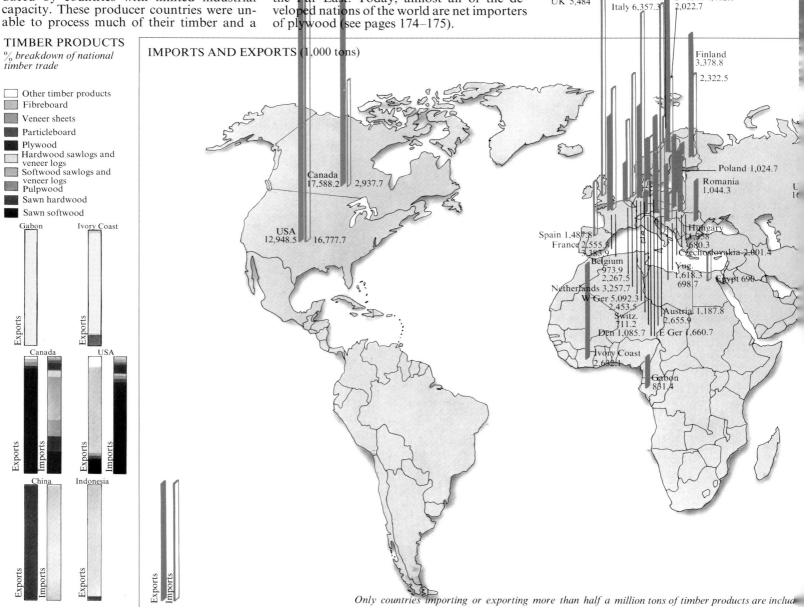

Only countries importing or exporting more than half a million tons of timber products are included

Below *The introduction of bulk carriers and of timber "packaged" to facilitate handling has meant increased efficiency in shipping methods during the last 20 years. But the transportation of bulky timber is still expensive and is avoided by traders wherever possible. Proximity to markets therefore plays an important role in determining trading partners. Europe, for example, imports most of its softwood requirements from Scandinavia and the USSR. The USA finds it cheaper to import large quantities of Canadian softwood for certain of its markets rather than transport domestic supplies over long distances, particularly where it would involve costly road or rail haulage. Movements of trade are also influenced by the traditional trading links between nations, particularly those established during European colonization of Africa, South America and southern Asia. France, for example, still imports large quantities of timber from its ex-colony Gabon. Political ideologies affect trading patterns too; much of the timber produced in the USSR, for example, is traded in eastern Europe.*

specialized than those for softwoods. The industrialized countries, particularly those with high populations and small land areas, are generally the largest importers of timber. Italy and the Netherlands are large European importers, and Great Britain imports 90 per cent of her timber needs. In Asia, industrial Japan is one of the largest importers of timber.

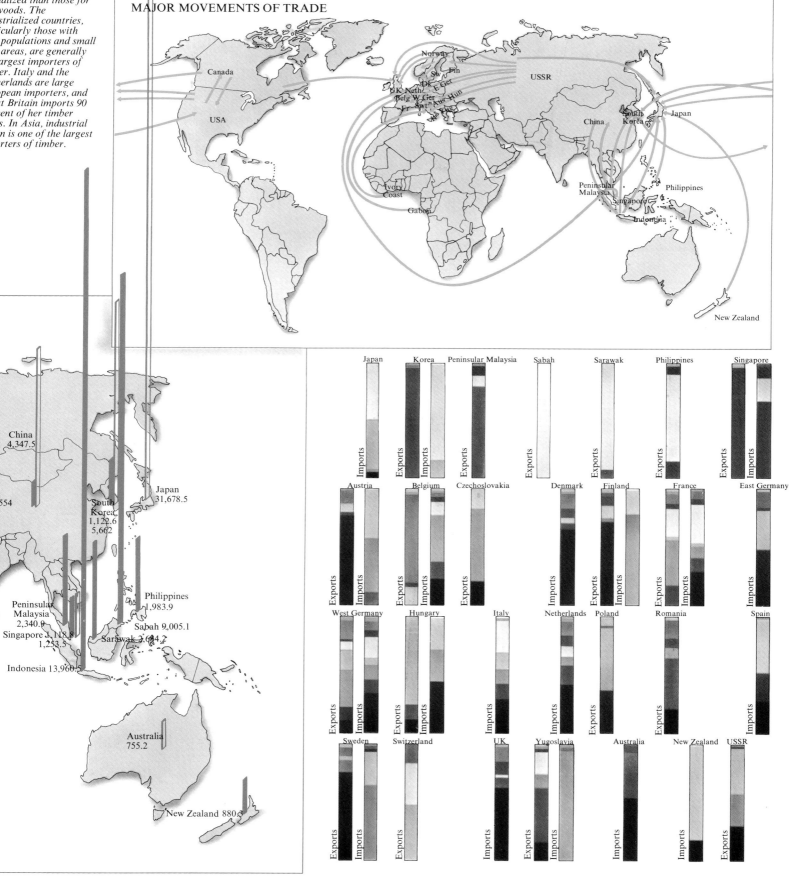

MAJOR MOVEMENTS OF TRADE

Commercial forestry

Left *Clearcutting is an ecologically sound harvesting method which is also essential for the regeneration of trees such as Douglas firs, which cannot tolerate shade.*

Below *The debris left after logging may be mulched back into the ground—a process which in itself aids regeneration.*

Right *Modern tree-planting machines can speed up the work that was once always done by hand. Two operators seated in a machine like this can release up to 10,000 seedlings in one working day. Manual planting skills are not yet dispensable, however, because machines are unsuitable for anything less than level ground.*

A hundred years ago trees were cut by hand and hauled from the forest by animals, and little or no attention was paid to managing timberland. The forests appeared endless and the demand for timber did not appear to be in danger of outstripping the supply. Today the demand for pulp, paper and solid wood products is growing at such a rate that it is essential to keep the forest's growth in step with human needs.

The modern forester manages the forest from site preparation and planting to the final harvest. Throughout the growing cycle of the forest he controls competing vegetation to make moisture and soil nutrients more available to young trees; controls the multitude of pests that inhabit the forest; prescribes fertilization and controlled burning; and periodically thins tree stands.

The forester now has modern science and technology at his command to improve the yield of the forest. One relatively new practice—the replanting of timberlands with genetically superior seedlings that grow taller and more rapidly with straight stems—has increased yields by up to twenty per cent.

By managing timberlands the quality and volume of harvested trees can be greatly increased. In an unmanaged coniferous forest in the north-eastern United States, for example, an average of 20,000 to 40,000 seedlings per acre may grow, and up to 240,000 seedlings

per acre have been known to regenerate after harvesting. But under these conditions tree growth is stunted and the forest is susceptible to disease and other natural hazards.

Conversely, in a managed forest 700 to 1,000 seedlings are planted per acre. Managing the forest speeds up the growing process by reducing the severe competition for sunlight and nutrients. In addition, a full stocking of the desired crop trees is achieved when each tree has room to grow but none to spare. Therefore, instead of waiting sixty to a hundred years to cut coniferous trees for pulpwood, in most northern latitudes they can be harvested in about thirty-five years. In the southern United States they can be harvested at about half this age. About fifteen per cent of the harvested forest areas in the United States and other industrialized nations are replanted; most forests regenerate naturally.

The first step a forester usually takes in establishing a tree plantation is preparing the site to facilitate correct seedling planting, or under less intensive preparation, natural regeneration. When an area has been logged, worthless trees and bushes remain alongside the debris of the logging operation—limbs, needles and twigs—which is known as "slash".

Foresters must dispose of the slash in order to plant seedlings or prepare the seedbed for natural regeneration. Although seedlings could be planted without removing the slash,

doing so increases cost and reduces the available planting area. There are three major methods of slash removal—moving it from the area, mulching it into the ground with heavy machinery or, the most efficient and widely used, burning. When burning slash foresters make detailed plans and prepare the site weeks before the actual burn date. This use of fire is particularly important in managing Douglas fir in North America.

Mulching the slash into the soil involves the use of heavy tractors and harrows, which also turn up the soil—a process known as scarification. The stirring up of the top-soil exposes it to the atmosphere and allows new seedlings to find moisture and mineral nutrients more easily. It is a technique that is no longer widely used in North America, although it is still used in the most northerly regions to help the natural regeneration of such species as yellow birch and white pine. It is impractical on less than gentle slopes and is now threatened by the increasing cost of motor fuel.

Tree plantations require strict control of pests and undesirable species of vegetation if the projected high demand for forest products is to be met. Pesticides and herbicides, both chemical and biological, have become an integral part of efficient forest management programmes. Herbicides help control broad-leaved tree species so that valuable softwood timber stands can be properly maintained.

Above *By reducing the build-up of flammable litter on the forest floor prescribed burning can protect trees from the destruction that could result from a full-scale forest fire.*

Below *Herbicides to control weeds and pesticides to protect trees against pests and diseases, here being sprayed from the air, are essential tools in modern forestry programmes.*

herbicides are also very important in seeding nurseries. Other forest chemicals protect against loss to insects, rodents and diseases, which annually destroy the equivalent of approximately forty per cent of the volume of wood harvested in North American forests.

Different types of tree harvesting techniques are employed when trees reach a marketable, mature age. Clearcutting, the practice of harvesting all the trees in a given area, is an accepted, fundamental forest management practice. In addition to its economical wisdom, clearcutting is ecologically sound in that it imitates nature's own approach to forest harvesting (wildfire may remove all the trees in a given area) while allowing use of the wood for products and fuel.

Because certain tree species—Douglas fir and pine, for example—cannot tolerate shade, clearcutting is particularly suited for their regeneration. It is also critical in plantation forestry, using genetically superior seedlings of intolerant species for reafforestation.

Another common harvesting method is selection cutting, which involves removing certain selected trees. This technique removes dead, overmature and overcrowded trees. Thinning might be thought of as a kind of pre-final harvest selective cutting that reduces the competition for sunlight and nourishment in a forest, ensuring more favourable growing conditions for the remaining trees.

Selective cutting also removes low-value trees as well as a number of higher value crop trees. In the past, this method of harvesting has been abused. Often, only the best trees were removed leaving the worst trees to generate the next forest. The abuse of this technique has resulted in the poor condition of many stands making up today's forests.

A third harvesting method is called seed tree cutting. This process involves leaving a small number (usually six to eight) of healthy, mature trees per acre to re-seed the surrounding land. Essentially a pine management practice, it is often less reliable than clearcutting followed by planting, and the marketable value of the seed trees left to stand would, in all probability, pay for the cost of planting in today's markets.

Another recognized harvesting technique is the shelterwood method. Somewhat between selective cutting and seed tree cutting, this method leaves about thirty to forty trees per acre to seed the area and provides some degree of shade for the young crop of seedlings.

Forestry has come a long way in the last century. New scientific and mechanical advances have enabled man to control carefully the quality and quantity of wood fibre. Modern techniques, along with a programme of conscientious stewardship of the land, will allow us to continue harvesting the renewable forest resource for centuries to come.

CLONING

A clone is an exact genetic duplication of a parent. Cloning has important advantages in the forest products industry: the technique can virtually assure a tree's growth structure and be used to mass produce genetically superior seedlings. While a forest of cloned trees could look more uniform than a natural forest, each tree would not look exactly alike; differences in environmental conditions would alter each tree's appearance. Tissue culture experts have been able to grow trees from cells taken from juvenile shoots in redwood, Douglas fir, pine, apple, citrus and poplar. Cloning's most important practical value to date is in the establishment of seed orchards.

Logging

Left *The shears of a mechanical harvester cutting through the base of a pine. Such machines can fell trees with a diameter up to 2 ft.*

Right *Felling with a powered chainsaw. Although less physically demanding than the old hand axe and saw, the same skill and precision is required to ensure that the tree falls to the ground in a controlled way.*

Left *Harvesting pulpwood in northern Canada. These machines drive into the forest, fell, delimb and buck the logs in one continuous cycle.*

Below *Water remains a cheap and convenient method of transport in Scandinavia and some parts of North America. Here a log jam is being broken up at the beginning of the spring drive after the snows have melted.*

Methods of logging vary according to the size and species of tree that is being cut, the terrain on which it grows, and the final use to which the felled timber is to be put. Logging a managed woodland for pulpwood is very different from the selective cutting of individual tropical rain forest trees for solid timber products.

The last thirty years have seen great changes in logging techniques, particularly in Scandinavia and North America. Buck saws and hand axes have been traded for powered chainsaws, and in the last ten years a whole family of new machines has stalked the forest, harvesting trees with a single cut. But perhaps more importantly the role of the logger has changed. He is no longer just "mining" trees and then moving on to new stands, but has become an integral part of the modern practice of forestry—for every tree felled at least five new ones are planted.

The move towards mechanization was stimulated by the lack of traditional skilled labour prepared to work in the forest far from home, especially in the most northerly regions where much of the world's pulpwood is harvested. Machines were designed to increase the efficiency of the cut, and to take away some of the physical hardship endured by the old-time loggers. Today a host of machines fell and debranch the trees and buck pulpwood logs into convenient lengths for use at the mill. More sophisticated machines now combine all three actions, taking only thirty seconds to reduce a growing tree to standard-length, small round-wood logs. The increasing use of purchased wood chips in the pulp industry has led to the development of "whole-tree chippers" that make chips in the forest, utilizing all parts of the tree and thereby eliminating waste.

The advent of the machine age in logging decreased the manpower requirements of

MOUNTAIN LOGGING

With the technique known as skyline logging (below) the yarder is guyed to the hillside. The skyline is attached to a winch that provides lift and tension, and is anchored to a tail block in the forest. Logs are drawn to the carriage by the tong line, then hauled by the main haul line up to the yarder on the hillside.

Running skyline
Main line (Haul-in line)
Front drum line
Guy lines
Tail block
Carriage
Chokers
Tong line

High lead logging (below) relies on the lifting power provided by a mobile, self-powered telescopic tower to keep the logs clear of the ground. Logs are attached by chokers to a short line, which is itself attached to a haul-in line. The haul-back lines run through fixed blocks and reposition the chokers after each run.

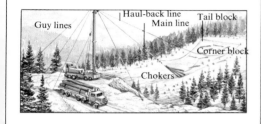

Guy lines
Haul-back line
Main line
Tail block
Corner block
Chokers

Below High lead logging in the north-west United States. Douglas fir logs are moved from the valley sides and bottom by the mobile tower, using a system of pulleys and guys, ready for loading on to a waiting truck.

Bottom Where access to logging operations is good, and the terrain is relatively flat, specially designed tractors known as skidders are used. These vehicles can drag logs down the narrow tracks without damaging standing trees.

Below Selective logging in Sarawak in Malaysia. Commercially desirable species of trees sometimes only occur at scattered intervals in such tropical rain forests. Because of poor access mechanization is not suitable.

Bottom Powerful elephants are trained to move logs from the teak forests of Assam State in north-east India. Here, logging technology has not changed, nor has it needed to change, for many hundreds of years.

some logging operations by a factor of ten. But the new breed of logger is still a highly skilled person and working on a shift basis areas can now be logged twenty-four hours a day, all year round. Another advantage is that trees are cut close to ground level, making it easier to replant clear-cut areas.

High technology, however, is expensive to buy and requires a team of engineers and mechanics for maintenance. The mechanical harvesters are only owned by large companies who combine logging, sawmill and paper-making operations. Moreover, such machines cannot handle trees with trunks more than two feet in diameter and, although some machines can now work on inclines of twenty-five degrees, most of them function best only on fairly flat, even terrain.

For the logging of large trees and those in mountainous regions, however, the skill of a team of loggers equipped with chainsaws is still required. Trees are felled by cutting out a wedge, and making a back cut slightly above the wedge cut, on the opposite side of the trunk, leaving a hinge somewhat off-centre so that the tree will fall in a controlled way. Once felled the tree is delimbed and bucked into convenient lengths ready for transport to the sawmill. Bucked logs are moved by special techniques of yarding from the valley bottoms and hillsides to a loading platform on the side of the logging roads cut into the contours of the mountain (see box above).

Both these mechanical and manual methods of harvesting work well when species that do not require separation are being harvested in a clear cut of maybe two or three hundred acres. In the tropical forest, however, much hardwood timber is selectively cut as the valuable commercial species such as obeche, mahogany and greenheart only occur at infrequent intervals. There may be only one of

these species to two hundred other trees in an acre. Usually this kind of harvesting, often called "creaming", means that the desirable species have a poor chance to regenerate, only being replaced by less soughtafter species. The logger moves on, deeper and deeper into the forest, searching longer and longer for his ever disappearing prize. In the tropical forest it is often still the traditional axe that does the job and beasts of burden—horses, oxen and elephants—that haul the felled timber. In recent years, however, large logging operations have adopted chainsaws and tractors.

More recently there have been attempts to harvest the tropical forest by mechanical means, utilizing all the wood available for sawn lumber, and the chips for particleboard or for pulp manufacture. If the forest is to be regenerated after these clear-cutting methods it is desirable for the ground to be replanted immediately, and a move towards the managed plantation of fast-growing species of either hardwood or softwood has already gathered momentum.

Once logs are extracted from the forest they are ready to begin their journey to the sawmill or pulpmill. The role of the railways diminished after the 1940s, when oil-based fuels were cheap, and most timber is moved by road on trucks that can carry heavy loads and negotiate the curves of a mountain logging road as well as travel along the highways. In many parts of Scandinavia and some places in North America water still remains a cheap and convenient method of transport. Large logs for the sawmill are usually dumped into the river and manoeuvred by special boats into log rafts that are then pulled along by tugs. Sometimes pulpwood, in eight- or four-foot logs, is put into the rivers and drifts downstream with the aid of the current and wind to be caught in booms at the mill.

The sawmill

Methods of converting round logs to lumber have changed considerably from the traditional sawpit and two-handed saw. A modern sawmill now utilizes computerized measuring and monitoring devices to ensure maximum economic value from each log, and mechanical handling systems to move the lumber through each stage of its manufacture. Yet, despite this modern technology, it is still the experienced and skilled judgement of the sawyer at every stage of the log's conversion that ensures the optimum use of each log.

Logs come from the forest to the sawmill yards and are stripped of their bark before being fed into the mill. As they enter the mill they are measured on a platform, or merchandizer, by electronic scanners linked to a computer that suggests the best use of the log and the lengths to which it should be cut. The operator, however, is able to override the computer if he sees defects such as crooks or large knots that are not picked up by the automated equipment, or that it has not been programmed to deal with. This information can be keyed into the instructions for the next automated stage in the process.

From the electronic scanners the logs are directed to the saws that cut the log into convenient lengths ("bucking") for processing. In a modern, integrated mill some logs may be passed to the plywood manufacturing line (see pages 172–173); large-diameter logs may be directed to the headrig saw; while smaller logs are passed to the smaller, or pony, headrig or to a recently developed machine, the chippercanter. This squares the log into a timber by chipping away the rounded surfaces of the log. The surplus wood chips from this operation are then used in the manufacture of wood pulp—for paper or cellulose production (see pages 180–187 and 188–191)—or for other wood products such as particleboard.

From the headrig, re-saws and edgers the individual lengths of lumber are sorted into sizes, trimmed to length and seasoned by drying in kilns to ensure stability. The lumber is then planed to standard dimensions, graded, banded and packaged ready for transport to the customer. Most of this work is automated and it is the large-diameter logs on the headrig saw that require the skill and expertise of the most experienced sawyers.

On the headrig the log is firmly clamped to a carriage that traverses backwards and forwards past the vertical blade of a bandsaw. The headrig sawyer sits in a control room above the log and has an assistant close to the log to guide the cut slabs of wood when each pass of the carriage is completed. On the first cut an irregular slab, rounded on one face, is removed and this is usually destined to be converted into chips for the pulping industry. Subsequent cuts usually remove boards in the knot-free outer zone of the log.

After this first series of cuts the sawyer rotates the massive timber through 90 or 180 degrees and makes another series of cuts of high-quality board lumber. All four sides of the log are worked in the same way until the centre of the log is left. Here the wood is more likely to carry knots and splits, and from this heartwood region heavy timbers and large beams are taken. As each cut is made the remaining part of the log is scanned by an electronic instrument that measures the diameter along its length and the degree of taper. A computer analyses the information and displays numerous recommended cutting patterns. The sawyer uses these as a guide but makes the final decision allowing for internal features of the log that are exposed by each cut. Three methods of working a log are illustrated (right). From the headrig the cut board is passed through the re-saw to be reduced to smaller sizes, seasoned in the drying kilns, planed and then sorted and graded ready for shipping to the customer.

Today nothing goes to waste. Stripped bark is used in the mill furnaces as a low-cost fuel, sawdust and trimmings are used in related wood product industries such as pulp, fibreboard and particleboard manufacture.

Above *Full-length roundwood logs are delivered by truck to the sawmill wood yard. Forklifts can unload a truck in one* "*bite*" *and a giant crane, with a massive lifting capacity, stacks the logs ready for feeding to the mill.*

Above *On the platform of the merchandizer the operator has determined the best lengths for sawing.*

Next, *circular saws swing down and cut across the log. Some of these logs will pass to a plywood veneer manufacturing line.*

Above *Planks are still cut by hand in Bangladesh, although diesel-powered* mills are beginning to replace such manual skills. Before mechanization a *man might have taken 20 years to become "top man" at the sawmill.*

Round the log sawing

Small timber

High-yield log

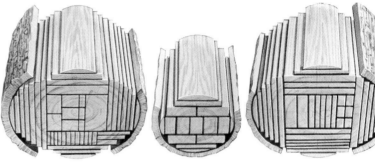

Each side of the log is worked in turn. The lower side was cut first to yield, after the slab, 6 high-grade boards. The right-hand side was then cut to give 2 boards and a timber, which was re-sawn into smaller sizes. The third side yielded more board, while the last side was cut into a large dimension timber. The heart of the log, now reduced to a 20-in-square, was converted into structural timbers in which knots do not reduce strength.

Some sawmills specialize in processing small-sized logs—passing the whole log, in one movement, through a series of bandsaws and circular saws that reduce it to 2- or 4-in-thick standard-width pieces. These are then turned flat and re-sawn to 2 × 2, 2 × 4 and 2 × 6 timber. The outside cuts, immediately after removal of the slabs, may yield wide, high-quality 1-in-thick boards.

The sawyer opened the log on the upper side and removed a number of high-grade boards, or selects. The log was then rotated through 180 degrees and the process repeated. This log consisted mainly of sound wood with very few knots and splits, so enabling the sawyer to cut a very high proportion of high-quality lumber.

Above *A large timber from the headrig passes through a multi-banded re-saw. The sawn lumber then passes along the* conveyor to be trimmed to length and sorted to size before entering the drying kilns for seasoning.

Above *Planed and seasoned lumber is automatically sorted into grades by a system of trapdoors in the overhead* conveyor. The lumber is then bound with steel bands and packaged for shipping from the mill by either road or rail.

Manufactured boards

Throughout history man has used wood—in solid form—for a variety of structural and decorative purposes. But as the twentieth century dawned it was found that solid wood could be "reconstituted" in the form of panels to provide a more versatile product. The first commercial panel product was plywood.

Commercial plywood makes use of an ancient technique of slicing or peeling logs to give veneers that are glued together, usually in an odd number of veneers, each laid with its grain running at right angles to the adjacent sheets. The result is a reasonably stable panel with a high strength to weight ratio. Most plywood today is made with "exterior" glues, which can be more durable than the wood they bind together. Plywood is used for purposes that range from aircraft to concrete formwork and packaging, and it is manufactured from both softwoods and hardwoods.

Blockboard is a variation on plywood, with a core of solid wood "strips" covered with wood veneers on the face and reverse sides. Laminboard and battenboard are variations of blockboard and are used in the craft-orientated joinery and furniture industries.

The second oldest member of the wood-based panel family is fibreboard, a more radically "reconstituted" product than plywood, in that the wood fibres are "blown" apart, using steam and pressure, or ground into fibres before being "hot-pressed" into panels. Fibreboards were for many years divided into hardboard, a dense form, and insulation board, a thicker, less dense board. In the past ten years, a new form—medium density fibreboard, or MDF—has had growing impact, notably in furniture manufacture.

Particleboard structure lies between plywood and fibreboard, as the wood raw material is cut into "chips"—fine chips for face and reverse sides of the panel with coarser chips for the centre core. A major outlet for particleboard has been in furniture manufacture, largely at the expense of plywood. It has also been strongly marketed for light construction work—particularly flooring.

A variant of particleboard is waferboard, fabricated from larger "wafers" of wood as opposed to smaller chips. The larger-sized wafers are said to give greater strength to the panels, which now compete with plywood for structural applications.

Wood-based panels are generally considered to have an expanding future, particularly particleboard and possibly waferboard and MDF. These panels use low-grade and waste wood that was previously burned, but plywood calls for logs large enough to be peeled or sliced—a possible inhibiting factor to future expansion. These raw material requirements mean that while particleboard and other "reconstituted" panels can be made in countries that are not timber rich, plywood producers need regular timber supplies.

A further reason for an expanding future for wood-based panel products is that as a man-made form of wood, they can be engineered to guaranteed and precise requirements. A recent example of this is Orientated Strand Board (OSB), a panel in which "strands" of wood are aligned to form a specified performance board.

Wood-based panel products can be manufactured with such additives as preservatives, fire retardants and stabilizers to give improved performance in use. Most of the defects that appeared in natural wood—knots, wild grain and splits—are eliminated in all man-made wood-based panels.

The fact that wood is one of mankind's few renewable raw materials, and that the fibre required for "reconstituted" panels can be grown relatively quickly in many parts of the world points to an expanding future for wood-based panel products.

Below *Plywood now plays an important part in construction because boards can be made in sizes not usually available as solid timber and, when they are used for walling and flooring, less jointing is required.*

Below *Logs are bucked to the correct length and stripped of their bark.*

They are then placed in steam baths to soften before being peeled on the

lathes. *Both hardwoods and softwoods can be used for board manufacture.*

Below *A log being peeled. The remaining central core will be sold as a fence post.*

Below *The peeled veneers are cut to standard size, then graded and sorted.*

Below *When the veneers have been glued and made into panels they enter*

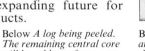

WORLD BOARD PRODUCTION

Production depends on three factors: the availability of raw materials, technology and labour. The three rarely coincide in any one country. New Zealand, for example, exports pulpwood for processing in Japan, only to buy it back as the finished product. Production of boards in the developing world, especially in Africa, is small because of lack of investment in machinery.

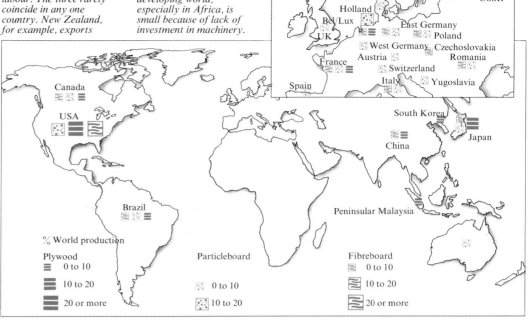

% World production

Plywood
- 0 to 10
- 10 to 20
- 20 or more

Particleboard
- 0 to 10
- 10 to 20

Fibreboard
- 0 to 10
- 10 to 20
- 20 or more

...team presses to set the adhesive. After gluing, the boards are trimmed to standard size and the faces are sanded before grading and packaging.

PARTICLEBOARD

In chipboard manufacture, wood is fragmented by machines—with fixed or stationary cutting edges—into regular-sized chips that pass through an air drier and are then screened and checked for size. The proportion of chips to resin glue is critical, and as the chips travel to the mixing chamber they are fed over a belt weigher whose signals vary the activity of the resin pump. A fine mist of resin drops released from a high-velocity spray-gun is mixed with the chips by centrally mounted rotating arms, and the sticky chips are spread into a mat. This then enters the press where heat and pressure determine the final character of the board.

FIBREBOARD

In fibreboard production strong chipping knives reduce wood to chips about one inch long. Pieces that are too large are recycled for a second chipping and wood dust that is too fine is collected for fuel. Then the chips are either steamed, passed through a mincer and fed out between two rough grinding discs—the "defibrator" method—or they are exploded into fibres by the release of high-pressure steam—the "masonite" process. The steam-softened lignin component of the fibres felts them into mats laid on a moving mesh. The mats are cut up into sheets that pass through light rollers to ovens (to make softboard) or heated presses (to make hardboard).

THE PLYWOOD FAMILY

The name plywood covers the various kinds of manufactured boards that are used in many industries, from construction work to furniture making. These boards are manufactured from wood and glue, the wood grain in each veneer lying at 90 degrees to those of the adjacent layers. This ensures an even distribution of strength with minimal movement and subsequent distortion. The uniform structure also facilitates impregnation with water-resistant and fire-retardant compounds.

Plywood is an assembly of an odd number of veneers with the grains alternating at 90 degrees.

Blockboard is an assembly of solid wood blocks set at 90 degrees to the facing panels. The wood blocks may be glued together.

Battenboard is a modification of blockboard with narrow wood core strips.

Laminboard has even thinner solid core strips. These are always glued together.

Decorative veneers

Below *West Germany has the largest veneer industry in the world, closely followed by Japan, Italy and the United States. Except in the USA, most veneer produced by these countries is cut from imported logs. In recent years veneer mills have been established close to the main sources of timber.*

Two thousand years ago Cleopatra presented Julius Caesar with a table "veneered and richly decorated with inlay". At that time the art of veneering was already an ancient craft in Egypt. Thin layers of precious wood backed with less valuable timber had been used for two thousand years to make furniture for the pharaohs: the throne from the tomb of Tutankhamun is of cedarwood overlaid with ebony and ivory. Walnut and olivewood were used as veneers by the craftsmen of Ancient Greece, and from Greece knowledge of the art spread to the rest of Europe.

Forgotten in medieval times, the technique of veneering was revived during the Renaissance and reached its height in the eighteenth century in France. During this period the purpose of veneer was entirely cosmetic; the furniture maker was not concerned with the cost of production or with the weight of individual pieces, since he generally worked under patronage. For centuries veneered objects remained the precious possessions of a privileged and wealthy few.

By the beginning of the twentieth century, however, an improvement in living standards created a growing demand for furniture for ordinary people. Veneers then became an integral part of modern furniture production, along with plywood, chipboard and spray finishing of surfaces.

Today, the production of veneers is a world-wide industry. Small by general industrial standards, it none the less employs experts throughout the world who select, buy and fell trees that will provide wood suitable for veneer work. Skilled selection is all important because in any one species the proportion of suitable trees is a small percentage of those available to the buyer.

Modern veneers are cut by one of two methods: peeling the log on a lathe (rotary cut veneers), or flat-cutting the wood with a piston-operated knife (sliced veneers). Veneers for construction purposes, such as ply-wood, are always peeled, but the lathe is rarely used for decorative veneers. More than ninety-five per cent of decorative veneers produced today are flat-cut.

The final appearance of a veneer is largely determined by the way in which a log is offered to the knife. It is the tree's annual growth rings that produce the desirable pattern or "figuring" of a veneer and it must therefore be decided at the mill how the log should be prepared. If a patterned effect, known as "crown", is required, the log is debarked, trimmed and offered to the knife in its entirety. If a straight grain, or stripe effect, is required, the log is quartered and each quarter, or "flitch", is offered to the knife separately, thus preserving the markings in parallel. Variation of figuring is also determined by the part of the tree from which the wood has been taken. Stumpwood produces a figure known as "butt"; "curls" are found in the wood between a branch and the main trunk; and delicately figured "burr" or "burl" veneers are sliced from cancerous outgrowths that form on certain species of tree.

After cutting, the veneers are maintained in strict log sequence and stacked to re-form approximately the shape of the original log. The grain variation from sheet to sheet is slight, but would be quite marked if the first and the last of a veneer stack were laid alongside one another. Furniture manufacturers therefore buy the veneers by the stack or "set" and the stacking order enables them to match the leaves exactly when they are bonded.

Veneered products are commonly considered to be inferior to those made from solid timber. However, this belief is close to the reverse of the truth because solid furniture remains hydroscopic—ever attempting to equate its moisture content with that of the surrounding air. It is therefore vulnerable to movement and distortion, and cracking can result. Scientists have applied themselves to the task of creating a substrate without ten-sions, and the modern chipboard, another undeservedly maligned material, has fulfilled this requirement.

Today a high-quality chipboard, correctly lipped and veneered on both sides, makes the finest warp-free panel for all furniture, and if Thomas Chippendale were alive today, he would be happy to use it. There are three attendant benefits from using this material. First, furniture can become lighter without loss of strength. Second, using modern veneer-cutting methods, the finest trees provide finishes for many more applications because a one-inch thickness of solid timber yields fifty sheets of decorative veneer. Third, the surface obtained by veneering with modern glues on to a suitable substrate is unique. The glue partly fills the pores of the veneer, which, after sanding, is ready to accept

SELECTING THE WOOD

The figuring, or natural patterning, on a veneer depends on the part of the tree from which the wood has been taken, on the cutting method employed and the environment in which the tree grew. Flat-cut, quartered and rotary-peeled veneers are generally cut from the main trunk wood. Burr or burl is taken from the cancerous outgrowths that develop on the trunks of some trees, and although they are usually flat cut, large burrs can also be peeled. Curls are sliced from the wood at the junction of a main branch and the trunk, and butt veneers are cut from the stumpwood, or roots of the tree.

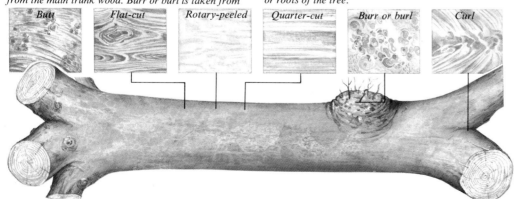

Butt Flat-cut Rotary-peeled Quarter-cut Burr or burl Curl

Newly delivered to the mill, logs are prepared for "half-round" cutting into veneers. As soon as logs are felled, they begin to lose their moisture. Left unprotected, the wood would have developed split or "checks" during the journey to the mill. The ends of the logs would have been heavily painted and, in some cases, fitted with "anti-checking" irons or

Debarking machine

Log fitted with "anti-checking" irons and iron bandages

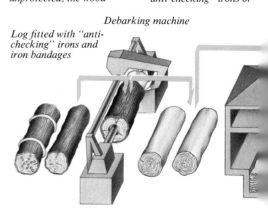

METHODS OF CUTTING VENEERS

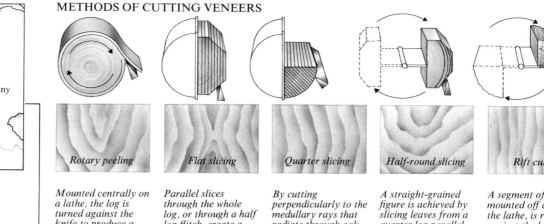

Rotary peeling — Mounted centrally on a lathe, the log is turned against the knife to produce a continuous sheet of veneer.

Flat slicing — Parallel slices through the whole log, or through a half log flitch, create a variegated figure known as "crown".

Quarter slicing — By cutting perpendicularly to the medullary rays that radiate through oak wood, a comb grain figure is achieved.

Half-round slicing — A straight-grained figure is achieved by slicing leaves from a quarter log parallel to the annual growth rings of the wood.

Rift cut — A segment of log, mounted off centre on the lathe, is rotated against the knife. A variegated figure is obtained.

an excellent finish by means of spraying or curtain coating. This reduces the cost of production by eliminating the lengthy finishing process of hand polishing the veneer.

In spite of the modernization of production techniques, the use of face veneer remains a craft, and as such it is in danger of disappearing. Simulations in the form of grained papers, vinyls and PVC (polyvinyl chloride) are now used on a vast scale. They create a "wood" effect, and are much easier to apply, often obviating the entire finishing process. Cheaper products are now often veneered with substitute materials, leaving only the upper end of the market to the real wood finish. In West Germany and the United States of America the wood veneer industry continues to thrive, but in Britain the craft of the veneerer has been put in jeopardy.

Above *Removing excess bark and irregularities in the wood with a bandsaw is one method of trimming veneer logs. The logs are then steamed or boiled (below) to prepare them for the final cutting process, when they are sliced or rotary peeled into thin veneers.*

VENEERS AND FASHION

Such master craftsmen of the eighteenth century as Chippendale and Sheraton perfected the art of inlaid veneer work. This George III mahogany card-table is decorated with a border of inlaid and etched satinwood, banded and edged with tulipwood. Satinwood and tulipwood are not especially popular today, but demand for veneers has always followed trends. These are influenced by availability of woods, the fashion of the time and, since the growth of a market for mass-produced furniture, the price. Since the Second World War, striped sapele mahogany, quartered oak and figured French walnut have been market leaders.

iron bandages. At the mill these irons are removed. The logs are then de-barked and trimmed. Half-round veneers can be cut from the whole log or from sections of log. If sections

are required, the log is sawn into flitches. Next, steaming or boiling tenderizes the wood and provides lubrication for the cutting process. Since this tends to darken timber,

white woods are cut without prior treatment and must be cut as soon as possible after felling. The log or flitch is then fitted off centre on the lathe, and is rotated against the edge

of the knife. At each turn of the lathe, a thin sheet of veneer is peeled from the log; the position of the knife is automatically corrected to allow for the reduction in log diameter. The veneer

sheets are run through a belt-dryer and are tested to ensure that a correct moisture level has been attained throughout each sheet. The ideal moisture content varies according to

the kind of wood. The veneers are then trimmed to a regular shape and stacked in strict cutting sequence to ensure continuity of figure when the sheets are matched.

Steaming pit   *Lathe and veneer knife*   *Trimming guillotine*

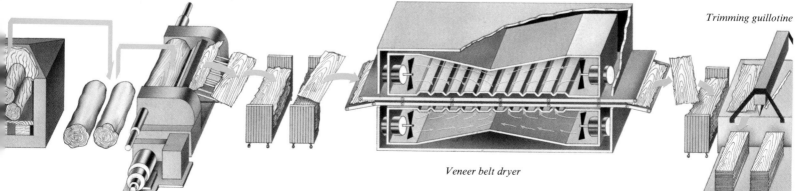

Veneer belt dryer

Wood for special uses

Below *The ribs of a piano's soundboard are glued and then pressed into position with "go-bars". Both the ribs and the soundboard are made of spruce, a lightweight timber with sufficient elasticity to give resonance to the strings. The keys are normally of basswood, a stable timber that resists distortion. The main beam is built of North American rock maple, and hornbeam, sapele or mahogany is used to manufacture the hammer heads.*

Right *Only oak can be used to make the casks that hold best-quality sherries and whiskies. American white oak is preferred for whisky casks and the wood that is chosen must be totally free of knots. The staves of a barrel are hand-cleft and then must be left to season before the cask can be built. Wooden wine and beer casks are made from a variety of different timbers including European oak and, in Australia, eucalyptus.*

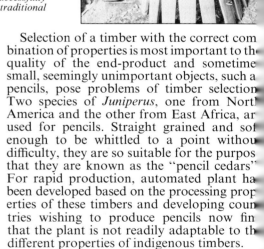

Left *Two layers of West African obeche are sandwiched between laminates of Honduras mahogany to form a cruiser hull that is strong, lightweight and resistant to decay. This particular combination of properties, difficult to achieve using man-made materials, is essential for all small ocean-going vessels. In recent years several tropical hardwood species have been successfully introduced to supplement the traditional boatbuilding timbers.*

The hundreds of different tree species provide a raw material with a vast range of potentially useful properties. From earliest times ship builders have made use of the special properties of a number of timbers, but throughout the northern hemisphere oak has long been, and still is, a most important ship-building timber (see pages 34–35). For boat planking, teak is one of the most highly prized woods, but larch, the mahoganies, West African agba, South American cedar and various other decay-resistant lightweight timbers are also widely used, usually as solid timber but sometimes as plywood for use in racing hulls.

More than one timber usually can be found for a particular end-use; but manufacturers of sports equipment, who use a number of specialized timbers, have been unable to find a satisfactory alternative to cricket-bat willow, a variety of the common willow, *Salix alba* var. *coerulea*, which has a toughness and resilience usually found only in much heavier timbers. Fortunately, it grows quickly and can continually be replaced. For tennis rackets and hockey sticks, ash is still favoured for its toughness, resilience, straight grain and good bending properties, although mulberry, *Morus alba*, first used on the Indian subcontinent, where it grows, has become a popular alternative for hockey sticks.

As in the sports goods industry, production of musical instruments depends upon the particular properties of certain woods, but the properties required are not the same for all instruments. The top side, or belly, of a violin, for example, has similar requirements to those of a piano soundboard. A lightweight timber with a high degree of elasticity is required, to enable the belly to vibrate and provide resonance to the strings. The spruces have been found most suitable for this purpose, but in some South American countries alerce, an unrelated timber of similar properties, has been used very successfully.

Organ soundboards are not required to be resonant, but they must be resistant to distortion, splitting, swelling or shrinking in changing atmospheric conditions, as this would affect the complicated movement of air to the various pipes. One of the most reliable timbers for this purpose is West African obeche, or samba. Keys for xylophones and Latin American marimbas are an example of a most unusual requirement—that the timber itself must produce a ringing, musical sound when struck. A very few high-density timbers have this property and among the best and most commonly selected for high-quality xylophones is rosewood, particularly Honduras rosewood, *Dalbergia stevensonii*.

Selection of a timber with the correct combination of properties is most important to the quality of the end-product and sometimes small, seemingly unimportant objects, such as pencils, pose problems of timber selection. Two species of *Juniperus*, one from North America and the other from East Africa, are used for pencils. Straight grained and soft enough to be whittled to a point without difficulty, they are so suitable for the purpose that they are known as the "pencil cedars". For rapid production, automated plant has been developed based on the processing properties of these timbers and developing countries wishing to produce pencils now find that the plant is not readily adaptable to the different properties of indigenous timbers.

Timber selection is also important for wood safety match production. Suitable timber is straight grained, able to take up just the right amount of wax and burn at the right rate. Poplar fulfils these needs in temperate regions but tropical countries need to find native timber that can be processed in industrial plant originally designed for poplar.

Timber remains an essential feedstock industries throughout the world and in spite of the growing number of man-made substitutes, a special-property timber is often still the most suitable raw material. The chemic

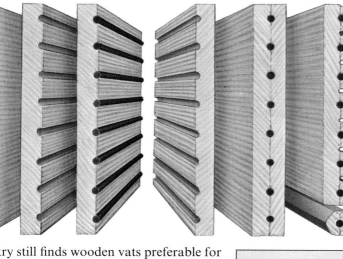

Left *Cricket-bat willow, the only timber used to make cricket-bat blades, is lightweight but strong and able to absorb high-impact shocks. The handle of a cricket bat is formed from 16 separate pieces of Sarawak cane.*

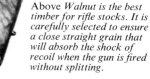

Above *Walnut is the best timber for rifle stocks. It is carefully selected to ensure a close straight grain that will absorb the shock of recoil when the gun is fired without splitting.*

ndustry still finds wooden vats preferable for certain acids and alkalis, and the industry also uses wooden filter-press plates. The timbers used vary according to the product, but they range from the softwood Douglas fir, favoured for its availability in long straight lengths, to the dense impermeable hardwoods, such as afzelia, greenheart and purpleheart, which can resist chemical attack.

Wooden casks for transporting liquids are still widely used and because their convex, or "bouged", shape makes them easy to roll, they have changed little in design since the ancient craft of cooperage began. Oak is the major cooperage timber and the only wood used for whisky, sherry, some red wines and for wooden beer casks. This is partly because the bending properties of oak are suitable for the convex shape required, and for whisky and wine cooperage because the timber is believed to affect the flavour of the product. The complicated biochemical interaction is not fully understood even now, but a research team at the University of California has succeeded in isolating flavouring components in wine that clearly derive from extractives in the oak. For whisky casks, however, the use of a suitable alternative would mean a change in the law in those countries requiring whisky to be held in bond in casks made specifically of oak.

Above *Balsa, the lightest of the commercially available timbers, has long been used by South American and Central American Indians for building canoes and rafts. But western boat builders also have found use for the timber. Methane-carrying tankers require large quantities of lightweight insulating material to keep their liquid loads cool and stable. Balsa wood, whose cellular structure makes it highly insulative as well as light in weight, has proved to be the most suitable material for this purpose. The lightness of balsa and its workability also make it the ideal material for making models, particularly aeroplanes.*

Building with timber

Early man soon found that timber was the most suitable building material: it was strong, easy to work with simple tools and readily available. The "beehive" hut was probably the first domestic dwelling in many parts of the world and it was almost certainly the earliest form of timber frame construction: the centre pole supporting a circle of sloping poles covered with palm fronds is reminiscent of the stem and branches of a sheltering tree.

The technique of adding a matrix of thin branches on which mud was daubed was soon developed and this modification proved so successful that it continued for centuries. This basic "tent" form of timber frame rapidly changed, however, as the development of tools and jointing methods enabled more sophisticated structures to be built.

In Europe decay-resistant oak was soon recognized as the most suitable timber for framing, because it could be left exposed and only the spaces between the posts required infilling. Materials used included wattle and daub, lathe and plaster, or the small bricks that had achieved limited popularity by the sixteenth century.

It was not until the eighteenth century that the growing scarcity of suitable framing timber created an upsurge in solid brick construction and caused the decline of the timber frame method of building in Europe. But timber was never entirely superseded: it continued to be used for roof trusses, rafters and joists, and even today the conventional European brick-built house requires as much as half a ton of timber.

While building practice in Europe changed, early North American and Australian settlers were clearing trees to make room for agriculture. Timber was the obvious building material and the early settlers continued the tradition of timber framing. The technique was further modified, until, in recent years, it has returned to Europe in modern form.

Timbers used for present-day framing, roofs and other general construction purposes are chosen for their straight grain, low cost and regular availability in the sizes required, and are often stress-graded to achieve economy without loss of safety. European and northern Asian countries use softwoods from the native forests, especially Scots pine, some hemlock and Douglas fir, where large dimensions are required. Hemlock and Douglas fir, with other indigenous conifers, are the major building timbers in Canada and the United States, while Australia, Chile, New Zealand and South Africa use *Pinus radiata* and species of eucalyptus.

Although not low in cost, teak has been widely used in India, Burma and Thailand because the warm, moist areas of every continent have the problem of combating termite attack. Termite-resistant timbers are not common, but iroko and afrormosia in Africa, and jarrah in Australia, are also highly resistant. Modern building methods and efficient preservative treatment, however, enable a wider range of timbers to be utilized.

Below *The Kirghiz of Afghanistan, like other nomadic peoples, still find timber the best material for building their mobile homes. Their "yurts" are constructed from lattices of poles, which are then covered with felt mats.*

TIMBER CLADDING

In North America weather boarding is widely used for cladding the walls of timber frame houses, and shingles and shakes are used both for walls and for roofing. In Europe,

Shakes are cleft by machine or mallet and froe.

Shingles are produced by sawing across the grain.

Overlapping shingles.

HEAVY CONSTRUCTION TIMBERS

Timber is still widely used for building heavy constructions such as docks, bridges and mine shafts. The timbers must be strong, durable and obtainable in large dimensions. Certain tropical timbers, such as basralocus and greenheart, are particularly suitable for marine work, but temperate hardwoods and some treated softwoods are also used. The recently built docks in Port Newark, New York City, have piles made from treated Douglas fir and fenders made of hard-wearing, decay-resistant oak. A variety of decay-resistant timbers can be used for bridge construction. The footbridge at Tintagel in Cornwall, made from laminates of iroko wood, is a relatively light construction but one that is strong, durable and capable of absorbing movement.

THE TIMBER FRAME

The "beehive" hut was probably the first form of timber frame construction. This simple structure consisted of an upright centre pole supporting a circle of diagonal poles. It was then modified to a rectangular "ridge-tent" frame that allowed more headroom than the circular design. Each end of the ridge pole was supported by two poles joined together to form an inverted "V" and from this basic construction the medieval "cruck" frame developed. Later, a second secondary structure of skirting wall was added and this eventually evolved into the post and truss frame building, whose roof supports were constructed separately from the wall frame. In the 18th century, a scarcity of suitable timber caused the decline of timber framing in Europe, although the tradition continued in North America. Two new framing techniques were developed to use the large quantities of North American softwood: the platform frame, which was built storey by storey, and the balloon frame, which used continuous lengths of vertical studding. The rigidity of the older European hardwood frame was achieved by placing the studs closer together and by bracing the whole frame. And from North America, the timber frame has now returned to western Europe.

however, timber cladding declined in popularity when the load-bearing brick wall construction superseded timber framing. Nevertheless, many examples of timber-clad buildings can still be found throughout northern

Europe. Perhaps the best-known examples of shingled roofing are the domes of the 18th-century Karelian Russian church (below), with traditional eastern European log walls and hand-cut shingles of aspen wood.

WORLD PRODUCTION OF SAWN WOOD

Much of the timber destined for building work is processed in the country of origin and enters the world market as sawnwood. More than 75 per cent of this is softwood produced by coniferous forests of the northern hemisphere. Hardwoods, although used for general construction in tropical countries, are used mainly for specialist building work in temperate regions.

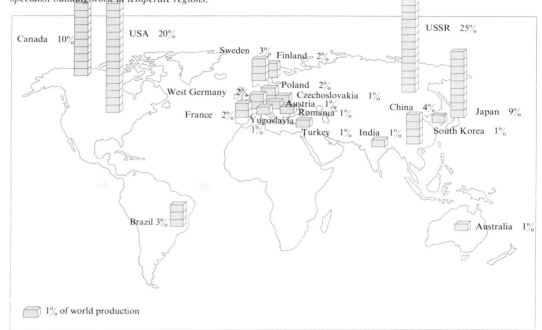

1% of world production

y ridge frame

Medieval cruck frame

Post and truss frame

Early American balloon frame

Resistance to decay is a particularly important quality for timber in contact with the ground or partly submerged in water. Heavy construction work for piles, bridge supports and dock gates requires either fully preservative-treated construction timbers such as pine or the natural durability, density and strength of some of the specialist tropical hardwood timbers. Greenheart from the Guyanas and Surinam, opepe and ekki from West Africa, very dense *Shorea* spp. from Indonesia and South East Asia and basralocus from the Guyanas and Brazil are widely used for these purposes. They are particularly suitable for construction work in harbours and estuaries, because they are resistant both to marine borers and to marine abrasion.

General joinery covers a wide range of purposes and the species of timber used varies from one country to another, and also according to fashion. Throughout the northern hemisphere, painted windows, doors and interior work are popular and the softwoods are most frequently used because they are generally easier to work and they also retain paint more readily than most hardwoods. The most commonly used timbers include the general construction timbers, as well as the lighter spruces of both Europe and North America.

Tropical hardwoods have been used increasingly for joinery in recent years in order to satisfy fashion's demand for the natural timber look. In France and Belgium, the earlier European tradition of hardwood windows has always been maintained, but tropical hardwoods, such as utile, mahogany and meranti, have in recent years supplemented supplies of traditional oak. North America also uses decay-resistant softwoods for unpainted joinery, particularly sequoia and western red cedar for exterior cladding of buildings.

Tropical countries use a wide variety of locally available hardwoods for exterior and interior joinery, and Brazil also uses and exports large quantities of the subtropical softwood Parana pine for interior work.

179

Paper: an ancient craft

Below *Papermaking began in China in the first century AD. The art travelled east to Japan and west through the Middle East, finally arriving in Europe by 1189. In 1690 the first papermill was set up in the USA.*

Man's earliest writings were inscribed on pieces of bone, tortoiseshell, woven cloth or clay tablets. As early as 3,500 BC the Egyptians were writing on papyrus scrolls made from a native sedge-like plant that grew prodigiously along the banks of the Nile, and from which the word paper is derived. But paper as we know it today, made from crushed vegetable matter and produced in sheets, was first invented in China.

History has long attributed the invention of papermaking to Ts'ai Lun, an official at the Imperial Court of China in AD 105. Recent archaeological finds, however, indicate that paper was being produced at least 200 years prior to Ts'ai Lun's first efforts. His paper was made from a mixture of the inner bark of the paper mulberry tree, *Broussonetia papyrifera*, old fishing nets, rags and hemp waste, all ground into fibre and laid on a mesh or screen of bamboo strips to drain and dry. Similar principles are employed today.

The Chinese method of papermaking soon spread to Korea and then to Japan. The civilizations of East and West developed simultaneously, but entirely separately, and so it was not until the eighth century, when Chinese prisoners were taken by the Arabs at Samarkand, that the art of papermaking began its slow progress across the continents. By AD 793 paper was being produced in Baghdad by Chinese workmen under Arab supervision. Damascus was the next centre of paper production and the finished sheets were exported throughout Europe. The art then travelled through Egypt, replacing papyrus, which had ruled supreme for more than 3,000 years, to Morocco. The Moorish invasion of Spain introduced papermaking to Europe and eventually, in 1690, the first papermill in the United States was constructed near Germantown near Philadelphia.

At that time paper was still made by hand, the process remaining virtually unchanged since its inception in China. But handmade paper had several disadvantages. The size of the sheet was determined by the size of the frame used and the ability of the papermaker to lift the frame from the stock. This was a slow and labour-intensive process, but at the end of the eighteenth century two major developments took place—the mechanization of papermaking and the substitution of new raw materials for old rags.

In 1799 Louis Robert, a clerk at the mill of Didot Frères at Essonnes in France, constructed a moving screen that delivered a continuous sheet of paper to a pair of squeeze rollers. This machine was not a success, but the idea was taken up by a London company of stationers, the brothers Henry and Sealy Fourdrinier, who employed the engineer Bryan Donkin to design and build a new machine. After much trial, and a certain amount of error, a machine was set up in 1803 at Frogmore in England. It is claimed that the expenses incurred nearly bankrupted the Fourdriniers, but they gave their name to modern papermaking machines.

Above *In this illustration from an early Chinese manuscript bamboo is being soaked before being boiled and beaten into pulp. Bamboo also served as the fuel for boiling and thin bamboo strips were used to make the screen on which the sheets were formed. Bamboo is still an important source of paper fibre in Asia.*

Copel

1376
1345

Elizabethtown, N.J. 1728
Milton, Mass. 1728

Hérault 1189
Toledo

Germantown, Pa.
1690

Mexico City 1575

Fès
Valencia 1150

Left *Cutting and sorting rags in the 18th century. Rags were sorted into linen or cotton and different proportions of each were used for different kinds of paper. By the beginning of the 19th century there was an acute shortage of rags and many mills were forced to close, even though the demand for paper was increasing every year. Wood pulp then began to take over as the essential source of fibre. Rags, however, are still used to manufacture paper with special characteristics notably bank-notes and legal documents.*

DONKIN'S PAPERMAKING MACHINE

Bryan Donkin set up his first successful papermaking machine in 1803 and in the following 10 years his company made and installed 13 more. Fifty years later he had made nearly 300 machines and they were exported throughout Europe, India and the USA. It was claimed that the machine, illustrated below in the catalogue of the London International Exhibition of 1862, could "make an endless sheet of paper about 20 miles long in 24 hours, and in that time cover an area of 17 acres, if kept at work".

Papermaking machine

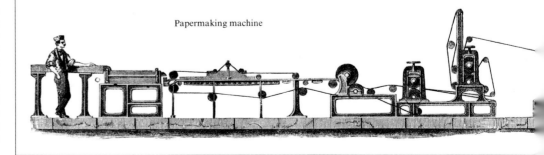

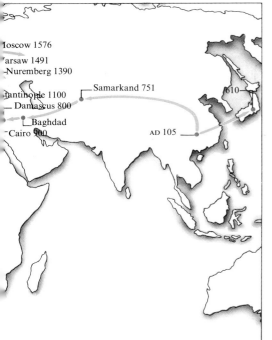

Hand in hand with mechanical improvements went the search for a viable alternative to rags as the source of pulp. Rags were increasingly in short supply and papermills, plagued by acute shortages, were openly advertising for them. In England alone twenty-four million pounds of rags were used in 1800. The industrial revolution, with its increase in population and spread of commerce and education, created a massive demand for paper, not only for export but also for internal consumption. The eighteenth century was a literary age: the educated classes read more books, the daily press was increasing its circulation and the new schools needed books.

Wood as a source of paper had already been suggested by the French scientist René de Réaumur early in the eighteenth century. He had observed a wasp build a nest from the fibres that it had taken from a dry post and mixed with its body secretions, and reasoned that man could learn from this. As with much scientific thought, however, it took a long time before this early hypothesis was put into practical use. The search for efficient methods of manufacturing paper from wood and vegetable pulps gathered momentum only after 1800. Several new pulping methods were evolved and these took two distinct pathways—mechanical and chemical.

Mechanically produced, or groundwood, pulp was first made in Germany in 1840 by Kellar, who held sticks of wood against a grindstone under a water shower, but did not come into extensive use until 1870. The same process is used today to make newsprint, but as the mechanical method produces pulp that contains all the components of wood it is not suitable for paper that requires high whiteness and permanence.

Chemical processing dissolves the lignin and other wood components to leave a pulp composed mostly of cellulose. Soda pulp was first manufactured from wood in England in 1852, and in 1867 a patent for the sulphite process was issued in the United States to the chemist B. C. Tilghman. The sulphite process was the chief method of pulping in the early days of the paper industry and spruce and fir were the preferred wood species. However, in 1884, Carl F. Dahl in Danzig, Germany, invented the sulphate, or kraft, process, which could utilize practically all species of trees, thus greatly expanding the potential supply of raw materials. Unlike the sulphite process that sewers all waste products, the kraft process has the advantage of recycling all chemicals used. This reduces the cost of raw materials and has a minimal impact on the environment. Since 1940 the kraft process has dominated the industry.

The use of trees as the primary source of pulp has tended to concentrate wood pulp and paper production in those countries that are highly industrialized and well forested with suitable tree species, particularly softwoods. Canada, the United States and Scandinavia now produce more than eighty per cent of the world's pulp and paper.

Despite the advances in engineering and invention that have transformed a skilled handicraft into a highly mechanized industry, the fundamental processes and principles have remained the same for 2,000 years.

Right *Papermaking by hand in the 18th century—as illustrated in Diderot's Encyclopédie (1751–72)—was a very labour-intensive industry. The vatman on the left is dipping the mould, or frame, into the stock while the next worker along presses the wet sheet in the mould to rid it of some of the water. The third man separates the sheet from the mould before putting it in the press to his left for further compressing. The size of the paper sheets was limited by the size of the mould and the vatman's ability to lift it.*

Drying machine

Cutting machine

Right *A patent for the sulphite pulping process was issued in the United States in 1867. This is the digester and blow tank belonging to the Duncan Company, Mechanicsville, New York, taken from an issue of the Scientific American of 1898.*

Trees into pulp

Papermaking begins in the forest where trees are harvested. From the serenity of the forest the cut trees are de-limbed and transported to the highly mechanized pulp mill. There they are stripped of their bark and reduced to small chips in seconds, before being cooked in chemicals—the chemical pulping process. Alternatively, they may be ground to pulp on giant grinding wheels or pulpstones. Hours later, whatever the pulping process, the cut trees may be part of a giant roll of paper ready for shipping to a customer.

The modern pulp mill runs for twenty-four hours a day and is highly automated, using sophisticated computer controls. Most pulp mills are situated in well-forested regions and are adjacent to papermills, so there is a continuous flow from trees to pulp and pulp to paper. Other mills may produce pulp that is shipped to papermills in unforested regions or made into other cellulose-based products such as cellophane and rayon (see pages 188–191). The purpose of the pulp mill is to extract cellulose fibres from trees by removing other components such as lignin. There are three major methods of producing pulp from wood.

Mechanical or groundwood pulp, as the name suggests, is made by physically grinding or pulling apart wood fibres. This pulp can be made from roundwood logs or chips. In the case of roundwood, short logs are pressed by hydraulic cylinders against a pulpstone made of a mixture of silicon carbide and aluminium oxide. Each stone can produce up to fifty tons of pulp in twenty-four hours.

From the grinders the pulp is screened to remove any knots, bark or dirt. As groundwood contains all the chemical constituents of wood, such as lignin, hemi-cellulose and resins, paper made from this stock is subject to yellowing when exposed to light and heat; as can be seen with old newspapers and many books. Also, groundwood fibres are very short and do not bond together very well so the papers produced do not have a high strength, although they are bulky and have good printing qualities.

Chemical wood pulp is produced by cooking wood chips in chemical solutions at high temperatures and pressures. There are two major processes: the sulphite and the kraft.

The sulphite process was the leader in chemical pulping for many years, but since 1940 it has given way to the kraft process.

THE KRAFT PAPERMILL

TRANSPORT

Pulpwood logs arrive at the pulp mill by road, rail, barge or, in some countries, by river. Up to 2,000 cords (150 truckloads) of wood may be delivered each day. In those parts of Canada and Scandinavia where river drives are the major method of transport all the timber has to be at the mill before the winter freeze.

CHIP PILE

Chip piles are supplemented by chips that are brought in by rail or road, usually from solid-wood product plants.

DEBARKERS

From the wood piles the logs are fed into the de-barking drums. The logs are tumbled against each other and the abrasive insides of the drum, until most of the bark is removed. The bark is directed to the furnaces, where it is burned to produce energy for the mill.

WOOD YARD

The logs are unloaded by crane into hardwood and softwood piles. Usually there are enough logs stored to keep the mill running for 1–6 months.

CHIPPERS

The barked logs are fed to the chippers and cut by rotating knives into chips approximately an inch square and a quarter-inch thick. The chips are then sorted. The small ones are burned with the bark and the large ones are recycled through the chippers. Chips are either fed to the digester or to chip piles.

DIGESTER

There are two kinds of digester in wide use today—batch and continuous. Batch digesters are giant pressur

Sulphite cooking liquor is usually made by dissolving sulphur dioxide in a solution of a sodium or calcium hydroxide. The wood chips are delivered to a digester (a large pressure cooker) and the acid liquor is added along with steam to provide heat.

After the cook the pressure is relieved with such force that it defibres the chips. Then, undesirable materials, such as knots, dirt and bark, are removed by screening based on particle size and density. The pulp is washed and acid chemicals are removed and sewered, posing a threat of pollution if not controlled properly. The resulting light-coloured pulp is strong and is used in an unbleached state for many printing papers, often in combination with groundwood pulp.

The modern kraft process was developed in 1884 as an improvement on the soda process that had been devised more than thirty years previously. Soda pulp was produced from hardwoods soaked with caustic soda (sodium hydroxide). This pulp was of low strength and was only useful as a filler pulp, often being mixed with stronger softwood fibres for printing paper. This process consumed large quantities of sodium hydroxide and the papermakers were forced to devise methods for recovering chemicals from the spent liquors. Fortunately, from this necessity there was an important development because chemical recovery and recycling have become an essential and integral part of kraft pulping.

The kraft process produced a much stronger pulp than soda pulp and derived its name from the German and Swedish word *kraft* meaning strong. It improved on the soda process by the use of a mixture of sodium hydroxide and sodium sulphide as the cooking liquor. However, the pulp produced was dark in colour and was therefore used for papers that did not require colour or brightness. This disadvantage was compensated for by the expansion of the packaging industry, which created a rapid growth in the demand for unbleached paper and board.

In the 1930s the colour disadvantage was eliminated when new bleaching techniques allowed pulp of high whiteness to be produced. The kraft process then became, and still is, the predominant pulping method. A major advantage is that pulp can be produced from a wide variety of tree species. High-resinous woods, such as loblolly, longleaf, shortleaf and slash pine, are not suitable for the sulphite process, but in the kraft process the pitch, or resin, is dissolved and can be separated from the pulp to provide a valuable by-product (see pages 194–195). The kraft process is described in detail below.

WASHERS

The spent cooking liquor, black liquor, is washed out. In a continuous digest process the black liquor is washed out before the mixture enters the blow tank. If brown packaging paper, such as grocery bags, is to be made the washed pulp is pumped directly to the papermill.

BLEACH PLANT

If white paper is to be made the pulp is sent to the bleach plant. First, chlorine gas is added to the pulp-water slurry to react with and solubilize the dark-coloured lignin derivatives that remain after cooking. Second, the chlorine is washed out and the pulp is treated with sodium hydroxide to extract any remaining lignin. The third stage is to add small quantities of chlorine dioxide, which brings the pulp to a medium level of whiteness. If higher brightness is required, the sodium hydroxide and chlorine dioxide steps are repeated.

BULK STORAGE

The pulp is then pumped into the bulk storage towers ready to be pumped to the adjacent papermill. Each tower can hold 50–500 tons of pulp, enough to keep the papermill running for up to 24 hours.

...ookers. Chips are fed into the top of the digester along with the cooking liquor of sodium hydroxide and sodium sulphide. The digester is sealed and steam is introduced at pressures up to 110 lb per square inch and the temperature can reach 170° C (345° F). The cook lasts for 2–2½ hours. In the most modern mills continuous digesters are in operation. These are huge towers more than 200 ft high with a number of zones. The chips and cooking liquor are fed continuously into the top of the tower and pass into successive zones of different temperature and pressure. This steady flow allows a greater uniformity in the quality of cooked chips. Cooking frees cellulose fibres from lignin.

CHEMICAL AND ENERGY RECOVERY

The modern pulp mill requires large amounts of energy to keep it running. Every effort is made to utilize waste material to fire the furnaces. Bark from the de-barking drums, undersized chips and the lignin from the cooking liquor are all used to generate steam to drive turbines that produce electricity.

Chemicals are also an expensive commodity, and if sewered they pose a pollution threat. In the kraft process up to ninety-five per cent of the chemicals used for the cooking, or white, liquor are recovered. The spent "black" liquor is washed from the defibred chips and pumped to the evaporating vessels. Here more than half the water is removed and the "strong" liquor is burned in a recovery furnace. The wood components in the lignin produce heat that is used to generate steam for the mill. The sodium sulphate and other sodium compounds formed during the cooking are converted to sodium sulphide and sodium carbonate. These are dissolved in water to form the "green" liquor. Calcium oxide from the lime kiln is added to the green liquor to form calcium carbonate and to reconstitute the original cooking liquor of sodium hydroxide and sodium sulphide. The calcium carbonate is allowed to settle out and is passed to a lime kiln, where carbon dioxide is driven off by heat to leave calcium oxide—the chemical added to the green liquor.

Pulp into paper

The papermill is supplied with either brown pulp or a bleached white pulp, depending on the kind of paper required. The final characteristics of that paper must now be decided upon because many of its properties are established at the next stage.

The pulp is pumped through blenders where ingredients are added to impart desired characteristics, such as colour, moisture resistance and opacity. Next, bonding strength is developed in the fibres by passing the pulp between rotating steel bars in machines called refiners. The degree of refining treatment determines the finished paper's strength and other qualities by breaking up the fibres to the required length and fraying them out. The difference between soft and porous paper, such as coffee filter paper, and dense printing paper is the result of beating or refining. The refined pulp is then diluted and sent through centrifugal cleaners to remove any foreign particles or dirt that may still remain.

The cleaned and refined pulp goes to the fourdrinier, or wet end, of the papermaking machine. It enters a pressurized headbox and emerges as a uniform fibre suspension through a narrow slit on to a rapidly moving wire or plastic screen, travelling as fast as 3,000 feet a minute. When the pulp first leaves the headbox it is about ninety-nine per cent water and only one per cent fibre. The water begins draining immediately so that the fibres settle on the screen and start to form a sheet.

The screen is usually supported by a forming board, which is followed by closely spaced table rolls, and most modern machines are supplemented with stationary supports called "foils". The movement of the screen over these table rolls and foils creates a suction effect, causing rapid drainage of the water through the screen. The screen then runs over a series of suction boxes where the remainder of the visible water is removed.

On some machines a dandy roll is located

on top of the screen between two of the suction boxes. This roll compresses the still wet sheet, distributing the fibres and improving the sheet formation. In some cases the surface of the roll contains lettering or a design, which can be used to produce a watermarked paper.

As the web of paper leaves the screen it is still about eighty per cent water. The wet web of paper is then supported by a felt and passes through a series of presses, which not only reduces the water content of the wet web of paper to about sixty-five per cent, but also compacts the sheet and levels the surface.

From the press section the paper enters the drying section, where the sheet is dried to the final moisture content. The driers are steam-heated cast-iron drums, four to six feet in diameter. They are generally arranged in two tiers with fifty or more tiers of driers on some of the larger machines. The paper is held tightly against the driers by a heavy felt and roughly two pounds of water are evaporated

THE HEADBOX

From the refiners the pulp is pumped to a pressurized headbox, where the pulp is discharged through a narrow slit across the whole width of the moving wire.

DANDY ROLL

This wire-wound roll is located over the wire and gently compresses the wet web of fibres on the wire. This roll smooths the top surface of the paper sheet and improves formation. Dandy rolls are sometimes used to impart a watermark on the paper.

PRESS SECTION

Felted presses squeeze out as much free water as possible before passing the sheet to the drying section. By the time the sheet leaves the press section it is only 65 per cent water.

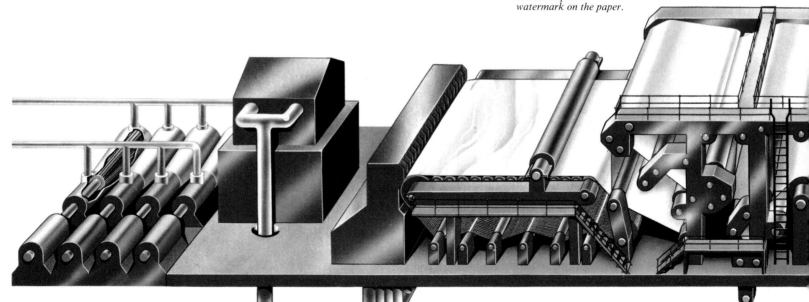

REFINERS AND BLENDERS

Pulp from the storage tanks is pumped through blenders, where the sizes, fillers and dyes are added, and then through refiners, where the fibres are rubbed against each other between steel plates. The fibres are shortened and their ends teased out so that they bond together better.

FOURDRINIER SECTION

The fourdrinier is an endless wire screen travelling over a series of rollers and suction boxes. The wire is made from a phosphor-bronze metal or synthetic fibres and the kind of paper to be produced determines the fineness of the wire mesh used. (Fine mesh for fine paper and coarse mesh for heavier board.) The wire may vary in width from 5 to 30 feet and can move at

for each pound of paper that is produced.

On some machines a pair of steel rollers, called a breaker stack, may be located within the drier section. These rollers press the paper and help to control its thickness, as well as accelerating the subsequent drying. An external sizing, when desired, may be applied at the size press, also located between sections of driers. This sizing imparts additional special properties such as water resistance.

From the drier section the sheet moves through the calender stacks, the last operation on the paper machine before the paper is rolled on the reel. Calender stacks are vertical stacks of cast steel rolls that have a highly polished smooth surface. The paper enters the stacks at the top and is compressed and smoothed as it travels down. Finally, a huge reel of paper weighing from fifteen to thirty-five tons is formed. This is removed and a new empty reel added simultaneously so that the sheet can be manufactured continuously.

REWIND AND CUTTING

Full reels are removed from the dry end of the papermaking machine and rewound evenly in a separate operation. During the rewind the paper can be cut to the width required by the customer by static knives slicing through the moving paper. From the rewind the paper is packaged ready for shipment.

If the customer does not require the material immediately the paper is rewound as full-width reels and then stored in an area where the humidity and temperature is controlled to ensure that the paper does not distort.

DRYING SECTION

Here the paper is wrapped round steam-heated drying drums to remove the rest of the moisture.

CALENDER STACKS

As the dry paper leaves the driers it passes through the smooth polished rolls of the calender stack. This smooths and compresses the paper before it is fed on to the final reel.

speeds of more than 30 miles an hour producing more than 1,000 tons of paper in an operating day. Water drains rapidly with the help of table rolls, foils and suction boxes. The wet web is approximately 80 per cent water when it leaves the wire. The fourdrinier here is the traditional kind, but in recent years new designs have appeared. The most important is the "twin-wire" former, where paper is formed between two wires.

THE REEL

Eight-foot-diameter reels weighing up to 35 tons are formed. The full reels are replaced by empty ones in such a way as to keep the web of paper running continuously.

Paper products

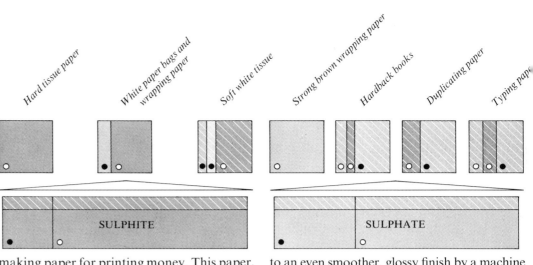

Hard tissue paper | White paper bags and wrapping paper | Soft white tissue | Strong brown wrapping paper | Hardback books | Duplicating paper | Typing paper

SULPHITE   SULPHATE

PROCESSES AND PRODUCTS

The papermaker first chooses a raw material—softwood, if he is making a strong paper, hardwood for a smoother but weaker paper. Then he selects the pulping process. Sulphite and sulphate methods produce strong but expensive pulps. Mechanical pulp is cheaper but produces a weak paper and is normally only used for short-life products. Soda pulp is very fine but so weak that it is used mainly as a filler for other pulps. Techniques such as bleaching and calendering then produce any further qualities required of the final paper product.

Paper is an ancient material, but it is at the same time one of the most pervasive symbols of contemporary life. Paper is an integral component of modernization. Without its ready availability for an infinity of purposes we would have to imagine a world without the registration of births and deaths, without money or prescription slips, without the fast and efficient distribution of food, and without learning, legislation or communication as we know it in the modern world.

It takes many different forms of paper to serve all these human needs and comforts, but the term paper is generally used to describe any kind of matted fibre sheeting. Vegetable fibre, or cellulose, is most commonly used, and most of this is obtained from wood, extracted by chemical or mechanical pulping processes (see pages 182–183).

There are, however, several other sources of papermaking pulps, including the seed hairs of the cotton plant, bast fibres, leaf fibres such as esparto and sisal, old rags, waste paper and straw. Each kind of pulp has its own distinctive characteristics, which determine the properties of the final paper product. And because of the many different uses of paper, papermakers must customize their products by using the right kind of pulp.

The quality of the pulp is a critical factor in making paper for printing money. This paper, called bank-note paper, or currency paper in the United States, must be manufactured from high-quality pulps that will help to make the paper strong and resistant to wear. New cotton rag trimmings and flax are used. The paper also contains some high-quality cotton fibre pulp, although sometimes pure chemical wood pulp is added instead.

The papermaker, as well as choosing the right kind of pulp, must also select the appropriate manufacturing processes and additives in order to produce the kind of paper desired. Sizing is added to the pulp to prevent the paper from being too absorbent. If sizing were not added to printing paper, for example, too much ink would penetrate the paper and leave it smeared. The paper used to form tubes that contain dynamite explosive, however, is unsized so that it will absorb waxes and other substances that protect the explosive against invading dampness.

Paper can also be coated. Quality books and magazines, especially those containing photographs, use papers coated with such pigments as kaolin clay or titanium dioxide. These coatings make the paper smoother and whiter and so allow both the print and the photographs to stand out on the page.

Magazine-quality papers are then polished to an even smoother, glossy finish by a machine called a supercalender, which irons the paper between large rollers at a pressure of 1,600 pounds to every linear inch. Most paper is simply calendered at a pressure of 300 pounds to the linear inch.

Sometimes a paper produced with qualities designed for one purpose may subsequently prove suitable for several other applications. Bond paper, an uncoated paper containing chemical pulp, which makes it strong and durable, was originally used for government bonds and legal documents. It then began to be used by businesses for stationery and forms, and since plain paper copying machines have been developed bond has been found ideal as duplicating paper.

One of the most important uses of paper is that of packaging. Although paper has been used to pack and protect goods from earliest times, modern mass production has created a huge increase in demand for boxes, cartons and wrappers of all kinds. In the United States, for example, more than half of all paper produced is paperboard, and nearly all of this is used as packaging. Rigid paperboard boxes have been in use in the United States since 1836, when a Colonel Andrew A. Dennison developed a box for jewellery, and today perfumes, confectionary, cameras, watches,

Left *Because of the fast turnover and short lifespan of newspapers, almost all newsprint can be made from cheap, mechanically produced softwood pulp. Hardback books, above, however, require a strong, high-quality chemical pulp. This is then bleached, coated and polished to a durable, glossy finished*

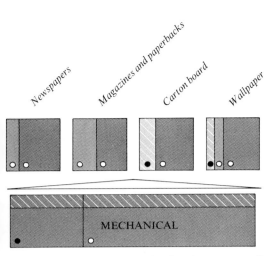

Newspapers | Magazines and paperbacks | Carton board | Wallpaper

Corrugated paper | Corrugated cases

● Hardwood   ○ Softwood

Bleached pulp

MECHANICAL

SEMI-CHEMICAL

SODA

shoes and a multitude of other items are all sold in solid rigid boxes made of paperboard.

Folding cartons, developed towards the end of the nineteenth century, are used to package perishable goods. Various frozen foods, such as ice-cream, meat products and pastries, are sold in folding cartons made of solid bleached sulphate (SBS), a paperboard manufactured from chemically produced pulp that has been bleached white.

Coated with plastic, SBS can also be used for liquid packaging, such as for dairy products or fruit juices. Some SBS is now polyester-coated to enable it to withstand temperatures of 425° Fahrenheit (218°C) or more. It is then used to make trays for food to be cooked in microwave ovens. Paper, unlike aluminium which has been used traditionally, does not reflect the microwaves.

Corrugated cardboard boxes are one of the least romantic, but one of the most important forms of paper packaging. They are made by sandwiching corrugated, or fluted, paper between flat sheets of paperboard. The corrugations give strength to the inner layer without adding too much weight to the container.

Corrugated paper was originally used to make sweatbands for British hats and it was not until 1874 that Oliver Long, an American, took the corrugated paper and put it between paper sheeting. Today, corrugated containers are used for shipping perishable products such as food and consumer durables such as television sets, washing machines and furniture.

Several different kinds of paper are suitable for packaging, but one of the most widely used is kraft. This is because the kraft chemical pulping process produces a very strong paper, in fact the name kraft comes from the German meaning strong. Unbleached kraft paper is brown and is used to make what is perhaps the best known of all forms of paper packaging, the brown paper bag.

The history of the paper bag can be traced back at least as far as the 1600s, but in 1852 in Pennsylvania, Francis Wolle invented a machine to produce paper bags in large quantities. The brown paper bag now takes many forms and sizes, ranging from the large, tough, multi-wall fertilizer sack to the small, convenient and widely used confectionery bag.

Paper tissue is another paper product that seems to have become an indispensable item of twentieth-century life. Toilet tissue, however, was reportedly used in China as early as AD 900. Tissue is a soft, clean, absorbent paper. The cellulose content of any paper naturally drinks up water, and so the pulps used for most kinds of paper have water-repellent materials added to them. For tissue manufac-

ture, however, it is important to keep these water repellents to a minimum. The paper machines that make tissues are the fastest in the paper industry; some of the machines in operation can produce as much as 6,000 feet of toilet tissue every minute.

World demand for paper is increasing. And while the market for traditional products such as newsprint, books and packaging materials is steadily growing, at the same time new uses and products are being developed. The use of paper as a building material is a recent innovation, at least in the western world. Paper is now used as an inner layer for interior doors and paper printed with a wood-grain pattern, and covered with a clear protective coating is now used as an alternative veneering for particleboard. Paper is also being used to manufacture a new kind of man-made composition building board. New forms of paper packaging are also being researched; development work is being carried out on a food or drink can that can be made entirely of paperboard.

Consumption of paper will probably continue to increase. The advantages of the material are many but possibly the most important is that, providing the forests are carefully managed, this eminently versatile product can continue to be obtained from an infinitely renewable resource.

...aper. The strength of corrugated cardboard boxes, above, is due partly to their inner layer of fluted paper and partly to the unbleached semi-chemical pulp used. Brown paper used to wrap parcels, above, is made from chemical pulp that is then machine polished on one side to give it wet strength. Wallpapers, right, are often vinyl-coated after printing to improve their wearing qualities.

Cellulose

Silk has always been an expensive and prestigious commodity and its producer, the silkworm, has presented a fascinating challenge to man. In 1664, Dr Robert Hook suggested in his *Micrographia* that "there might be a way found out to make an artificial glutinous composition, much resembling, if not full as good, nay better than that excrement or whatever other substance it be out of which the silkworm wiredraws his clew". The desire to emulate the silkworm's ability to produce fibres led to the discovery that useful man-made fibres could be made from cellulose, and that chemicals derived from cellulose could be used to make films and plastics, as well as providing feedstock for many other products and their manufacturing processes.

The many historical accounts of these developments attach varying significance to individual events. One of the most important discoveries was made in 1846 by a German chemist, Christian Frederick Schonbein, when he used a cotton apron to mop up a spillage of sulphuric acid and saltpetre. He left the apron to dry, it exploded, and gun cotton had been discovered. But perhaps more important was his discovery that the cellulose in the cotton had been converted into cellulose nitrate, which unlike pure cellulose is soluble.

Schonbein had therefore discovered the first cellulose derivative that could be used as a raw material for manufacturing fibres and plastics. At first interest in this unstable compound was directed entirely towards its potential as an explosive, but in 1868 an American, J. W. Hyatt, won a prize of ten thousand dollars for successfully making a billiard ball from a mixture of nitro-cellulose and camphor. He had created the first plastic, which became known as celluloid.

Cellulose nitrate was first manufactured into filaments in 1883–84 by Sir Joseph Swan, who used it to form the elements of electric light bulbs. He spun cellulose nitrate yarn, and then de-nitrated it to reduce its inflammability. In 1892 three British chemists,

Cross, Bevan and Beadle, patented another process for dissolving cellulose, by converting it into sodium cellulose xanthate, a term derived from the Greek word *xanthos*, meaning yellow, the colour of the solution.

During the next few years this process was developed for spinning filaments and also for casting films. Two years after they had patented the viscose process, Cross and Bevan discovered a method for producing cellulose acetate, another soluble cellulose chemical that could be spun into fibres or formed into solid plastic products.

Cellulose ethers were the last of the important cellulose derivatives to be developed. They now have an extensive variety of commercial uses, ranging from glue production to the manufacture of foodstuffs. Interest in developing this family of derivatives for commercial purposes began in 1912.

At first, all the cellulose derivatives—acetate, nitrate, viscose and ethers—depended on cotton linters for their source of cellulose. The quantities available, however, were soon insufficient to meet the increasing demand for raw material and linters are now used only for specialist purposes, such as the production of food-grade ethers, and for nitro-cellulose that is to be used to make certain explosives.

Dissolving-grade wood pulp provides the bulk of cellulosic raw material for the industries today. This is produced mainly by the sulphite pulping process, but some use is made of sulphate or kraft pulps (see pages 182–183). Until recently almost all dissolving pulps were obtained from the temperate forests of Europe and North America. Tropical and subtropical woods such as *Eucalyptus* were not used because they produce shorter fibres. These faster-growing woods, however, now form a substantial part of the source of dissolving pulps used for plastics and fibres.

Pulp is supplied to the fibre industry in a relatively pure sheet form, which resembles thick blotting paper. Viscose for making fibres or films is produced by first steeping the pulp

At first, the compound aroused interest as a potential explosive, but it was soon realized that because it was soluble, it could also be used to make plastics and fibres. This was the foundation for the modern cellulose industry.

THE CELLULOSE PRODUCERS

At one time the producers of cellulosic plastics and fibres relied exclusively on the cellulose obtained from waste cotton floss. But, as demand for the material increased, wood pulp supplemented supplies and now it provides most of the industry's raw material. Until recently most of this was derived from spruce, Monterey pine and western hemlock as well as some temperate hardwoods. Faster-growing tropical and subtropical timbers were rarely used, but eucalyptus from South Africa is now an important source of cellulose pulp.

Ame
swee

VISCOSE

Viscose, or sodium cellulose xanthate, is one of the most important chemicals used to make plastic films and rayon fibres. It is sometimes made from cotton linters, the short fibres that adhere to cotton seeds, but more frequently from high-cellulose-content wood pulp such as northern spruce. Present-day production is based on the experiments carried out by Cross, Bevan and Beadle in 1892.

Above right Wood pulp is continuously converted to alkali-cellulose slurry in a large solvo-pulper. In older plant, sheets of wood pulp are soaked in the caustic soda in steeping presses and are discharged as sheets of alkali-cellulose.

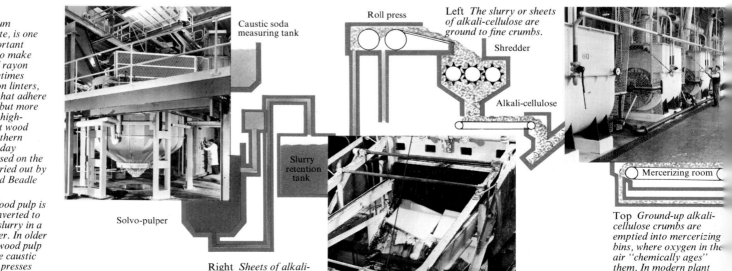

Caustic soda measuring tank

Roll press

Left The slurry or sheets of alkali-cellulose are ground to fine crumbs.

Shredder

Alkali-cellulose

Slurry retention tank

Solvo-pulper

Mercerizing room

Right Sheets of alkali-cellulose passing from press.

Top Ground-up alkali-cellulose crumbs are emptied into mercerizing bins, where oxygen in the air "chemically ages" them. In modern plant (above) an automatic ageing room is used.

WORLD PRODUCTION AND TRADE OF DISSOLVING-GRADE WOOD PULP

Dissolving-grade wood pulp provides most of the cellulose used for the production of viscose and cellulose acetate, nitrate and ethers. Most of the pulp is produced by the sulphite method. Despite increased South African production, the USA is still the world's largest producer of dissolving-grade wood pulp.

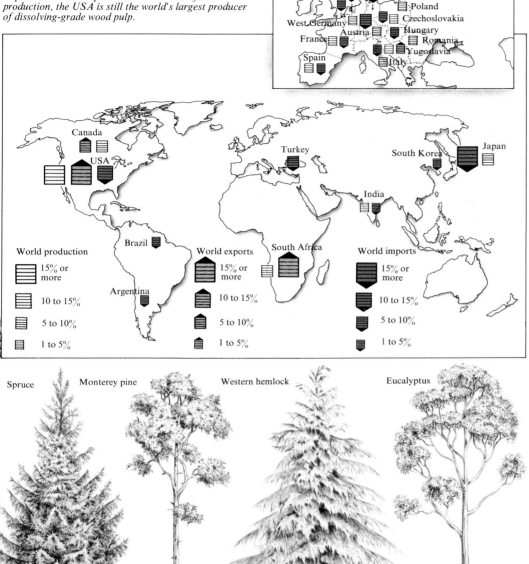

World production
- 15% or more
- 10 to 15%
- 5 to 10%
- 1 to 5%

World exports
- 15% or more
- 10 to 15%
- 5 to 10%
- 1 to 5%

World imports
- 15% or more
- 10 to 15%
- 5 to 10%
- 1 to 5%

Spruce   Monterey pine   Western hemlock   Eucalyptus

in caustic soda solution. This converts the cellulose into alkali cellulose and also removes any residual impurities in the pulp. Excess liquid is pressed out and the sheets are ground up to a fluffy crumb-like consistency. These crumbs are then added to another chemical, carbon disulphide. They react to form sodium cellulose xanthate. This compound is dissolved in more caustic soda solution, and, after careful conditioning and filtration, the liquid is then ready to be extruded through a die to form fibres or plastic films.

The manufacture of cellulose ethers also begins with the conversion of wood pulp into fluffy alkali cellulose crumbs. These are first dried, then mixed with compounds such as methyl chloride, to form methyl cellulose, or with monochloracetic acid, to make sodium carboxymethyl cellulose.

For cellulose acetate production, the sheets of pulp are shredded and mixed with their own weight of acetic acid. This is then mixed with acetic anhydride, in the presence of a catalyst and a solvent. The reaction produces a viscous solution of almost completely acetylated cellulose, cellulose triacetate. By adding water to the solution, carefully washing it and then drying, solid granular flakes of cellulose triacetate are obtained. If cellulose acetate, rather than triacetate, is required, viscous triacetate solution is further processed to partially reverse the acetylation before the water is removed from the solution.

Nitro-cellulose is also made with different levels of nitration. These vary from sixty to ninety per cent nitration depending on the end use of the compound. The purified cellulose from wood pulp or cotton linters is mixed with sulphuric acid, nitric acid and a ratio of water according to the nitration level required. The reacted mass is then released into a "drowning tank" of water and boiled to stabilize the product. The product may be bleached before it is finally dehydrated by washing in alcohol. It is then packaged and transported to the manufacturers of nitro-cellulose plastics.

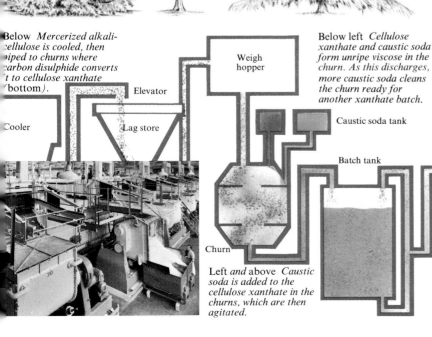

Below Mercerized alkali-cellulose is cooled, then piped to churns where carbon disulphide converts it to cellulose xanthate (bottom).

Cooler
Elevator
Lag store
Weigh hopper
Caustic soda tank
Batch tank
Churn
Storage tank

Below left Cellulose xanthate and caustic soda form unripe viscose in the churn. As this discharges, more caustic soda cleans the churn ready for another xanthate batch.

Left and above Caustic soda is added to the cellulose xanthate in the churns, which are then agitated.

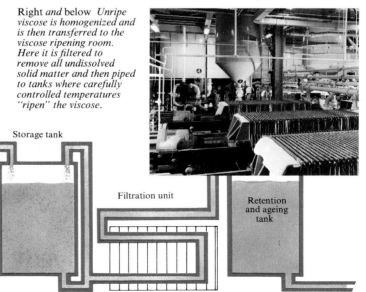

Right and below Unripe viscose is homogenized and is then transferred to the viscose ripening room. Here it is filtered to remove all undissolved solid matter and then piped to tanks where carefully controlled temperatures "ripen" the viscose.

Filtration unit

Retention and ageing tank

Plastics and textiles

Once described as "the chemical that grows", cellulose from the forests of the world is a plentiful, renewable and eminently versatile chemical. The various cellulose derivatives— viscose, cellulose acetate, tri-acetate, nitrate and the ethers—have an enormous diversity of commercial applications, ranging from man-made fibres and plastics to paints and explosives. The production of man-made fibres is one of the most important of the cellulose-based industries, and cellulose fibres still form a significant part of the textile market despite the availability of a vast range of alternative man-made fibres.

The essential feature of cellulose fibre production is the spinneret, or jet, through which the viscous cellulose liquid is extruded to produce filaments. Viscose fibres are made by extruding a solution of cellulose xanthate into a spinning bath containing sulphuric acid and certain salts that make the filaments solidify. Acetate and tri-acetate fibres are also produced by extruding them in solution, but the filaments are not solidified in an acid bath, but are solidified by allowing the solvent in the spinning solution to evaporate.

At one time all cellulose-derived fabrics were woven directly from the filaments. In the 1930s, however, staple or "cut-fibre" viscose was introduced for spinning into yarns in the same way as the short fibres of cotton or wool are spun. Many varieties of viscose have been produced since then. The standard continuous filament yarns have been used principally for dress-making fabrics and furnishings, but the staple fibres have also been used for carpets. Other speciality viscose yarns have included high-strength fibres for use in tyre cords and conveyor belts, and a soft absorbent fibre, used for surgical dressings.

Cellulose acetate fibres are finer and more glossy than viscose. They are therefore rarely used as staple fibres but are ideal for continuous filament-spinning into fine soft dresswear fabrics. Acetate fibres are also used to make the filter tips of cigarettes. For this purpose, the continuous filaments are drawn together into long ropes known as tows.

The manufacture of moulded plastic is another traditionally important use of cellulose chemicals. Viscose cannot be used because it is not mouldable, but both cellulose nitrate and acetate are used for the purpose. Celluloid, produced from cellulose nitrate and camphor, was in fact the first of all plastics to be developed and throughout its history it has had many uses, ranging from knife handles and fountain pens to table tennis balls and bicycle mudguards. Celluloid, however, has not retained a large share of the plastics market because of its inflammability.

Cellulose acetate is the most important of the two cellulose plastics. Sheets can be sliced from blocks of the material or, alternatively, they can be obtained by heating granules of acetate that are then extruded through a die and pressed between rollers to the required thickness. Granules are also melted into moulds of various shapes. Cellulose acetate

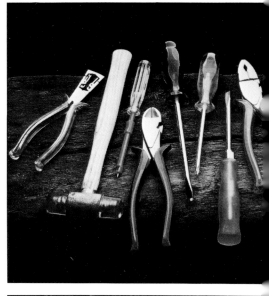

Left *Viscose fibres are produced from sodium cellulose xanthate. This chemical is dissolved in caustic soda to form a thick spinning solution known as viscose. Filaments are formed by extruding the viscose through the fine holes of a spinning jet, or spinneret. The head of the jet is submerged in a bath containing sulphuric acid and salts. These chemicals react with and coagulate the viscose issuing from the spinneret to form cellulose filaments. If staple, or "cut-fibre", viscose is to be produced the filaments are then drawn together to form a rope, or tow. This is then fed to a cutter, which produces fibres of the desired length. These are washed, dried and spun like cotton into a yarn.*

PLASTIC FILM FROM CELLULOSE

Below right *Sodium cellulose xanthate is used to produce transparent plastic film. A thick solution of the chemical (viscose) is first filtered.*

Below left *After filtration, the viscose is passed through a vacuum that de-aerates the solution and creates the correct consistency for film production.*

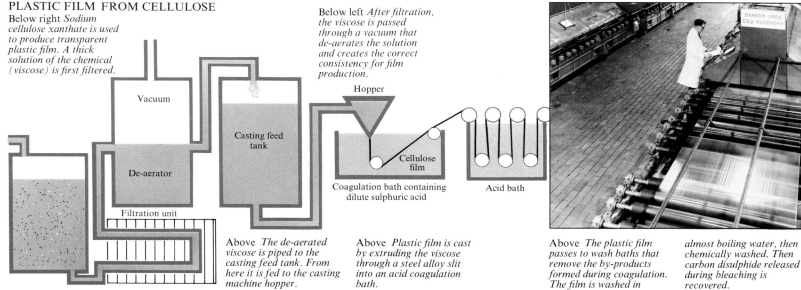

Vacuum

Casting feed tank

De-aerator

Hopper

Cellulose film

Coagulation bath containing dilute sulphuric acid

Acid bath

Filtration unit

Above *The de-aerated viscose is piped to the casting feed tank. From here it is fed to the casting machine hopper.*

Above *Plastic film is cast by extruding the viscose through a steel alloy slit into an acid coagulation bath.*

Above *The plastic film passes to wash baths that remove the by-products formed during coagulation. The film is washed in* almost boiling water, then chemically washed. Then carbon disulphide released during bleaching is recovered.

plastics are used in many familiar ways: for spectacle frames and screwdrivers, combs and toothbrushes, car steering wheels, lampshades and knitting needles, pens, toys and buttons. Industrially they are used for protective goggles, light filters and transparent screens. Easily worked and capable of holding colours well, cellulose plastics are also valued for their great resistance to shattering.

Production of plastic film is perhaps the best known use of cellulose plastic and in some countries, such as Great Britain, it is still the most commercially significant. For this purpose viscose is by far the most important of the cellulose chemicals. The film is formed by casting cellulose xanthate through a long narrow slit into a bath containing sulphuric acid and sodium sulphate. The film is then passed by rollers through a series of baths that wash, bleach, apply a softener, such as glycerine, and an anchoring agent if the film is to be coated. The film is then fed through a dryer.

Much of the film that is produced is coated with nitrocellulose or vinyl polymer to make it moisture-proof or heat sealable. Cellulose film is used in many forms of packaging and several different varieties are produced to meet the large range of requirements dictated by commodity and climate.

Cellulose acetates and nitrates are also used to make certain specialist kinds of film. Cellulose tri-acetate film is the basis of many photographic films including cine, although film for x-rays and professional use is now mainly polyester. Cellulose acetate film is used extensively in packaging and display, in sound and television recording tapes, and in a matt form for adhesive cellulose tape. The films are formed by casting a solution of acetate or nitrate on a large drum or a wide conveyor belt and the film forms as the solvent is allowed to evaporate.

The cellulose ethers are the most recently developed of the cellulose derivatives. Perhaps the best known is carboxy methyl cellulose, CMC. The ethers have a wide range of applications. They are used as the powder for making wallpaper paste and as thickeners in paint strippers. They act as thickeners, binders and stabilizers in shampoos and toothpaste, as soil suspenders in detergents and as thickeners and suspenders in soft drinks, pie fillings, creams, confectionery and other foods. Emulsion paints, pencil and crayon leads and many pharmaceuticals include a cellulose ether component. Ethers also have important industrial roles, as mud stabilizers in oil well drilling, in textile, paper and leather processing, in building products and in agriculture and horticulture.

Finally, cellulose in the form of cellulose nitrate is also an important raw material for the explosives industry. There are two major kinds of explosives—blasting agents for mining and quarrying, and propellants for projectiles and bullets. It is a minor component of blasting formulations but it forms as much as sixty per cent of the explosive material in bullets and projectiles.

Left *Cellulose acetate and cellulose nitrate are used for making a large range of products, from tool handles to lightweight but sturdy chairs. Such articles as pens and spectacle frames are extruded or moulded from granules. Cellulose plastics are easily worked, hold colours well and are more resistant to shattering than other plastic materials.*

Right *The Sopwith camel, like other early timber framed aircraft, was clad with lacquered, or "doped" linen. The outbreak of war in 1914 created an urgent need for non-flammable dope. Research produced cellulose acetate not only as dope, but as a future raw material for fibre and plastic industries.*

Below *After bleaching, the web of plastic is washed with water. The brittle inelastic material is then softened with chemical agents such as glycerine or glycols.*

Below *The film now contains more than three times its weight of water. Most of this is removed by passing the plastic through heated rollers within a hot air dryer that regulates the* moisture removal. *The film is next fed through a steam-filled humidity chamber to ensure a correct moisture level and is then wound into a mill roll.*

Below right *Most cellulose plastic film is coated with nitro-cellulose or polymers before use. These ensure that the film is heat-sealable and moisture-proof.*

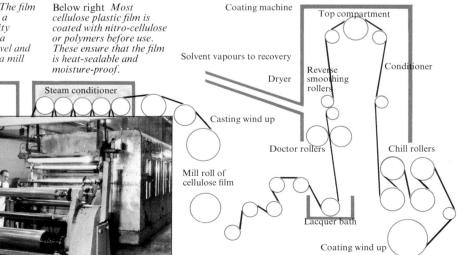

Right *Cellulose plastic film is wound on to mill rolls at the end of the casting machine. Before being wound, the film is automatically checked for correct weight, thickness and moisture level.*

Above *Film is fed through a lacquer bath. Rollers smooth the coating. The* film passes through a *dryer, then a conditioner restores lost moisture.*

Charcoal

Charcoal is charred or incompletely burned wood, produced in the absence of adequate oxygen so that a concentration of carbon is formed. The preparation and use of charcoal has been known for six thousand years and is probably the oldest of the wood-based chemical industries. During all this time it remained an essential raw material to the metallurgical industries of the world, until the eighteenth century when an alternative metal-refining agent, coke, took over its role.

Until this time, however, a steadily increasing demand for charcoal resulted in the large-scale devastation of the forests of Europe, especially those in which iron ore could be mined. South-eastern England, for example, which had been an almost impenetrable forest, was exploited with particular ruthlessness. There, the process was encouraged by the abundance of three of the most suitable European trees for producing iron-refining charcoal: alder, sweet chestnut and oak. The early American iron industries in the eastern states favoured charcoal produced from the several species of oak that are still plentiful in the region. In the west, the industry used Utah juniper, singleleaf pinyon, oak and willow.

The quality of charcoal depends on the kind of wood of which it is composed. Hardwoods make heavier and generally better charcoal than softwoods. Certain woods produce charcoal best suited for certain purposes. In India, for example, some trees are favoured for charcoal to be used in iron-smelting, others for lime-burning, others for making gun-powder, and yet other species for use by goldsmiths. In the Tropics quick-growing species of *Eucalyptus* provide much of the wood used for making industrial charcoal, but as it burns quickly it is often mixed with the harder, slow-burning charcoal from species of *Acacia*. For blast furnaces in Australia, however, one of the best charcoals is from the very hard wood of the slow-growing *Eucalyptus marginata*, and the best European charcoal is said to be

Above Variations of the traditional earth or stack kiln are still used to make charcoal in the Third World, but, in developed countries, the stack has given way to metal and masonry kilns, retorts and furnaces. The last English woodcollier continued to make charcoal in earth kilns until 1948. The traditional stack was about 15 ft in diameter with a "chimney", about 6 ft high and constructed of split logs, in its centre. Logs were tightly piled around the chimney and then covered in a layer of turf or soil. When the stack had been built, burning charcoal and dry tindering of twigs and straw were dropped down the chimney, which was then sealed. The fire in the stack would burn steadily for ten days, reducing the logs to charcoal.

PRODUCTION AND TRADE

Less than 300,000 tons of charcoal enter in to world trade each year. Approximately one-third of this is produced in South East Asia, but the USA is also one of the world's largest exporters. Most of world production, particularly in the Third World, does not enter in to world trade; it is manufactured on a small scale and consumed locally. It is difficult, therefore, to quantify world production, but more than half of all wood harvested each year is used for fuel and it has been suggested that more than three million tons is converted into charcoal first.

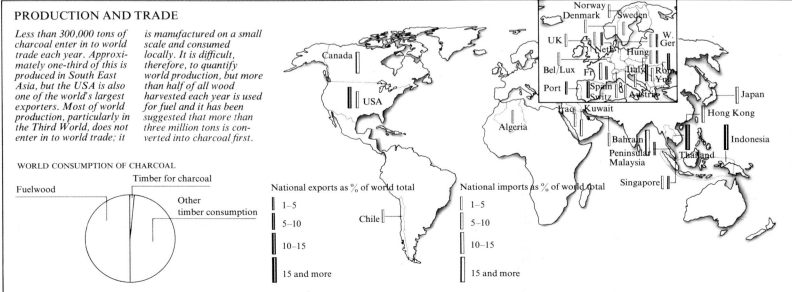

WORLD CONSUMPTION OF CHARCOAL

Fuelwood

Timber for charcoal

Other timber consumption

National exports as % of world total

1–5
5–10
10–15
15 and more

National imports as % of world total

1–5
5–10
10–15
15 and more

made from alder buckthorn, *Rhamnus frangula*.

In developing countries, particularly in the Tropics, charcoal is still produced in traditional hearths, or earth kilns, formed of stacked logs covered with a layer of soil. In western countries, however, this cheap but labour-intensive method has been replaced entirely by mechanized processes. Even in Third World countries the earth kiln is now being superseded by metal kilns, among the simplest of which are small portable models made from sheet steel. Large masonry kilns have also been developed and although they require greater capital expenditure and a permanent supply of timber, they produce a better and more standardized product, and also offer opportunities for mechanization.

The retort, a more complex method of manufacturing charcoal, generally operates near large sawmills, using mill waste sawdust, shavings and wood chips as feedstock. Retorts are, in essence, ovens in which the wood is reduced to charcoal by great heat. They are expensive to install but have the advantage that they can be designed to collect the by-products of wood carbonization, such as acetic acid, methyl alcohol and pitch. The cheapness of hydrocarbon by-products derived from coal and oil has, however, made the marketing of these charcoal by-products uneconomic; at least for the present.

Charcoal itself is far from being an obsolescent material. Nearly three hundred thousand tons enter into world trade each year. But much of charcoal production, particularly in the Third World, does not enter into world trade; it is produced on a small scale and consumed locally.

Although consumption of charcoal in developed countries is relatively small, its uses are extraordinarily varied. In recent years it has become best known as a fuel for barbecues and grills, but it can also be used in stoves. In combination with limestone it plays an important role in the manufacture of quicklime and cement. And despite the introduction of coke in the eighteenth century, charcoal is still used by the metallurgical industries for local and specialist purposes such as the production of cobalt, magnesium, purified arsenic and antimony where, as a high-purity refining agent, charcoal is invaluable.

In the agricultural world it is used as a fuel for drying fish, hops and tobacco; horticulturally it is a beneficial top-dressing for lawns and flower beds. After undergoing a process known as activation it extends its property of combining with other substances to a much wider range of items, and can be used for purifying water, air and sewage, and will absorb surplus insecticides and herbicides. Activated charcoal is also used by the food and wine industries as a de-colouriser and de-odouriser and in medicine as an antidote to drug poisoning. Walnut hulls are said to produce the best activated charcoal.

Charcoal is used as a pigment in printing inks, paints and rubber, and in the production of fireworks and gunpowder. A recently developed application for charcoal is the manufacture of charcoal-impregnated cloth for surgical and protective use.

The future undoubtedly holds many new uses for this extremely versatile substance but its most important role could well be as an alternative fuel. It has great potential in those developing countries with forest resources and insufficient foreign exchange to buy other hydrocarbon fuels for their nascent industries. And, as coal and oil reserves become scarcer and more costly to extract, western economies, in their search for alternative fuels, may consider more seriously the possibilities of charcoal and its by-products. With careful management of the world's forests, wood and its derived fuel charcoal could provide a renewable source of energy for the future.

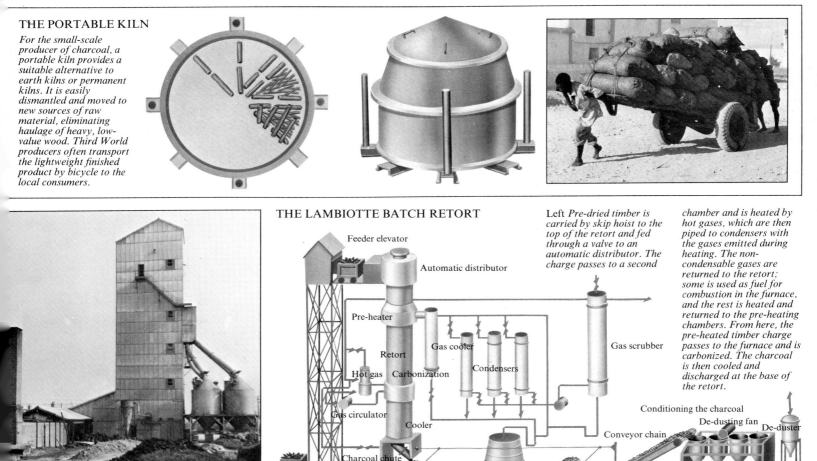

THE PORTABLE KILN

For the small-scale producer of charcoal, a portable kiln provides a suitable alternative to earth kilns or permanent kilns. It is easily dismantled and moved to new sources of raw material, eliminating haulage of heavy, low-value wood. Third World producers often transport the lightweight finished product by bicycle to the local consumers.

Above Retorts such as this operate in several parts of Europe and the USA. Wood gas by-products are recycled as fuel for the kiln and the wood-drying furnaces.

THE LAMBIOTTE BATCH RETORT

Feeder elevator

Automatic distributor

Pre-heater

Retort

Hot gas   Carbonization

Gas cooler

Condensers

Gas scrubber

Gas circulator

Cooler

Charcoal chute

Pyroligneous products collector

Conveyor chain

Conditioning the charcoal

De-dusting fan   De-duster

Left *Pre-dried timber is carried by skip hoist to the top of the retort and fed through a valve to an automatic distributor. The charge passes to a second chamber and is heated by hot gases, which are then piped to condensers with the gases emitted during heating. The non-condensable gases are returned to the retort; some is used as fuel for combustion in the furnace, and the rest is heated and returned to the pre-heating chambers. From here, the pre-heated timber charge passes to the furnace and is carbonized. The charcoal is then cooled and discharged at the base of the retort.*

Naval stores

Below *In 1652, the outbreak of the Anglo-Dutch sea war blocked England's supplies of naval stores from the Baltic region. This and the shipping monopoly held by Sweden caused England to turn to the USA.*

Below *More than 80 per cent of American naval stores production is obtained as a by-product of the sulphate papermaking process, but China obtains large quantities of gum turpentine by tapping pine trees. In parts of Africa,* *where suitable trees and a large supply of labour are available, attempts to establish gum turpentine industries have not been successful. The map illustrates world turpentine and rosin production in 1977.*

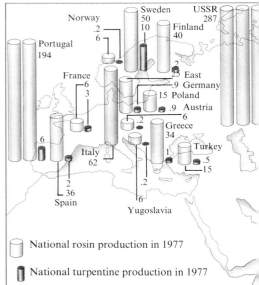

National rosin production in 1977

National turpentine production in 1977

PRESENT-DAY METHODS OF TAPPING GUM TURPENTINE

Crude gum turpentine occurs in a system of interconnecting resin ducts in the wood of certain pine trees. It is collected by chipping bark from the tree's trunk. This severs minor ducts close to the surface. Metal spouts or gutters guide the exuding gum into cups. Chipping faces today are never so deep as to damage the tree.

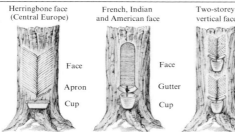

Herringbone face (Central Europe) — Face, Apron, Cup

French, Indian and American face — Face, Gutter, Cup

Two-storey vertical face

Two-storey echelon face

BY-PRODUCTS OF PAPERMAKING

Digester: pressure, heat and chemical solvent reduce wood chips to pulp and dissolve pine resin in the wood.

Black liquor is removed from the digester after pulp is formed and its tall oil (liquid rosin content) is separated from the solvent chemicals.

Header

Condens...

Digester

Cyclone sepa...
Cyclone sepa... turpentine, s... and non-condensable... relieved duri... venting of di... are separate... any black liq... pulp carried... by the pressu...

Black liquor

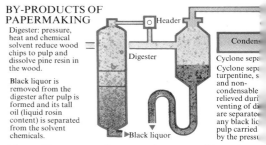

Above Turpentine and rosin can be extracted from the pulped pine wood used to make paper. The "sulphate" method of papermaking enables these naval stores to be recovered as by-products of the process.

The ancient Egyptians used the natural resin produced by certain pine trees to seal the mummy casings of their dead. But it was the Greeks of the first millennium BC who were among the first people to realize the product's potential in ship building. They used resin to caulk their war boats, the wooden ships that protected their city-state against the persistent threat of Persian invasion.

Pine resin proved to be of lasting significance to the ship-building industries of Europe. By medieval times seafaring nations depended upon supplies of the tar and crude resin, or pitch, extracted from pine logs, to caulk the hulls and decks and to seal the ropes and lines of their growing fleets. These products of pine wood became known as naval stores, a term still used today to describe the various derivatives of pine resin.

Until the end of the seventeenth century most of Europe's naval stores were obtained from the dense stands of pine trees that surrounded the Baltic Sea. But in the late 1600s sea warfare blocked merchant routes and drastically reduced England's supplies. This, and the shipping monopoly held by the Swedish producers, encouraged England to look to America for naval stores.

Naval stores production became the first export industry in the United States. As early as 1608, settlers in Virginia were producing and exporting to England small quantities of crude resin and tar. By 1700 the industry had spread to North Carolina and even today

North Carolinians are known as "tar heels" after the men who worked in the industry, shovelling tar and crude resin from the fires used to collect exudates from pine logs.

This method of extraction, now known as destructive distillation, was the earliest known technique of producing naval stores. Pine logs were burned in enclosed pits so that the heat of the fire would release the tar and crude resin from the wood. When the fire had burned out, the exudates were scraped from the pit.

But resin and tar were the only fruits of this primitive process. The volatile fraction of the pine resin—turpentine—was lost during burning. In the late seventeenth century, however, a new method of collecting the exudate was developed in the United States, which eliminated the need for burning pine logs to produce naval stores. By directly tapping the live tree, it was found that the whole resin product could be collected and this could be distilled and the two separate fractions, turpentine spirit and crystalline rosin, recovered.

The early resin tapping method, known as "boxing", damaged and seriously weakened trees, however, because it involved hacking a deep hollow in the base of a tree trunk into which pine resin, exuding from wounds made in the bark above, flowed. Today more scientific tapping techniques have been developed, whereby only a thin layer of bark is chipped from the tree to produce a tapping "face". The resin is fed through a metal gutter attached to the trunk in to a cup suspended beneath. By

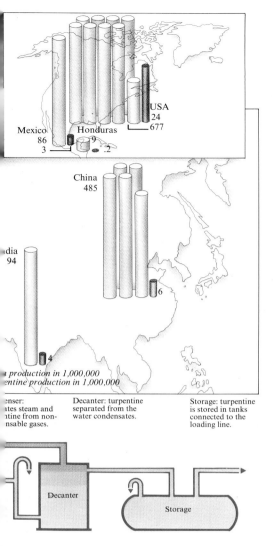

Mexico
86
3

Honduras
9
.2

USA
24
677

China
485

ndia
94

6

4

production in 1,000,000
ntine production in 1,000,000

nser:
tes steam and
ntine from non-
nsable gases.

Decanter: turpentine
separated from the
water condensates.

Storage: turpentine
is stored in tanks
connected to the
loading line.

Decanter

Storage

Below These southern yellow pines, like other turpentine-producing trees of warm temperate regions, can only be tapped during the late spring and summer when the gum is sufficiently liquid to flow from the chipping face.

Below Turpentine is an important material for the perfume industry because it contains chemicals known as pinenes. B-pinene is used for synthetically producing the scent-creating chemicals found naturally in certain essential oils, such as lemongrass. Turpentine from the Monterey pines of New Zealand (right) contains 65 per cent B-pinene. Dextro-pinene is found in turpentine from the Aleppo pines of Greece (far right).

Above Pine resin is added to retsina to produce the distinctive flavour of this famous Greek wine. This is a traditional use of resin in Greece, a country with a long history of pine resin production.

Above Dancers apply rosin to their shoe soles before performing. The ability of rosin to give "grip" to slippery surfaces is also made use of by baseball players who use it on their hands and by violinists for their bows.

carefully regulating the depth of the chipping face, a mature pine tree can continue to be productive for most of its natural life.

Tapped resin became the most important source of naval stores until the nineteenth century, when another method of producing turpentine and rosin was developed in the United States. Now known as wood distillation, it involved chipping the stumpwood of pine trees that had long since been felled and chemically distilling the chips to separate the two fractions. Wood distillation enabled producers to utilize previously useless pine wood and the technique was rapidly adopted.

In the 1940s yet another technique of producing naval stores was introduced in the United States. Paper manufacturers discovered that when using the sulphate, or kraft, method of pulping pine wood for paper production (see pages 182–183) the turpentine and rosin released from the wood could be collected as a by-product.

Destructive wood distillation is no longer practised because, since the demise of the wooden ship, there has been little demand for pitch and tar. More recently distillation of wood chips from pine stumps has also declined as supplies of old pine stumps have grown scarce. Tapped resin is still important in some countries. Yields have been doubled by careful breeding of trees, and by the use of stimulants sprayed on the tapping faces of trees to encourage resin flow. Nevertheless production is labour intensive and the method is proving increasingly uneconomic. Sulphate production is now the most important method of producing turpentine and rosin.

Although naval stores are no longer used by the ship builder, they are essential raw materials for many other industries throughout the world. Papermakers are the largest consumers of rosin, using it to "size" so that it can be printed on without smearing the inks. Considerable amounts of rosin are used as a drying agent in varnishes, paints and other surface coatings. It is also used in printing inks, in the production of rubber, soaps, detergents and adhesives and in the processing of various mineral ores.

At one time the major use of turpentine was as a paint solvent, but since the introduction of synthetic solvents its use by paint producers has been confined to certain specialized paints and varnishes. Today, turpentine is used mainly as a source of chemicals. These highly refined and valuable chemicals, known as pinenes, are important to a variety of industries, including perfume producers, manufacturers of disinfectants, food processers and producers of food flavourings.

Gums, resins and oils

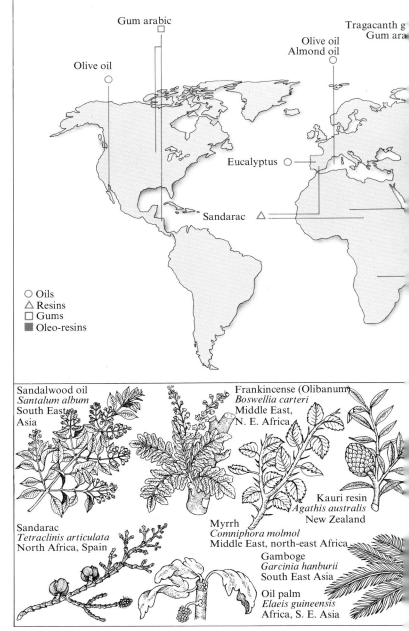

Sandalwood oil
Santalum album
South East
Asia

Frankincense (Olibanum)
Boswellia carteri
Middle East,
N. E. Africa

Kauri resin
Agathis australis
New Zealand

Sandarac
Tetraclinis articulata
North Africa, Spain

Myrrh
Comniphora molmol
Middle East, north-east Africa

Gamboge
Garcinia hanburii
South East Asia

Oil palm
Elaeis guineensis
Africa, S. E. Asia

Gum arabic
Olive oil
Tragacanth g
Gum ara
Olive oil
Almond oil
Eucalyptus
Sandarac

○ Oils
△ Resins
□ Gums
■ Oleo-resins

Above Tapping chicle, the basic ingredient *of chewing gum, from the chicozapote tree, which grows in the tropical rain* *forests of Guatemala. The sap is boiled and forms a solid residue, which is then transported by aircraft.*

Gums, resins and oils have always been important in preparing food, fragrance and soap, but in more recent years their unique properties—gums are able to absorb water to form gelatinous pastes, and resins and oils are insoluble in water—have made them essential substances in many modern industries.

Most gums and resins are saps that gradually ooze from the bark of the trunks and lower branches of certain tree species. The trees are usually stimulated to produce more of these exudates by deliberate wounding, either through the act of tapping with a sharp implement that pierces or removes the bark, by beating, or by scorching the tree.

There has been some controversy as to why and how trees actually produce these precious saps. The best tapping trees grow wild, and if they are cultivated they do not give good yields of sap. It seems that some gums, gum arabic, for example, are purely pathological products, formed by trees only when their tissues are in an unhealthy state, due to drought or poor soil, and have become infected by fungi or micro-organisms. Most resins, however, form naturally in special

ducts that are designed for healing damaged tree tissues and preventing desiccation and this function gives them their characteristic decay-resistant and antiseptic properties.

Sometimes volatile oil is a constituent of gums and resins and those containing large amounts of it are termed oleo-gums or oleo-resins. Pure oils are different, however, and they are not tapped from an incised trunk or stem but are expressed from the leaves or seeds of trees, often palms. The oil palm, *Elaeis guineensis*, which is native to the wetter parts of tropical Africa, has become the most important oil-producing plant. Increasing demands for it in the plastics, lubricants and food industries has led to successful cultivation of oil palms in huge plantations in Africa and Malaya, now the major exporter.

Two thousand years ago, frankincense and myrrh, oleo-gum resins that are tapped from trees found only in north-east Africa and Arabia, were luxury commodities, highly esteemed and ranking with gold in price. The ancient Egyptian queen Hatsheput used myrrh to make her legs smell sweet and had thirty-one myrrh trees from Somaliland plan-

ted in her garden. They did not survive but retained a reputation as the world's first forest plantation. Myrrh trees are still popular today for fragrances and incense.

Gums, having a similar composition to carbohydrates, a sweet smell and a pleasant taste and texture are ideal as additives in food and cosmetics. Thus, world demand for the highest grades of gum for a variety of purposes in the food industry—thickening lozenges and pastilles, stabilizing ice-cream, producing frothy beer—is steadily increasing.

Gum arabic is exported in large quantities to Europe and North America from Africa where the spiny acacia trees, whose sap has so many commercial uses, are found growing erratically in the wild. It was first used by the ancient Egyptians for preparing ink colours and it is still an important ingredient in the manufacture of smudge-proof water colours. Gum arabic was vital for the invention of the lithographic printing technique in 1768 and it remains indispensable in this field today.

Since its osmotic pressure and colloida content are equal to those of blood, it ha been used in medicine for maintaining bloo

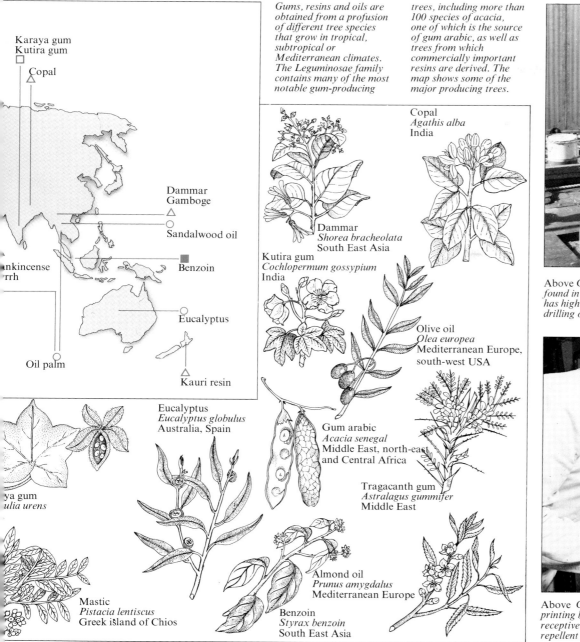

Gums, resins and oils are obtained from a profusion of different tree species that grow in tropical, subtropical or Mediterranean climates. The Leguminosae family contains many of the most notable gum-producing trees, including more than 100 species of acacia, one of which is the source of gum arabic, as well as trees from which commercially important resins are derived. The map shows some of the major producing trees.

Karaya gum
Kutira gum
Copal

Dammar
Gamboge
Sandalwood oil
Benzoin
Frankincense
Myrrh
Eucalyptus
Oil palm
Kauri resin

Copal
Agathis alba
India

Dammar
Shorea bracheolata
South East Asia

Kutira gum
Cochlopermum gossypium
India

Olive oil
Olea europea
Mediterranean Europe,
south-west USA

Gum arabic
Acacia senegal
Middle East, north-east
and Central Africa

Tragacanth gum
Astralagus gummifer
Middle East

Eucalyptus
Eucalyptus globulus
Australia, Spain

Almond oil
Prunus amygdalus
Mediterranean Europe

Benzoin
Styrax benzoin
South East Asia

Karaya gum
Sterculia urens

Mastic
Pistacia lentiscus
Greek island of Chios

Above *Gum ghatti from Anogeissus latifolia, a tree found in the dry deciduous forests of India and Ceylon, has high powers of absorption and is used in oil-well drilling operations to prevent fluid loss.*

Above *Gum arabic acts as a desensitizing agent in printing by making the image to be printed grease receptive, and thus distinguishing it from the grease-repellent non-printing area.*

pressure, and also as a surgical adhesive to graft severed peripheral nerves together. Gum arabic was the traditional adhesive for stamps, but due to increasingly high demand, it has become uneconomical for this purpose and has to some extent been replaced by modern synthetic adhesives.

As new technologies develop, gums from different parts of the world are continually being introduced, primarily as inexpensive substitutes for the traditionally valued types. Many, particularly from India and Ceylon, have become popular in their own right for specific uses.

Fossil resins, such as copal and amber, and fossil gums are often found in the continental interiors of Africa and Australia, or washed up on beaches by the sea. They are relics of exudates from flourishing forests of past epochs that were buried by soil or sea (see pages 20–21). They are extremely hard due to eons of desiccation and thermal treatment is usually necessary to make them oil- or water-soluble again. Since fossilized resins and gums are never found in great quantities they have become uneconomic to collect commercially.

Vegetable laxative tablets
Sugarless fruit drops for diabetics
Cough pastilles
Indigestion tablets
Cough linctus
Sugarless pastilles for diabetics

Above *Gums, resins and oils are used extensively in the pharmaceutical industry. Resins have antiseptic properties and are used to make cough mixtures and mouth washes. Some gums act as laxatives, but they are more frequently used as suspending agents for insoluble powders, as binding agents for pills and tablets, or for thickening pastilles. Olive oil has pharmaceutical applications in making medical plasters.*

Rubber: the plantation

Christopher Columbus, during his fifteenth-century voyage to America, was probably the first European to see the curious elastic material obtained from the milky exudate, or latex, of certain tropical trees. Subsequently named rubber by the eighteenth-century scientist Joseph Priestley, because of its ability to rub out pencil marks, there is evidence that this material had been used by the natives of Belize in Central America for their ball games as early as the eleventh century.

Rubber latex has been found in some 1,800 species of plants, ranging in size from that of fungi and small shrubs to forest trees. Until the end of the nineteenth century it was obtained from a range of tropical trees including various species of *Hevea*; the ceara rubber tree, *Manihot glaziovii*; *Funtumia elastica*; several species of *Castilla* called the hula tree; and the India rubber tree *Ficus elastica*, as well as from some tropical vines. For various reasons none of these, except *Hevea brasiliensis*, is now used, and all the natural rubber of commerce comes from plantations of this single species.

Plantation cultivation was developed in the late nineteenth century when the British Government began to investigate the possibilities of growing rubber as a crop in their equatorial colonies. As a result Henry Wickham, who had previously tried unsuccessfully to establish rubber plantations in the Amazon basin, was asked to collect seeds of *Hevea brasiliensis* for germination in England. Wickham was paid £700 for the 70,000 seeds, which he duly delivered to Kew Gardens in London, where they were planted, in June 1876.

Popular accounts of Wickham's achievement suggest that he smuggled the precious seeds out of Brazil illegally, but this romantic belief has never been substantiated. Owing to the inevitable delay in planting the seeds, less than four per cent of them germinated. The resulting two thousand seedlings, carefully protected by miniature greenhouses, were then shipped to various destinations in South East Asia. From such small beginnings the whole of the *Hevea brasiliensis* population of South East Asia has been grown; an estimated three billion trees. In 1978 these trees produced nearly three and a half million tons of rubber and accounted for ninety-four per cent of the world's supply of natural rubber. In South America, the native home of *Hevea*, production has remained low, mainly due to the incidence of a fungal leaf blight that attacks the rubber trees.

Grown as a crop, *Hevea* trees are cultivated either on large estates or on smallholdings of one hundred acres or less. A typical smallholding is approximately ten acres in extent and cultivated by a self-employed farmer with the help of his family. Smallholdings make an important contribution to the world's supply of natural rubber, accounting for seventy-one per cent of production in Indonesia and fifty-eight per cent in peninsular Malaysia, although in Vietnam and parts of Africa, much more of the output comes from large

Below *Rubber trees on a plantation are tapped every 2–3 days. The tapper shaves a thin diagonal groove in the bark of the tree trunk to release the latex from the inner layers of the bark. He then connects a metal spout to the lower end of the groove. A cup is suspended beneath the spout to collect the exuding latex. After 3–4 hours the latex stops flowing and about one-third of a pint of the milky white liquid will have collected in the cup.*

Right *Rubber has been obtained from various plants, including the South American Castilla and Manihot trees. Castilla, once more important than Hevea, proved uneconomic as a plantation tree because of the difficulties involved in tapping its latex content. Hevea is the only source of natural rubber used today, but a Mexican desert shrub, guayale, and a species of dandelion grown in the USSR both show potential.*

Right *Early tapping methods involved cutting into the tree with knives or axes. These tools did not provide clean channels for the latex flow and often damaged the tree as the depth of the incision was difficult to control.*

Metal plates slotted into the coagulation tanks divide the latex and cau it to form thick sheets a solidifies (4). After coagulation has taken place the metal plates ar removed and the sheets coagulum passed throug power-operated mills to remove water. In many modern processes crumb rubber is then produced adding a small amount castor oil to the sheets o coagulum and passing them through a series of rollers (5). The crumble rubber is thoroughly washed, placed in large trays and dried in hot-a ovens for 2–3 hours, aft which it is compressed i bales that are wrapped polythene (6) and crate for export.

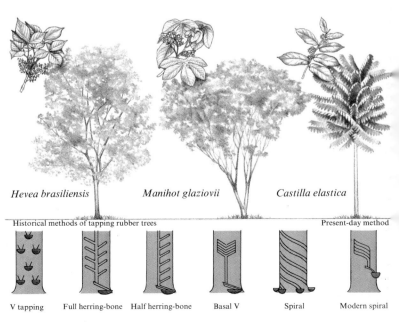

Hevea brasiliensis   *Manihot glaziovii*   *Castilla elastica*

Historical methods of tapping rubber trees   Present-day method

V tapping   Full herring-bone   Half herring-bone   Basal V   Spiral   Modern spiral

World production of natural rubber amounted to more than three and a half million tons in 1978 and South East Asia accounted for more than 90 per cent of this total. Careful selection and breeding of trees to increase yields have helped rubber producers keep pace with the growth in world demand (bottom).

China 34
Burma 20
Thailand 460
Cambodia 18
Vietnam 39
Brunei 75
Philippines 62
Indonesia 888
Peninsular Malaysia 1,529

Nigeria 57
Liberia 77

■ Centres of production

Limits of production   Brazil 24

○ Producing countries in 1978 (1,000 tons)

Ivory Coast 18
Ghana 5
Cameroon 17
Zaïre 25
Sri Lanka 154
India 131

Other producing countries 25

1967
1971
1976

0 2 4 6 8 10 12 14 16 18 20 22 24 26 28 30 32 34 36
100,000 tons

Above *Unlike the large rubber estates, smallholdings rarely have their own processing plants. Smallholders bring their latex to group processing centres for* coagulation. *The sheets of coagulum are then hung up to dry in the open and the finished product is then exported as "air-dried sheet" rubber.*

estates. Between 160 and 280 trees are planted to each acre of plantation and intercropping is practised to improve the fertility of the soil and provide an income for the farmer while the rubber trees mature. The young trees produced in nurseries, either from selected seed, or from high-yielding clonal material budded on to seedlings, are ready for latex tapping after about six years.

The pre-eminence of *Hevea brasiliensis* as the rubber-producing tree is partly because the latex is formed in an interconnecting system of tubular vessels, the most important of which occur in the inner bark of the trunk. When the trees are "tapped", by cutting an oblique groove round part of the trunk, the vessels are cut and latex flows out to be collected in a cup attached to the trunk. The flow ceases in a few hours, but the *Hevea* tree, unlike other rubber-producing trees, will replenish the supply of latex in the bark within a day. By removing a thin sliver of bark from the bottom of the groove, the process can be repeated many times during the twenty to

twenty-five years of the useful life of the tree.

Tapping is a highly skilled process because the best yielding vessels are nearest to the growth cambium, which if damaged will impair the regeneration of the bark and shorten the productive life of the tree. Marks are painted on the bark at monthly intervals to indicate the rate of bark removal. When the tapping panel nears ground level on one side of the tree a fresh panel is opened on the other side, and by the time this is exhausted the first panel will have completely regenerated so that it may be used over again. A more modern technique uses several small puncture holes in place of a continuous cut. With this method it is necessary to treat the bark chemically to stimulate a sufficient flow of latex, but it has the advantage of reducing bark consumption.

Rubber yields have been greatly improved over the years by the careful selection and breeding of trees. In the 1920s an acre of plantation produced less than 3,000 pounds, whereas the best clones today will yield more than 10,000 pounds of rubber in a year.

Chemical stimulants painted on to the trunks increase the yield by a further fifty per cent.

Most of the product from the trees is converted into dry rubber, but about seven and a half per cent is shipped as concentrated latex for use in the manufacture of dipped goods such as rubber gloves, adhesives and foam rubber. The old process of converting the latex to rubber by drying it into a ball over a smoky fire is no longer used commercially: latex today is coagulated by the addition of formic acid. The resulting sheets of rubber are treated in one of two ways—in the traditional method the washed sheets are dried in a smoke-house. This also helps to preserve the raw rubber. The sheets are then formed into bales weighing 250 pounds. In a more modern process the wet sheets are washed and broken down into particles; the loose crumbs are then rewashed, dried and compressed into smaller bales of thirty-three and one-third kilogrammes before being wrapped in polythene. The bales of raw rubber are tested and graded before shipment to the makers of rubber products.

Rubber products

Useful rubber products were first made in Europe and North America in the early nineteenth century, by which time modest quantities of rubber derived from wild trees in the Amazonian forests were being exported from South America.

But rubber proved to be an awkward material to process and shape satisfactorily: some means of softening the material was necessary so that it could be mixed with other substances. The invention of the masticator, by the Englishman Thomas Hancock in 1820, resolved this difficulty because it enabled rubber to be dissolved in solvents and consequently used to make such products as the waterproof raincoat.

These products, however, still had the inconvenient attribute of becoming stiff when cold, and soft and sticky when hot. This happened because the very long, unconnected molecules within rubber's chemical structure were responding to temperature changes by altering their relative positions slightly. The cure for this—vulcanization—was discovered by the American, Charles Goodyear in 1839. Vulcanization involves heating rubber with sulphur to produce stabilizing chemical linkages between the rubber molecules.

As soon as mastication and vulcanization had become established as methods of processing the raw material the modern rubber industry could really get under way and, from the 1850s onwards, a wide range of products came on to the market. With one major exception, they included most of those still made today: hose, conveyor and transmission belts, footwear, flooring and cable insulation. The exception was the pneumatic tyre. The tyre, in fact, had been invented by a Scotsman R. W. Thomson in 1845, but as he was concerned with wheels for horse-drawn vehicles, his patent fell into oblivion. The pneumatic tyre was re-invented by John Boyd Dunlop in 1888 for bicycles. By the turn of the century the motor industry became established, and the tyre became the major product of the rubber industry, a position it still holds.

The basics of rubber processing today resemble those of a century ago. The raw rubber arrives at the factory in bales. When it has been cut into manageable pieces it is fed into a mixer, an evolution of Hancock's masticator, and then on to a two-roll mill, to enable the rubber to be mixed with sulphur and other ingredients. These always include chemicals to assist vulcanization, and also will usually include chemicals to protect the rubber against environmental damage such as heat, light and ozone in the air. Fillers such as carbon black are frequently incorporated to produce the required strength and stiffness. The commonest filler is carbon black, which darkens the rubber to the familiar black coloration of tyres; raw rubber is pale or dark brown.

For the simplest kind of product—a shoe sole for example—the mix is simultaneously vulcanized and shaped into the product by heating it under pressure in a mould to about 150°C (300°F). Tube-shaped products (hose,

Production of a tyre begins by masticating the raw rubber and compounding it with various chemicals in a Banbury mixer. The compound is then distributed to the component-producing areas of the factory. Tyre components are manufactured in various ways: laminates are produced by calendering; bulky components such as tread are "hot-feed" extruded through a die, and for this

Raw rubber is fed into a Banbury mixer

tubing, rubber pipes) are made by extruding the mix through a die with subsequent vulcanization in steam. For a tyre, which is a complex product to manufacture, the various components, tread, sidewall, carcass and other smaller items, are separately shaped from the mix and are brought together in a "building" operation. After this the united components are vulcanized by heating in a mould in which such features as the tread pattern are developed.

Most rubber products are made from solid rubber, which has been produced by coagulating liquid latex from the *Hevea* tree, or has been manufactured synthetically from coal and oil by-products. A smaller group of products is made directly from liquid latex itself; by dipping a "former" into the latex to produce "dipped goods" such as gloves, by beating in air to form latex foam, or by extruding the latex as a filament known as latex thread. In all cases the shaping process is then followed by coagulation and vulcanization: the vulcanizing ingredients are incorporated with the latex as suspensions in water.

Until the Second World War all rubber products were made from natural rubber obtained from *Hevea brasiliensis* plantations. But the Japanese take-over of the rubber plantations in Malaysia, Indonesia and Thailand in 1941 engendered a rapid development in the United States of oil-derived synthetic rubbers. Subsequently, the post-war motoring boom stimulated a fast growth in demand for rubber, and output from trees could no longer keep up with demand. This resulted in a world-wide expansion of synthetic rubber production, which was further encouraged by the availability of cheap and plentiful oil. Today natural rubber accounts for only one-third of the world's rubber supply.

There are many kinds of rubber, and each kind has its own attributes, including price. If the need is for a very strong rubber, able to withstand extreme stresses (as in an aircraft

process the rubber must first be warmed and made pliable by milling it. "Cold-feed" extrusion is used for small components such as tyre-walls. The various constituent parts of the tyre are then assembled. First, a cylindrical tyre-casing is formed. This is then attached to a "shaping diaphragm" which is inflated to expand and stretch the casing into a tyre shape. Bracing strips and a laminate of

Milling the rubber before "hot-feed" extrusion

The inflated diaphragm shapes a tyre casing

tyre) then the choice is natural rubber; if the need is for a material able to resist hot oil, such as a seal in a jet engine, then one of the special and expensive heat- and oil-resistant synthetics would be used. Treads of tyres are normally made from the standard general-purpose synthetic rubber, styrene/butadiene rubber, because it imparts excellent wear and grip on wet roads. Interestingly, the modern radial-ply tyre requires a higher proportion of natural rubber than does the older cross-ply tyre because of the extra stress that it places on the thinner sidewalls.

At present synthetic rubber is cheaper than natural, but as oil prices rise, this situation will probably change. There are also obvious merits in favour of the natural material, which comes from renewable resources—sunlight, water and carbon dioxide—over one that comes from a depleting resource. These merits are strengthened by the fact that several developing countries are heavily committed to the production of natural rubber because it sustains their economies. Since most natural rubber comes from smallholdings, a faster development of its production is seen as a way to assist rural development in tropical countries

BREAKDOWN OF THE END-USES OF RUBBER IN INDUSTRIALIZED COUNTRIES

Left Three-fifths of all synthetic and natural rubber consumed in industrialized countries is used for tyre production. The next most important end use of these materials is the manufacture of footwear.

100%

the tread and its lining are added to the tyre, which is then removed from the diaphragm and spray-coated with black silicon-based paint, which will prevent it sticking to its curing mould. The tyre is given its final shape and tread pattern when it is steam-cured in a mould for 20 minutes. Rigorous quality control tests, including x-rays, finally check the finished product for faults.

Calendering applies the undertread to the tread

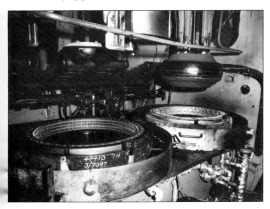

A tyre enters the curing mould

WORLD RUBBER CONSUMPTION IN 1978 (1,000 TONS)

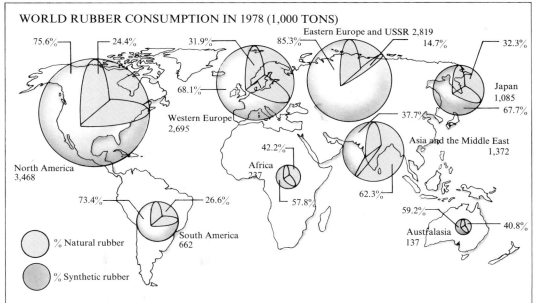

75.6% — 24.4%
31.9%
Eastern Europe and USSR 2,819
85.3% — 14.7%
32.3%
68.1%
Japan 1,085 — 67.7%
Western Europe 2,695
37.7%
Asia and the Middle East 1,372
Africa 237 — 42.2%
North America 3,468
73.4% — 26.6%
57.8%
62.3%
59.2% — 40.8%
South America 662
Australasia 137

○ % Natural rubber
● % Synthetic rubber

Total world consumption of rubber amounted to 12 million tons in 1978. The United States, the largest consumer nation, had a domestic demand of 3 million tons, more than the total consumption in western Europe that year. Synthetic rubber's share in the world market has been steadily increasing since the material was first commercially developed during the Second World War, and in 1978 it accounted for 70 per cent of world rubber consumption. Recycled synthetic and natural rubber accounts for about 4 per cent of the world's consumption every year.

X-raying the tyre for structural faults

STRUCTURE OF A CROSS-PLY TYRE

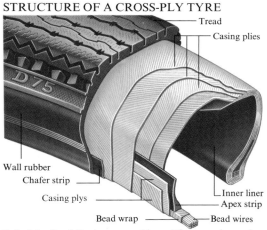

Tread
Casing plies
Wall rubber
Chafer strip
Casing plys
Inner liner
Apex strip
Bead wrap
Bead wires

Left John Boyd Dunlop developed the first successful pneumatic tyres in 1888. Fitted to a frame, they were given a public trial at a cycling race in 1889, and the bicycle easily won against the solid-tyred cycles. From then onwards Dunlop's invention gradually gained acceptance.

Above The many-layered structure of a tyre is produced in a complex building process that requires step-by-step addition of each component. Radial tyres, because of the different arrangement of casing plys, require an additional tread-bracing layer to give the casing enough rigidity.

LATEX PRODUCTS

About 8 per cent of all rubber products are manufactured directly from liquid latex. Foam rubber is produced by beating air into the latex, which is then poured into a mould (above), coagulated and vulcanized. There is also another method of producing foam; by adding a chemical to the latex, which creates pockets of gas throughout the liquid. Liquid latex is also used to produce "dipped" goods such as rubber gloves, and is extruded to form latex thread.

Tannins and dyes

Thousands of species of plants and trees produce dyes, and several hundreds are potential sources of tannin. Their use and extraction have been an integral part of human culture for centuries, for without dyes textiles could not be coloured and without tannins leather would not exist. Tanning is probably the older of the two crafts: archaeological evidence suggests that as long ago as 10,000 BC leather was being produced by soaking animal skins in extracts of tannin.

Tannins are chemical substances, compounds of carbon, hydrogen and oxygen, that are found in the wood, bark, leaves, roots or seeds of various plants. They are extracted by soaking or boiling the plant material: wood or bark is usually chipped or shredded first to allow maximum release of the tannin. The tan liquor is then evaporated to produce the desired concentration. First, a very weak solution of tan liquor is used to soak the hides and prevent the outer layers hardening to impervious leather before the centre layers have been penetrated. A more concentrated liquor then cures the leather thoroughly.

It was not until the middle of the nineteenth century that tannins became a significant item of international trade and until this time leather industries depended on local sources. One of the first trees to be utilized for commerce was the valonea oak, *Quercus aegilops*, whose acorn cups are a rich source of tannin. Found in the Middle East, this oak still features in world trade.

In England the bark of the sweet chestnut, *Castanea sativa*, had long been a familiar, though inferior, alternative to the traditional oak bark. But in about 1820 it was discovered that the finely chipped wood of the tree was considerably more productive of tannin than the bark and, after this, trade in chestnut wood steadily increased, both in Europe and North America. In the United States the allied American chestnut, *Castanea dentata*, was the species that was used until an introduced disease, chestnut blight, virtually exterminated it.

Above *The Xingu of Brazil paint themselves with red "urucum" dye from Bixa orellana.*

Below *By the 19th century large-scale felling of brazilwood for dyes had decimated supplies.*

Above *In Morocco, as in other developing countries, the tanning and dyeing industries have remained unchanged for centuries. Vegetable dyes are still used for colouring*

NATURAL PRODUCERS OF TANNINS AND DYES

Right *The thousands of dye-producing plants range from small arctic lichens to forest trees of the Tropics. Many traditional European vegetable dyes were obtained from herbaceous plants such as indigo, madder and woad, but the most significant dye trade was in tropical woods. Tannin is present, in small quantities, in many plants, but is more common in flowering species, particularly trees, than in the lower plant forms. It also occurs freely in many coniferous trees and in various species of palms. Tannin-rich plants are distributed throughout the world, but commercially important species tend to be found in warmer climates.*

The quebracho tree from South America was a commercially important tannin producer during the 19th and early 20th centuries. Tannin was extracted from two species, Schinopsis balansae and S. lorentzii.

Mangrove trees are found throughout swampy regions of the Tropics and subtropics. Tannin from mangrove bark is not only used by leather industries but also by American oil-producers as a lubricant in well-drilling muds.

Annatto is a South American woody shrub. The seeds and fruit produce an orange-red dye, which is used for fabrics in Brazil, India and the West Indies and is still used to colour butter and cheese in Europe and the USA.

The logwood tree is native to South and Central America and was also introduced to the West Indies. Until recently blue and black logwood dyes were widely used for fabrics, leathers and printing inks.

The osage orange is a shrubby North American tree, the wood of which produces a yellow fabric dye still in use in the USA. Because of the wood's high tannin content, it is also used to produce dyed leather.

For much of the present century, the world tannin supplies have been dominated by certain species of the quebracho tree, found in subtropical Argentina and Paraguay. The trade assumed such dimensions that the stands of quebracho became seriously depleted, and because this tree grows very slowly plantations of fast-growing black wattle trees, established in South Africa, have replaced it.

Several species of mangrove are also efficient producers of tannin. Their bark has been used in the East for hundreds of years and in the nineteenth century it was exported to Europe under various names, the one most widely employed being "mangrove cutch". This tree still occupies a role in the international tannin market.

Predictably, synthetic substitutes for vegetable tannins, known as syntans, have been developed in recent years, and these, along with mineral tanstuffs, have eroded much of the demand for the natural material.

Dyeing, like tanning, is an ancient and ubiquitous craft which was practised by the oldest civilizations: the Persians, the Egyptians, the Phoenicians and the people of ancient China. Dyes were produced from locally available plants and trees. The traditional dye-woods of Europe, for example, were derived from indigenous trees such as alder, birch, oak, walnut and flowering ash. Then, during the Middle Ages, the European dyer's colour spectrum was broadened by the introduction of tree dyes from Asia.

The most significant dye-wood trade, however, began after the discovery of America and its native dye-producing trees such as brazil-wood, *Caesalpinia echinata*. Another species of this tree, *Caesalpinia sappan*, had been exported from India, Malaya and Sri Lanka since medieval times, but only in limited quantities. When Europeans landed in South America in 1500, they encountered vast tracts of the American brazilwoods and from these trees the region was named Brazil. Large quantities of the red and orange brazilwood dyes were exported to Europe and later to North America. By the nineteenth century, however, the supplies had been severely reduced and other red dye-woods replaced them.

Another form of brazilwood, *Haematoxylon brasiletto*, was exported from Central America from the 1850s onwards. Camwood from West Africa, barwood from Sierre Leone and sanderswood from tropical Asia, all trees of the genus *Pterocarpus*, also provided considerable quantities of red dye during the eighteenth and nineteenth centuries.

Blue and black dyes were obtained from logwood, which was exported from Central and South America from the seventeenth century onwards, and another native of South America, the fustic tree, *Chlorophora tinctoria*, was a provider of yellow dye, as was the North American black oak.

Since the middle of the nineteenth century, however, the trade in vegetable dyes has steadily declined and present-day dyeing industries in industrialized countries are based entirely on cheaply produced, standardized aniline dyes derived from coal-tar. The traditional dye-woods are now only used for specialist purposes. A small amount of *Haematoxylon brasiletto* dye is used as a stain in the preparation of microscope slides, and as a leather colorant in the United States. Barwood serves as a dye for a particular kind of leather in Britain, and camwood has limited use in the United States as a fabric dye, as pigment for artists' paint and as pencils used for marking dimension stone. Logwood was used in printing inks until the 1950s, and the last logwood dye factory in Yucatan, Mexico, which produced black silk dyes, remained in operation until the 1960s.

Natural dyes still play a significant role in developing countries where local craftsmen, who account for most of the textile production, are unable to obtain or afford synthetic fabric colorants. In these regions dye-plants and dye-woods retain their age-old importance as essential feedstocks to the textile industry.

the locally produced fabrics, and at the tanners' souk in Fez, leather is still produced in traditional stonework tanning pits, from local materials.

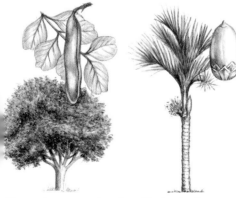

The carob tree, a native of the Middle East, is now distributed throughout the Mediterranean region. The bark and leaves were once an important local source of tannin and the wood of the tree was used as a source of brown dye.

The betel palm grows in tropical Asia. In India, silks are still dyed brown using "cutch" derived from betel nuts. Rich in tannin, cutch is also used to produce cream-coloured leather and to make fishing nets rot-proof.

THE VERSATILE OAK

The bark and the heartwood of English and durmast oak, are traditional sources of tannin in Europe. The tannin-rich acorn cups of the valonea oak have been exported from the Middle East since the 19th century. In the USA, the white, black, Californian tan bark and chestnut oaks, and in southern Europe the evergreen and kermes oaks were commonly used tan barks. The kermes oak is also the source of a scarlet dye, produced from a small insect that lives on the tree. Various oak barks and oak galls have been used to produce black, brown and yellow dyes.

English oak
Quercus robur

English oak bark produces tannin and dyes. The heartwood also yields tannin.

Kermes oak
Quercus coccifera

An insect that lives on the kermes oak yields red dye.

Valonea oak
Quercus aegilops

The large dried acorn cups of the valonea oak are a rich source of tannin.

Turkey oak
Quercus cerris

Gall nuts from the Turkey oak yield tannin and dye.

Cork

For more than two thousand years cork has been harvested from the forests of cork oak that surround the Mediterranean Sea. The cork oak was described by Pliny the Elder in the first century AD. He wrote: "Its only useful product is its bark which is very thick and which when cut grows again." And yet the Romans and the Greeks understood the unique qualities of this tree's "only useful product"—its lightness, impermeability, buoyancy and resistance to decay. They used it as floats for their fishing nets, for soleing their sandals, and for sealing their caskets of oil and wine. In medieval times cork kept buildings cool in summer and warm in winter.

By the late seventeenth century, the commercial development of glass bottles created an increase in demand for cork as stoppers. This encouraged the first attempts to cultivate the wild cork oak and to improve harvests by careful management of the natural forests. Forest management techniques were first introduced into Spain in about 1760 and by 1820 their practice had extended to France, Portugal, Italy and North Africa.

The growing of cork is a long-term investment: a cork oak must grow for about fifteen years before the thick, spongy bark is first stripped. This stripping is called virgin cork. After this the tree can be stripped every eight to ten years and will produce the better quality cork known as reproduction cork. The tree must be periodically pruned to improve growth, which is slowed down by stripping, and to allow the maximum production of cork that can be removed in large regular sheets.

Virgin cork is rough, uneven and of poor quality. Reproduction cork is thicker and does not have the deep ridges and furrows of virgin cork. Only by the third stripping, thirty to thirty-five years after planting, is first-quality cork obtained.

The tree is stripped in summer, when it is growing, and the cork is stacked and allowed to season for a few weeks. This curing allows

PRODUCING ARE

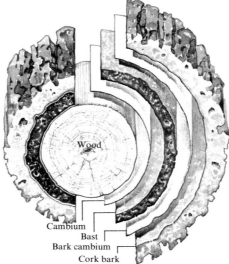

Wood

Cambium
Bast
Bark cambium
Cork bark

Above *Quercus suber is a small, broadleaved evergreen tree which grows to a height of 40–60 ft and lives for 150 years or more. It thrives in the Mediterranean climate where there is little rain, much light and a fairly high atmospheric humidity.*

Left *The formation of a corky outer bark is common on many trees. The cork oak is unique because its thick outer bark can be removed without harming the tree, providing no damage is done to the delicate underlying tissues, the layer of bast, which carries sap around the tree and the cambium cells, which produce new wood and regenerate the protective layer of cork bark.*

Above *Almost all commercially produced cork is derived from the cork forests that surround the Mediterranean Sea. Most of it comes from the species of oak known as Quercus suber, but the closely related Quercus occidentalis is sometimes grown in parts of northern Spain and Portugal as it is more resistant to the cold Atlantic winds and lower winter temperatures.*

Nearly one-third of the world's cork-producing forests are located in Portugal, where most of the large tracts are now state owned. Nevertheless, a significant percentage of Portugal's cork is still produced by small farmers who supplement their incomes by cropping the cork oaks on their land.

CORK AND THE BOTTLE

Impermeable, colourless, odourless, tasteless and able to form a completely hermetical seal, cork is an ideal material for stoppering bottles. From earliest times bottles of wine have been sealed with cork. This has proved so effective that excavated bottles have been found to contain 1,000-year-old wine that is palatable.

Present-day production of corks is a multi-million-dollar industry. At one time shaped entirely by hand, almost all cork stoppers today are mechanically cut into the many specialized shapes that are needed: square-cut vintage wine corks, champagne corks, tapering whisky bottle stoppers and the cylindrical wine corks, which are the most widely used. After being cut, a cork must be washed, bleached, inspected for flaws and finally sterilized before being used by the bottling industry.

Bottling is also a highly mechanized industry today. This corking machine is automatically inserting stoppers into bottles of Spanish "champagne".

PRODUCTION

Spain 28%

Portugal 51%

Italy 6%
Algeria 5%
Morocco 5%
France 3%
Tunisia 2%

Total world production of cork is estimated at 390,000 tons every year. Portugal produces more than half of the world's supply.

moisture to evaporate and helps flatten the pieces. The cork bark is then steamed or boiled to soften the cells and dissolve tannins and dirt. The woody outer cork—called hardback—can then be scraped away and the sheets pressed flat. These sheets are then charred to seal the surfaces, trimmed, graded, baled and marketed. The grading is crucial because the value varies according to it.

Much of the high-quality reproduction cork is consumed by the bottling industry. Natural cork is also used for floats, fishing-rod handles, life-jackets, buoys, baseballs, golf, cricket and hockey balls, dartboards and fireworks.

Cork compositions were first commercially produced in 1910 and had a lasting impact on the industry. Cork particles, ground from natural cork waste, when bonded with suitable adhesives were found to possess many of the qualities of natural cork. Present-day producers of manufactured and natural cork are mutually dependent: natural cork waste is the feedstock of the manufactured cork industry and a valuable source of revenue for producers of natural cork. Today almost all virgin cork, low-quality reproduction cork and remnants obtained from cutting and slicing corkwood are ground into small particles and used to make agglomerates.

There are several forms of manufactured cork. Pure expanded agglomerates are made by compressing the granules at high temperatures. Natural resins are forced out of the cork and these bond the granules together. Used to make cork tiles for interior decorating and insulated corkboard, pure agglomerated cork is probably the most important sector of the industry. It acts as a thermal, acoustic and vibration insulator. As a thermal insulator for refrigerator plants, it does not decay, or contract under constant freezing and thawing and is impermeable to water. It is also used as an acoustic insulator in schools, hospitals and theatres and as a vibration insulator under heavy machinery such as drop hammers.

Composite agglomerates are made by adding adhesives such as resins or plasticizers at lower temperatures, so that the general appearance and colour of the bark is maintained. These can then be coloured with a fine coating of plastic for decorative use.

Another composition cork product is cork-rubber—granulated cork bonded by natural or synthetic rubber. Stronger and more flexible than standard composition cork, it is also denser and more expensive.

Composition cork is used extensively for bottle cap liners; it is essential to the aircraft and car industries; and is used to make gaskets of all kinds. New markets for cork include the space and nuclear industries. From the 1960s, specially bonded composition cork has been used as a thermal and insulation shield for space vehicles. Cork was used on the first manned journey around the moon.

Transportation of radioactive isotopes carries the serious hazard of radioactive contamination in the event of fire. The use of cork-lined containers has greatly reduced this risk. The isotope is stored in a small container with an outer capsule lined with cork. Tests carried out at more than 800°C (1,500°F) charred the outside of the cork, but left the inside container undamaged.

In spite of efforts to introduce the cork oak into North America, the Soviet Union and elsewhere, the Mediterranean countries of Europe and Africa remain the source of world supplies of natural cork. California has the most suitable climate for the cork oak in North America, but the high labour requirements involved in cork farming discourages businessmen from taking advantage of it.

In recent years cork has lost some of its markets to substitute materials, but the loss has been balanced by increasing consumption in other fields. World demand for cork and its products continues to grow, however, and in fact it is in danger of outstripping the supplies available in the future.

Left *A special axe or curved saw is used to make longitudinal and horizontal cuts in the cork bark. The layer of cork is then carefully peeled away from the tree with the axe's wedge end.*

Above *Stripped bark is hauled to a central collecting station where it is stacked and left to season. After a few weeks the cured cork is ready to be boiled, cleaned and baled for shipment.*

Left *The scrap cork generated by the natural cork industry is basic feedstock to the composition industry. Collected waste is ground up and bonded into blocks of composition cork.*

Above *Now used throughout the world as thermal and acoustic insulation for buildings, cork has lined walls and floors in southern Europe since the time of the medieval monasteries.*

Bamboo

Although botanically a grass, bamboo forms large "forests" in many parts of the world. Several hundred species of bamboo are distributed throughout the tropical, subtropical and mild-temperate regions.

From time immemorial the people of Asia have cultivated and utilized selected species in almost every aspect of their daily lives. A unique combination of qualities—lightness, hollowness, flexibility and strength—makes bamboo a highly adaptable material. Its use can be observed in the village life of Malaysia today, serving as a reminder of the important role it has played in so many Asian civilizations—from the Tang dynasty of imperial China to the heroic age of the samurai in medieval Japan.

Present-day villagers use large stems, or culms, of bamboo for the main structures of their houses. Other varieties are split vertically along one side and flattened to make raised floors. Light bamboos are used as roofing material, or woven into varying criss-cross patterns to form the walls of a house. Short lengths of bamboo, once the cross-wall at the node, or joint, has been removed, are used as multipurpose receptacles in the home.

In Java certain species of bamboo are particularly valued for making flutes and other forms of wind and percussion instruments. Bows and arrows are also made from bamboo, as are small sharp knives made from a species with much silica in the surface cells. Single internodes of bamboo are used for making blow-pipes in Malaya.

The ubiquitous basket is also made of bamboo in South East Asia. Thin flexible strips are obtained by a series of diagonal cuts in the culm. These strips can then be woven to form the sides of a basket. Other kinds of bamboo with suitable properties are used for making mats, fishing rods and fish traps—the diverse catalogue of uses for this material is endless.

A bamboo culm, or stem, grows quickly to its full height. It then produces leafy branches and gradually strengthens its woody tissues over the three to five years it takes to reach full maturity. For structural purposes fully mature culms are needed; for papermaking they are felled at an earlier stage. Mature culms are air dried before use, but in Java bamboo destined for building work is sometimes soaked in water before drying to make it less vulnerable to insect attack. Throughout South East Asia bamboo is grown locally and most villages have definite preferences for certain species. If a species grows at some distance from the village, the bamboo is often formed into a raft and transported by river: the hollow internodes of the culms ensure their buoyancy.

Each new bamboo culm starts as a bud rising out of the base of an old culm. The bud grows gradually to a large size before it begins to elongate and form a new culm. When fully grown, but just before it elongates, the bud is packed with firm edible tissue. At this stage it can be cut off to provide human food in the form of bamboo shoots. Certain species have especially good-quality shoots while others are unpalatably bitter. Young bamboo leaves provide animal fodder. The seeds of certain species can also be used as a famine crop in areas with regular and prolonged dry seasons. Bamboos that are native to these climatic regions will sometimes flower in a year of drought (see pages 98–99). The plants flower on all culms, produce a large crop of seeds and die. Since rice cannot be grown in this season the seeds are a valuable source of food. These factors are important considerations in local selection of bamboos to be cultivated.

It is only in Japan, and to some extent in China and India, that bamboos have been selected for large-scale commercial plantation. In China *Arundinaria amabilis* was carefully cultivated for many years and widely exported for the special purpose of constructing fishing rods. Due to economic and political pressures, and the development of suitable substitute materials, this trade stopped after the Second World War. There are now signs, however, that the unique properties of this particular bamboo will find new markets in the future. There is little record of the systematic cultivation of other bamboos in China, but certainly many species are known and used locally. In Japan and Taiwan modern techniques, such as lamination, have enabled manufacturers to use bamboo for an increasing range of products and especially for many domestic articles.

On the Indian subcontinent a few species of bamboo occur in almost pure stands over wide areas. *Melocanna bambusoides* is used extensively in Bangladesh for paper pulp and for building purposes. In 1966 it was estimated that nearly 700 square miles were covered by this bamboo, yielding 350,000 tons of air-dried culms annually.

In drier parts of India *Dendrocalamus strictus* occurs over large areas. Mainly natural, but increasingly cultivated in recent years, it is valued for the production of paper pulp and for poles used in a variety of ways. The culms of this type of bamboo are slender but have very thick walls.

Much remains to be done to develop the full potential of bamboos, especially in Malaysia, Melanesia and Burma. The native bamboos of this region are not yet fully known or exploited; those most prized in Java, for example, have still not come into general use in other countries. Research is necessary to unravel the relationships between bamboo species and their classification as applied research and scientific selection and cultivation could well have immense implications. Already, Japanese scientists have successfully demonstrated the possibilities for bamboo and its by-products as a chemical catalyst, and as a culture medium for bacteria in the pharmaceutical industry. And the properties of natural bamboo—a cheap and plentiful resource in many poor countries—as a material strong in tension, and therefore useful as a reinforcement for concrete, is just one example of its great potential.

Joints, or nodes, occur at regular intervals along the length of a bamboo culm whose unique structure produces many of its most useful qualities: hollow internodes sealed at each node by a cross-wall create a flexible, lightweight, strong and eminently adaptable material.

METHODS OF PLANTING BAMBOO

Monopodial species: cuttings taken from rhizomes with or without sections of culm attached.

Sympodial species: cuttings taken from sections of culm with or without rhizome.

Bamboos are divided into two classes according to their growth habits. Monopodial species have widely spaced culms; every culm has a long rhizome which develops buds at each of its joints every year. Some of these buds grow into new culms. Sympodial species have short rhizomes, and new culms grow close to the parent bamboo in a clump formation. Because bamboos rarely flower and seed, cultivation is generally carried out by taking cuttings of either rhizomes or culms, depending on the species.

A native of South America, *Guadua angustifolia* has culms, or stems, that grow to 60 or even 100 ft in height. They are used for general building work.

Gigantochloa verticillata reaches a height of 50 ft or more. It is used, particularly in Java, for building purposes and as a source of edible shoots.

The largest bamboo in Japan, but most widely distributed in China, *Phyllostachys pubescens* grows to 60 ft and is valued for its edible shoots.

The Chinese bamboo *Arundinaria amabilis* grows to a height of 40 ft. Until the early 1940s China exported it to Germany, England and the USA.

Below *Designed to transport fighting cocks, these Balinese baskets are woven from thin, flexible strips of bamboo cut diagonally from a large culm.*

Below *Serving as containers for transportation and as communal drinking vessels, bamboo culms filled with beer are carried to market in Sulawesi, Indonesia.*

Above *Traditional housing for the Dayak of Sarawak, the village longhouse accommodates up to 400 people and is often constructed almost entirely of bamboo.*

Left *Bamboo is not just a traditional building material but an integral part of modern-day construction industries in Asia. Whole culms of bamboo are used as scaffolding for building. Intersections of the scaffolding are formed by binding the culms together with wetted rattan. The lashings contract as they dry, so forming tight and secure joints.*

NATIVE BAMBOOS

Bamboos are unevenly distributed throughout tropical, subtropical and warm-temperate regions of the world. Of the hundreds of species, by far the greatest diversity occurs in southern and south-eastern Asia, many of the most useful kinds occurring on the mainland. There are only a few native species in Africa and their distribution is limited mainly to the West African lowlands, Kenya and Uganda. Madagascar, in fact, has a greater variety of species than Africa. Bamboos are found in tropical and temperate regions of the American continents, but are far more abundant in South America than in the temperate North. In many parts of the world, especially in North and Central America, natural stands of bamboo have been destroyed by clearance of land for agriculture. These losses have been partly balanced by the introduction of bamboos, particularly useful Asian species, in parts of Euirope, Africa and the USA.

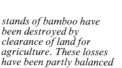

Above *Bamboo can be forced to grow square by placing a frame, based on an estimate of the culm's eventual diameter, around a young shoot. Square bamboo is highly valued in Japan for use as ornamental posts.*

Natural fibres

Attalea funifera

Raphia ruffia

Leopoldinia piassaba

Left *Among the most important of the fibre-producing palms today is Attalea funifera, a native of the dry forests of Bahia, and Leopoldinia piassaba, which is also indigenous to Brazil. Other commercial sources of palm fibre include the jaggery palm, Caroyta urens, from Sri Lanka, Borassus flabellifer from India, Vonitra fibrosa from Madagascar, and Raphia graolis and R. hookeri, which are harvested mainly in Sierra Leone. Raphia ruffia from Malagasy produces much of the raffia used for horticultural purposes. Palm fibres are extracted from the portion of the leaf stalk that remains on the tree after the leaves have fallen.*

Forest trees and forest plants provide fibrous materials that have been used for centuries by local inhabitants. Few of these trees and plants are as well-known as the fibre producers, such as cotton, flax, sisal and jute, that are native to grassland environments. But forest fibres play an important role in local economies for use as thatching, cordage, matting, hats, fishing nets and brushes and some of them also enter international trade.

The inner bark of certain forest trees was used to manufacture a form of fibrous cloth long before man had learned to extract fibres from plants and then re-combine them by weaving. The bark of the tree was removed in strips that were first soaked in water to make them pliant and then pounded with wooden mallets to separate the fibrous layer from the epidermis, or outer skin. The paper mulberry, *Broussonetia papyrifera*, cultivated in Japan, China and Polynesia, is particularly well-known as the traditional source of raw material for Polynesian "tapa" cloth. Tapa is still manufactured today, although mainly for ceremonial purposes. The fibrous barks of certain other trees however, such as the baobab, *Adansonia digitata*, of Africa and some species of *Bombax*, still provide a local source of fibres for cordage and similar products.

Unlike bark fibre, some of the fibres obtained from the leaf stems of palm trees have important industrial uses, particularly for brush- and broommaking. These fibres enter the world fibre market and, in fact, have played an important part in the development of international brush industries. Their introduction, however, was initially accidental.

Hog bristles were for centuries the most important brushmaking material, and the best-quality bristles were obtained from wild boar, or from pigs that were between five and ten years old. But by the middle of the nineteenth century new breeds of pig had been developed that produced more meat at an earlier age. Few pigs, therefore, survived long enough to develop high-quality bristles, and supplies became progressively scarce and expensive.

Until this time palm fibre was used as a cargo packing material and was discarded as waste after ships had been unloaded. It was then offered cheaply to some brushmakers in Great Britain who soon recognized its possibilities. It was cheaper than bristles and also filled an important gap in supplies, so fibres soon became an important brushmaking material. Even today, despite the impact on the market of synthetic substitutes, palm fibres remain an essential raw material for the brush and broom industries.

The fibres produced by palms are extracted from the portion of the petiole, or leaf base, that remains attached to the palm trunk after the leaf has fallen. This part of the leaf base gradually decays, leaving a mass of fibres that can be extracted by crushing, beating or scraping the surrounding tissue. In some countries, such as Sierra Leone, the natural decaying process is accelerated by "retting" the petioles—submerging them in water until the unwanted tissue decomposes and the fibres are released. The yield of fibre from a palm varies according to its species and its age. The palm *Attalea funifera* reaches its full productive capacity by the time it is eight years of age and will then yield about twenty pounds of fibre every year. Throughout the world, about ten thousand tons of brushmaking fibre are harvested from palms every year. Much of this is exported and provides important foreign exchange for the developing countries that produce palm fibre.

Perhaps the best-known of the fibre-yielding palms is the coconut tree, *Cocos nucifera*, but unlike most other palms, its useful fibre is found in the husk surrounding the large seed, the coconut. Exported in large quantities from tropical countries, particularly India and Sri Lanka, coir, or coconut fibre, is used to manufacture matting, cordage, mattresses and also brushes.

Rattans, the fibrous materials used to make woven furniture, are also derived from species of forest palm—the *Calamus* palms. Natives of

Left *The fibres extracted from palm petioles are important brush- and broommaking materials. The extracted fibres are first heckled, or combed, over steel pins to clean them and remove any weak strands. They are then* *automatically inserted into broom or brush stocks (above). The brush-making machine rapidly bores holes in the stock, doubles a tuft of fibre which it punches into the hole, and anchors it with a wire staple.*

the tropical rain forests, these leafy climbers have spiky stems that wind their way over other trees to a length of 150 feet or more. The two-inch-thick stems are cut just above the ground and pulled clear from the trees that support them. The leaves, spikes and branches are removed from the vines, which are then cut into lengths of about fifteen feet. These are then allowed to dry for about a month, after which they are bundled and sent to traders who bleach them with sulphur ready for export. If the rattans are to be used for furniture or mattings the outer layer may be removed and the stem cut into long strips by machine. Indonesia is the main source of supply of rattans and exports thousands of tons every year.

The kapok, *Ceiba pentandra*, is one of the few forest fibre-producers that is not a palm. It is one of the tallest trees in the tropical forest and is indigenous to a number of countries as a component of secondary, or non-climax, forest. Kapok fibre, or floss, is produced in the tree's spindle-shaped pods. These must be collected when they are ripe, just before they burst and scatter their contents. The hulls of the harvested pods are removed and the floss is spread out to dry in the heat of the sun before the seeds are extracted.

The cells of the kapok fibre are full of air but the cell walls are impervious both to water and air. Kapok is therefore buoyant and resilient and a suitable stuffing material for products such as life-jackets, cushions and mattresses. It is also used as an insulating material against heat and sound. Thailand, now the world's largest producer, exports some 17,000 tons of kapok every year for these purposes.

Some species of *Chorisia* and *Bombax* also produce floss in their seed pods. Small quantities of floss from the silk cotton tree, *Bombax malabaricum*, are exported from India, while floss from the South American *Chorisia speciosa* is exported from Brazil to various countries. Commercially, however, flosses from these other trees are generally not considered as good as true kapok.

Left *The kapok tree, Ceiba pentandra, a native of the tropical forests of Asia and Africa, is also grown in Indonesia and the Philippines. The large pods produced by the tree are lined with floss that is used to fill sleeping bags,* *insulated clothing and life-jackets. Similar flosses are produced by the Indian tree, Bombax malabarica, and the South American Chorisia speciosa, but commercially these flosses are considered inferior to true kapok.*

FIBRES FROM AN EPIPHYTE

Spanish moss, *Tillandsia usnedoides*, a common epiphyte of the swamp forests around the Gulf of Mexico, is used as a stuffing material. The whole plant is gathered and retted by being left in a moistened heap.

SILK FROM THE FOREST

One of the most valuable fibres produced by the forest is wild silk, also known as tasar silk. Wild silk cocoons are harvested from the forests of sal trees, Shorea robusta, in China and northern India. Unlike the common silkworm, which feeds only on mulberry leaves, the tasar worm has an exclusive diet of sal leaves, but recent research has produced a hybrid tasar worm that will also eat oak. In India the wild silk cocoons are collected by local tribespeople who sell them to buy rice.

Food from the forest

For thousands of years prehistoric man was a hunter-gatherer who depended entirely upon the forest for food. Then, 10,000 years ago, the first agricultural revolution took place. Farming techniques were developed and the open grasslands were used to grow the first crops—cereals that could provide a regular, abundant and storable supply of food. From this time onwards wherever agriculture was practised, the nuts, fruits, roots, shoots and leaves gathered from the forest became supplementary foodstuffs, adding variety and nutritional balance to a staple diet of grain. They also served as famine foods in times of crop failure and shortages.

During the last century, however, the development of food processing, storing and distribution reduced the dependence of the people of the western world on local harvests. The availability and food value of forest foods were forgotten and many of the traditionally important forest products were transferred to commercial orchards and plantations. In developing regions, however, particularly in the Tropics and where hunter-gatherers still exist, the forest remains a vital food resource.

Nuts and seeds, for example, are appreciated in these contexts, especially when meat, fish or dairy products are luxury items or are prohibited for cultural reasons, because many kinds of nuts are a rich source of fat and protein. One of the most widely grown tropical nut trees is the coconut but other locally and commercially important species include the cashew nut tree, *Anarcardium occidentale*,

and the brazil nut tree, *Bertholletia excelsa*. Brazil nuts are both a valued local resource and an export crop; nearly 50,000 tons, all from the wild, are exported every year.

Nuts and seeds from the temperate deciduous and coniferous forests may no longer be essential foodstuffs, but thousands of tons of them are still harvested from the mature forests and commercial orchards of these regions each year. Several species of southern conifers produce edible pine kernels, almost all of which are still collected from the wild, both for local consumption and export. Deciduous forests produce a variety of nuts including hazels, walnuts and beech nuts, pecans from North America and pistachios and almonds from Asia. All of these trees have been under cultivation for many centuries but their nuts are still also collected from the natural forests (see pages 122–123).

Acorns are no longer considered as one of the forest's edible products but at one time they were regularly used as food, once they had been leached of their bitter and poisonous tannic acid. In Europe they mainly served as a famine food when bread was scarce, but in North America they were the staple food of forest Indian tribes, particularly for the Pomo Indians of California who used leached and ground acorns as flour for making soups, gruels and bread. Roasted and ground acorns also produce a substitute for coffee, one that was widely used in Europe during the food shortages of the Second World War.

Fruits and berries, along with nuts, are

probably the best-known of the forest foods. Many common fruits such as bananas, strawberries, blackberries and oranges—which are now grown in large commercial orchards or on farms—originated as forest trees or plants of the forest floor.

In parts of the world, particularly where farming has been difficult or where crops have been insufficient, starchy fruits such as dates and bananas are basic sources of carbohydrate. Similarly, starchy root plants from the forest floor such as manioc and yam and the carbohydrate-rich pith of the sago palm tree, which grows in tropical forest swamps, are important staple foodstuffs. The beans of the carob tree, *Ceratonia siliqua*, and algoroba tree, *Prosopis juliflora*, are especially valuable because they contain protein as well as carbohydrate. Carob bean flour is particularly suitable as a baby food and flour ground from algoroba beans has proved an ideal substitute for maize in times of bad harvest.

Sugar is one of the most important of carbohydrate foods and although the crops of sugar cane and sugar beet are the most important commercial source of sugars, the forest has its sugar producers too. The sugar maple of the eastern United States, tapped for its sweet sap, maple syrup, is the only temperate forest sugar producer but tropical forests have a range of trees which can be tapped for sugar. These include the sugar palm, *Arenga saccharifera*, which grows wild and under cultivation in Malaysia and Indonesia, the borassus palm, *Borassus flabellifer*, and the

1 Papayas *Carica papaya*
2 Mangoes *Mangifera indica*
3 Rambutan *Nephelium lappaceum*
4 Passion fruit *Passiflora edulis*
5 Pine kernels *Pinus* spp.
6 Yam *Dioscorea* spp.
7 Capsicums *Capsicum annuum*
8 Cloves *Eugenia caryophyllus*
9 Juniper berries *Junipus communis*
10 Coconuts *Cocos nucifera*
11 Cardamoms *Elettaria cardamomum*
12 Cinnamon *Cinnamomum zeylanicum*
13 Nutmeg *Myristica fragrans*
14 Dates *Phoenix dactylifera*
15 Bay leaves *Laurus nobilis*
16 Peppercorns *Piper nigrum*
17 Allspice *Pimenta dioica*
18 Mace *Myristica fragrans*
19 Coffee beans *Coffea arabica*
20 Vanilla pods *Vanilla planifolia*
21 Limes *Citrus aurantifolia*
22 Lemons *Citrus limon*
23 Oranges *Citrus sinensis*
24 Capsicums *Capsicum annuum*
25 Breadfruit *Artocarpus communis*

Starchy fruits and roots from the forest such as breadfruit, yams and bananas are staple foodstuffs in many parts of the Tropics. The Bantu people of Africa, for example, depend upon bananas as their major source of carbohydrate. The banana plant is native to the tropical forests of Asia but it has long been cultivated in other parts of the tropical world. Citrus fruits such as oranges, lemons and limes are also natives of Asia. Originally subtropical species, their fruits are now a major orchard crop in many tropical and warm temperate regions. The pineapple plant, the small guava tree, the papaya tree and the passion fruit plant are all indigenous to the tropical forests of South America although all of these fruits are now grown throughout the Tropics. The capsicum is another South American plant. Capsicums are the fruit of the plant, but, like tomatoes, they are generally eaten as a vegetable. Mangoes are used both as vegetables and as fruit. The mango tree, indigenous to southern Asia, has been cultivated in India for thousands of years. The rambutan is another Asian fruit but less familiar to Europeans. It is native to the rain forests of Malaysia. Grapes, one of the oldest of cultivated fruits, are also thought to have originated in Asia. Many of the most prized forest fruits are native to temperate woodlands. Both raspberries and strawberries can be found in European woodlands. Like fruits and berries, edible nuts and seeds are an important source of forest food. Among the most popular forest nuts are the pine kernels obtained from various coniferous trees,

wild date palm, *Phoenix sylvestris*, which is grown mainly in India.

Unlike fruits, seeds, roots and saps, the leaves of forest trees and bushes are not generally recognized as major sources of human food. Leaves of various species have formed a small but traditional part in many peoples' diets but they have never been consumed in quantity because of the human gut's inability to digest them adequately.

Indirectly, however, leaves are an essential foodstuff because they provide large quantities of fodder for meat- and milk-producing ruminants such as cattle, goats and sheep. In fact, it has been estimated that forest foliage provides more fodder than all the grasslands and pastures of the world. But this is a relatively inefficient method of food production and research is now being carried out to find methods of producing usable human food from foliage without the need for passing it through a ruminant's digestive system first.

Forests produce an abundance of foodstuffs, several of which are of world-wide commercial importance and many of which are of local importance. Many hundreds more, however, have been forgotten, or have never been exploited. Much could be done to improve the efficiency of the food harvest from the forest and with the world's population growing by seventy million every year, and the limited extent of agricultural land, the forest may become, as it was in prehistoric times, the greatest human food resource (see pages 216–217).

(see pages 216–217).

26 Raspberries *Rubus idaeus*
27 Hazel nuts *Corylus avellana*
28 Brazil nuts *Bertholletia excelsa*
29 Strawberries *Fragaria* spp.
30 Guavas *Psidium guajava*

Below *Cranberry vines are still to be found growing wild in damp, open woodlands in northern Europe, Asia and eastern United States. The berries are collected in autumn and used to make sauerkraut, jellies and pies.*

Many shrubs that form undergrowth in northern and temperate forests are prized for their fruits and berries. Black currants and red currants grow wild in the wet woodlands of Europe, while the gooseberry bush prefers rocky forest land. The little cloudberry herb is found in scrubby woodlands, especially in Scandinavia, and huckleberries grow in light, sandy thickets and woodland areas in North America.

Below *Tapioca is prepared from the roots of the manioc plant, a native of Brazil now grown throughout the Tropics. The poisonous prussic acid must first be removed by washing, boiling or drying the roots in the sun.*

Left *Wild honey is an important source of food to the forest-dwelling tribes of northern India. The best-flavoured honey is produced by bees of the species Apis indica, which build their hives in the branches of trees.*

31 Grapes *Vitis vinifera*
32 Pineapple *Ananas comosus*

33 Bananas *Musa* spp.
34 Walnuts *Juglans regia*

Above *Roasted, boiled or ground into a flour, chestnuts were at one time an important forest food. The roast chestnut vendor is a familiar figure in many European cities.*

23
25
22
21
24
20
19
16
18
27
29
30
3
26
32
33
34

hazel nuts and walnuts from temperate woodlands and brazil nuts from the Tropics. Forest plants and forest trees also produce

many spices, herbs and the raw material for beverages. Most of the world's coffee is obtained from the berries of the

small South American Arabica coffee tree. Mace and nutmeg are the fruit and the seed of a tall tropical tree native to

Indonesia, cloves are the dried flower buds of another Indonesian tree. Cardamoms are the berries of a small plant indigenous

to Indian forests, and cinnamon is ground from the bark of a tree still found wild in India and Sri Lanka. Vanilla pods are produced by a climbing orchid that is native to Central America and bay

leaves are obtained from the Mediterranean bay laurel tree. Allspice is ground from the berries of a species of European cypress and black pepper corns are the seeds of a vine found in the tropical forests of southern Asia.

Pharmaceuticals

From earliest times people learned how to use the wide variety of plants that grew in the forests. Leaves, fruits, seeds and roots were usually gathered for food, but a knowledge of specific plants that cured certain illnesses quickly developed. These were the first drugs.

This vital knowledge has remained, relatively unchanged, throughout recorded history. A third of the forest plants mentioned by the ancient Egyptians, for example, are still in common use. The ancient Greeks used extracts of willow, *Salix alba*, to relieve pain and their contemporaries in American forests, the Houmas and Alabamas, are known to have used willow bark for the treatment of similar ailments. It was not until the nineteenth century, however, that its active ingredient, salicin, was isolated and renamed "aspirin". Today, apart from alcohol and nicotine, it is the most widely used drug in the world. It is mostly synthesized, but the main commercial sources are still derived from the two willow species, *Salix fragilis* and *Salix purpurea*, that are native to Europe and Asia.

As people became more remote from the trees that surrounded them many of the early remedies were forgotten. By the Middle Ages the basis of all known drugs was still the *Materia Medica*, a catalogue of 600 medicinal plants that had been written in the first year AD. The fact that people had no idea how the plants actually worked led to a dark era and this long stagnant period in the history of medicine only ended when pharmacists began to receive specimens of all kinds of new healing plants from the tropical forests of South America, imported by early explorers (see pages 114–115).

A sinister substance, now commonly known as curare, which is derived from a species of climbing vine, *Chondodendron tomentosum*, became the most feared of all poisons. It was not until 1942, however, some four and a half centuries after the first Spanish explorer fell to his "flying death" from the curare-tipped arrows of his Indian adversaries, that it finally made its début in western medicine. An obscure Canadian doctor used it successfully as an anaesthetic prior to an appendix operation, thus making modern sophisticated techniques in surgery possible. Similarly, seeds from the *Strophanthus* tree of eastern Africa, which were first sent to England by Livingstone in 1860, became of inestimable value to modern medicine for stimulating the heart after a heart attack.

Today, increasingly aware of the side effects and of the cost of producing synthetic drugs, the pharmaceutical industry is searching the plant world for naturally occurring active ingredients. Due to the growth in demand, almost all the raw material needed to produce the contraceptive pill, for example, is now derived from common forest plants. Some companies have huge arboretums as part of their research and development programmes, and many trees, such as the cinchona tree that supplies the raw material for quinine, are specially bred and grown in plantations.

Chemicals from plants that act on the heart are called cardiac glycosides. They are widely distributed in nature but only a few sources are important in western medicine. Plants used to treat common infections of the respiratory tract either act as expectorants or cough depressants.

Drugs may act in several ways on the gastro-intestinal tract. The popular purgatives, such as senna and cascara, contain anthraquinones that reduce constipation by stimulating peristaltic action. Bitters increase the amount of gastric juices and emetics induce vomiting.

Many plants can eliminate toxic products from the kidneys by inducing a loss of fluid from the body via the urinary tract.

The autonomic nervous system supplies the smooth muscles and glands that either gear the body for immediate action or else produce effects that are more associated with energy conservation or sleep.

This group of drugs has either a stimulatory or a depressant effect on the brain and spinal cord. Cocaine, coffee, tea, cocoa and kola all stimulate mental activity, whereas plants such as Rauwolfia containing reserpine and atropine depress mental activity and are used in psychiatric treatment.

Many extracts, particularly oils, have antiflammatory and healing properties that are used to treat skin infections. Bark tissue from toothbrush trees is incorporated into toothpastes because it contains large amounts of chlorine and vitamin C.

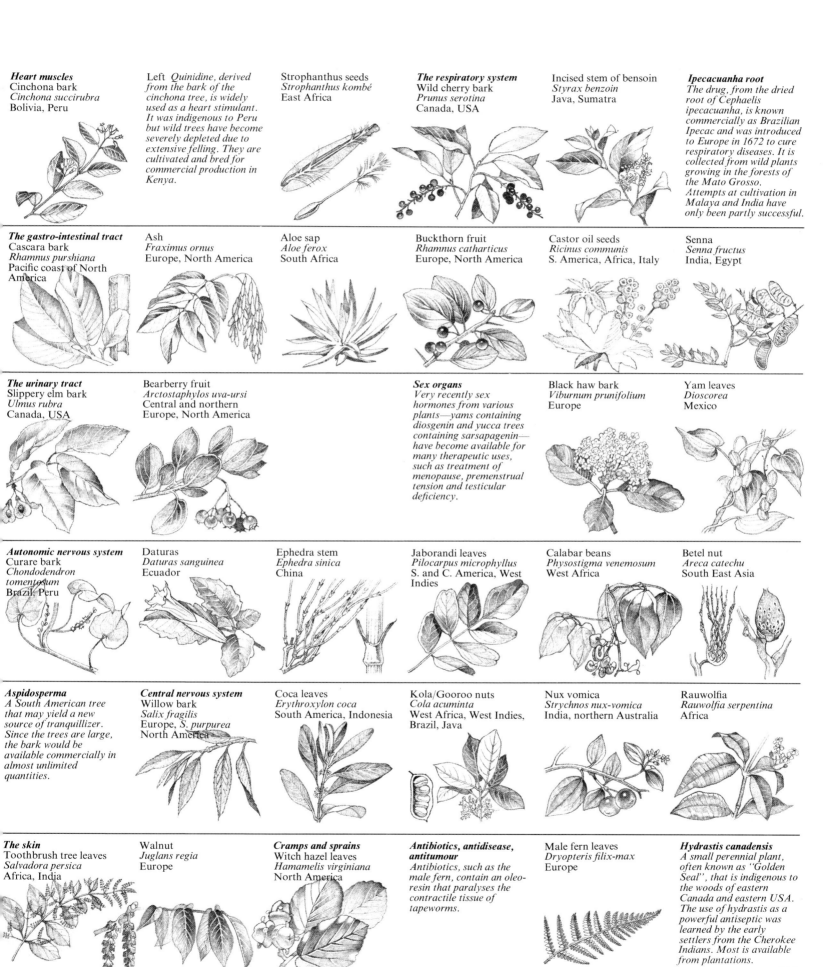

Heart muscles
Cinchona bark
Cinchona succirubra
Bolivia, Peru

Left *Quinidine, derived from the bark of the cinchona tree, is widely used as a heart stimulant. It was indigenous to Peru but wild trees have become severely depleted due to extensive felling. They are cultivated and bred for commercial production in Kenya.*

Strophanthus seeds
Strophanthus kombé
East Africa

The respiratory system
Wild cherry bark
Prunus serotina
Canada, USA

Incised stem of bensoin
Styrax benzoin
Java, Sumatra

Ipecacuanha root
The drug, from the dried root of Cephaelis ipecacuanha, is known commercially as Brazilian Ipecac and was introduced to Europe in 1672 to cure respiratory diseases. It is collected from wild plants growing in the forests of the Mato Grosso. Attempts at cultivation in Malaya and India have only been partly successful.

The gastro-intestinal tract
Cascara bark
Rhamnus purshiana
Pacific coast of North America

Ash
Fraximus ornus
Europe, North America

Aloe sap
Aloe ferox
South Africa

Buckthorn fruit
Rhamnus catharticus
Europe, North America

Castor oil seeds
Ricinus communis
S. America, Africa, Italy

Senna
Senna fructus
India, Egypt

The urinary tract
Slippery elm bark
Ulmus rubra
Canada, USA

Bearberry fruit
Arctostaphylos uva-ursi
Central and northern Europe, North America

Sex organs
Very recently sex hormones from various plants—yams containing diosgenin and yucca trees containing sarsapagenin—have become available for many therapeutic uses, such as treatment of menopause, premenstrual tension and testicular deficiency.

Black haw bark
Viburnum prunifolium
Europe

Yam leaves
Dioscorea
Mexico

Autonomic nervous system
Curare bark
Chondodendron tomentosum
Brazil, Peru

Daturas
Daturas sanguinea
Ecuador

Ephedra stem
Ephedra sinica
China

Jaborandi leaves
Pilocarpus microphyllus
S. and C. America, West Indies

Calabar beans
Physostigma venemosum
West Africa

Betel nut
Areca catechu
South East Asia

Aspidosperma
A South American tree that may yield a new source of tranquillizer. Since the trees are large, the bark would be available commercially in almost unlimited quantities.

Central nervous system
Willow bark
Salix fragilis
Europe, *S. purpurea*
North America

Coca leaves
Erythroxylon coca
South America, Indonesia

Kola/Gooroo nuts
Cola acuminta
West Africa, West Indies, Brazil, Java

Nux vomica
Strychnos nux-vomica
India, northern Australia

Rauwolfia
Rauwolfia serpentina
Africa

The skin
Toothbrush tree leaves
Salvadora persica
Africa, India

Walnut
Juglans regia
Europe

Cramps and sprains
Witch hazel leaves
Hamamelis virginiana
North America

Antibiotics, antidisease, antitumour
Antibiotics, such as the male fern, contain an oleo-resin that paralyses the contractile tissue of tapeworms.

Male fern leaves
Dryopteris filix-max
Europe

Hydrastis canadensis
A small perennial plant, often known as "Golden Seal", that is indigenous to the woods of eastern Canada and eastern USA. The use of hydrastis as a powerful antiseptic was learned by the early settlers from the Cherokee Indians. Most is available from plantations.

Recreation

The idea of recreation is only as old as the idea of work. Centuries ago, a farming peasant would have naturally integrated what we call recreation—sport, rest and culture—into an outdoor working day that was determined by how long the sun shone. But today, with more and more people living and working in cities according to clock time, it has become necessary to set aside time for recreation and the forest has come into yet another role as a natural and beautiful arena for a variety of such activities, from birdwatching to fishing.

In the great hunting forests of medieval Europe recreational activity was once combined with a practical search for food, but the woodlands protected in order to house game also fulfilled many other human needs (see pages 142–143). This was an early practice of the principle that a managed forest is a multiple resource, and a "working" forest can be a beautiful environment. The modern forester actively sees selective cutting, clean air, pure water, stable soils, the study of growth and plant disease, abundant wildlife, natural beauty and recreational pleasure as mutually supporting goals, but now the recreational dimension is no longer for the exclusive enjoyment of a tiny aristocratic minority.

Different types of forest afford specific pleasures and the availability of time, money and mobility also influence how people enjoy the forest, from the photographer's rapture at the New England fall to the skier's delight in the snow-covered slopes so often embraced by the forest. But the most economical pleasure is that of simply walking through peaceful and natural surroundings.

Even the walker through a seemingly "wild" forest needs the forester, however, because the use of a forest exclusively as a recreational resource and as a conservation area needs modern fire-fighting expertise and vigilance. But the forester operating in a commercially productive forest also serves the recreation seeker. The felling of trees, for example, can, by reducing competition in the forest, enable those trees remaining to grow taller and stronger and allow young seedlings to push forth. Such harvesting results in those welcome sunny clearings where grass, herbs and flowers can grow to sustain wildlife and provide attractive picnic spots.

The watercourses within the forest—rivers, lakes and streams—have proved to be a major attraction and the forester has a role to play in maintaining the forest as the guardian of the headwaters of major waterways that feed our cities and land. If trees do not grow along mountain forest streamsides, for example, resulting soil erosion can lead to heavy siltation of water, and fish—the symptom of clean water—cannot live. There are, from the tree harvester's point of view, usually enough "low value" trees to provide such protection so here the angler and the forester can gain from the forest in harmony.

The compatibility of the working timber-yielding forest with the forest as a recreational resource is not in doubt. More often the forester's task lies in ensuring that different recreational pleasures in the forest—that of a waterskier versus the fisherman, for example—do not conflict. The forester must also help visitors to the forest to learn its secrets and its lore so that the natural recreational resource can be enjoyed by being understood and the myriad other human needs it meets—from water to paper—can also be appreciated.

Below *The green and shady setting of the forest is ideal for picnics. Logging roads provide access, tables and seats provide comfort, while specially designed open fireplaces can reduce the risk of fire hazard.*

Below *By keeping the ecological carrying capacity of the forest for each animal species in balance, hunting is compatible with forestry. Logging roads provide access to otherwise inaccessible areas and* shooting parties on foot can move easily through the regularly planted stands. Some clear-cut areas provide the grass and young hardwood tree sprouts that are the favoured food of deer and small game.

Left *The forest can be surveyed very comfortably from horseback, but care must be taken to design trails that do not encourage shortcutting at the expense of the environment. Horseback riding trails often serve as snowmobile trails in winter.*

Right *In August and September the forest walker can enjoy the additional pleasure of collecting elderberries, which are rich in vitamin C and ideal for home winemaking.*

Below *Ski-ing is a major forest winter sport. Old timber-felling roads and fire trails can be linked together with connector trails to form various patterns of loops.*

Above *Ornithologists delight in the forest's feathered population, which varies according to tree species and season.* This enthusiast is camouflaged so that he can approach the birds without disturbing them. Birdwatching, however, is becoming such a popular outdoor hobby that in some forests specially designed hides, or "blinds", are now provided.

The future resource

Above *Most of the trees in this pine plantation in Guatemala have already been felled. Between the remaining trees, fields of Indian corn have been planted. Intercropping, for example by harvesting annual food crops between timber trees in this way, is an extremely* *efficient and economical way of using forest land. And if the world's ever-increasing population is to be fed as well as being supplied with fuel and other forest products, such methods of agri-silviculture may well become essential in strategies for survival in the future.*

The forests of the future may become one of mankind's most valuable resources, one that provides not only the traditionally derived products such as writing paper, packaging material and solid wood products, but also energy, chemicals, food, medicines and many other products that at present rely in one way or another on the fossil fuels.

At first glance, the forest does not appear to have much potential as a source of energy. Wood fuel is less efficient and more labour intensive than conventional energy sources. It is also difficult to handle, and requires a collection and distribution network. But wood has one quality that could make it regain much of its former importance: unlike the fossil fuels, it is a renewable resource.

The commercial forests of the United States alone contain about 200 quadrillion BTUS (British Thermal Units) of energy, enough to satisfy total world energy demand for a year. And every year these forests "capture" another five quadrillion BTUs above ground. But this increase is small; basically because so much of the forest is in natural mature stands that have little net growth. It is estimated that with intensive silvicultural management, yearly solar energy "capture" could be increased five-fold, enough to satisfy one-third of the total energy requirement in the United States in 1978. And this yearly rate could even be increased with further genetic advancements.

At present, it is not economically attractive to manage all of the forest for energy production. But the economic break-even point—the point at which it is economically feasible to harvest some trees for direct use as industrial fuel—has already arrived, based on current harvesting and combustion technology. Such harvesting will become increasingly attractive as fossil fuel costs rise and technology develops.

In the future a part of our energy may be obtained from wood grown on "energy farms". These farms would be plantations where trees were grown in much the same way as corn.

RECYCLING PAPER

World demand for forest products is increasing every year. Improved forestry techniques and more efficient production and utilization of these materials have so far enabled the industry to keep pace with demand. But one aspect of the industry that would help to cope with future demand is the full development of recycling materials after their first useful lives. Paper, for example, is one of the most important products of the forest: more than 150 million tons of paper and paperboard are produced each year. At present, relatively small amounts of this are recycled even though paper is one of the forest's products most adapted to recycling after use. Not all kinds of paper, however, can be made from recycled pulp. High-quality printing paper, for example, would "age" too quickly if it used secondary fibre. But all newsprint, which has a very short life and is then discarded can be made entirely of recycled pulp.

Fast-growing biomass plantations of this sort would become an economical source of energy after the first crop rotation—which could take as little as five years if *Eucalyptus deglupta* were planted—chiefly because, after this point, site preparation costs would be reduced.

The use of wood energy at present is largely confined to the forest products industry, which burns wood residuals for power, but shows promise for much wider future use. Forest products industry experts foresee that, in the short term, wood energy will continue to be used primarily in the form of solid fuel such as sawdust, mill waste or wood chips.

There should be some development in the capacity for producing methanol, an alcohol that can be obtained from wood by destructive distillation, and which, when mixed with gasoline, produces "gasahol" as a liquid fuel for cars. There will also probably be an increase in the production of high-energy compressed wood forms such as pelletized wood. Gasification, the process used to form a combustible gas, could also be further developed.

At some point it may also become economically feasible to extract oil from wood chips. Researchers in the United States are already processing Douglas fir chips into oil by first drying the wood and grinding it into a flour-like consistency. The chips are then either slurried with water or a low-grade oil, which helps to break down the composition of the chips, or fed directly into a pressurized reactor. Sodium carbonate is added as a catalyst to the mixture while carbon hydroxide is used to compress the material. The pressure is reduced as the process comes to an end and the oil is separated from the solid matter that remains. The resulting product can be used as fuel to run electric power facilities and, as it is low in sulphur content, it has only a negligible effect on the environment. Genetic engineering, an important factor in the future potential of wood energy, may also provide a means of obtaining raw materials and food.

About one-third of all the weight of the Earth's annual plant growth is cellulose, and starch is also abundant. Both of these plant polymers are glucose compounds, a sugar that microbes and most animals, including man, can use as an energy-rich food. There is great potential to provide much-needed food for the populations of developing nations from these sources.

Research has already been carried out with high-temperature anaerobic bacteria (bacteria that live in high temperatures without oxygen) that break down cellulose and starch. One kind of bacterium converts starch to ethanol and lactic acid—both important chemicals. Another produces a potent cellulose-degrading enzyme, which could be used to convert cellulose to glucose to feed animals and humans. Bacteria could also convert the glucose to acetic acid and ethanol. The present problem is that lignin, the substance that gives plants their rigidity, makes the cellulose fibres resistant to microbial attacks. But with research, bacteria with an appetite for lignin might be discovered or genetically engineered. Rapid conversion of wood fibre, as well as other plants, could then be carried out.

For many years such by-products as rosins, turpentine, pine oil, vanillin, torula high-protein food yeast and activated charcoal have been recovered from the papermaking process. In a world looking for ways to provide renewable resources, greater attention will be paid to efficient recovery of by-product silvi-chemicals from pulping liquors and effluents. At the same time, reconstituted wood products introduced in recent years such as wafer-board—made from thin wooden wafers held together by a resin compound—and composite panels—made with a core of particleboard sandwiched between veneers—should experience steady growth as man tries to obtain more building materials from the forest.

The forest also offers man many beneficial medicinal products (see pages 212–213). Many of these, used as folk medicine for centuries, are only now being rediscovered. The development of others are the result of present-day scientific knowledge and research.

Pine needles, for example, are now being used in pioneering efforts in Russia for commercial production of vitamins A and E, and in several species of trees, including yellow poplar and prickly ash, substances with anti-tumour properties have been isolated. Anti-microbial substances have been isolated from aspen and an anti-leukemic compound has been isolated from *Maytenus ovata*.

The forests have enormous potential as a future resource but they must be carefully managed. Possibly the most important and most basic question facing the forester of the future, is: how much of today's forests will remain by the year 2000?

The question is most relevant to tropical, less-developed nations where slash and burn agriculture and the use of wood for fuel have contributed, at least temporarily, to an enormous loss of forest cover. After a few years of agricultural activity on this land, sunshine, rain and unstable soil conditions make it unsuitable for forests as well as for crops.

There are, however, many pioneer tree species that adapt to these impoverished soils: and if given enough time, they can heal an area. Although geographically confined to the Tropics, this forest depletion may have global implications. Some scientists believe that the world's forests are critical to the proper carbon dioxide balance in the atmosphere as trees are net producers of oxygen and net absorbers of carbon dioxide (see pages 116–117).

Even if the world's forests are fully utilized they may not readily, or easily, provide everything that we want and need from them. But if forests are to serve all of society's needs, from energy and chemicals to building materials, pulp and paper, and if they are to provide recreational opportunities, scenic beauty and wildlife protection, then sound planning will have to resolve what may be incompatible needs.

Left *Forests have the potential to become the world's major food resource. Trees' leaves contain valuable protein, but, because humans are unable to digest leaf matter efficiently, these leaves must first be processed, by pulping, pressing and coagulating the juice. Prototype leaf pulpers have been designed at Rothamsted Experimental Station, England, and the product obtained has been shown to be as nutritionally valuable as meat.*

Right *In Brazil, cars are already converted to run on vegetable alcohol derived from sugar cane. Alcohol from wood can also be used, and probably will be in the future. If so, forests may well become a fuel resource.*

Index

Acknowledgements

The publishers would like to extend their thanks to the following individuals and organizations who have helped in the production of this book.

International Paper Company: Thomas Amidon, Carl Ashcraft, Henry Berry, James Blanck, Charles Bossier, James Buckner, Linda Cello, Mary Cockerline, Curt Copenhagen, Esther Dorfman, Darwin Fender, Thomas Finch, Warren Goldsmith, Keith Hall, Clarence Haltom, Paul A. Johnston, David Mote, William Olsen, Asha Palta, Thomas Pierce, William R. Pollert, Peter C. Quast, James Ralston, Chuck Riekert, Rita Rochon, Harry "Swede" Roller, Thomas Saviello, John J. Stephens, John Stone, Charles Webb, Bill Will, Charles Willhoite
Canadian International Paper Company: Donald Gilliam, Robert Goodfellow, Bernard LeClare
John Blackwell, Western Forestry Research Center, Portland, OR. Chet Makinster, Longview Booming Co., Longview, WA. Elizabeth Ogilvie, Millicent Trowbridge, Meg Price-Whitlock, Paddy Poynder, Ken Hewis.
The Librarians, Australia House, Aldwich, WC2. The Librarian, New Zealand House, High Commission, Haymarket, SW1. Library Staff, British Museum (Natural History), South Kensington and Tring, Herts. Librarians, Royal Horticultural Society, Vincent Square, SW1.
Brine Veneer Mills Ltd., Stratford, E15. Dunlop Limited, Tyre Division, Fort Dunlop, Birmingham. Lake and Cruikshank, Berkhampstead, Herts. Reliance Veneer Co Ltd., London. Miss R. Angel, Economic Botany Collection, Royal Botanic Gardens, Kew. Dr Clinton Green, Tropical Products Institute, London.
George Philip and Son Ltd. for information on pages 162–163.
The Bamboos: A New Perspective by F. A. Maclure, Harvard University Press, 1966.

ARTISTS
John Davis Pages 59, 96–7, 133 bottom, 102–3, 204, 212–213
Brian Delf Pages 33, 56–7, 122–3, 124–5, 127, Butterfly sequence 128, 137 illustration, 150–1
Chris Forsey Pages 16–17, 18–19, 23, Top right 28–29, 34–35, 38, 55, Middle 63, Top 110–111, 114, 120–1, 127, Robin 171, 173, 174–5, 188–9, 190–1, 198–9, Centre 206–7
Vana Haggerty Pages 196–7 plants
Peter Hayman Page 157
Tim Hayward Pages 108–9, 130–1 Centre
Ingrid Jacobs Pages 31 Bottom, 198 Bottom
Peter Morter Pages 100–1
Richard Orr Pages 24–5
Colin Salmon Pages 23, Middle 27, Top 30–1, Middle 35, Middle 55, Top 133, Middle 156, 174–5 Middle 179 Top right 6–7, 192, 194–5 Middle
Mick Saunders Pages 20–1, 26–7 Maps 80–1, 107, 148–9, 158–9, 162–3, 164–5, 180–1 Map, 193, 199, 201, 202–3, 204–5 Map
Venner Artists Pages 178–9, Centre 182–3, 184–5, 201 Bottom
Marilyn Bruce Maps Pages 68–9, 84, 86, 88, 90, 94, 95, 97, 137, 138, 140, 152, 196–7
Photo Retouching Roy Flooks Pages 1–13, 38–9, 160–1, 177

PICTURE CREDITS
The publishers acknowledge the co-operation of photographers, photographic agencies and organizations as listed below.
Abbreviations used are:
t top; c centre; b bottom; l left; r right; u upper; lw lower; AA – Animals, Animals; B – Biofotos; BC – Bruce Coleman; IP – International Paper Co; MEPL – Mary Evans Picture Library; NHPA – Natural Science Photographic Agency; NSP – Natural Science Photos; OSF – Oxford Scientific Films; VN – Valan Naturefotos.

Page 1: VN/Harold V. Green; Pp. 2–3: OSF; Pp. 4–5: Luiz Claudio Marigo; Pp. 6–7: Claire Leimbach; Pp. 8–9: NHPA/Dr. Ivan Polunin; Pp. 10–11: VN/Albert Kuhnigk; Pp. 12–13: John Sims; Pp. 14–15: Franco–Flemish tapestry, *c*. 1500, from the Château of Verteuil. Photo © Metropolitan Museum of Art, Cloisters Collection, Gift of John D. Rockefeller, Jr., courtesy Robert Harding Associates 17l B/Heather Angel, r John Sims; 18 and 19ur B/Heather Angel; 19lwr Biophoto Associates; 21l Biophoto Associates, cand r B/Heather Angel; 22–3 Popperfoto; 23bl Camera Press, bc and br National Coal Board; 25 Black Star Photos/John Launois; 27 Mansell Collection; 28tl Natur-fotograferna; 29lr Ronald Sheridan, ur MEPL; 30 Lebanese Tourist Board; 31 Ronald Sheridan; 32l Mansell Collection, b MEPL, r British Library/Ms. Kings 24, f. 47v from medieval Ms. of Virgil's Georgics; 33ul Barnaby's Picture Library, bl Dr. Alan Beaumont, br © Mitchell Beazley/Photo: Mike Busselle; 34 BC/Robert P. Carr; 35 National Gallery, London; 36tl Peter Newark's Western Americana, tc MEPL, bl Mansell Collection, br and 36–7t © American Museum in Britain, 36–7b M. Gold Archiv; 37t and c Sean Keogh Collection, br USDA Forest Service Photo; 38tl Mansell Collection, c Cadbury Schweppes, Birmingham; 39tr J. Allan Cash; 38–9 (background) Peter Newark's Western Americana; 40–1t and 40bl USDA Forest Service Photo, 40br Royal Botanic Gardens, Kew; 41t from *Des Divers Styles de Jardins*, by M. Fouquier and A. Duchêne/ Royal Horticultural Society/Photo: Christopher Barker, b Forestry Commission; 42t *Lower Falls of the Yellowstone River*, by Thomas Moran/Photo ©Thomas Gilcrease Institute of American History of Art, Tulsa, Oklahoma, b Reflejo/Susan Griggs Agency; 43l BC/Jane Burton, r BC; 44–5 Bildagentur Mauritius; 45b Alan Hutchison Library, c Dr. Alan Beaumont, lwc John Topham Picture Library, rc Gerald Cubitt, tr IP; 46–7 IP; 47tl Rex Features, tr Robert Harding Picture Library/Walter Rawlings, b BC; 48–9 Camera Press/Edward P. Leahy/ GEO; 48b John Topham Picture Library; 49bl and tr United Nations Photo Library, rc Victor Englebert/Susan Griggs Agency, br Douglas Dickins; 50–1t Loren McIntyre/ Susan Griggs Agency, b IP; 51b IP; 52–3 Adam Woolfitt/Susan Griggs Agency; 54t Ardea, b Douglas Botting; 55l, lwc B/ Heather Angel, l, uc VN/Brian Milne; 57 John Sims; 58–9 John Hillelson/ © Ernst Haas, Magnum; 58bl BC, br Naturfotograferna/© Clarence Newton; 59ur and br BC/Charlie Ott; 60l VN/Taylor, tr BC/Jane Burton, cr BC/S. C. Bisserot; 61t BC/Antti Leinonen; 62t OSF/ AA/ Mark Newman, b BC/Hans Reinhard; 62–3 NHPA/E. Murtomaki; 63tr Naturfotograferna, br Novosti Press; 64 NHPA/E. Murtomaki; 65tr BC/Bob and Clara Calhoun, c Naturfotograferna/P. Roland Johanson, bl Brian Hawkes, br OSF/Earth Sciences/Breck P. Kent; 66–7 Scott Leathart; 67tl Ardea, tr VN/Brian Milne, cl BC/Hans Reinhard, cr Jacana/ Pissavini, b Vision International/Paolo Koch; 68 B/Heather Angel; 69tl Haroldo and Flavia de Faria Castro, tr Jacana, c and br B/Heather Angel, b Royal Naval College, Greenwich; 70 BC/Charlie Ott; 70–1 BC; 71tl and tr NSP/Yendall, tc BC/ Charlie Ott, rc BC/Joe Van Wormer, br OSF; 72l OSF, r B/Heather Angel; 73l BC/ Gene Ahrens, tr Photri, br Popperfoto; 75ul IP, tr OSF/AA/Dan Suzio, lwl BC, br Bryan and Cherry Alexander; 76l Peter Newark's Western Americana, r MEPL; 77ul ZEFA/Hans Reinhard, lwl IP, ur John Stevenson, br Mansell Collection; 78–9 Luiz Claudio Marigo; 80 Douglas Dickins; 81l J. Allan Cash, br P. Villiers Le Moy; 82l Walter Rawlings, r Tony Morrison; 83l and r NHPA/Ivan Polunin; 84tr Roger Perry; 84–5b Luiz Claudio Marigo; 85tl Tony Morrison, tr Malaysian Rubber Producers Research Association; 86b BC/K. and D. Bartlett; 86–7 BC/Simon Trevor; 87 B/Heather Angel; 88 Chris Grey-Wilson; 88–9 BC/G. D. Plage; 89 NHPA/Ivan Polunin; 90 Australian Picture Library; 90–1 BC/Brian Coates; 91tl Jacana, tr J. Allan Cash; 92t Stephen Benson; 92–3 Andrew Sugden; 93t and b BC/G. Ziesler; 94 Cris Grey-Wilson; 95 Hans Hoefer/APA/Susan Griggs Agency; 96–7 Claire Leimbach; 97tl NHPA/E. H. Rao, lwl Jacana/La Boute, r NHPA/Ivan Polunin; 98–9 OSF/AA/Kojo Tanaka; 99t Tony Stone Associates, cr Walter Rawlings, b BC/Lee Lyon; 100 Marion Morrison; 101t Luiz Claudio Marigo, b Image Bank; 102 Tony Morrison; 103l Jacana/Gerard, c Ecology Pictures/ M. P. L. Fogden, r OSF/AA/Z. Leszczynski; 104ur John Hoke, lwl Jacana/M. Moisnard, t OSF; 105r BC/G. D. Plage, b BC/M. T. O'Keefe; 106–7 Colorific!/Dmitri Kessel © Time, Inc.; 106 NHPA/Roy D. MacKay; 107bl NSP/C. Banks, tr NSP, cr NHPA/Ivan Polunin, br OSF; 109t Ardea/Don Hadden, c OSF/AA/Z. Leszczynski; 108–9 sequence, all Leonard Lee Rue III; 109bc Collection Dr. Barbara Harrison, br Alan Hutchison; 110t Ardea/John Mason; 111c Ecology Pictures/M. P. L. Fogden, tr Ardea/ C. McDougal, bl Jacana; 112 and 113tl and lwl Su Braden; 113 tr Alan Hutchison Library, br Dr. Michael Yorke; 114t Mansell Collection, c MEPL, b from *Vues des Cordillères* by Humboldt and Bonpland, Royal Geographical Society/Robert Harding Picture Library; 115tl Royal College of Surgeons/Medical Illustration Support Service Ltd., cl from *The Naturalist in the River Amazons* [*sic*] by Henry Walter Bates, John Murray 1892, tr Mansell Collection, bl Brian Fawcett, br Popperfoto; 116t Alan Hutchison Library/Jesco von Puttkamer; 117t BC/Brian Coates, b BC/Neyla Freeman; 118–9 John Sims; 120–1 John Sims; 123t ZEFA/M. Becker; 124 John Sims; 125 BC/Leonard Lee Rue III; 126t John Sims, lw BC/Leonard Lee Rue III; 127 BC/Eric Crichton, tc Naturfotograferna/ L. Mathiasson, b BC/M. P. L. Fogden; 128t Ardea/W. Curth, b OSF/AA/Ralph A. Reinhold; 129l Jacana, r OSF/AA/ Leonard Lee Rue III; 130l VN/John Fowler, br John Sims; 131bl ZEFA, ur OSF/AA/ Breck P. Kent, br NHPA/Brian Hawkes; 132l Gallegos, r NHPA/M. Savonius; 134l BC/John A. Burton, r B/Heather Angel; 135tl B/Heather Angel, tc Ronald Sheridan, tr B/Heather Angel, b BC/Jen and Des Bartlett; 136–7 Paul Miles; 136b Michael Freeman; 137 IP; 139t Barnaby's Picture Library/Loescher, bl Geoslides/G. and P. Corrigan, bc B/Heather Angel, br BC/John Markham; 140t Orion; 140–1t Tony Stone Associates; 141r Tony Stone Associates; 142l Ms. Française 616, f. 85, *Livre de la Chasse que fist le Comte Gaston Phébus de Foys*, Seigneur de Béart, 14 – 15th century/ Photo © Bibliothèque Nationale; 142–3 John Hillelson/© Leonard Freed, Magnum; 143ur ZEFA/E. Harstrick, br Barnaby's Picture Library; 144 Mansell Collection; 145t Richard W. Brown, b Vautier-De Nanxe; 146–7 ZEFA/Erwin Christian; 148t and c G. R. Roberts, b BC; 149t *Whispered Words* by Paul Gauguin/Private Collection, b *Captain Cook* by Dance/Photo: National Maritime Museum; 151bl G. R. Roberts, br Derek Fell; 152br OSF; 153tr NHPA/ Douglass Baglin, bl B/Heather Angel, c and br Fritz Prenzel; 154l BC/John R. Brownlie, r OSF/A. G. Wells; 155l Ardea/Jean Paul Ferrero, r Ardea/Don Hadden; 156l Geoff Moon, r G. R. Roberts; 157tl and tr Geoff Moon, bl British Museum/Photo: C. M. Dixon; 158–9 ZEFA/B. Benjamin; 159t DerekFell, b BC/George Laycock; 160–1 J. Allan Cash; 166l G. R. Roberts, r IP; 167l and tr and b IP; 168lwr Robert Harding Picture Library, tl and lwl IP, tr John Hillelson/Ted Spiegel; 168–9 Commonwealth Institute; 169tc and lwc IP, tr Abril; 171tr Mireille Vautier; all others 171–2 IP; 172–3t Council of Forest Industries of British Columbia, all others 172–3 IP; 175r Sotheby's, all other photos © Mitchell Beazley/Naru Inui; 176tl and lwr © Mitchell Beazley, tr Alfred Knight Ltd.; 177tl Wilkinson Match Co., tr © Museum of English Rural Life, cr courtesy Holland & Holland/Photo: Sean Keogh, b Mireille Vautier; 178t Alan Hutchison Library/ André Singer, c Port Authority of New York and New Jersey, b Timber Research and Development Association; 179 Barnaby's Picture Library; 180t Fotomas Index, c Mansell Collection; 180–1b Mansell Collection; 181c Mansell Collection, br Ann Ronan Picture Library; 182t M. Thatcher Archive, b IP; 183 IP; 184 Australian Information Service; 185 all IP; 186l IP, c Mitchell Beazley London; 186–7 IP; 187c Post Office, r Arthur Sanderson & Sons; 188t Ann Ronan Picture Library, all others Courtaulds Ltd.; 189 all Courtaulds Ltd; 190l and br Courtaulds Ltd., tr Bayer; 191tl Bayer, tr Royal Aeronautical Society, b Courtaulds Ltd.; 192 John Topham Picture Library; 193 Vautier-De Nanxe, l Photo © Aldred Process Plant Ltd.; 194t MEPL; 194–5b G. R. Roberts; 195t Geoff Howard, c © Mitchell Beazley/Photo: Sean Keogh, r Bush Boake Allen; 196 Anne Bolt; 197t Shell Photographic Service, c 3M Co., b © Mitchell Beazley/Photo: Naru Inui; 198 Dunlop; 199tl Vautier-De Nanxe, all others Malaysian Rubber Producers Research Association; 200 © Mitchell Beazley/ Photos: Naru Inui; 201tl, cl and c © Mitchell Beazley/Photos: Naru Inui, bl and br Dunlop, cr Malaysian Rubber Producers Research Association; 202t Mireille Vautier, c Ann Ronan Picture Library; 202–3 Mireille Vautier; 204bl Firo-Foto, br Shell Photographic Unit; 205bl Shell Photographic Unit, bc Daily Telegraph Colour Library/J. G. Mason; br Portuguese Trade Office; 207tl, tr and lwr Mireille Vautier, second from bottom Anglo-Chinese Educational Institute Library, b © Dana Levy; 208bl and br Briton Chadwick; 209t ZEFA, c Mireille Vautier, bl Dr. Michael Yorke, br Walter Rawlings; 211tl Finnish Tourist Board, lwl Dr. Michael Yorke, tr Alan Hutchison Library, lwr J. Allan Cash; 210– 1 © Mitchell Beazley/Photos: Naru Inui; 214 IP; 215tl, cl, tr and br IP, bl Eric Hosking, cr John Wallace; 216t Gallegos, bl Camera Press/ D. Newell Smith; 216–17 N. W. Pirie/ Rothamsted Experimental Station; 217r V. A. G. (U.K.) Ltd., Milton Keynes, Audi Volkswagen Concessionaires